The High Church Revival in the Church of England

Anglican-Episcopal Theology and History

Edited by

Paul Avis (*University of Exeter*)

Editorial Board

VOLUME 2

The titles published in this series are listed at *brill.com/aeth*

The High Church Revival in the Church of England

Arguments and Identities

By

Jeremy Morris

BRILL

LEIDEN | BOSTON

Cover illustration: Two acolytes censing – Pentecost (1863), by Simeon Solomon. Courtesy of the Ashmolean Museum.

The Library of Congress Cataloging-in-Publication Data is available online at http://catalog.loc.gov
LC record available at http://lccn.loc.gov/2016034427

Typeface for the Latin, Greek, and Cyrillic scripts: "Brill". See and download: brill.com/brill-typeface.

ISSN 2405-7576
ISBN 978-90-04-32679-8 (paperback)
ISBN 978-90-04-32680-4 (e-book)

Contents

Preface

Even by its own admirers Anglo-Catholicism is commonly thought to be one of the more exotic expressions of Protestant Christianity. Its love of colourful vestments, rich and elaborate ritual and Catholic devotionalism sit uneasily inside a liturgical tradition rooted in the Reformation. Its language of Catholicity, and its apparent affinity with the vastness of Roman Catholicism and Eastern Orthodoxy, belies its character as a minority movement within Anglicanism. It has brought colour, commitment, theological inventiveness and evangelistic enthusiasm to the worldwide Anglican Communion, and yet it has also carried with it factionalism, division, enmity and at times a sterile or a reactionary traditionalism. It is probably true that no movement of opinion inside the Church – or any other human institution, for that matter – can possibly make its way without controversy and contradiction altogether. But Anglo-Catholicism does seem to have provoked more than the usual share of these things. Despite its pervasive influence over late-nineteenth and twentieth century Anglicanism, it has never been more than a minority presence in Christianity in modern Britain, and the general decline in Anglican congregational numbers in recent decades has if anything made its particular preoccupations and style seem more arcane and even irrelevant to the broad mass of churchgoers, such as they are.

Its history is, then, a troubled history, and the enthusiasm of its supporters is often matched by the puzzlement, suspicion or straight incomprehension of others. And yet its pathology – if I can perhaps use that term here – certainly merits careful investigation, not least because its study can both illuminate important aspects of the experience of Anglicanism over the last two centuries or so and, taken along with other elements of Anglican history, highlight lasting tensions and anomalies in the very notion of a distinctive 'Anglican' way of being Christian. Although it sometimes seems as if Anglo-Catholicism remains stuck in a nineteenth-century, neo-Gothic time-warp, nevertheless it continues to have startling effects and wider resonances in Anglicanism, to say nothing of its often provocative interactions ecumenically. All these considerations are further complicated by the troubling question of terminology. My subject in this book goes beyond the very sharp form in which Anglican High Churchmanship came to be encountered or experienced by many in the nineteenth century, namely Anglo-Catholicism, the term I have used so far. It embraces questions bearing on a rather broader movement which, following others, I have called the 'High Church revival'. I have preferred this term over the more common 'Catholic revival', because the latter has tended to be used exclusively in connection with Tractarianism and Ritualism. There certainly were, and are, Anglicans who would consider themselves 'High Church', but not 'Anglo-Catholic'. Yet the exact relationship between these terms is not straightforward, and attempts to delineate clearer definitional boundaries almost invariably founder when they are brought to bear on particular individuals, whose views often could not be easily pigeonholed.

It is one thing to assert the complexity and internal tensions of a religious movement, however, but quite another to map out a viable way, as a historian, of studying it. For all the enthusiasm of its followers, High Churchmanship has a troubled historiography, as I shall demonstrate in the first chapter. It is, to be sure, at once over-studied and under-studied. If we accept at face value one of its own dominant founding myths, namely that its 'origins' as a modern movement lie mainly in Oxford, in the vigorous assertion of a 'Catholic' Anglicanism by Newman, Keble, Pusey and others in the 'twelve years' from 1833, it is surely the case that library shelves are groaning almost to breaking point with relevant studies, many of them very fine indeed and used much by me here. There will be many, I am sure, whose first thought, seeing the title of this book, will be, 'Not *another* book on Anglo-Catholicism!' And yet, as I shall argue, much of this existing literature is curiously unrelated to some of the central concerns of a quite different set of historians whose interest, one way or another, has also been centred on the religious history of modern Britain. That either suggests the irrelevance of Anglo-Catholic history – to some a tempting, but I think ultimately implausible position – or a limitation in the way that this history has been written.

This book is an attempt to find a way of broadening out the study of this apparently exotic or eccentric movement, both to discern some of its wider connections with the religious history of Britain, and indeed of Europe, and to explore some of its more complex and subtle interactions with other aspects of modern British social and religious history. It is in part a reflection on historiography, but it is also an attempt to expand the field of study in various ways. It is based in part on a number of pieces I have written over the last twenty years, all of which however have been revised for this book, and in some cases extensively recast. It is absolutely not a narrative history of High Churchmanship, nor is it in any way comprehensive. It is a series of studies of, or rather segments cut through, the historical material, to try to uncover aspects, connections and themes which are rarely disclosed by the more conventional narratives or research monographs. There are certainly many significant gaps, and I hope to explore a parallel and related set of issues in a further volume looking at the triangular relationship of religion, society and the State.

My intellectual debts here are many and various, and perhaps surprising, because they include those with whom I have often strongly disagreed. They are of course too many to mention here, and inasmuch as they are helpful for the reader, they are I hope adequately indicated in the notes or in the text itself. But I would like to thank a number of people who have been particularly helpful to me over the years – Paul Avis, Angela Berlis, Georgina Byrne, Jonathan Clark, Cally Hammond, Tim Jenkins, Charlotte Methuen, Peter Nockles, John Pollard, John Prest, Richard Rex, Jaakko Rusama, Nicholas Sagovsky, Tom Seville, Rowan Strong, and the late Nigel Yates, amongst others. I also need to thank Ben King for saving me from a number of errors, and likewise Paul Avis in particular, both for specific points and for his general observations as series editor. I have recorded before now my debts to three academic mentors who have been long dead but whose work and influence continue to make me think – Dan Hardy, Peter Hinchliff, and Colin Matthew. My own view of Anglicanism has been profoundly shaped by my experience of other churches in ecumenical dialogue, particularly through the Anglican-Old Catholic International Coordinating Council, the Malines Conversations Group, the Porvoo Study Network, and the members of the Strasbourg Ecumenical Institute's Klingenthal seminar. It is usual, but important, to thank the staff of various libraries and archives; I am especially indebted to the Bodleian Library, the Cambridge University Library, Lambeth Palace Library, Pusey House, the Cambridgeshire, Nottinghamshire and Somerset County Record Offices, and the Bibliothèque Nationale de France. I should also thank, for support over the years, Trinity Hall, and King's College, Cambridge, and for a great deal of stimulation, members of the Faith and Order Commission of the Church of England, and its predecessor body, the Faith and Order Group.

My greatest debt as ever is to my wife, Alex, and to my children.

I should credit the publications in which earlier versions of many of these chapters appeared. An earlier version of chapter two appeared as 'The Regional Growth of Tractarianism: Some Reflections', in Paul Vaiss (ed.), *From Oxford to the People: Reconsidering Newman and the Oxford Movement* (Leominster: Gracewing 1996). Chapter three draws on a private publication by the Anglo-Catholic History Society, *Communicants' Guilds in the Late Nineteenth Century: Implanting Anglo-Catholicism in the Parishes* (2007). Chapter four is an extended version of an article which appeared in the *Journal of Ecclesiastical History* in 2015 as 'British High Churchmen, continental church tourism and the Roman connection in the nineteenth century', and chapter five is likewise a longer form of an essay which appeared in S. J. Brown and P. Nockles (eds), *The Oxford Movement: Europe and the Wider World 1830–1930* (Cambridge: Cambridge University Press, 2012). Chapter six is based on an essay in W.

Gibson & K. Francis (eds), *The Oxford Handbook of the British Sermon, 1689–1901* (Oxford: Oxford University Press, 2012). Chapter seven is a revised version of 'Newman and Maurice on the *Via Media* of the Anglican Church: Contrasts and Affinities', published in the *Anglican Theological Review*, Vol. 85 (2003). Chapter eight draws on a much shorter piece published in *Studies in Church History* by the Ecclesiastical History Society: '"An infallible fact-factory going full blast": Austin Farrer, Marian doctrine and the travails of Anglo-Catholicism', in R. N. Swanson (ed.), *Studies in Church History*, Vol. 39 (Woodbridge: Boydell, 2004).

List of Abbreviations

ARCIC	Anglican-Roman Catholic International Commission
CambsRO	Cambridgeshire Record Office
CBS	Confraternity of the Blessed Sacrament
CHP	Church House Press
COERS	Church of England Record Society
CTS	Catholic Truth Society
CUL	Cambridge University Library
CUP	Cambridge University Press
FHS	*French Historical Studies*
HJ	*The Historical Journal*
IVP	Inter-Varsity Press
JBS	*The Journal of British Studies*
JEH	*The Journal of Ecclesiastical History*
LPL	Lambeth Palace Library
ODNB	*The Oxford Dictionary of National Biography*
OUP	Oxford University Press
PCC	Parochial Church Council
RCC	Representative Church Council
RCED	Royal Commission on Ecclesiastical Discipline (1906)
SPG	Society for the Propagation of the Gospel
SRO	Somerset Record Office
SSC	Societas Sanctae Crucis
StaffsRO	Staffordshire Record Office
VS	*Victorian Studies*

Rewriting the Historiography of the High Church Revival

The High Church revival in the Church of England is surely one of the most intensively studied aspects of modern British religious history. It is not difficult to imagine why. Many of those contributing to the literature on the revival are either themselves Anglicans inspired by the revival, or friendly critics disposed to welcome and criticize aspects of a movement which has touched elements of their own religious tradition. Study of High Church Anglicanism echoes the 'confessionalism' supposedly re-discovered in Reformation historiography, though it had never entirely disappeared even there.[1] It thus seems to fall foul of the temptation Diarmaid MacCulloch has lamented for historians to indulge in 'ancestor worship'.[2] This is particularly true of Roman Catholic scholars interested primarily in Newman – indeed one might almost speak of a 'Newman' industry, such is the profusion of books on him, his associates, and his role in the Oxford Movement and in Roman Catholicism.[3]

Mass need not mean quality or originality, however. While the abiding interest in the subject is evident, is there much more to say? After all, the general outline of the revival is familiar enough, at least in the form it has come to be commonly understood. That view – the 'conventional account' – could be sketched in the following way. High Churchmanship, as it came to be understood in the nineteenth century, had largely disappeared from view in the previous century, as successive constitutional crises over the royal succession in the late seventeenth and early eighteenth centuries had forced the episcopate to make accommodations with the 'Whig' establishment, driving 'divine right' High Churchmanship underground, or at least into isolated parishes. There were indeed High Churchmen in the Hanoverian Church of England, but not many, and they were not very influential. The piety of Hanoverian England was not sacramental, but rational, ordered, and practical. High Church teaching on the liturgy, the sacraments, and church order was not altogether forgotten, however, and in the ancient universities – Oxford in particular – it

---

1   See the comments of Peter Marshall, '(Re)defining the English Reformation'.

2   D. MacCulloch, 'Protestantism in Mainland Europe: New Directions', as cited in Marshall, '(Re) defining the English Reformation', p. 571.

3   Cf. L. N. Crumb, *The Oxford Movement and its Leaders: A bibliography of secondary and lesser primary sources*.

© KONINKLIJKE BRILL NV, LEIDEN, 2016 | DOI 10.1163/9789004326804_002

continued to be taught. It was in Oxford, then, that the roots of the High Church revival were to be found when, in 1833, a growing sense of unease at a series of constitutional measures forced through in the late 1820s and early 1830s, which bore badly on the Church of England's traditional relationship with the State, came to a head over the Whig government's plans to suppress ten Irish bishoprics in the interests of stabilizing Roman Catholic opinion in Ireland. Led by John Henry Newman (1801–1890), John Keble (1792–1866), Richard Hurrell Froude (1803–1836) and Edward Bouverie Pusey (1800–1882), a movement of opinion rapidly gained ground in favour of reasserting the spiritual independence of the Church of England, of recovering and restating its historic spiritual resources (and especially its doctrine and liturgy), and of galvanizing its fading energies. The 'Oxford Movement' ran until Newman's conversion to Roman Catholicism in 1845, and in the course of these twelve years the movement's wider reception changed from cautious sympathy to outright hostility. The loss of Newman only served to confirm popular suspicion that Oxford principles led to the Roman yoke.

The year 1845 was a low point, and destroyed the credibility of the movement in Oxford itself, so the conventional account runs. Yet, paradoxically, it marked the beginning of widening and intensifying influence in the Church of England at large. The removal of Newman and other extreme voices stabilised and moderated Anglo-Catholicism, as it was increasingly called, and under the leadership of Pusey and Keble (Froude had died in 1836) High Church principles gradually gained ground in the parishes and in the hierarchy. High Churchmanship diversified. One edge was drawn increasingly into a flamboyant and rich revival of quasi-medieval ritual, art and music. The 'Ritualists' faced concerted opposition from Evangelicals, tested in a series of bruising law suits, and triggered Disraeli's belated and fruitless attempt to contain them through the Public Worship Regulation Act of 1874. Other High Churchmen, not so interested in ritual, created a credible body of High Church or Anglo-Catholic theology, though divisions came later in the century over questions of historical and biblical interpretation, so that a conservative versus liberal fissure opened up. Others still concentrated on pastoral responsibilities, creating, through a cult of celibacy and priestly sacrifice, a tradition of 'slum priests' who helped to transform the standing of the Church of England in many of the poorest parts of the cities. In all these ways, opposition was gradually overcome, and much for which Anglo-Catholics had fought came to be accepted by the Church of England at large. The movement went from strength to strength in the twentieth century, checked only by the failure of Parliament to endorse the revised *Prayer Book* in 1927–28 – until, that is, mounting divisions over the ordination of women and over human sexuality brought about a prolonged internal crisis in Anglo-Catholicism from the 1980s onwards.

This view cannot stand up to critical scrutiny now. It was a construct, an idealised view carefully crafted and honed over many years by a succession of writers. As we shall see, much of it goes right back to the narrative that the Oxford Movement's leaders provided as justification. Through Warre Cornish's detailed and authoritative *English Church in the Nineteenth Century* (1910), with its unashamed reliance on the accounts of Newman himself and R. W. Church, it passed into the bloodstream of twentieth-century ecclesiastical history.[4]

The popular and influential *History of the Modern Church* (1930) by J. W. C. Wand, later Bishop of London, is a useful illustration.[5] Covering the history of Christianity in its entirety, it devoted a whole chapter to the Oxford Movement – an extraordinary imbalance in perspective which highlighted first British Christianity within the worldwide Church, then the Church of England within that, and then in turn Anglo-Catholicism. The chapter opened by claiming that, at the beginning of the nineteenth century, 'the Church of England was in a bad way'; it went on to claim there was a 'remnant of the old High-Church party' at this time; the Whig government's proposals for the Irish Church 'stirred the Church to its depths, and the movement that now began in Oxford seemed the expression of all that was felt by those who were at all affected by these dangers to religion'; *Tract 90*, Newman's reinterpretation of the Thirty-Nine Articles in a sense compatible with Tridentine Catholicism, 'aroused against him so great a storm as to turn the success of his movement into contempt'; Newman's conversion broke the Tractarian party 'in pieces'; yet, even after 1845, there could be no doubt but that 'it was the Tractarians more than any others who fostered the new impulse which has renewed the strength of the whole Church in this country'.[6] This is a chain of quotations carefully chosen to make the point, of course. Nevertheless the general thrust is clear, and it is also telling that this was uncontentious on its publication at the end of the 1920s, a decade that is often seen as the highpoint of Anglo-Catholicism's influ-

---

4   'It is impossible to tell anew in fitting terms a story which has been told by Newman and Church, and with which the world still rings': F. Warre Cornish, *A History of the English Church in the Nineteenth Century*, Vol. 1, p. 213.

5   J. W. C. Wand, *A History of the Modern Church from 1500 to the Present Day*; it was reprinted eleven times over the next thirty-five years. On Wand, an 'acknowledged Anglo-Catholic', according to H. Riley, 'Wand, (John) William Charles, 1885–1977', ODNB, see J. S. Peart-Binns, *Wand of London*.

6   Wand, *History of the Modern Church*, pp. 205, 210, 216, 217, 219.

ence in the Church of England.[7] Wand's much later *Anglicanism in History and Today* (1961) provided a more critical gloss on the impact of the Oxford Movement, but even so he could still claim that by the early twentieth-century 'the vast majority of the clergy were indebted in varying degrees' to it.[8] Another popular text – Stephen Neill's *Anglicanism* (1958), in print at least until 1978 – echoed the usual view ('England had gone far to pull itself together after the lethargy of the eighteenth century').[9]

The conventional view outlined above retained scholarly credibility well into the 1970s, and even now can be found from time to time. There were always dissident voices, however, even from within the ranks of those who called themselves High Churchmen. There was a substantial body of clergy who professed much in common with the Tractarians, but who were reluctant to be identified with them. These are the people who were the real heirs of the 'Orthodox High Churchmen' whom Peter Nockles has shown to have remained active and influential throughout the eighteenth century.[10] I will come back to Nockles's book in due course; it is a landmark in the recent historiography. It built on earlier work by Norman Sykes, who was carefully undermining conventional views well back in the 1920s and 1930s, showing a much more complex and mixed assessment of the fortunes of the eighteenth century church.[11] The clues were there, however, even in things published in the nineteenth century – in, for example, William Palmer's *Narrative of Events* (1843) and J. W. Burgon's *Lives of Twelve Good Men* (1888).[12] Palmer (1803–1885) was an ally of Newman in the early stages of the Oxford Movement, but came to believe that Newman and others had taken it in an extreme and factional

---

7   Some contemporary reviews were critical of Wand's Anglo-centrism: cf. R. H. Nichols's comment, in the *Journal of Educational Sociology*, that Wand evidently 'has written for English readers. His outlook is emphatically English and Anglican': Vol. 5, No. 3 (Nov., 1931), p. 198. For Adrian Hastings, the 1920s were the 'start of the golden age of Anglo-Catholicism': *A History of English Christianity 1920–1985*, p. 195.

8   J. W. C. Wand, *Anglicanism in History and Today*, p. 143; on the Oxford Movement, pp. 100–3.

9   S. C. Neill, *Anglicanism*, p. 262.

10   P. B. Nockles, *The Oxford Movement in Context: Anglican High Churchmanship 1760–1857*.

11   The most pertinent books here are N. Sykes, *Edmund Gibson, Bishop of London, 1669–1748: A study in politics & religion in the eighteenth century*; idem, *The Church of England and Non-episcopal Churches in the Sixteenth and Seventeenth Centuries: An essay towards an historical interpretation of the Anglican tradition from Whitgift to Wake*; and above all, idem, *Old Priest and New Presbyter: Episcopacy and Presbyterianism since the Reformation*.

12   W. Palmer, *Narrative of Events Connected with the Publication of the Tracts for the Times*; J. W. Burgon, *Lives of Twelve Good Men*.

direction. Burgon (1813–1888) was a High Churchman of the old school who was 'as opposed to Romanism and ritualism as he was to rationalism and every form of liberalism'; his aim was to displace Newman, Keble and Pusey in the story of the High Church revival, and emphasize instead a group of men whose views reflected the older High Church tradition but who had also been energetic and instrumental in church reform in his lifetime.[13]

Yet Palmer's and Burgon's accounts, and those of others, simply did not attract much attention from historians until recently.[14] The 'golden age' of Anglo-Catholicism, which lasted seemingly until the 1950s or so, if such it was, supplied a much more intoxicating context for the reception of Anglo-Catholic history, and as a result it was the dramatic, colourful, intense and (depending on your point of view) heroic or tragic elements of the revival that came to prominence. A lingering distortion of perspective is evident even in the work of Owen Chadwick, who in other ways did so much to redress simplistic generalisations. His influential essay on 'The Mind of the Oxford Movement' (1960) demonstrated an acute awareness of the complex relations between different strands of Anglican opinion underlying the sensibilities of the leaders of the Oxford Movement, and his two-volume work on *The Victorian Church* (1966–70), for long regarded as the authoritative statement on the subject, displayed an extraordinary breadth of knowledge of nineteenth-century Anglicanism.[15] Yet the main outlines of the conventional account remained largely intact there, and perhaps through the absence of any more recent, comparable survey, have continued to affect the way Anglicans think about their history.[16]

Historical scholarship never stands still, however. The careful re-examination of source material and the challenging of established arguments and orthodoxies by professional historians have opened up significant gaps between the popular view and what can confidently be said on the basis of the evidence. Even modern scholars have their biases, and there is no guarantee that the shifts of perspective achieved by historians in the last half-century will not in turn undergo change. One of my aims is this book is to try to anticipate some

---

13   G. Martin Murphy, 'Burgon, John William', *ODNB*.

14   We could include, for example, also Frederick Oakeley's brief lecture *Personal Reminiscences of the 'Oxford Movement'* and his *Historical Notes on the Tractarian Movement*.

15   Chadwick later gathered together 'The Mind of the Oxford Movement' with a number of other essays into *The Spirit of the Oxford Movement: Tractarian Essays*, which remains a vital starting point for anyone interested in reading their way into the history of the Oxford Movement; see also W. O. Chadwick, *The Victorian Church*.

16   Trevor Beeson, for example, has claimed that no one 'attempting to write sensibly and accurately about the Church of England in the nineteenth century can afford to be without Owen Chadwick's two-volume classic': *The Bishops*, p. 237.

of the ways in which future research might develop. But before I can outline
these ways, it is necessary to examine in more detail the main lines of recent
historical work.

Varieties of High Churchmanship[17]

Given the weight conventionally placed on the role of the Oxford Movement in
the High Church revival, it is hardly surprising that scholarly attention has
tended to focus there. There are, arguably, three main lines of historical enquiry
which need to be considered, however, and the Oxford Movement, though the
first to which I shall attend, is but one of the three, the others being the older
High Church tradition, and the Anglo-Catholic movement after Tractarianism.
As I suggested above, critical interest in the history of the Oxford Movement
has been intense, sustained by fascination with the theology and spirituality of
John Henry Newman, and recently by the campaign for his canonisation. At
the risk of simplification, there were three overlapping dimensions of the historiography. The first was the 'heroic' interpretation of Tractarianism as a story
of struggle by an embattled group of religious reformers, who pioneered the
revival of High Church principles and practice, and thus gave birth to what
was, by the late nineteenth century, being called the 'Anglo-Catholic' wing of
the Church of England. Though not the first of its kind, Richard Church's history of the movement, *The Oxford Movement: Twelve Years 1833–1845* (1891),
which broadly followed Newman's chronology in his *Apologia Pro Vita Sua*, was
perhaps the most influential historical account, albeit unfinished and published posthumously.[18] Church (1815–1890) fell under Newman's spell while at
Oxford, and though he never considered converting to Rome (one of his biographers considered that his interest in history for itself rather than as a quarry
for doctrine 'saved him from the tendency to turn every difficulty into a crisis',
a judgement extraordinarily patronizing in its implications for theologians),
nevertheless he continued to hold Newman in the highest regard throughout
his life.[19] As Chadwick asserted, Church 'owed his soul' to Newman, and after

---

17   Cf. Matthias Ploeger, *High Church Varieties: Three Essays on Continuity and Discontinuity
      in Nineteenth-Century Anglican Catholic Thought.*

18   R. W. Church, *The Oxford Movement: Twelve Years 1833–1845*; the broad outline, and chro-
      nology, followed by Church was already evident in part, for example, in Frederick Oake-
      ley's four articles on Tractarianism for the *Dublin Review* in 1863–4, republished as
      Historical Notes, and which anticipated Newman's *Apologia.*

19   G. Martin Murphy, 'Church, Richard William, 1815–1890', ODNB. Chadwick has speculated

his secession 'could not believe that Newman went because he chose' but rather that he went 'because he was driven'.[20] Church not only accepted Newman's reckoning of Keble's Assize Sermon on 14 July 1833 as the true beginning of the Movement, but also considered Newman's secession a catastrophe which effectively marked its end as a university-based, academic movement.[21] The *Apologia* had done its work well. Church's book might not be the comprehensive history he was fitted to write – Chadwick calls it a 'failure' because it is stained by its author's rancour at the treatment of Newman by Oxford, yet also a 'very influential piece of history' – but this chronology was buttressed by various books which appeared in or around the centenary year of 1933.[22] Yet the combined influence of Newman's and Church's books was evident even within a few years of Church's account in George Worley's popular *Catholic Revival of the Nineteenth Century* (1894), which followed Church's account in all essentials.[23] With some qualification and nuance, the prominence this gave to the Oxford leaders and the 'twelve years' has remained crucial for some scholars who have added immeasurably to our understanding of High Church Anglicanism.[24]

But almost coincidental with this was an alternative stream of interpretation, which emphasised the alien character of the Oxford Movement in Anglicanism. Drawing in particular on contemporary Evangelicals' hostility, and on popular anti-Catholicism, this received its most notorious expression in the 'conspiracy' view of the *Secret History of the Oxford Movement* (1898), written by the ultra-Protestant controversialist and journalist Walter Walsh.[25] Walsh's book was factually rich, and certainly highly readable; coloured as it was by a tendency to see all religious forms and expressions from which he dissented as traceable to Rome, however, it was not critically astute.[26] It was part and

that Church's book was 'so good that it blinds': Chadwick, *Spirit of the Oxford Movement*, p. 146.

20 Chadwick, *Spirit of the Oxford Movement*, pp. 151–2.

21 Church, *Oxford Movement*, p. 272.

22 Chadwick, *Spirit of the Oxford Movement*, 153. Cf. G. Faber, *Oxford Apostles*; S. Leslie, *The Oxford Movement, 1833–1933*; J. L. May, *The Oxford Movement: Its history and future.*

23 G. Worley, *The Catholic Revival of the Nineteenth Century: A brief popular account of its origin, history, literature, and general results.*

24 See in particular G. Rowell, *The Vision Glorious: Themes and Personalities of the Catholic Revival in Anglicanism*, and Chadwick, *Spirit of the Oxford Movement.*

25 W. Walsh, *The Secret History of the Oxford Movement*. For an effective study of the way in which anti-Catholicism could morph into anti-Tractarianism, see A. Atherstone, 'The Martyrs' Memorial at Oxford'.

26 Cf. G. I. T. Machin, 'The Last Victorian Anti-Ritualist Campaign, 1895–1906'.

parcel of a stream of ultra-Protestant literature which never unquestioningly accepted the Oxford Movement's agenda.[27] The most remarkable expression of this sceptical strand – paying the Oxford leaders the backhanded compliment of acknowledging their influence even as it regretted it – was the Evangelical bishop Edmund Knox's *The Tractarian Movement, 1833–1845* (1933), which for all its critical shortcomings at least was influenced by its author's anti-Catholic leanings to depict the Movement as an expression of a continent-wide Catholic revival – something to which I shall return.[28] This second 'phase' of interpretation for much of the twentieth century was a minority view, but a persistent one. It was given a novel twist by Frank Turner's controversial biography of Newman, which argued that the anti-Liberal campaign Newman claimed as characteristic of the Oxford Movement was in fact a later re-interpretation of what had been originally a campaign against Evangelicalism.[29] The confessional anxieties which underlay Evangelical historians' treatment of High Church Anglicanism have perhaps been reinforced recently by a robust criticism of the way in which Anglo-Catholic interpretations of church order distorted Anglicanism's ecumenical priorities.[30]

There is a connection of sorts here with the third strand, the 'revisionist' phase which has emerged particularly in the last quarter century. Signalled above all by the work of Peter Nockles, this has moved beyond Tractarian 'hagiography' to look much more critically at the Oxford Movement's relationship to Evangelicalism and traditional Anglican High Churchmanship, in the process widening both the focus of Tractarian studies to include many figures and aspects formerly neglected, and the chronology of the movement, to question

---

27   Walsh went on to pursue this critical line in his *History of the Romeward Movement in the Church of England: 1833–1864*. For a more recent discussion, see P. Toon, *Evangelical Theology, 1833–1856: A Response to Tractarianism*; on Evangelical opposition more broadly to Anglo-Catholicism, see M. Wellings, *Evangelicals Embattled: Responses of Evangelicals in the Church of England to Ritualism, Darwinism and Theological Liberalism*.

28   Note the full title: E. A. Knox, *The Tractarian Movement, 1833–1845: A study of the Oxford movement as a phase of the religious revival in Western Europe in the second quarter of the nineteenth century*.

29   F. M. Turner, *John Henry Newman: The Challenge to Evangelical Religion*; for an exchange on the nature of Turner's thesis, see S. A. Skinner, 'History *versus* Hagiography: The Reception of Turner's *Newman*', and E. Duffy, 'The reception of Turner's Newman: a reply to Simon Skinner', and S. A. Skinner, 'A response to Eamon Duffy'.

30   Two examples may suffice: 'The classic nineteenth-century disputes between rival church parties have imparted to Anglicans a see-saw view of ecumenism, according to which a tilt in one direction implies a tilt away from another': S. W. Sykes, *Unashamed Anglicanism*, p. 176; 'the apostolic paradigm of Anglicanism was ecumenically sterile': P. D. L. Avis, *The Anglican Understanding of the Church*, p. 37.

the 'twelve years' mythology which Newman, largely, dictated, and which so strongly influenced Church and others.[31] Nockles, a Roman Catholic scholar whose *forte* has proved to be a meticulous reading of contemporary texts, allied with a formidable breadth of knowledge of eighteenth and nineteenth-century High Anglican networks, in *The Oxford Movement in Context* (1992) published probably the single most important study of High Church Anglicanism to have appeared in almost half a century (if, that is, Sykes's *Old Priest and New Presbyter* is recognised for the landmark that it is). Here Nockles demonstrated the continuing vitality and influence of High Church Anglicanism in the eighteenth and nineteenth centuries, clear elements of continuity between that tradition and Tractarianism, and at the same time the sharpness and intensity with which the Tractarian hyper-emphasis on the doctrine of apostolic succession (exemplified in Newman's *Tract 1*, 'On the Ministerial Commission') effectively 'unchurched' non-episcopal churches.[32] Nockles has broadened his description to encompass High Church Anglicanism in Scotland and Ireland, and a careful re-reading of the origins of the Oxford Movement in Oxford University, but his re-description of the field has been confirmed by a growing number of historians.[33]

It is worth dwelling a little on some of the implications of this revisionism, as its broad conclusions lie behind much of what I shall cover in later chapters. As Nockles has argued, it was not that Tractarianism simply recovered long-lost aspects of Anglican divinity, as the Oxford leaders often claimed themselves, but rather that it represented a new emphasis within Anglican ecclesiology, placing so much weight on the 'linkage of the validity of sacraments to the [apostolic] succession', that it also required new or intensified considerations of practical devotion, including penance, sanctification, and

---

31   Cf. Nockles, *Oxford Movement in Context*; J. Pereiro, *'Ethos' and the Oxford Movement: At the heart of Tractarianism*; S. Skinner, *Tractarians and the 'Condition of England': The social and political thought of the Oxford Movement*.

32   Cf. Nockles, *Oxford Movement in Context*, chapter 3, 'Ecclesiology: the apostolic paradigm', pp. 146–83.

33   P. B. Nockles, 'Church of Protestant Sect? The Church of Ireland, High Churchmanship, and the Oxford Movement, 1822–1869'; idem, "Our brethren of the north': The Scottish Episcopal Church and the Oxford Movement'; idem, "Lost Causes and … Impossible Loyalties': The Oxford Movement and the University', in M. G. Brock & M. C. Curthoys (eds), *The History of the University of Oxford*, VI: *Nineteenth-Century Oxford, Part I*; R. Strong, *Alexander Forbes of Brechin: The First Tractarian Bishop*; idem, *Episcopalianism in Nineteenth-Century Scotland: Religious Responses to a Modernising Society*; Pereiro, *'Ethos' and the Oxford Movement*; Skinner, *Tractarians and the 'Condition of England'*.

communion.[34] However, in turn this has thrown up points of continuity between the existing High Church tradition of Anglicanism and Evangelicals, and so the very notion that one can trace distinct church 'party' labels in early nineteenth-century Anglicanism has come under close scrutiny. Critics sometimes tended to imply that Anglo-Catholicism (including Tractarianism) was principally, or merely, preoccupied with ritual and doctrine, but this was far from the case. Pastoral, parochial renewal was really at the heart of the Tractarian enterprise, and not incidental to it. But this was an agenda shared with others: studying Tractarian pastoral practice has brought to light again striking continuities with other Anglican efforts, as well as dissonances. Much Tractarian preaching, as I shall show in chapter six, displayed themes and moods highly characteristic of Evangelicalism, including a strong appeal to emotion and religious experience, a sharp contrast between the Church and the world, a conviction of the importance of conversion, and constant appeal to the authority of the Bible. Yet it also appealed to what it called 'Church principles' in a way characteristic of the older High Church tradition. It is true that what was not shared with others were the ritual and ceremonial changes that eventually issued out of the theological changes engineered by the Tractarians. Tractarian preaching touched on these from time to time, though it is also true – as often observed – that what became Ritualism was to some extent a development beyond what the Oxford leaders themselves practised.[35]

The growing recognition of elements of continuity and discontinuity has raised profound questions about the identity of the Oxford Movement. At the most basic level, what was it, and who composed it? Newman's *Apologia*, one of the most influential spiritual autobiographies in the English language, has cast a long shadow over these questions. His depiction of a movement generated in Oriel Common Room, triggered by Keble's clarion call to defend the Church against the depredations of the State, and led above all by a small group of friends, has proved so attractive to subsequent generations that it has largely deterred revision. And yet even Newman's narrative – hastily constructed in a few fevered weeks in 1864 – itself acknowledged a much wider, larger movement of opinion, which not only drew on changing currents of sentiment and intellectual life at the beginning of the nineteenth century, but also sought to gather wide support amongst the parochial clergy.[36] If we follow Nockles's lead in recognizing the ecclesiological innovations of the Oxford Movement, what emerges from his description is a distinct group *within* High

---

34   Nockles, *Oxford Movement in Context*, p. 152.

35   Cf. J. S. Reed, *Glorious Battle: The Cultural Politics of Victorian Anglo-Catholicism*, pp. 14–16.

36   J. H. Newman, *Apologia Pro Vita Sua*, p. 43.

Church opinion, marked off by its wariness of the term 'Protestant' and of the Reformation heritage of the Church of England, by its readiness to accept loudly-condemned elements of Roman Catholic devotional practice, and by the concentrated emphasis it placed on apostolical succession.[37] The most detailed study of Tractarian numbers, by George Herring, reckoned on some 950 clergy in all by the mid-nineteenth century, the vast majority of whom were parish clergy.[38] If scepticism about the Reformation differentiated the Tractarians, on one side, from Evangelicals and those 'middle' Anglicans later to be termed the 'Broad Church', nevertheless it also differentiated them, on the other side, from those traditional High Churchmen with whom they otherwise had much in common.

Herring took his analysis well beyond 1845, and implied that no account of the Oxford Movement which accepted Newman's conversion as a *terminus ad quem* could hope adequately to explain the Tractarians' impact on the Church of England. There could be no chronological end-point as such, when, leaving to one side the further difficulty that many of the later Anglo-Catholics traced a direct lineage from the Tractarians even as they embraced Ritual change with an enthusiasm from which Pusey and Keble shrank, many clergy in the late Victorian period continued to profess the principles of the Oxford Movement, not least Henry Liddon (1829–1890), Pusey's great friend and disciple, without whom no consideration of Tractarianism in the nineteenth century could be complete.[39] Just as the end of the Movement is problematic, however, so too is the beginning. Here, Nockles above all has indicated how the determining theological and ecclesiological opinions adopted by the leaders of the Movement really emerged in the late 1820s. The struggle over Catholic Emancipation in Oxford was decisive for clarifying the ideas of those who were later regarded as the 'leaders' of the Oxford Movement, though much recent scholarship, including Nockles's own, also recognizes distinct shifts of opinion even from the mid-1820s within the intellectual development of Pusey and Newman.[40] Keble's Oxford 'Assize Sermon' of 14 July 1833 may have been kept by Newman as the start of the Oxford Movement, but in practice any discussion of

---

37   This theme is also explored in P. D. L. Avis, *Anglicanism and the Christian Church*, passim.

38   G. W. Herring, 'From Tractarianism to Ritualism: A Study of Some Aspects of Tractarianism outside Oxford, from the time of Newman's conversion in 1845 until the First Ritual Commission in 1867', DPhil, Oxford University, 1984, p. 39.

39   J. O. Johnston, *The Life and Letters of Henry Parry Liddon*; M. Chandler, *The Life and Work of Henry Parry Liddon*; cf. also, B. A. Orford, *H. P. Liddon and the Priestly Ideal*.

40   Cf. Nockles, "Lost Causes and ... Impossible Loyalties".

Tractarianism inevitably has to cover a much longer period of time, from roughly the mid- or late 1820s, onwards into the late-nineteenth century.

A broadening of the chronology of the Oxford Movement has been accompanied also by a broadening of its geography. To Newman, Church and later writers such as Faber, the Movement was so closely identified with Oxford University that the world beyond the dreaming spires seemed to recede into an indistinct haze. There were clues even in the *Apologia* itself that this was never satisfactory: Newman makes play of the support the Oxford leaders sought amongst parish clergy, of the great petition presented to Archbishop Howley, of the conference at Hadleigh Rectory in 1833, and of the role of the religious press, amongst other things.[41] Contemporaries were well aware of a parallel movement of opinion, albeit smaller, at Cambridge, and of the role Tractarian views were to play in the work of the 'Ecclesiologists', such as John Mason Neale (1818–1866).[42] The work of Nockles and of Rowan Strong has highlighted Tractarian sympathies amongst clergy in other parts of the British Isles, and Nigel Yates, albeit with a principal focus on Ritualism, and assisted by essays by Frances Knight and the present author, has helped to flesh out our knowledge of Tractarianism in the parishes.[43] It would be too easy, and too misleading, to suggest that the principles of the Oxford Movement simply 'rippled out' from Oxford itself, not least because – as I shall demonstrate in chapter two – in practice the growth of Tractarian and later Anglo-Catholic opinion in Church of England parishes depended on a complex interaction between local ēlites, popular opinion, clerical hierarchies, and ecclesiastical administration, and was rarely without conflict. Nevertheless, we can safely put to bed the notion that the Oxford Movement was somehow confined largely to Oxford.

Some of this new research on the Oxford Movement has come forward in the form of biography, and a passing acknowledgement of that is important. Anyone coming fresh to the subject must reckon with three significant lives of

---

41   'I called upon clergy in various parts of the country, whether I was acquainted with them or not': Newman, *Apologia*, p. 43.

42   J. F. White, *The Cambridge Movement: the ecclesiologists and the gothic revival*; C. Webster & J. Elliott (eds.), *'A church as it should be': the Cambridge Camden Society and its influence*; L. Litvack, *John Mason Neale and the quest for sobornost*; M. Chandler, *The Life and Work of John Mason Neale, 1818–1866*.

43   Nockles, *Oxford Movement in Context*; Strong, *Episcopalianism in Nineteenth-Century Scotland*; W. N. Yates, *Anglican Ritualism in Victorian Britain, 1830–1910*; F. Knight, 'The influence of the Oxford Movement in the Parishes: a Reassessment', in P. Vaiss, *From Oxford to the People. Reconsidering Newman and the Oxford Movement*; J. N. Morris, 'The Regional Growth of Tractarianism', in Vaiss, *From Oxford to the People*.

Newman to set beside the *Apologia*, namely those by Ker, Gilley and Turner.[44] Each – though in sharply different ways – has qualified Newman's own picture, not only of his spiritual journey, but of his relationship with his fellow Tractarians. But a number of recent biographies of others have also somewhat undermined the conventional narrative, addressing the lives of Pusey, Manning, Wood, Oakeley, Liddon and Neale.[45] When set beside some earlier biographies – including Battiscombe on Keble, and Brendon on Hurrell Froude – the biographical testimony adds up to a formidable scholarly achievement itself, even if it would hardly be possible to claim any sort of emergent consensus on the role of particular individuals in the Movement.[46] At the very least, it forces us to acknowledge that bringing particular figures to the fore tends to fill out the somewhat sketchy impressions one might otherwise deduce from the 'classic' accounts of Newman and Church. What is striking is that no one yet has sought to examine in depth the *autobiography* of the Oxford Movement.[47] If the *Apologia* has cast a long shadow, nonetheless it is not for the want of first-person testimony from many other participants in the Movement, including Isaac Williams, Frederick Oakeley, Thomas Mozley, and William Palmer.[48] Closer consideration of these and other accounts might serve not so much to modify the narrative tradition about the Oxford Movement, as to help us to understand better the process of retrospective interpretation and reception of the Movement as those who were involved in it, like Newman himself, changed and grew older.

So far I have concentrated mainly on the ways in which recent historical scholarship has changed received views of the Oxford Movement. What of High Church Anglicanism more broadly? To move the discussion on, we have to make arbitrary and rather unsatisfactory distinctions, which would not

44   I. Ker, *John Henry Newman. A Biography*; S. Gilley, *Newman and his Age*; Turner, *Newman*.
45   A. M. Allchin, *Participation in God: a Forgotten Strand in Anglican Tradition*; R. Strong & C. Engelhardt Herringer (eds.), *Edward Bouverie Pusey and the Oxford Movement*; J. Pereiro, *Cardinal Manning: An Intellectual Biography*; idem, *'Ethos' and the Oxford Movement*; P. Galloway, *A Passionate Humility: Frederick Oakeley and the Oxford Movement*; Chandler, *Liddon*; Chandler, *Neale*.
46   G. Battiscombe, *John Keble. A Study in Limitations*; but see also Owen Chadwick's critical reply, 'The limitations of Keble', in idem, *Spirit of the Oxford Movement*; P. Brendon, *Hurrell Froude and the Oxford Movement*.
47   Though I note an important step towards this in P. Nockles, 'Newman's Tractarian Reception', in F. D. Aquino & B. King (eds.), *Receptions of Newman*.
48   G. Prevost (ed.), *The Autobiography of Isaac Williams*; T. Mozley, *Reminiscences chiefly of Oriel College and the Oxford Movement*; Oakeley, *Personal Reminiscences*, and *Historical Notes*; Palmer, *Narrative*.

always have seemed obvious to contemporaries. The older High Church tradition, to which Nockles and others have drawn our attention, represented by
Palmer and Burgon, amongst many others, is arguably misrepresented by the
comparative word 'older', if that signifies a precursor which at some point in
the early nineteenth century ceased to exercise much influence. Far from being
in some way occluded by the Tractarians, this more moderate and cautious
form of High Churchmanship was if anything emboldened and challenged to
assert its influence more widely. The 'Hackney Phalanx' of High Churchmen
which gathered around the layman Joshua Watson (1771–1855) formed a bridge
between the High Churchmanship of the eighteenth century, and the more
reform-minded figures of the mid- and late nineteenth century.[49] This tradition included, for example, from the earlier period, William Jones (1726–1800),
Vicar of Nayland, William van Mildert (1765–1836), bishop successively of
Llandaff and Durham, and Christopher Wordsworth (1774–1846), brother of
the poet and master of Trinity College, Cambridge, but also influential later
figures such as Walter Farquhar Hook (1798–1875), the reforming vicar of Leeds
and later dean of Chichester, and George Augustus Selwyn (1809–1878), missionary bishop of New Zealand and later of Lichfield.[50] These later figures have
often been associated by historians with the Tractarians, but the relationship
was never entirely straightforward. Hook's High Churchmanship was formed
long before he knew any of the Oxford leaders or their work; at first he welcomed the Movement, and even defended the publication of Tract 90, but in
time 'his reservations matured into distrust'.[51] Selwyn is often cast as a disciple
of the Oxford Movement, but his opposition to State interference in Church
affairs in the colonies should not be taken as a sign that he accepted the
Movement's standpoint in its entirety; recent scholarship has concluded he is
much better described as a traditional or 'orthodox' High Churchman.[52]

Nockles has shown us how pervasive and lasting the influence of these men
really was, but many of them await full critical study. The persistence of moderate High Churchmanship in the nineteenth century has been overshadowed
by the literature on Tractarianism and Ritualism. A number of studies, however, have drawn attention to its influence in the reform and revival of the
Church of England in mid-century. Books by Philip Barrett and Clive Dewey in

---

49   A. Webster, *Joshua Watson: the story of a layman*.
50   These connections are briefly referenced in P. B. Nockles, 'Watson, Joshua (1771–1855)', *ODNB*.
51   G. Herring, 'Hook, Walter Farquhar (1998–1855)', *ODNB*.
52   R. A. Wilson, 'G. A. Selwyn, the colonial episcopate and the formation of the Anglican Communion', Cambridge University PhD thesis, 2010.

the early 1990s, both using Trollope's Barchester as a reference point, explored the key role played by High Churchmen in transforming the pastoral and liturgical ministry of the cathedrals.[53] As Dewey puts it, perhaps a little too sharply, like 'most reforms in England, [the Anglican recovery] was a defensive reaction on the part of a conservative establishment'; the old high churchmen galvanised the clergy by bringing ability to the fore.[54] Geoffrey Best's monumental study of Queen Anne's Bounty and the Ecclesiastical Commissioners, still an essential guide to the intricacies of nineteenth-century church reform, similarly yielded much insight into the work of traditional High Churchmen such as Charles Blomfield (1766–1857), Bishop of London, and loathed by the Tractarians for his willingness to support church reform.[55] Best's work has been complemented by that of Arthur Burns, whose study of diocesan reform drew particular attention to the influence of traditional High Churchmen, in contrast to that of the Oxford leaders.[56] As Burns pointed out, the controversy which surrounded the Oxford Movement 'vitiated its effectiveness as an ideology underpinning practical reform', for few orthodox High Churchmen could reconcile 'the theoretical emphasis on episcopal authority in the *Tracts* with what they regarded as the authors' repeated provocation and defiance of an episcopate bravely resisting strong pressure to act decisively against Puseyism.'[57] Burns emphasised the close 'fit' between the 'coherent theological and ecclesiological tradition' of orthodox Anglican High Churchmanship, with its support for episcopacy and historic continuities in Anglicanism, and the 'emphases which characterised the Diocesan Revival and its accompanying legitimation'.[58] For Burns, then, it was *not* predominantly the Oxford Movement which transformed the pastoral practice and ecclesiastical administration of the Church of England, but rather the very group they mightily disparaged, the more moderate, or conservative, orthodox High Churchmen. Burns's account has not been seriously challenged; his description of the practical aspects of diocesan reform, which stops effectively in the 1870s, urgently needs to be extended into the early twentieth century, when almost all the trends he

---

53   P. Barrett, *Barchester: English Cathedral Life in the Nineteenth Century*; C. Dewey, *The Passing of Barchester*.

54   Dewey, *Passing of Barchester*, p. 3.

55   G. F. A.Best, *Temporal Pillars: Queen Anne's Bounty, the ecclesiastical commissioners and the Church of England*; see also O. Brose, *Church and Parliament, the reshaping of the Church of England, 1828–1860*; and P. J. Welch, 'Blomfield and Peel: a study in co-operation between Church and State, 1841–46'.

56   R. A. Burns, *The Diocesan Revival in the Church of England c. 1800–1870*.

57   Burns, *Diocesan Revival*, p. 18.

58   Burns, *Diocesan Revival*, p. 19.

described were carried even further. Such an account would uncover even more complex sets of relationships between different strands of High Churchmanship, and indeed other Anglican opinion, than can be described in the early and mid-nineteenth century. It would need to register, for example, the influence of the Christian Socialism of F. D. Maurice and its sacramental followers, the philosophical Idealism of T. H. Green's Oxford, the more flamboyant elements of Ritualism and Anglo-Catholicism, and the inheritors (though there is no adequate term) of mid-century 'Broad Church' opinion.

Each of these elements has its own historiographical challenges. The relationship of Christian Socialism to Anglican High Churchmanship was at first glance relatively marginal. The first phase ran from 1848 to approximately 1854, and is associated particularly with F. D. Maurice (1805–1872), best known as Chaplain of Lincoln's Inn, Charles Kingsley (1819–1874), Rector of Eversley, and John Malcolm Ludlow (1821–1911), layman and lawyer. Literature on this phase has ranged from the admiring (Charles Raven), through the sceptical (Torben Christensen) to the downright critical (Edward Norman).[59] It has been complicated by the question of the movement's relationship to the rise of socialism in Britain.[60] Maurice in particular is conventionally depicted as the fountainhead of modern Anglican social theology.[61] It is misleading, however, to interpret Maurice according to later language of socialism with its overtones (influenced by Marx) of an economic and class analysis with which he had little sympathy.[62] Maurice's 'Christian Socialism' – a term which he did not actually adopt until 1850 – was principally an expression of his ecclesiology, an ecumenical vision of Catholicity encompassing major separated schools of Christianity but represented most fully in Anglicanism.[63] His description of the objective 'signs of a spiritual society', or marks of Catholicity, included baptism, the eucharist, the Catholic creeds, the Scriptures, the threefold order of ministry, and a fixed liturgical tradition; the consonance of these with High Churchmanship is evident.[64] His defence of the Thirty-Nine Articles and of

---

59   C. E. Raven, *Christian Socialism 1848–54*; T. Christensen, *The Origins and History of Christian Socialism 1848–1854*; E. R. Norman, *The Victorian Christian Socialists*.

60   See, for a general overview, C. Bryant, *Possible Dreams: A Personal History of British Christian Socialists*; and also A. Wilkinson, *Christian Socialism: From Scott Holland to Tony Blair*.

61   M. B. Reckitt, *Maurice to Temple: A Century of the Social Movement in the Church of England*.

62   J. N. Morris, *F. D. Maurice and the Crisis of Christian Authority*, pp. 130–60.

63   Maurice claimed 'Christian Socialist' was the 'only title which will define our object', since it would commit them to conflict with the 'unsocial Christians and the unchristian Socialists': F. Maurice, *The Life and Letters of Frederick Denison Maurice*, vol. 2, p. 34.

64   See in particular F. D. Maurice, *The Kingdom of Christ, or Hints to a Quaker respecting the Principles, Constitution and Ordinances of the Catholic Church*.

the Prayer Book naturally attracted admiration from some High Churchmen.[65] Maurice himself, however, strongly rejected Tractarianism when he read Pusey's *Tracts* on baptism, and Kingsley's relationship with Tractarianism was always critical, and later tainted by the taunt which provoked Newman to write his *Apologia*. Historians have been tempted to include them, not under High Churchmanship, but under the term 'Broad Church'.[66] Many later followers of Maurice's theology, however, such as Stewart Headlam (1847–1924), and even Charles Gore (1853–1932) were to see in his appreciation of the doctrine of the Incarnation, in his social theology and in his understanding of church order a theology well suited to High Church sacramentalism; Mauricean theology was patient of Anglo-Catholic development.[67]

But there was a second phase of Christian Socialism, which owed much to Maurice but also arose in response to the economic and social ills of the 1870s and 1880s, and arguably lasted at least until the beginning of the First World War.[68] It is associated with two organisations, the Guild of St Matthew, founded by Stewart Headlam, and the Christian Social Union (CSU), established by Charles Gore, Henry Scott Holland (1847–1918), and James Adderley (1861–1942), and later absorbed into the Industrial Christian Fellowship. The first was an openly sacramental and Ritualist association. The second was a national organisation which promoted the study of industrial and social problems from a Christian perspective and drew into its membership a wide range of theological opinion, including some Evangelicals and Liberals as well as High Churchmen. Study of this second phase has been influenced by admiration for Stewart Headlam's courageous and somewhat quixotic radicalism, and by impatience with the CSU's apparently vague and ineffectual intellectualism.[69] The details of the historiographical debate do not concern me directly here, since my interest for the moment is specifically on the relationship with Anglican High Churchmanship. Suffice it to say that the second phase of

---

65 F. D. Maurice, *Subscription no Bondage, or the Practical Advantages Afforded by the Thirty-Nine Articles as Guides in all the Branches of Academical Education*; idem, *The Prayer-Book Considered Especially in Reference to the Romish System*.

66 C. R. Sanders, *Coleridge and the Broad Church Movement: Studies in S. T. Coleridge, Dr Arnold of Rugby, J. C. Hare, Thomas Carlyle, and F. D. Maurice*; T. E. Jones, *The Broad Church: A biography of a movement*.

67 J. Orens, *Stewart Headlam's Radical Anglicanism: The Mass, the masses, and the music hall*; J. Carpenter, *Gore: a study in Liberal Catholic thought*; P. D. L. Avis, *Gore: Construction and Conflict*.

68 P. D'A. Jones, *The Christian Socialist Revival 1877–1914: Religion, Class and Social Conscience in Late Victorian England*.

69 A particularly telling contrast emerges in the pages of E. R. Norman, *Church and Society in England, 1770–1970*, pp. 179–82.

Christian Socialism attracted many Anglo-Catholics, and indicated how High Churchmanship was adaptable to currents of opinion and contexts distinct from the initial interests of the Oxford Movement. If anything, this conclusion can be carried even further, into the twentieth century, when account is taken of the radical sacramental tradition that manifested itself in, for example, the Catholic Crusade, founded by the Thaxted priest Conrad Noel (1869–1942).[70] Noel identified himself with the theological tradition of Maurice and Kingsley, but like Headlam he allied it, or rather fused it, with a high sacramental practice that owed everything to the ritual and liturgical developments of the late nineteenth century: 'What I found ... was a beauty manifested principally in the Mass, with its employment of all the senses: the colour of roses, the scent of incense, and the rich harmonies of music'.[71]

In the same way, late-nineteenth century High Churchmanship was also capable of development in and through the particular vein of Philosophical Idealism sponsored in Oxford by, among others, T. H. Green (1836–1882). By no stretch of the imagination was Green a High Churchman: he was closely associated with Benjamin Jowett, the 'Broad Church' Master of Balliol forever tainted by the controversy over his participation in the writing of *Essays and Reviews* (1860), and religiously unorthodox. But Green's combination of a Hegelian metaphysic with a broadly Christian ethics proved immensely attractive to High Churchmen seeking some way of reconciling traditional belief with contemporary scholarship. The nature, influence, strengths and weaknesses of Philosophical Idealism as it bore on Anglicanism in the late nineteenth and early twentieth centuries have been the subject of much discussion, and again need not detain us much here.[72] Nevertheless, the appearance of this pervasive metaphysical or speculative approach to questions of faith was a powerful instrument in the hands of High Churchmen who feared that Anglicanism could not afford to rest on the mere repetition of the dogmatic conclusions reached by Pusey and others in deliberate resistance to the methods of 'modern' biblical and historical criticism. Philosophical Idealism – even if admittedly not in any particularly systematic or rigorous fashion – enabled High Churchmen to square a circle, affirming the authenticity of primitive

---

70   Cf. R. A. Burns, 'Beyond the "Red Vicar": Community and Christian Socialism in Thaxted, Essex, 1910–84'.

71   S. Dark (ed.), *Conrad Noel: An Autobiography*, p. 37.

72   Important recent works include A. Vincent & R. Plant, *Philosophy, Politics and Citizenship: The Life and Thought of British Idealists*; A. P. F. Sell, *Philosophical Idealism and Christian Belief*; T. Gouldstone, *The Rise and Decline of Anglican Idealism in the Nineteenth Century*; see also C. Tyler (ed.) *Unpublished Manuscripts in British Idealism: Political Philosophy, Theology, and Social Thought*.

tradition, and at the same time acknowledging the force and effects of modern scholarship. This they thought they could do by adapting the historicizing, evolutionary structure of Green's understanding of human ideas to Christian doctrine, taking as their central presupposition the presence of Christ in history through the doctrine of the incarnation. Most famously, and notoriously, the volume *Lux Mundi* (1889) gathered together contributions from a group of young Anglo-Catholic theologians – they called themselves the 'Holy party' – who, as it seemed subsequently, almost single-handedly dragged Anglo-Catholicism into the world of contemporary critical scholarship.[73] As others have pointed out, in fact the 'older' generation of Liddon, Pusey and others were not as immune to critical scholarship as is commonly supposed.[74] Nor is it the case, as is sometimes assumed, that the 'Holy party' put incarnational theology on the map in Anglicanism: the 'incarnational turn' about which Boyd Hilton has written occurred rather earlier, and in the hands of theologians such as F. D. Maurice who owed little or nothing to T. H. Green.[75]

Yet *Lux Mundi* did conveniently mark the arrival of what came to be called 'Liberal Catholicism', accentuating the doctrine of the incarnation in High Church theology. But this opened up influences and associations in many different directions, ranging from the 'Cambridge' school of Westcott, Hort and Lightfoot, to the doctrinally cautious but socially alert and passionate Anglo-Catholicism of Frank Weston (1871–1924).[76] The designation 'Liberal Catholicism' was certainly professed by Charles Gore, who was no friend of Modernism, whether Anglican or otherwise, as was demonstrated in his polemic against R. J. Campbell's 'New Theology'.[77] This breadth of connection arguably suggests that 'Liberal Catholicism' was not a clearly-identifiable position, sharply marked off from that of others, but rather a mood of response, a tendency to assimilate an Anglican High Churchmanship conservative in its liturgical, doctrinal and devotional emphases to a willingness to entertain speculatively questions raised against Christian traditionalism by others, if only to

---

73   C. Gore et al., *Lux Mundi: A series of studies in the religion of the Incarnation.*

74   See for example the chapter on Pusey's biblical scholarship in T. Larsen, *A People of One Book: the Bible and the Victorians*; but for a different view, P. B. Hinchliff, *God and History: Aspects of British theology, 1875–1914.*

75   B. Hilton, *The Age of Atonement: The influence of evangelicalism on social and economic thought, 1795–1865.*

76   Cf. D. Newsome, *Two Classes of Men: Platonism and English Romantic Thought*; Hinchliff, *God and History*, pp. 73–98; F. Weston, *The one Christ: An inquiry into the manner of the Incarnation*; A. M. Ramsey, *From Gore to Temple: The Development of Anglican Theology between Lux Mundi and the Second World War 1889–1939.*

77   C. Gore, *The New Theology and the Old Religion* (London, 1907).

reinterpret and thus in some measure reject them. The distinction some scholars have assumed existed between the 'static' approach of churchmen such as
the dogmatic historian Darwell Stone (1859–1941) and the progressiveness of
Gore and others in practice amounted to little, at least in theological terms.[78]

The distinction is not irrelevant, however. Gore was quintessentially an
English Anglo-Catholic, wary of the ritual and liturgical influences of Rome;
that was not at all Stone's position. By the end of the nineteenth century, a
real fissure had opened up in High Churchmanship over reactions to Rome.
This takes us into the troubled history of Ritualism, a particularly slippery
term which came into common use partly as a form of abuse. Apart from the
Oxford Movement itself, Ritualism is probably the aspect of nineteenth-century Anglican High Churchmanship which has attracted most attention, not
least because attempted prosecutions of Ritualist clergy gave the impression
they were a cohesive or compact group.[79] This misperception was facilitated
by the fact that the prosecutions focused mostly on particular ritual acts, and it
was easy, then, to analyse the distribution and advance of the Ritualist threat.
The historiography of Ritualism has been dominated by the late Nigel Yates,
who produced a series of illuminating local studies of Ritualist conflict, and
then finally a comprehensive study, *Anglican Ritualism in Victorian Britain*
(1999). By the 1850s and 60s there was indeed a cluster of specific practices
which parishes were encouraged to adopt by 'Ritualist' clergy, and which
were used commonly as a barometer of Anglo-Catholic orthodoxy, through
such publications as the *Tourist's Church Guide*.[80] The publication in 1858 of
Directorium Anglicanum, a manual of ritual and liturgical directions for the
celebration of the eucharist compiled by John Purchas (1823–1872), who was
later the subject of a notorious ritual prosecution himself, was a significant
stage in this development, completed later in the century by the even more
detailed and elaborate *Ritual Notes* (1890).[81] 'Advanced' Anglo-Catholic clergy
promoted the ritual 'six points' – the eastward-facing position of the celebrant,
incense, the mixing of water and wine in the chalice, wafer bread, eucharistic

---

78   On Stone, see F. L. Cross, 'Stone, Darwell (1859–1941', *ODNB*; also, A. Nichols, *The Panther and the Hind: A Theological History of Anglicanism*, pp. 128 & 140.

79   J. Bentley, *Ritualism and Politics in Victorian Britain: The Attempt to Legislate for Belief*.

80   The *Tourist's Church Guides* were published regularly from the 1870s, mostly by the Eng-lish Church Union, as a directory of 'advanced' or Ritualist churches, with details of ser-vices.

81   J. Purchas, *Directorium Anglicanum: Being a Manual of Directions for the right Celebration of the Holy Communion, for the Saying of Matins and Evensong, and for the Performance of the other Rites and Ceremonies of the Church*; Anonymous, *Ritual Notes on the Order of Divine Service*.

vestments, and lit candles on the altar during the eucharist ('altar lights'). The controversies generated by adoption of these and other practices were fuelled by persistent anti-Catholic sentiment.[82] They also triggered a largely abortive attempt to stamp out Ritualism by legislation, the Public Worship Regulation Act adopted reluctantly in 1874 by Benjamin Disraeli under pressure from the Evangelical peer Lord Shaftesbury and others, and given a lukewarm welcome by Archbishop Tait.[83] The provocative nature of Ritualist practices, the strong current of anti-Catholicism running through conventional British Protestantism, and the flamboyance of many Anglo-Catholics, has led John Shelton Reed, in one of the most comprehensive historical studies of the phenomenon so far, to emphasize the counter-cultural dimension of Anglo-Catholicism.[84] This has never seemed a satisfactory description to me, however, taking into account the social and educational background of most Anglo-Catholic clergy, and their ease of penetration into the upper ranks of the Established Church by the late nineteenth century. It is not without its use, certainly: aspects of Anglo-Catholicism were profoundly disturbing for many Victorians – including the apparent effeminacy of many Ritualist clergy – but it implies a systematic subversion of Victorian society which does not match the complexity both of High Church Anglicanism itself and of its surrounding culture.[85]

By the late nineteenth century, Ritualism had developed in two quite distinct and even opposed ways. In order to protect Anglican High Churchmanship from the 'taint' of Rome, one stream tended to emphasize the authentic English roots of Ritualism. 'Prayer Book Catholicism', as it came to be called, affirmed the *Book of Common Prayer*, even as it sought to situate it in a ritual, sacramental and devotional culture that owed much to a pseudo-Gothic fantasy about the medieval past. Its most famous exponent was Percy Dearmer (1867–1936), who popularised the principles of Prayer Book Catholicism in his best-selling *The Parson's Handbook*, first published in 1899.[86] Dearmer, no mean scholar, was a propagandist as much as an original thinker: his work drew on clear precursors, including J. M. Neale and William Palmer, whose

---

82   On Victorian Anti-Catholicism, see E. R. Norman, *Anti-Catholicism in Victorian England* ; D. G. Paz, *Popular Anti-Catholicism in Mid-Victorian England*; J. Wolffe, *The Protestant Crusade in Great Britain, 1829–1860*.

83   Bentley, *Ritualism and Politics*; cf. also P. T. Marsh, *The Victorian Church in Decline: Archbishop Tait and the Church of England*.

84   Reed, *Glorious Battle*.

85   Cf. D. Hilliard, 'Unenglish and unmanly: Anglo-Catholicism and Homosexuality'; also, D. Janes, *Victorian Reformation: The Fight over Idolatry in the Church of England, 1840–1860*.

86   See D. Gray, *Percy Dearmer: A parson's pilgrimage*.

own works of architectural and liturgical archaeology earlier in the century had helped recover awareness of the history of the 'English use'.[87] In terms of design, and also the liturgical arrangement of church interiors, it was impossible to escape the influence of Augustus Welby Pugin (1812–1852), a convert to Roman Catholicism who was profoundly influenced by Continental Gothic. It was obvious to many, however, that the *Prayer Book* was a poor vehicle for Anglo-Catholic sacramentalism, even with the liturgical elaborations with which the eucharistic rite in particular came to be surrounded, and by the end of the nineteenth century pressure was emerging for a modification of the communion rite in order to express more effectively the eucharistic theology of High Church Anglicanism.[88] This was eventually to lead, in the 1920s, after protracted discussion, to the proposals contained in the revised Prayer Book submitted to Parliament in 1927.[89] Decisive in the process of beginning formal liturgical revision was the report of the Royal Commission on Ecclesiastical Discipline, issued in 1906, which marked the abandonment of the policy of attempting to extirpate Ritualism by regulating or penalizing Ritualist clergy, and which admitted that Anglican order needed to accommodate the liturgical and ceremonial ambitions of Anglo-Catholicism.[90] The 1906 report could be said, then, to mark the institutional acceptance of Ritualism, but largely on 'English' lines.

Always in a minority were those clergy and parishes inclined to discern theological and liturgical norms within Roman Catholicism, and to shape their vision of Anglican worship accordingly. I have already mentioned Darwell Stone, for example. Stone was unabashed about citing Roman precedent in favour of certain liturgical and ritual practices. In his short popular manual on Reservation, he drew attention to the 'devout use' of the reserved sacrament by the Roman Catholic Church 'inheriting a long tradition of Western Christendom' and clearly approved of the following of this Western norm, whilst also arguing for tolerance for those who inclined towards the more cautious use of the Christian East.[91] Use of the Roman rite in Anglo-Catholic worship remained

---

87   See, for example, J. M. Neale, *A few words to Church Wardens on Churches and Church Ornaments: No. 1. Suited to country parishes*; and W. Palmer, *Origines Liturgicae: Or, Antiquities of the English Ritual.*

88   Cf. R. C. D. Jasper, *Prayer Book Revision in England, 1800–1900.*

89   See D. Gray, *The 1927–28 Prayer Book Crisis*; also J. Maiden, *National Religion and the Prayer-Book Controversy, 1927–8.*

90   There is as yet no comprehensive study of the Royal Commission, but a number of authors, including Nigel Yates and John S. Reed, have drawn heavily on its findings.

91   D. Stone, *Reservation of the Blessed Sacrament*, pp. 11 & 14. Another, later, example would be Dom Gregory Dix; cf. Dix, *A Detection of Aumbries.*

relatively scarce, perhaps with the exception of the fairly common practice of inserting an expanded prayer of consecration and oblation, drawing on the Roman Canon, though also on pre-Reformation precedent, into the eucharistic prayer. Yet in other ways – even minor questions of style of vestment and dress, for example – the Roman example was an attractive one. Nonetheless, it was always controversial. Conrad Noel, for example, hailed Dearmer's development of a 'magnificent ceremonial' harking back to the pre-Reformation Church of England to replace the 'trashy ceremonies of the Romish movement'.[92]

No sooner has the existence of this distinction within late-nineteenth century Anglo-Catholicism been noted, however, than it is necessary to complicate it and blur it in various ways. It would be wrong to think that, from the roots of the Oxford Movement, stemmed two separate branches of Ritualism or Anglo-Catholicism, one 'English', the other 'Roman'. Despite growing interest in the churches of Eastern Orthodoxy and the Old Catholic churches of the (later) Union of Utrecht, Roman Catholicism remained, to all intents and purposes, the one extensive, close by, living model of Catholic Christianity, despite all its apparent faults.[93] Its religious orders naturally influenced the revival of orders within Anglicanism.[94] Elements of its devotional life were received and adapted in Anglicanism, including confraternities and guilds, the practice of retreats, and the use of the confessional. Anglican High Churchmen were generally prepared to 'pick and mix' from Roman models, but the extent to which they did so, and the thoroughness with which they did it, varied enormously.

One further dimension of the post-Oxford Movement legacy needs to be considered, at least as far it bears upon the historiography of Anglo-Catholicism. That is the myth of the slum priest. I say 'myth', but this is not meant to deny that there were many Anglo-Catholic clergy who devoted themselves selflessly to service amongst the poor in the great cities and towns of nineteenth and twentieth century England. Amongst the most famous were Arthur Mackonochie (1825–1887), Charles Lowder (1820–1880), Robert Dolling (1851–1902), Richard Enraght (1837–1898) and Arthur Stanton (1839–1913).[95] There

---

92   Dark, *Conrad Noel: An Autobiography*, 79.

93   Cf. M. Chapman, *The Fantasy of Reunion: Anglicans, Catholics, and Ecumenism, 1833–1882*.

94   Cf. P. F. Anson, *The Call of the Cloister: Religious communities and kindred bodies in Anglicanism*; A. M. Allchin, *The Silent Rebellion: Anglican religious communities, 1845–1900*; S. Mumm, *Stolen daughters, virgin mothers: Anglican sisterhoods in Victorian Britain*.

95   M. Reynolds, *Martyr of ritualism: Father Mackonochie of St Alban's, Holborn*; L. Ellsworth, *Charles Lowder and the Ritualist Movement*; B. Palmer, *Reverend rebels: Five Victorian clerics and their fight against authority*; C. Osborne, *The life of Father Dolling*; G. W. E. Russell, *Arthur Stanton: a memoir*.

have been more recent examples, too.[96] Time and again, biographers and historians have tended to emphasize the uncomplicated Catholic spirituality of these men, seeing them as natural heirs of the Oxford Movement, but rather in the development and exemplification of the pastoral ideals of the movement, and in the efflorescence of the more colourful aspects of Catholic liturgical practice, than in any developed system of doctrine as such. The idea that the devotional ideals of the Tractarians were fulfilled in the *unique* commitment of these men to work in the slums needs severe adjustment, however. There was nothing unique about their pastoral zeal, which was matched by any number of Evangelical and 'Broad Church' clergy. Here, for example, is his wife's description of Charles Kingsley's work amongst the poor of Eversley during the cholera outbreak of 1849:

> The parishioners got frightened; so that it was difficult to get nurses for the sick, and he was with them at all hours. After sitting up a whole night by the bedside of a poor labourer's wife ... that he himself might give her the nourishment every half-hour on which her life depended, he once more broke down.[97]

The phenomenon of dedicated celibate priests exercizing a self-sacrificial ministry in the poorest parts of Britain cannot be read as uniquely distinctive of Anglo-Catholicism, nor as alone the reason why, by the beginning of the twentieth century, popular hostility to the alleged 'Romanizing' tendency of Anglo-Catholics had become largely a thing of the past. Here, it is sobering to bear in mind Brian Heeney's criticism of Lida Ellsworth's study of Charles Lowder, 'One would gather, as one often does from books which are rooted in this tradition, that the main thrust of the Church in this period in the slums was, in fact, ritualistic and ceremonialist ... This is a false impression and ought to be corrected by books of this sort'.[98]

Heeney's comment takes us back to the problem of the confessional basis of so much writing on High Churchmanship, the point at which I began. With the exception of the strongly critical writing of Evangelical authors such as Walter Walsh and Edmund Knox, and the few more recent studies by scholars such as

---

96   For example, David Diamond (1935–1992), Rector of Deptford; one of his obituaries said of him, 'He was, unfashionably, an out-and-out Anglo-Catholic, an incense, biretta and Benediction priest': *Independent*, 9 September 1992.

97   F. E. Kingsley, *Charles Kingsley: His Letters and Memories of his Life*, 81.

98   B. Heeney, review of Ellsworth, *Lowder*, in *Albion: A Quarterly Journal Concerned with British Studies*, Vol. 15, No. 3 (Autumn, 1983), p. 254.

Peter Toon and Martin Wellings, the historiography of Anglican High Church-manship has mostly been dominated by Catholics, Anglican and Roman. Even granted the complexity of the historiography I have described, the historical writing on Anglican High Churchmanship has tended to concentrate on influ-ential individuals rather than social movements, on clergy rather than High Church laity, on heroism and struggle rather than the routine, inglorious stuff of administration and parish management, on liturgical practice rather than the theology of pastoral care, and on what is unique and striking rather than what is mundane yet pervasive. It is not that these commonly-described fea-tures are irrelevant and ought to be ignored, but that, time and again, they lack integration into a wider understanding of British religion and society, and iron-ically therefore distort the very phenomenon they seek to explain. This is perhaps even more telling when the history of High Churchmanship is carried on into the mid and late twentieth century, for here, apart from certain theo-logical studies and biographies, there is very little serious examination as yet of the main currents of Anglo-Catholic opinion, and the historiography of the movement has the appearance of a mist out of which a few isolated peaks loom – the 1927–8 Prayer Book crisis, the controversy over the Church of South India, Dix's *Shape of the Liturgy*, Michael Ramsey, the divisions and secessions over women's ordination.[99]

High Churchmanship and Social History

The historiography of Anglo-Catholicism is thus attended, on the one hand, by a series of fine studies, stretching over many decades, which has given us what looks like an almost exhaustive picture of the Oxford Movement and its lead-ers, and by a growing awareness of other dimensions of High Churchmanship, long neglected; and on the other hand, by a persistent tendency to describe High Churchmanship in ways that are peculiarly remote or distinct from the wider currents of British, and indeed European, social and religious history. The chapters that follow are intended to help correct this imbalance, and to that end they try to open up and interrelate questions of ecclesiastical, social and theological history. Methodologically, that is probably my most heartfelt proposal. British church history all too often has slotted into neat disciplinary

---

99　Thus a history of sorts can be reconstructed from unpublished theses and clerical biogra-phies, including: Alan Piggot, '"An educated sense of fitness": Liberal Anglo-Catholicism 1900–1940', unpublished DPhil thesis, Oxford, 2004; Alex Hughes, 'The gospel of divine action: Oliver Chase Quick and the search for a Christocentric metaphysic', unpublished PhD thesis, Cambridge, 2011; W. O. Chadwick, *Michael Ramsey: A Life*; Simon Bailey, *A Tactful God: Gregory Dix Priest, Monk and Scholar*; E. L. Mascall, *Saraband*.

grooves. But this is hardly a satisfactory approach to matters which, to Christians, bore as much on common life as they did on some peculiarly discrete realm of the 'churchly'. Here, then, even as I try to re-read theological or institutional developments, I aim to be porous, to be open to the possibility that significant questions come at this material from angles outside the conventionally ecclesiastical. In particular, a number of general observations underlie my thinking, and these help to provide a broader context.

First, I do not mean to exaggerate the influence of High Churchmanship in this period, nor to suggest that it represented a normative default in Anglicanism as a whole. Nothing of what follows should be read without the realisation that I see British church history in the nineteenth century as profoundly and fundamentally reshaped by the revolution in personal piety in Western Protestantism which historians have called, variously, the Great Awakening, the Evangelical Revival, and Pietism.[100] As I shall show at various points, High Churchmen were influenced positively as well as negatively by Evangelicalism, and even when that was not obviously true, Evangelicalism had effected a transformation in religious opinion.[101] The seriousness with which the Tractarians approached almost every question of church life shared profound affinities with Evangelical views of the world, and unsurprisingly even as Newman criticised and resisted Evangelical theology, he continued to appreciate its impact even on his own soul.[102] The same goes for many High Churchmen – perhaps most famously Gladstone.[103] Evangelical historiography is alive and well, and no historian of British religion can afford to ignore it. So Evangelicalism is a sort of ghost at the banquet here. This is a series of studies of High Churchmanship, not Evangelicalism, and yet the power and prominence of the latter in the nineteenth century, particularly at local level, cannot be ignored, even as it seemed largely absent from the bench of bishops.

A second observation concerns the broad intellectual context of the early nineteenth century. In a famous passage of the *Apologia*, Newman himself drew attention to the influence of what we now call Romanticism, speaking of 'a re-action from the dry and superficial character of the religious teaching and

---

100   Cf. W. R. Ward, *The Protestant Evangelical Awakening*.

101   For all its weaknesses, Ford. K. Brown's influential study of British Evangelicalism does effectively demonstrate the Evangelical reshaping of Victorian society: *Fathers of the Victorians: The age of Wilberforce*; however a more reliable reading can be found in the work of various contemporary scholars, including David Bebbington, John Wolffe and Mark Noll; see, for example, J. Wolffe, *The Expansion of Evangelicalism: The age of Wilberforce, More, Chalmers and Finney*.

102   Newman, *Apologia*, pp. 4–6.

103   Cf. H. C. G. Matthew, *Gladstone 1809–1874*, pp. 6–9.

the literature of the last generation, or century, and as a result of the need which was felt both by the hearts and the intellects of the nation for a deeper philosophy'.[104] The affinity of Romanticism with the 'heart' religion of Evangelicalism is evident, and needs to be affirmed even as we mark David Bebbington's observation that Evangelicalism in other aspects – including its methodical and rational approach to spiritual formation – was a child of the Enlightenment.[105] Romanticism was a broad movement of sensibility which shaped not only art and literature in the nineteenth century, but philosophy, theology and anthropology, critically challenging what had come to be seen as the orthodoxies of an earlier age. Despite its consonance with what is sometimes assumed to be a distinct English tradition, it also helped to undermine notions of national distinctiveness, highlighting or recovering aspects of a vision of Catholicity in particular that instead drew attention to affinities with other historic church traditions such as Eastern Orthodoxy and of course Roman Catholicism, and with the medieval past.

A third observation concerns social history. Elsewhere I have called for an account of religious experience which resists the implicit reductionism of much that has passed for the social history of religion in Britain in the last half century.[106] Discussions of religion in the work of social historians have frequently assumed, following the sociological theory of secularisation, that religious belief has a residual or quantum dimension, for which causes of erosion (such as alternative forms of leisure, resistance to paternalism, and ideas of political and social action, amongst others) can readily be identified, but which does not presume an internal conceptual sophistication. This is obviously flawed as an approach to studying popular belief, and historians need to pay careful attention to the complexity of different manifestations of religious belief and practice in the past in order to understand how our predecessors thought and felt. But by the same token ecclesiastical history does need to register the *social* sophistication of religious belief, and here inspiration can be found, not in the work of secularisation theorists, but in that of religious ethnographers and anthropologists of religion whose primary concern is with understanding how particular religious communities actually work.[107] High Church Anglicanism is, or was, a social movement, whose members, recruit-

---

104   Newman, *Apologia*, p. 99.

105   Cf. D. W. Bebbington, *Evangelicalism in Modern Britain: A History from the 1730s to the 1980s*, pp. 20–74.

106   J. N. Morris 'Secularization and Religious Experience: Arguments in the Historiography of Modern British Religion'.

107   Cf. T. D. Jenkins, *Religion in English Everyday Life: An Ethnographic Approach*, which contains a rich and provocative methodological proposal.

ment, policies, strategies, and economics are important considerations if we wish to understand the phenomenon itself well.

Talk of social history does also raise a number of specific issues that it is as well to note in passing. If the almost pervasive spirituality and ethos of Evangelicalism in the nineteenth and early twentieth centuries is registered, following not only the work of W. R. Ward, but also more controversially that of Callum Brown in his provocative reframing of secularisation theory, *The Death of Christian Britain* (2000), then we are already some way on from the simplistic generalisations of conventional secularisation theory.[108] As I shall note in a moment, the critique of that theory has opened up alternative ways of seeing religion in the nineteenth century than the 'decline' model, and that in turn has implications for the social history of High Churchmanship, which might be better interpreted as a response to general religious revival as much as a last-ditch resistance to the advance of the secular. Its ecumenical awareness – albeit facing a particular direction, namely that of churches conforming to the historic threefold order of deacon, priest and bishop – likewise need not be interpreted as a strategy merely of defence.[109]

I do not specifically cover the role of women here. A more comprehensive account would surely require a feminist perspective – both an analysis alert to the implications of history for the status of women, and a substantial historical argument that attends to the actual place and treatment of women in the past. It is embarrassing to note this, because so little of the literature on Anglo-Catholicism is by women and about women.[110] 'High' churches were no different in their gender composition from other churches in this period: by far the majority of their active congregants were women.[111] This simple observation opens up a very wide and important field of enquiry, not least for a

---

108   Cf. Ward, *Protestant Evangelical Awakening*; and C. G. Brown, *The Death of Christian Britain. Understanding Secularisation 1800–2000*.

109   In the conventional sociological literature on secularisation, ecumenism was commonly interpreted as a strategy for combatting church decline, as in B. R. Wilson, *Religion in Secular Society: A Sociological Comment*; also R. Currie, *Methodism Divided: A Study in the Sociology of Ecumenicalism*.

110   Reed outlines some key issues in a chapter on 'Women and Anglo-Catholicism': *Glorious Battle*, pp. 186–209.

111   Women historians of Anglo-Catholicism include the biographers Georgina Battiscombe, *John Keble*, and Ellsworth, *Lowder*, and also Susan Mumm, *Stolen Daughters, Virgin Mothers*; apart from the female religious orders, probably the most significant female *subject* of writing in this area is the novelist Charlotte M. Yonge, for which see, *inter alia*, E. Jay, 'Charlotte Mary Yonge and Tractarian Aesthetics'; also G. Budge, *Charlotte M. Yonge: Religion, Feminism and Realism in the Victorian Novel*.

theological and devotional movement which placed so much emphasis on a theory of ministry which – at that time – assumed that only men could be ordained. The movement was mainly led by men, and its implications for arguments about gender in ministry – arguments which some think were tested to destruction at the end of the twentieth century – and about celibacy cannot be separated naturally from our understanding of the long history of changing views of the role of women in society.[112] I intend to return to this theme of gender in the future, just as I think there is some mileage to be gained from a consideration of the place and treatment of children, and childhood, along with education, in High Churchmanship.

Fourth, a number of historians, reaching for a succinct way of characterizing Anglo-Catholicism, have formulated interpretations which deem it in some way counter-cultural. Reed certainly did so, as I noted above. So too did J. R. Griffin, whose attempt to align Tractarianism with political radicalism has not commanded much assent, despite some affinities with the much more sophisticated description offered by Simon Skinner of the movement's social radicalism.[113] An earlier discussion of Tractarian literature by Raymond Chapman also picked up the note of cultural dissent.[114] Unfortunately these characterisations, unless heavily qualified, have the potential to mislead seriously. Most High Church clergy in the nineteenth century were politically and socially conservative, and drawn from the same social world as clergy of widely different opinions. They went (largely) to the same schools and universities, and to all intents and purposes displayed the same values and assumptions of the professional middle classes. Their counter-culturalism, such as it was, was not so much symptomatic of an irreducible, intrinsic identity, as of the tensions that resulted from competing religious loyalties within the overarching framework of establishment.

A fifth observation is related. Paradoxically, one underplayed aspect of High Church Anglicanism is precisely its *theological* history, and in turn its situation in the theological evolution of Anglicanism. We are not short of specific theological studies. Amongst the best are those of Yngve Brilioth, A. M.

---

112 This is a significant field of enquiry in its own right, but some measure of its importance can be grasped from the prominence religion occupies in what is now regarded as one of the pioneering works of British feminist history, namely L. Davidoff & C. Hall, *Family Fortunes. Men and Women of the English Middle Class 1780–1850*; cf. especially pp. 76–148.

113 J. R. Griffin, *The Oxford Movement: A revision*; Skinner, *Tractarians and the Condition of England*.

114 R. Chapman, *Faith and Revolt: Studies in the literary influence of the Oxford Movement*.

Allchin, Peter Nockles and Brian Douglas.[115] To these we should add the many rich studies now to hand of aspects of Newman's theology, though these often focus as much on his Roman Catholic period as on his Anglican.[116] Nor are we altogether without some useful general accounts of Anglican theology in this period, which do pay some attention specifically to Anglo-Catholic arguments.[117] But there are still many *lacunae* – no comprehensive study of High Church ecclesiology, for example, nor of its sacramental theology, nor of its soteriology. Again, my aim here is not so much to plug one or two of these gaps, however, as to sketch an approach to High Church Anglicanism which refuses to separate doctrinal and theological history from social history and the history of church institutions. This is something that David Thompson has pursued in his illuminating study of baptism in the nineteenth century.[118] It is also illustrated by R. W. Franklin's monograph on the 'new Catholicism' of Germany, England and France, which traces interconnections between the Catholic theological school of Tübingen, the liturgical theology of Prosper Guéranger, and Pusey's theology.[119] Franklin does not simply describe doctrinal influences: rather, he explores the social and political implications of these developments, hinting at a reading of High Church Anglicanism in the broader context of European Christianity. Though the term is perhaps problematic in relation to British church history, a similar conclusion emerges from the preoccupation of some European historians with the notion of 'culture wars' in the nineteenth century.[120]

Finally, I am convinced that the long shadow of arguments over secularisation and over the supposed uniqueness of British constitutional, political and social development has prevented historians from grasping clearly the reli-

---

115   Y. Brilioth, *The Anglican Revival: Studies in the Oxford Movement*; Allchin, *Participation in God*; Nockles, *Oxford Movement in Context*; B. Douglas, *The Eucharistic Theology of Edward Bouverie Pusey*.

116   These are too many to list here, though I would include, amongst notable recent books, B. King, *Newman and the Alexandrian Fathers: Shaping doctrine in Nineteenth-Century England*.

117   See especially Hinchliff, *God and History*; B. M. G. Reardon, *Religious Thought in the Victorian Age: A survey from Coleridge to Gore*; and D. M. Thompson, *Cambridge Theology in the Nineteenth Century: Enquiry, controversy and truth*.

118   D. M. Thompson, *Baptism, Church and Society in Modern Britain: From the Evangelical Revival to* Baptism, Eucharist and Ministry.

119   R. W. Franklin, *Nineteenth-century Churches: The history of a new Catholicism in Württemberg, England, and France*.

120   See, for example, C. Clark & W. Kaiser, *Culture Wars: Secular-Catholic Conflict in Nineteenth-Century Europe*.

gious character of the nineteenth century. An image of revolt and resistance served Anglo-Catholic historians well against the background of a historiography that presupposed the essential incompatibility of religion and the modern world. Perceptions of church decline, buttressed by the new science of statistics, were endemic in the nineteenth century. But they were fuelled by the very theological and pastoral impulses which informed the culture of renewal to which the Evangelical Revival gave rise, and which provided a rationale for the monumental efforts the British churches poured into church building and philanthropy in the nineteenth century. The 1851 Religious Census – the only complete official census of church attendance ever undertaken in Britain – profoundly influenced the second half of the century, with its apparent conclusion that less than half of the population attended church regularly, and that the Church of England was outnumbered by Dissent and other churches.[121] Clergy and church workers of all denominations struggled to reconcile the perception that the masses of the great towns and cities were unchurched with the obvious truth that congregations and religious causes were multiplying around them throughout the century, and put it all down to ignorance and indifference, a 'falling away' from an assumed point, long in the past, when practically everyone was pious, God-fearing and church-attending. Their insecurity was certainly fed by interdenominational rivalry, by the political controversies surrounding the abolition of discriminatory legislation against Dissenters and Roman Catholics in 1828 and 1829, and by those writers, artists and intellectuals who modified or abandoned their orthodox Christian convictions, giving rise to the frequently-used sobriquets 'Crisis of Faith' or 'Age of Doubt'.[122] Historians have thus been tempted to characterize the Victorian age as just that, an age of threat to religion and of incipient religious decline.[123] But how can one really sustain such a view, when churchgoing was rising inexorably for most of the century, when the churches pervaded almost every aspect of social life, performing vital welfare and educational functions that were later taken over by the State, and when almost all the leading figures in politics and the professions were active members of their denominations?

---

121 Cf. K. D. Snell & P. S. Ell, *Rival Jerusalems: The Geography of Victorian Religion*; but useful still as a summary is B. I. Coleman, *The Church of England in the Mid-Nineteenth century: A Social Geography*. The actual returns have been published in full for many English and Welsh counties, and these editions are too numerous to list here.

122 Both phrases have been widely adopted in the critical literature; cf. T. Larsen, *Crisis of Doubt: Honest faith in nineteenth-century England*, pp. 1–17.

123 Owen Chadwick underlined this view in his influential survey of the origins of modern doubt, *The Secularization of the European Mind in the Nineteenth Century*.

This was admittedly the period in which the roots of European scepticism, nurtured in the Enlightenment, grew to maturity in the humanism, material- ism and atheism of the great modern 'masters of suspicion', such as Feuerbach, Marx, Nietzsche and Freud.[124] But though British churchmen were sometimes tempted to contrast British piety with continental 'Infidelity', just as, in a mirror image, continental Roman Catholics commonly contrasted their own devotion with British heresy and indifference, across Europe as a whole it was scarcely possible to see the hundred years from 1815 as anything other than a period in which the churches generally flourished. In France, the Low Countries, and other parts of Europe in which years of revolutionary turmoil had scoured away much of the ecclesiastical paraphernalia of the *Ancien Régime*, the recov- ery of the churches was little short of remarkable. France, for example, saw the numbers of male clergy leap from 45,000 in 1830 to 75,000 in a little over thirty years, though in the same period the growth of female religious was even more spectacular, from 31,000 to almost 90,000.[125] Continental historiography in some ways remains as preoccupied with the narrative of secularisation as does that of Britain. But this, taking the evidence as a whole, is perverse. As histori- ans increasingly have recognised, the nineteenth century was not a period of religious decline in general, but of great religious revival, and probably the greatest period of institutional church revival since the Middle Ages.[126] *That* is the overarching context for the Anglican High Church revival. Across Britain and Europe throughout the nineteenth century, Christians were restoring and rebuilding their parish churches, building new ones for new or neglected con- gregations, overhauling their administrative structures and hierarchies, and reinvigorating and transforming their pastoral and liturgical practices. They certainly did this with much anxiety about the future. They were alarmed by confessional rivalries. They were also consumed by fear of the recurrence of revolution. That was a vital motivation for mission, but not only in the social historian's presumed 'social control', for it was peasants, artisans and clerks as well as notables who were actors in this drama, and their support for their

---

124   The phrase is Paul Ricoeur's, as used in idem, *Freud and Philosophy: An Essay on Interpre- tation.*

125   H. M. Mills, 'Negotiating the Divide: Women, Philanthropy and the "Public Sphere" in Nineteenth-Century France', p. 44; Mills' figures are derived from C. Langlois, 'Les effectifs des congregations féminin au XIXe siècle: De l'enquête statistique à l'histoire quantita- tive', pp. 44–53.

126   A useful brief assessment of the evidence in Catholic Europe is N. Atkin & F. Tallett, *Priests, Prelates and People: A History of European Catholicism since 1750*, pp. 110–20; an earlier and influential statement of the case for interpreting the nineteenth century over- all this way was D. H. McLeod, *Religion and the People of Western Europe 1789–1970.*

churches was certainly a statement of political intent, a determination to recast and re-form local communities that they thought had been sundered by the vicious cycle of revolutionary militancy.

Reading the nineteenth century in this way runs more compellingly with the grain of the evidence than does the narrative of decline, and should transform our ways of viewing modern British church history. It does not exclude important elements of threat to the churches or of failure in their aspirations. Failure is a motivating principle of Christian action: almost all evangelism is a response to a perceived absence, whether unfamiliar and new (the situation of mission in Africa and Asia in the nineteenth century), or old, habitual and recurrent, as in the Old World. Revivalism generates its own stories of failure even as it recasts or reshapes pious identities and promotes them.[127] In most of its historical incarnations Christianity is also a project for reshaping the self, and so failure in the sense of falling short or falling back from aspiration is endemic to its very existence. By implication, the High Church revival is better read, not so much as a counter-cultural phenomenon, but as a distinct development within the panorama of European religious vitality in this period, one which shared much of its ecclesial character with parallel movements both in Britain and abroad, and yet also had its own unique features.[128] This is not to downgrade its Anglicanism (though, as I have indicated above, its Anglican identity was open to contestation); but there are, or were, correspondences that we might otherwise miss between this current in British Anglicanism and developments on the continent of Europe, and these are most obviously found in sacramental theology and practice.[129] Noting this fact helps to foreground the theological articulation of Anglican High Churchmanship in a way which also does justice to its social and ecclesiastical presence.

What follows, then, is offered as a series of reflections pursuing some of the themes mentioned above. It does not offer a new interpretation as such, but new emphases, and it can be characterised perhaps by four main assertions. First, I want to complicate, rather than simplify, our understanding of High Churchmanship, because only by drawing out the many different strands of action and interaction can we begin to understand the whole picture. But this

---

127   Cf. Morris, 'Secularization and Religious Experience'; also D. Erdozain, 'The secularisation of sin in the nineteenth century', pp. 59–88.

128   This is a point noted also by Pereiro, 'Ethos' and the Oxford Movement, pp. 60–2.

129   An instance of this theme in the historiography was N. P. Williams and C. Harris (eds), Northern Catholicism; however, this volume proposed a distinctive 'North European' form of Catholicism which sits uneasily with the evidence put forward here and elsewhere that the main lines of influence between Anglican High Churchmanship and Continental Catholicism ran through France and Italy.

requires, second, a recognition of, and attention to, the local, and to the implications of change in churches as they are encountered and experienced locally.
But third, I also want to draw out wider international comparisons, and to
demonstrate that what is at issue is not merely a small subset of one nation's
religious history, but rather common currents and responses that were experienced across Europe, as in Britain, in varying ways. Much more could be said
on this theme, and what I do here is no more than to offer some observations
on a perspective that I hope to open out in future work. Fourth, these currents
are validly explored as theological (I appreciate some will say 'ideological')
aperçus, which nevertheless cast light on the social placing and ambitions of
High Churchmanship.

The Language of Church Party and Revivalism

However, there are two difficulties. The first is that of church 'party' language,
or rather terminology. This is peculiarly slippery in relation to Anglican High
Churchmanship. The designation 'High Churchman' is a broad one which
includes many subsets, and I have generally stuck to it as a way of capturing the
whole field of study. And yet historians sometimes use the term in a restricted
sense too, in contrast to, for example, Tractarianism or Ritualism, qualifying it
by the adjectives 'orthodox', 'older' or 'traditional'. The qualifiers are helpful, if
only because they indicate that there were High Churchmen who considered
themselves to be loyal to an inherited tradition which the Tractarians and others were abandoning or distorting; that was the position taken up by Palmer of
Worcester College, and Burgon, for example. It is confusing to use the same
term as the general description for a whole phenomenon as is used for a particular element, however. The same difficulty arises with the common term
'Catholic revival', and can bedevil even the terms 'Anglo-Catholic' or 'Anglo-
Catholicism', or even (less commonly in the historical literature) 'Catholic
Anglicanism'. If Anglo-Catholicism is a subset of High Churchmanship, how
can it at the same time usefully be used as a catch-all term? The Liberal Broad
Churchman H. L. Jackson, Vicar of St Mary's, Huntingdon, writing to his con-
gregation in 1899 about Ritualism seems to have largely conflated the terms
'High Church' and 'Anglo-Catholic', conceding the victory of the 'High
Churchman' – 'Very patiently, very courageously has he worked. Most of the
opposition he has met with has been fatuous to the last degree.'[130] Once again,

---

130   H. L. Jackson, *Liberalism and Loyalty: Or Some Plain Words on the (so-called) Crisis in the
       Church* (1899), quoted in R. Lloyd, *The Church of England in the Twentieth Century*, Vol. 1,
       p. 121.

we are trapped by the complexity of individuals, as earlier when I discussed Walter Hook in passing. Was Charles Gore, to take another example, a High Churchman (definitely 'English' and even Protestant rather than 'Roman' in his sense of theological and liturgical norms), or an Anglo-Catholic (profoundly influenced by the Oxford Movement), or a Ritualist (vestments, mixed chalice, etc), or a Liberal Catholic (in his acceptance of critical scholarship)? Or all four? It does not seem to me helpful to impose rigid boundaries on the scope of these terms, and so the reader may think that sometimes I slip too easily from 'High Church' to 'Anglo-Catholic'. But a few broad guidelines may help.

'High Church' is by far the most comprehensive term used here, and it covers the 'orthodox' or old High Church, the Tractarians and their followers, Ritualists, Liberal Catholics, and all others who form the subject of this book. But its distinctness as a term is compromised by its breadth: in general, it means those Anglicans who upheld the threefold order of ministry and the doctrine of the apostolic succession of the ministry, who valued the tradition of the Church, and who emphasized the importance of the sacraments in the life and worship of the Church. It is not helpful or important to try to press the term more closely than this, though its sheer breadth means that it could be used to cover, for example, F. D. Maurice, who is often also described as a Liberal Anglican or a Broad Churchman, as well as someone of an altogether different persuasion such as Henry Liddon. Nonetheless, the broadest sense of the term remains the most significant first step in noting a movement of opinion marked off in its approach to matters of faith and order from the Low Church or 'Evangelical' wing of the Church of England, and from many aspects of the 'middle' or 'Broad' church.

Some of the difficulties of adopting this broader perspective have been indicated by James Pereiro, who prefers a sharper distinction between Tractarianism and the older High Church tradition than I am altogether comfortable with. As Pereiro pointed out, following Nockles, the Oxford Movement was both born 'within a High Church intellectual context' and yet contained at its heart a 'radical theory [of apostolic succession] which would drastically transform their [i.e. High Church] shared theological, disciplinary, and ascetical positions'.[131] Accordingly, tensions rapidly widened between the 'older' High Church tradition and the Tractarians, and by the early 1840s there was a clear attempt on the part of the High Church (a 'determined High Church counter-offensive') to reassert the Anglican, even 'Protestant' character of the movement of 1833, and to distance it as much as possible from the more extreme 'Roman' development to which, by 1843, it seemed to be subject.[132] In time, as Pereiro

---

131   Pereiro, 'Ethos' and the Oxford Movement, p. 72.
132   Pereiro, 'Ethos' and the Oxford Movement, p. 75.

recognizes, many High Churchmen were to see the Oxford Movement as 'a hindrance rather than a help'.[133] On a longer perspective, however, these terms became, later in the nineteenth century, somewhat slippery, and weighed down by polemical connotations. As even Pereiro admits, the claim 'that the advance of High Church principles had taken place in spite of the Oxford Movement bears all the marks of an anxious effort to disclaim a connection which by then had become odious'.[134] Nonetheless Tractarianism *was* a subset of a broader category we may call Anglican 'High Churchmanship' – a category subject to many internal tensions and divisions – and it was a part, if nonetheless a very salient and dynamic one, of a High Church revival that began before 1833 and continued on through the century, long after the apparent 'collapse' of the Oxford Movement in 1845.

If, for all the ambiguities, the term 'High Church' is the most useful overall term, specific emphases or moods within it require more restricted labels, though again contemporary description was not always as nicely discriminating as historians would have it. 'Oxford Movement', 'Puseyite', and 'Tractarian' all serve to highlight the particular strand of High Churchmanship represented by the Tractarians and their followers. Frederick Oakeley noted perceptively the difficulties posed by all of these descriptors, opting himself for the 'modest term Tractarian'.[135] The tendency to use the term 'Ritualist' to denote those who were especially noteworthy for liturgical and ceremonial innovations is helpful in describing a particular set of controversies in the third quarter of the nineteenth century, but there was a complex relation to Tractarianism (more on that in the next chapter), and again the term must not be taken in an absolute, ring-fenced, definitive sense.

Finally, there is the term 'Anglo-Catholic'. Most common usage suggests that, by the end of the nineteenth century, it had come to be applied in a more restricted way than 'High Church'. Anglo-Catholics were definitely High Church, but not all High Churchmen were content to be called Anglo-Catholics, assuming that the phrase implied a more militant shade of High Churchmanship. Nonetheless, once again the distinction has only to be pointed out to demand qualification: there was a difference of emphasis, or even in some respects of opinion (for example on attitudes to the Roman Catholic Church), so that in practice to describe someone as a High Churchman but definitely not an Anglo-Catholic has a certain 'common sense' accuracy. But there were many people who simply could not comfortably be pigeonholed one way or another,

---

133   Pereiro, *'Ethos' and the Oxford Movement*, p. 77.

134   Pereiro, *'Ethos' and the Oxford Movement*, loc. cit.

135   Oakeley, *Historical Notes*, p. 3.

such as R. F. Littledale (1833–1890), a definite Ritualist who was, nonetheless, a determined critic of Roman Catholicism.[136] The linguistic or terminological problem resists easy resolution, and for the sake of convenience I have retained 'High Church' as the dominant term, mostly resorting to 'Anglo-Catholic' for those circumstances in which I wish to point to an individual or set of views influenced by the more 'advanced' sacramentalism of those who were followers of the Tractarians.

The second difficulty concerns the question of revival. This is a study of a movement of revival, and the term may seem unproblematic. But as I have already indicated, therein lies a major historiographical complication. Whatever else they were advocating, the Tractarians certainly saw themselves as *reviving* principles and practices long neglected in the Church of England. Yet recent scholarship has cast doubt on their assumption that the High Church tradition had fallen into decay in the Church of England by the early nineteenth century. Was there, then, a High Church revival at all, in any meaningful, objective sense in the nineteenth century? My contention, *pace* recent scholarship, is that there was – a revival of confidence, a revival of many ritual and ceremonial practices, a revival of sacramental convictions and principles not altogether lost to previous generations, but still neglected or at times poorly integrated into wider ecclesial practice, amongst other things. Whether or not this was, strictly, a numerical revival is hard to establish. But we should be wary of dispensing with the term 'revival' altogether. Contemporaries knew it was happening, and would have looked askance at the suggestion that it was largely an illusion. They knew that what was at stake was nothing less than the theological identity of the Church of England. A great deal of energy, in print and in practice, was spent in promoting the High Church revival. Nevertheless what exactly the revival was, and how far one can assume it to have been a question of numeric strength and growth, is a question that will surface a various points in this book.[137]

In this interconnected series of studies I present the High Church revival in the Church of England as more central to the modern experience of

---

136   George Herring, 'Littledale, Richard Frederick (1833–1890)', ODNB.

137   There is an extensive literature on revival*ism* in the nineteenth century, but this for the most part concerns the particular cluster of opinions and practices typical of Evangelical revivalism, and receives little direct attention here. For a useful discussion of the overlap between Evangelical revivalism and High Churchmanship, see D. Voll, *Catholic Evangelicalism: The acceptance of Evangelical traditions by the Oxford Movement during the second half of the nineteenth century*; also, J. Kent, *Holding the Fort: Studies in Victorian Revivalism*, pp. 236–94. I attempted a brief, overall history of modern revivalism in J. N. Morris, *Renewed by the Word: The Bible and Christian Revival since the Reformation*.

Anglicanism than many historical critics have presented it, and yet also more closely related to broader currents of European religious history. Part 1 covers the key characteristics of the revival itself. In the second chapter, I explore the local dynamics of the revival through a number of case studies, indicating both its regional complexity and its dependence upon a variety of factors stretching well beyond the role of 'heroic' individuals. In chapter three, I draw a number of broader themes together to depict the revival as a movement of sacramental renewal which sought to present a new way of understanding church community in England as, first and foremost, eucharistic community, and yet which encountered significant, even decisive resistance. Part 2 opens up a European perspective. Chapter four explores the ways in which British High Churchmen toured the Continent and commented on what they observed in Roman Catholic churches, bringing back their perceptions into Anglican commentary. Chapter five traces common interests and common perceptions, if at the same time critical counter-currents, between French Catholics and the Tractarians. In the remaining chapters I show something of the internal theological complexity of the revival, and at the same time distinct elements of its identity as a movement within Anglicanism. Chapter six involves a discussion of the way Tractarianism was preached. This forms a bridge to two more closely theological chapters, exploring successively the ecclesiological 'boundaries' with the Broad Church, and with Marian devotion. A final chapter considers the twentieth-century destiny of High Churchmanship, and the reasons for its 'failure', that is its inability to transform the identity of the Church of England so decisively and completely that its theological perceptions could be accepted broadly and without controversy. Its failure in some degree set the scene for its late-twentieth century conflicts over human sexuality and women's ministry.

PART 1

Growth, Renewal and Society

∴

Movements and Regions: Dynamics of Local Religious Change

Whatever the cross-currents of historical interpretation, the High Church revival in the Church of England was at least an unquestioned fact by the early twentieth century. Its prominence could be measured externally in terms of changing ritual and liturgical practice, with a growing frequency of communion services, an increasingly elaborate liturgical style, and a rising confidence in asserting doctrinal positions and emphases on controverted points that would have shocked many Anglicans two or three generations before. Its institutional base, after the failure of the strategy of containing Ritualism through legislative and penal means, was secure by the 1890s and 1900s. The founding of theological colleges such as those at Chichester (1839), Wells (1840), Salisbury (1861) and St Stephen's House, Oxford (1876) provided a theological and vocational grounding in High Church principles. National associations such as the English Church Union (founded in 1859 as the Church of England Protection Society), the Society of the Holy Cross (or SSC, from the Latin Societas Sanctae Crucis, founded 1855 for clergy), and the Confraternity of the Blessed Sacrament (first formed 1857, but refounded 1862, as a society dedicated to eucharistic devotion) could draw together Anglo-Catholic opinion, and represent its interests. Although its more extreme adherents, with their enthusiasm for devotional practices going beyond the canonical or authorised norms of Anglicanism, continued to be a headache for bishops, nevertheless there was growing acceptance by the church hierarchy of the distinct theological position advocated by Anglo-Catholics.

Some have even argued that this growing acceptance represented a 'respectable' or increasingly 'middle class' trend that was tantamount to a betrayal of its roots.[1] By the time of the *British Weekly* London church census of 1886–7, for example, the building of distinctly Ritualist or Anglo-Catholic churches in the London suburbs had easily begun to outpace the congregations built up by several decades of intensive slum ministry in East London – contrast St Augustine's, Kilburn (consecrated in 1880), with its morning congregation of 866, with Charles Lowder's St Peter's, London Docks (consecrated in 1866; Lowder, by then, was dead, and his former curate Lincoln Wainwright was in

---

1   Cf. J. S. Reed, *Glorious Battle: The Cultural Politics of Victorian Anglo-Catholicism*, pp. 263–4.

© KONINKLIJKE BRILL NV, LEIDEN, 2016 | DOI 10.1163/9789004326804_003

charge), with its morning congregation of 226.[2] But there is actually little evidence that middle-class adhesion to High Churchmanship was a late-nineteenth century phenomenon: churches completed or consecrated in the last quarter of the century could take a long time, even up to twenty years, to reach that point, from the conception of a mission district through to the acquisition of land, the building of a mission hall, and the raising of funds. Moreover, suburban strength compared with inner-city weakness was hardly a feature unique to Anglo-Catholicism, at least in modern British religious history, and the very existence of the comparison points to the importance of scrutinizing closely the various regional and local factors that contributed to the changing fortunes of the movement. The nature and scope of the revival cannot adequately be assessed from congregational numbers alone – no more than it can by concentrating exclusively on personalities and opinions. The local dynamics of change – the multiple interactions between people at local level which facilitated or impeded church life – constitute an essential dimension in any attempt to understand a religious movement.

In this chapter, I shall explore these dynamics through a number of telling examples, drawn from various regions. I aim to demonstrate how the study of Anglican High Churchmanship in this period is part of the wider social history of religion in Britain, in order to outline the complex processes by which Anglican ecclesial culture was transformed in the nineteenth and early twentieth centuries. Initial reflections on the theme of growth qualify the more outlandish assumptions often made about the impact of the Oxford Movement in particular, emphasizing its location within a broader movement of church renewal. As one social historian of religion acknowledged, the growth of the Church of England in the nineteenth and early twentieth centuries represented 'the one prolonged period after the Restoration in which [it] succeeded in improving its quantitative position within English society'.[3] In that context, it is clear that the High Church revival took place *within*, rather than over and against, the broader recovery of the Church of England in the period. A second section considers the more troublesome question of the relationship of Tractarianism and Ritualism within the revival, and essentially argues for their treatment as a single phenomenon. The third and fourth sections turn to a more detailed exploration of local patterns of change, focusing particularly on urban areas, taking into account particularly the work of the late Nigel Yates,

2   *The Religious Census of London, Reprinted from the British Weekly*, pp. 22 & 32.
3   A. D. Gilbert, *Religion and Society in Industrial England: Church, Chapel and Social Change 1740–1914*, p. 29.

who surpassed all other researchers in the field in his detailed local studies of Tractarianism.

Revival and Church Growth

When historians, theologians and others speak about the Evangelical revival, invariably what they actually mean by that is numerical expansion, from the first appearance of recognizably Evangelical principles in the hands of a relatively small number of Anglican clergy in the mid-eighteenth century, who had to fight prejudice and suspicion, through a great period of growth and consolidation to a secure position of prominence by the middle of the nineteenth century.[4] Even in relation to Evangelical history, however, the notion of 'revival' has always entailed something more complex than mere numeric growth, including as it does *both* the renewal of vitality *and* changing patterns of piety on the part of many who would always have considered themselves in some sense 'Low' church. Similar ambiguities are involved in High Churchmanship. The complications of 'party' identity are relevant, too: it is much less easy to assume a simple model of numeric expansion when party rivalries which were fast solidifying by the mid-nineteenth century were much less certain, much more fluid, just a generation or two back. To grasp the nature of this complexity, it is necessary to undergo a brief immersion again into the historiography of the High Church revival.

Before the work of Nockles and others began to appear in the 1990s, our understanding of the High Church revival, and especially of the Oxford Movement, was seen from a vantage point – the early twentieth century – when Anglo-Catholicism was on the verge of becoming the largest and most vigorous wing of the Established Church. If, as Owen Chadwick has suggested, the first, influential series of studies of Tractarianism were those, not by 'its heirs but its critics and renegades', which appeared in the 1880s and prompted the writing and posthumous publication of Church's history, nevertheless books such as Ollard's *Short History of the Oxford Movement* (1915), Brilioth's *Anglican Revival* (1925), Webb's *Religious Thought in the Oxford Movement* (1928), and Faber's *Oxford Apostles* (1933) for two generations or so heavily

---

4   The point is neatly made by the title of the second volume of the IVP four volume series, *A History of Evangelicalism*, namely John Wolffe's *The Expansion of Evangelicalism*, which sits between Mark Noll's *The Rise of Evangelicalism*, and David Bebbington's *The Dominance of Evangelicalism*.

influenced historians' views.[5] These were all published around what Pickering called the 'triumphal period' of Anglo-Catholicism, when numbers of clergy and laity enrolled at the Anglo-Catholic congresses jumped from 13,000 in 1920 to some 70,000 in the centenary year of 1933.[6] With the partial exception of Brilioth's more nuanced account, they tended to reinforce the common view of the High Church revival as both a crescendo from a rather isolated 'rump' in the mid-1840s and, paradoxically, as a direct consequence of the inspiration and actions of the early Tractarian leaders. Numerical and other evidence appeared to back up this view. Palmer's *Narrative* describes how the petition to Archbishop Howley in 1834 raised apprehension and opposition from some clergy who might otherwise have sympathised with its views; nevertheless, some 7,000 did sign, and in the *Apologia* Newman described his own efforts to rally local clergy 'in favour of the Church'.[7] Both Newman's and Palmer's narratives saw 1845 as a watershed, a crisis from which the Movement took many years to recover.[8] The impression of Tractarianism as embattled in mid-century was underlined by the Gorham judgement, further secessions, and popular hostility as exemplified by the surplice riots in Exeter. George Herring's research claimed that Tractarianism was a relatively small, albeit growing clerical movement in mid-century, some 81 Tractarian incumbents in 1840 rising to 442 in 1870 by his reckoning.[9] It was certainly a very different picture by the end of the Victorian period: the *Tourist's Church Guide* of 1902 reckoned that some 1,526 churches in England and Wales, for example, possessed and were using eucharistic vestments, a sure mark of 'advanced' Anglo-Catholic or Ritualistic practice.[10]

For all the apparent precision of such figures, accurate assessment of the real strength of Anglo-Catholicism throughout this period is difficult, though, and positions such as Herring's on Tractarianism imply a monolithic movement sharply differentiated from the rest of the Church. The controversial nature of Tractarianism and Ritualism itself encouraged many clergy to dis-

---

5   W. O. Chadwick, *The Spirit of the Oxford Movement*, p. 139.

6   W. S. F. Pickering, *Anglo-Catholicism: A Study in Ambiguity*, pp. 48 & 56.

7   W. Palmer, *Narrative of events connected with the Tracts for the Times*, pp. 108–9; J. H. Newman, *Apologia Pro Vita Sua*, p. 43.

8   In Palmer's case, the 1883 edition is vital here; see Palmer, 'Supplement to the Narrative', pp. 233–43, on the fall of the 'Romanizing party'.

9   G. W. Herring, 'From Tractarianism to Ritualism: A Study of Some Aspects of Tractarianism outside Oxford, from the time of Newman's conversion in 1845 until the First Ritual Commission in 1867', D.Phil. thesis, University of Oxford, 1984, p. 43.

10   Royal Commission on Ecclesiastical Discipline [RCED], *Report of the Royal Commission on Ecclesiastical Discipline*, Vol. 1, para. 88.

tance themselves from such labels, however, even though in practice they promoted many of the same liturgical and sacramental principles, misleading contemporaries about the real nature of the difference. Conybeare's survey of 'Church Parties' in the *Edinburgh Review* in 1853 reckoned some 7,000 clergymen out of 18,000 were 'High Church', though of these only 1,000 were the 'more noisy than numerous' Tractarians.[11] This was nothing more than an estimate, based on an extrapolation from 500 clergymen on the *Clergy List* whom Conybeare happened to know.[12] Herring's identification of 958 Tractarian clergymen in the period 1845 to 1867 is probably an underestimate. Since he included figures such as Charles Lowder and Alexander Mackonochie, men commonly described as Ritualists, it must be assumed that his Appendix listing these clergymen embraced *both* Ritualism *and* Tractarianism, movements which in the main body of his thesis he tended to distinguish from each other, and yet in my own doctoral research on Croydon I found that of eleven priests-in-charge and five incumbents at Tractarian and Ritualist churches in Croydon and Norwood before 1870, none was listed by Herring.[13] This does at least indicate the nature of the problem of counting. If we take into account the complications of terminology and typological analysis described in the previous chapter, the High Church revival can seem peculiarly elusive. At one end of the spectrum of speculative descriptions of growth, one might indeed see a triumphant progress from the presumed 'rump' of 1845 to the thousands attending the Anglo-Catholic congresses in the 1920s and 30s; but at the other end, registering the numerical density of High Church clergy in the mid-nineteenth century, one might almost see no significant numerical 'growth' at all over the ensuing half century.

The safest course – or rather, the most plausible one – seems to be a 'middle' way. The High Church revival brought renewed confidence and energy to sacramental Anglicanism, but it depended on the continual activity and influence of clergy and laity who were definitely 'High Church' but not necessarily Tractarian or Ritualist, as well as on the more sharply-articulated opinions of the Tractarians and their 'heirs'. Identifying the various component strands of the revival is something that can be done only at the local level. Here it may be

---

11   W. Conybeare, 'Church Parties', originally published in 1853 in the *Edinburgh Review*, but amended and reprinted several times; there is a full critical edition, edited by R. A. Burns, in S. Taylor (ed.), *From Cranmer to Davidson: A Church of England Miscellany*, pp. 245–385; references here pp. 329 & 357.

12   Conybeare, 'Church Parties', p. 356. For a useful discussion of Conybeare's use of sources, see R. A. Burns's introduction to 'Church Parties', in Taylor, *From Cranmer to Davidson*.

13   Herring, 'Tractarianism to Ritualism', pp. 37–9, & Appendix.

possible to recognize distinctively Tractarian or Ritualist churches, but the influence of the revival or development of High Church doctrines, of liturgical renewal, and of greater provision of services, especially communion, to take but a few features, was far wider and far more diffused. Croydon Parish Church, for example, was scarcely in the forefront of Ritualist innovation in the 1860s and 1870s, and yet it introduced a surplice choir, used lighted altar candles, and introduced weekly communion and then daily offices, all of which modest charges led to accusations that the vicar of Croydon had compromised his opposition to Ritualism.[14] What precisely was the relationship between this kind of moderate change, and the sharper, more focused practice and ecclesiology of Ritualism? Whilst not ruling out altogether some limited notion of Anglo-Catholic expansion within the Church of England as a whole, the revival is much more helpfully characterised in terms of distinctive changes and shifts within High Churchmanship. If the High Church revival in its broadest sense meant a renewal of confidence and vitality on the part of those who professed to be High Church Anglicans, that renewal was to a considerable degree driven by the 'revival' in a narrower sense, namely the growing adoption of the version of apostolic sacramentalism promoted by the Tractarians and their heirs.

The Relationship of Tractarianism and Ritualism

Yet is it even possible to assume that Tractarianism and Ritualism essentially constituted one movement? My contention is that it is. Yet to say as much does go against some influential voices. Nigel Yates claimed that Ritualism was the 'logical outcome' of the Oxford Movement – a practical outworking of Tractarian sacramental principles.[15] This was denied by the Ritual Commission of 1906, which took the pragmatic line that the theological positions of the Oxford Movement leaders did not directly imply or require the ritual elaborations of later Anglo-Catholics.[16] Herring followed suit, arguing that the very extremism of Ritualist clergy in the late 1850s and 1860s marked them out from the Tractarians, who had elevated the practice of caution and moderation, he says, into a distinctive pastoral practice.[17] Herring pointed out that many Tractarian clergymen were critical of Ritualist innovations and did not themselves see these as a 'logical outcome' of their own views. W. J. Butler, for example, thought

---

14   Anon, 'John Hodgson', in *Croydon Crayons* (Croydon, 1873), p. 10.

15   W. N. Yates, *The Oxford Movement and Anglican Ritualism*, p. 22.

16   RCED, *Report*, Vol. 1, paras 300–4.

17   Herring, 'Tractarianism to Ritualism', especially chapter 13.

Alexander Mackonochie was 'trying to force into the use of the Church of England that which the Church in no way authorizes'.[18] Ritualism chiefly arose, as Herring saw it, in the wake of the publication of the first edition of the *Directorium Anglicanum* in 1858.[19]

Herring – amongst others – thus sharpened up a distinction between Tractarianism and Ritualism which needs to be blunted again. As he acknowledged, both Protestant and Roman Catholic critics drew a direct connection between the two, on both accounts ironically because Tractarian teaching was assumed to lead to Rome.[20] Furthermore, whilst citing Tractarian critics of Ritualism such as Pusey, Butler, William Gresley and Thomas Stevens, he also supplied a number of instances of Tractarians who did support Ritualism and did assume a direct connection – J. M. Neale, T. T. Carter, W. J. E. Bennett, and J. W. H. Molyneux, amongst others.[21] If caution and moderation were to be taken as distinctive Tractarian hallmarks, then where did Neale and Bennett fit in, provocative and 'advanced' as they were? Herring used what was essentially a pastoral distinction to prise apart liturgical practice from sacramental theology, but there is much evidence to suggest that contemporaries recognised that this could not be done. Newman, for one, looked back on his views in the 1840s in the following way:

> I considered that to make the *Via Media* concrete and substantive, it must be much more than it was in outline; that the Anglican Church must have a ceremonial, a ritual, and a fullness of doctrine and devotion, which it had not at present, if it were to compete with the Roman Church with any prospect of success. Such additions would not remove it from its proper basis [presumably the *Prayer Book*], but would merely strengthen and beautify it: such, for instance, would be confraternities, particular devotions, reverences for the Blessed Virgin, prayers for the dead, beautiful churches, rich offerings to them and in them, monastic houses, and many other observances and institutions, which I used to say belonged to us as much as to Rome.[22]

---

18   Herring, 'Tractarianism to Ritualism', p. 203, quoting A. J. Butler (ed.), *Life and Letters of William John Butler* (1897).

19   Herring, 'Tractarianism to Ritualism', p. 286.

20   Herring, 'Tractarianism to Ritualism', pp. 309 & 399.

21   See, for example, T. T. Carter's assertion in 1878 that 'there were real, vital links binding the one to the other, – a substantial unity of faith and purpose': Herring, 'Tractarianism to Ritualism', p. 312.

22   Newman, *Apologia*, p. 173.

James Bentley quotes Newman, again, writing to Manning in 1839: 'Give us more services, more vestments and decorations in worship.'[23] As chapter 4 will demonstrate, a number of Tractarians were drawn to the elaborate ritual and devotional practices of continental Catholicism, and brought back their excitement at what they had seen abroad to Britain. Pusey may have been cautious in his approach to liturgical matters – and his difficulties with St Saviour's, Leeds, were to convince him of the strategic importance of making haste slowly in ritual affairs – but he was, if anything, unusual in that respect.

It is not, all in all, convincing to argue that Ritualism represented a sharp break from an earlier phase of the revival. Liturgical revival and reform were well under way before the publication of the *Directorium Anglicanum*. Works such as William Palmer's *Origines Liturgicae* (1832) and William Maskell's *Monumenta Ritualia Ecclesiae Anglicanae* (1846) drew attention to continuities between the *Book of Common Prayer* and the historic rites and liturgies of the Western Church. J. M. Neale's *Hierurgia Anglicana* (1843), itself a principal source for the *Directorium*, assembled a battery of evidence about the rites and ceremonies of the post-Reformation Church. Even the word 'ritualist' was in use from the 1830s to describe someone who favoured more elaborate ceremonial in worship: Palmer, for example, used it in the Preface to *Origines Liturgicae*, and Maskell used it in his letters *On the Present Position of the High Church Party* in 1850.[24] It seems likely that the *Directorium* no more than focused ritualistic tendencies which were already in existence by the late 1850s. Two sources or trends in particular served to intensify the movement towards ritual revival and innovation. One, quite simply, was the response to controversy, and particularly to legal prosecution. The Denison and Westerton versus Liddell cases, for example, prompted a flurry of publications on either side, including Thomas Perry's *Lawful Church Ornaments* (1857), yet another of the principal sources for the *Directorium*.[25] Perry's enormous volume anticipated the *Directorium*'s assertion that the Ornaments Rubric of the Prayer Book referred to existing common practice in the second year of Edward VI, and not solely to the ordinances of the first Prayer Book; it and the Denison case illustrated the

---

23   J. Bentley, *Ritualism and Politics in Victorian Britain: The Attempt to Legislate for Belief,* p. 26.

24   W. Palmer, *Origines Liturgicae or Antiquities of the English Ritual,* 'Preface' to 1st edn., p. vi; W. Maskell, *A Second Letter on the Present Position of the High Church Party in the Church of England,* p. 61.

25   T. W. Perry, *Lawful Church Ornaments: Being an historical examination of the Judgement of the Right Hon. Stephen Lushington.*

other trend, namely the developing Tractarian understanding of the eucharist, particularly the doctrines of real presence and eucharistic sacrifice.[26] Indeed it may have been not so much the ritual directions contained in the *Directorium* which caused so much offence, thoroughly in line in the main with published Tractarian teaching as they were, as its uncompromising language of eucharistic sacrifice: 'the principal worship of the Church on earth ... [is objective and contains] a great action, even the perpetuation of the Sacrifice made on the Cross, in an unbloody manner on the altar'.[27] If, as Härdelin argued, the change was first marked by the appearance of Robert Wilberforce's *Doctrine of the Holy Eucharist* in 1853, nevertheless this was not a novel or isolated theological stance. As Newsome suggested, Wilberforce's book came 'as manna in the wilderness' to Manning, Gladstone, Philpotts and others like them.[28]

Herring's argument claimed, then, that the term 'Ritualism' was effectively shorthand for a liturgical extremism detached to some degree from the sacramental theology of which it was an expression. Certainly evidence can be found for contemporary Tractarian or High Church clergymen wishing to distance themselves from unashamed Ritualists. But these distinctions did not carry much weight for local clergy and laity, nor indeed for local journalists, for whom the terms 'Tractarian', 'Ritualist', 'Anglo-Catholic' and even simply 'High Church' were often largely interchangeable. In retrospect, there were many differences between certain Anglo-Catholic 'Romish' positions, Prayer Book Catholicism, and Tractarianism proper, at least as professed by individuals who could be identified as such, but in general they hardly constituted discrete, firmly-defined 'parties within a party'. The patterns of interaction were complicated, and perhaps the best that can be said, along with the Royal Commission on Ecclesiastical Discipline, is the vague but adequate statement that 'If on the one hand it is true to say that what is called Ritualism is a development of the Tractarian Movement, it is on the other hand as true to say that it represented a great change ... a new departure in that movement.'[29]

---

26   Perry, *Lawful Church Ornaments*, p. 7; on Tractarian views of the eucharist, see A. Härdelin, *The Tractarian Understanding of the Eucharist*.

27   Purchas, *Directorium Anglicanum*, p. x.

28   D. Newsome, *The Parting of Friends: A Study of the Wilberforces and Henry Manning*, p. 380.

29   RCED, *Report*, Vol. 1, para. 302, echoing Archbishop Davidson's evidence at Vol. 2, paras 12851–2.

Regional Variations of Religious Belief and Practice

The general implication of the foregoing section is that the varieties of High Churchmanship to be encountered within nineteenth-century Anglicanism did not nevertheless negate a larger, essential unity within the revival. That makes the prospect of some generalisations about patterns of revival much stronger than might otherwise be the case. Here the regional dimension is pertinent, and I need to make some preliminary observations about the regional analysis of religious practice in Britain. It has long been a commonplace of commentary on British religion that different denominations had varying regional strengths and weaknesses. The social commentator Geoffrey Gorer's mid-twentieth century reflections on English character, for example, drew on familiar enough observations about religion in asserting that after Anglicanism, the 'nominal creed' of the north-east was Methodism, whereas that of the north-west was Roman Catholicism.[30] But such comments rarely went beyond broad generalisation. It was the ending of the 100-year ban on access to the detailed returns of the 1851 census of church attendance in the 1950s which provided the spur to much more careful analysis of regional patterns of religious affiliation. This, the only ever official survey of church attendance in England and Wales, had provoked enormous controversy when its summary results were published in 1853 and had suggested not only that Anglicanism barely registered an advantage over Nonconformity in terms of numbers attending public worship on the census day, but that a significant number of people – some 42% – who could have attended church did not go anywhere at all.[31] The summary tables did provide data rich enough to enable some conclusions to be drawn about the regional and social strengths and weaknesses of the various Christian denominations, but in fact little was done with them until the mid-twentieth century. One of the earliest attempts to analyse the social strengths and weaknesses of the churches was E. R. Wickham's *Church and People in an Industrial City* (1957), a pioneering book which focused on Sheffield and concluded that Anglicanism in industrial areas was hampered by its middle-class character and failed to reach the industrial working class.[32] But Wickham did not actually use the detailed census returns, which would

---

30   G. Gorer, 'English Character in the Twentieth Century', p. 76.

31   *Census of Great Britain, 1851: Religious Worship (England and Wales), Report and Tables*; an abridged edition was published by Horace Mann, the barrister tasked with organizing the census, as H. Mann (ed.), *Census of Religious Worship in England and Wales*.

32   E. R. Wickham, *Church and People in an Industrial City*; for a critique, see J. N. Morris, 'Church and People Thirty-Three Years On: A Historical Critique', pp. 92–101.

have given his research a more finely-grained picture of local religious life. Growing awareness, from the 1950s, of the availability of the local returns stimulated debate about the methodological complexities of studying this kind of data, but it also fitted in with a growing interest in the kind of religious sociology being pursued in France by Gabriel le Bras and others.[33] Another foray into this kind of regional, religious sociology was John Gay's *Geography of Religion in England* (1971), which observed that Anglicanism generally appeared to be stronger in the mid-nineteenth century in a belt crossing the country from the south-west, running eastwards through the midlands and encompassing the south-east and eastern counties. North of this line – formed, very roughly, by high ground and by historic patterns of parish formation going back even to the Danelaw – the machinery for enforcing conformity had been weaker, parishes were generally poorer, and the greater distance from the capital discouraged more ambitious clergy.[34] Gay's description reinforced the assumption – still powerful in the 1970s – that the eighteenth and early nineteenth centuries had been a time of stasis or even decline for Anglicanism in parts of the country. As we saw in the first chapter, much of that view needs qualification, as historians have uncovered a high degree of pastoral diligence on the part of the Georgian clergy. Philip Tovey's recent work on confirmation, for example, argued forcefully for a consistent pattern of catechizing by parish clergy and efforts to confirm large numbers of people (with the strong implication that large numbers *wanted* to be confirmed) across the country. His cases studies of York, Lincoln, Canterbury, Worcester and Exeter dioceses imply that despite some long-term causes for later regional variations in Anglicanism, still until the mid to late eighteenth century the established Church was functioning relatively efficiently.[35] It was, almost certainly, the substantial growth of manufacturing districts from the mid-eighteenth century, and the accompanying growth of Dissent both 'new' (Methodist) and 'old' (Independents and Baptists especially), that left Anglicanism in the midlands and north seemingly vulnerable.

Greater complexity in processes of regional religious development has been acknowledged by historians in the last forty years. A ground-breaking study of Dissent in rural areas by Alan Everitt, drawing on the local census returns from

---

33   K. S. Inglis, 'Patterns of religious worship in 1851', pp. 74–86; William Pickering, 'The 1851 religious census: a useless experiment?', pp. 382–407; David Thompson, 'The 1851 religious census: problems and possibilities', pp. 7–97.

34   J. D. Gay, *The Geography of Religion in England*, chapter 4., 'The Church of England', pp. 64–80.

35   P. Tovey, *Anglican Confirmation 1662–1820*, pp. 111–36.

1851, demonstrated how patterns of religious growth and denominational competition could be affected by such diverse factors as forms of property ownership, proximity to populous districts, transport, and even types of agriculture.[36] James Obelkevich, in a study of South Lindsey in Lincolnshire, similarly drew attention to the complexity of social and economic relations as formative influences on processes of evangelisation and religious belonging.[37] But the most detailed and authoritative survey of the 1851 census returns, whilst confirming the overall picture of Anglican strength in the south, at the same time showed surprisingly resilient pastoral strategies in evidence across the country, and particularly in towns and cities – contexts that a long tradition of English historiography, stemming from nineteenth-century convictions of pastoral failure and reinforced by the emphases of the new social history of the 1960s and on, had assumed were hostile to the Established Church: 'it did better in urban locations than most of its rivals, despite its longer rural traditions and inheritance.'[38]

A number of points can be drawn from this brief – and selective – survey of recent work that bear upon the scope of the High Church revival. Anglicanism was certainly stronger in some areas than in others, but the contrasts between regions were probably not so sharp as to indicate some sort of pastoral collapse in those contexts in which the Established Church was, relatively, weaker. There is good evidence to suggest it had held up well across the country for much of the eighteenth century. If it struggled to adapt its historic structures to the rapid growth of industrial centres in the midlands, the north, and south Wales in the early nineteenth century, by the middle of the century it was recovering its position strongly. Gay, like others, acknowledged this when suggesting it was at its peak in the 1870s (though in fact numbers of churchgoing Anglicans continued to rise well into the twentieth century).[39] The High Church revival was thus part of a broader process of institutional recovery for Anglicanism, which affected all parts of the country and which meant that High Churchmen (again, despite clear local and regional variations, as we shall see) could be found almost everywhere to some degree at least. This last point needs to be refined a little more, to reflect the various circles of revival I outlined earlier: traditional High Churchmen may have been found almost everywhere, more or less, throughout the nineteenth century, but the more specific strands that were influenced particularly by the theological and devotional impulses of the Oxford Movement could also be found, by the end of the

---

36   A. M. Everitt, *The Pattern of Rural Dissent : the Nineteenth Century*.

37   J. Obelkevich, *Religion and Society: South Lindsey 1825–1875*.

38   K. D. Snell & P. S. Ell, *Rival Jerusalems: The Geography of Victorian Religion*, p. 399.

39   J. D. Gay, *The Geography of Religion in England*, p. 78.

century, to have spread throughout the country. But this has not always been acknowledged. The notion that Anglo-Catholicism was confined largely – with the exception of a few 'slum' parishes – to the fashionable suburbs, to London and the south coast of England lodged itself firmly in the minds of commentators early on.[40] It has remained a powerful one. 'High Church devotion was essentially an elite phenomenon', asserted David Bebbington, which percolated further down the social scale only in the twentieth century, when the Romantic sensibility that nurtured the High Church revival in the nineteenth century was diffused to 'larger numbers and lower down the social scale'.[41] There is some truth in this: by the late nineteenth century, advanced Ritualist or Anglo-Catholic churches were particularly prevalent in parts of southern England, and especially in the newly-created parishes of the suburbs. But the generalisation needs much qualification, and it is local studies in particular which help us to do this.

The foremost historian of the local growth of Anglo-Catholicism – as we have seen, a key component of the High Church revival – was Nigel Yates. By background and training an archivist as well as historian, Yates used his extensive knowledge of county record offices to compile a formidable series of case studies examining the growth of Tractarianism and Ritualism in the nineteenth century. Some of these covered the familiar 'London, Brighton and South Coast', but many did not.[42] Yates gathered up the results of his studies into a monograph of great importance for studying the High Church revival, *Anglican Ritualism in Victorian Britain 1830–1910* (1999). The book is not without its flaws. Though Yates acknowledged continuities between Ritualism and broader High Church opinion, his delineation of the regional patterns of Ritual growth depended upon contemporary practices that were particularly associated with 'advanced' ritual, and especially the 'six points', and as a result many nuances of local colour were almost certainly obscured or elided in his account.[43] In particular, Yates's methodology tended to displace doctrine in favour of practice, since the latter could be measured and featured

---

40   This was a point picked up by Nigel Yates in his article 'Bells and Smells: London, Brighton and South Coast Religion Reconsidered', pp. 122–53. The familiar characterisation of Anglo-Catholicism evoked in Yates's title deliberately echoed the name of the pre-Beeching London, Brighton and South Coast Railway. Cf. R. Cowl, '"London, Brighton and South Coast Religion"? Tractarianism and ritualism in Brighton, Hove and Worthing', unpublished PhD thesis, University of Keele, 1996.

41   D. Bebbington, *Holiness in Nineteenth-Century England*, p. 28.

42   Cf. W. N. Yates, *Ritual Conflict at Farlington and Wymering*; *The Anglican Revival in Portsmouth*; idem, 'Bells and Smells'.

43   For Yates's discussion of the connections between Tractarianism, Ritualism and Ecclesiology, see idem, *Anglican Ritualism in Victorian Britain, 1830–1910*, pp. 48–63.

prominently in contemporary sources such as the *Tourist's Church Guide*. He even suggested that some High Churchmen may have made 'ceremonial moves' first, influenced perhaps by the fashionable medievalism of the age.[44] However this seems *prima facie* unlikely in more than a small handful of cases, especially given the controversy which ritual innovation courted. Nonetheless, Yates's concentration on external signs at least indicated a reliable core of parishes that can be taken as a minimum outline of the regional strength of Anglo-Catholicism. As he argued, the assumption that Ritualist churches were largely confined to large towns and seaside resorts, and absent from the countryside, 'has been greatly exaggerated'.[45] Few large towns and cities, even in the north, were altogether without Ritualist churches by the 1870s, but even more significant is the fact that a 'high proportion' of Tractarian and Ritualist incumbents (Yates here fused Herring's research on Tractarian clergy with the *Tourist's Church Guide*) held parishes 'with very small populations', most of which were in villages or small market towns.[46] They were mostly scattered, rather than concentrated, though there were certainly significant variations between dioceses. Dioceses and areas which later, in the twentieth century, were considered strongholds of Anglo-Catholicism, such as Chichester, London, Wakefield and Truro, were already displaying something of this tendency in the late nineteenth century, if not earlier.

Yates's more detailed work on Leeds and its environs can stand as a model case study contradicting the lazy 'London, Brighton and South Coast' generalisation. Leeds was one of the more famous cases of what was called, in the nineteenth century, 'church extension', namely the subdivision of parishes to provide new churches for the growing populations of towns and cities. Almost all urban areas could provide similar examples. I shall explore an outer London example, Croydon, shortly, but an inner London example would be the old parish of Battersea, which was subdivided under the long incumbency of John Erskine Clarke, Vicar from 1872 to 1909, to create fifteen new parishes by the beginning of the twentieth century, covering a population of 170,000.[47] Church extension could be impeded by a hostile or indolent clergyman, or facilitated by an energetic one. Leeds got a famously energetic one, Walter Hook, Vicar for twenty-two years from 1837 until his appointment as Dean of Chichester. Like other northern industrial towns, the city grew bewilderingly fast in the early

---

44   Yates, *Anglican Ritualism*, p. 376.

45   Yates, *Anglican Ritualism*, p. 85.

46   Yates, *Anglican Ritualism*, p. 88.

47   R. Mudie Smith, *The Religious Life of London*, p. 253. There is as yet no detailed local study of Battersea church extension, but there are some references in J. G. Taylor, *Our Lady of Batersey*.

nineteenth century, reaching the quarter of a million mark by 1851. At the time of Hook's appointment, Leeds was a startling example of the difficulties of adapting the historic parish structures of the Church of England to the new industrial age, with 150,000 people catered for by the historic parish of Leeds; within this one parish, eighteen churches were in effect 'chapels of ease', that is church buildings serving a district but without permanent parochial existence.[48] Anglicanism had lost much ground to Nonconformity. At the time of the 1851 religious census, it seems that Anglican church attendances, at 34.5% of all the attendances registered in Leeds on the census Sunday, were easily outdistanced by Methodist attendances alone, at 41.9%.[49] Hook arrived determined to put into practice his vision of High Church Anglicanism, sympathetic as he was to the ideals of the Tractarians. In his first few years at Leeds, he rebuilt the parish church, making the new church almost the model of Tractarian ideals, with a high altar, weekly communion, a surpliced choir, and candles before the altar.[50] He also sponsored a major programme of church extension, obtaining the passage of the Leeds Vicarage Act of 1844 which led to the division of the historic parish, and eventually to the building of new churches, some 31 in all by the end of his incumbency. His determination to provide for the spiritual needs of the people ensured that Leeds remained a bastion of High Church Anglicanism into the twentieth century. The mechanism through which this happened was, essentially, patronage. Through the Leeds Vicarage Act, Hook retained the patronage of a number of the newly-created Leeds parishes, enabling him to make appointments sympathetic to his views across the city. This was not without difficulty, most notoriously at the parish of St Saviour's, Richmond Hill, a church built at the expense of Pusey himself, but where a succession of conversions to Roman Catholicism caused Hook immense grief.[51] Indeed, Hook's experiences with St Saviour's were an important factor in turning him against Tractarianism – or at least against the more extreme manifestations of it. Yet he remained a staunch High Churchman and his language about Tractarianism in the late 1840s and 1850s seemed to change markedly depending on whether he was defending the principles he had taken it to represent in the 1830s and early 1840s, or attacking its 'Romanizing' tendencies.[52] Hook is thus an excellent example both of the internal tensions and ambiguities in High Churchmanship and of the relative

48   W. R. W. Stephens, *The Life and Letters of Walter Farquhar Hook*, pp. 376–9.
49   Coleman, *The Church of England in the Mid-Nineteenth Century*, p. 41; cf. also W. N. Yates, 'The Religious Life of Victorian Leeds', pp. 250–69.
50   W. N. Yates, *Leeds and the Oxford Movement*, pp. 15–6.
51   W. N. Yates, *The Oxford Movement and Parish Life: St Saviour's, Leeds, 1839–1929*.
52   Stephens, *Life and Letters of Hook*, pp. 447–8.

success with which, in specific localities, the right combination of opportunity, energy, and resources could engineer circumstances favourable to the High Church revival even in an industrial city.

Hook's combination of unwavering High Churchmanship and variable, expressed support for Tractarianism (and Ritualism) points back to my earlier argument about 'revival within revival'. Leeds, as Yates demonstrated, displayed almost all the usual variants of Anglican High Churchmanship in the second half of the nineteenth century. At the same time, however, even the more moderate forms of High Churchmanship were shifting, as the doctrinal, devotional and liturgical changes inspired by the Oxford Movement worked their way through the Church of England. If we must assume something of a 'ripple' effect, by which liturgical practices originally advocated by a seeming minority gradually became adopted throughout High Church circles, then we must presumably assume a continuation of that effect throughout the rest of the Church, weakening as it worked its way through the Broad Church to liberal Evangelicalism, and disappearing altogether at the Evangelical or Low Church extreme. This is a thoroughly limited image, mechanistic, even; nevertheless its appropriateness in some contexts – the spread of surpliced choirs, the increasing frequency of communion, for example – is undeniable. As Leeds showed, urban expansion presented all denominations in the Victorian period with almost unparalleled opportunities for growth and mission.

As a contrast to Leeds, and drawing on my own work, the outer London borough of Croydon is a good case in point. The area of Surrey, and now south London, once covered by the old parish of Croydon, was indeed an area of spectacular growth in the nineteenth century, its population leaping from some 12,000 in 1831 to over 134,000 by 1901.[53] The old parish was enormous, thirty-six miles in circumference, largely rural apart from the market town of Croydon itself at the beginning of the nineteenth century, and almost entirely integrated into the London sprawl by 1914. Its one parish, with its parish church and two district churches in the 1830s, had subdivided to form twenty-nine Anglican churches in nineteen parishes by 1901. High Church Anglicanism had become a powerful presence by then: seven parishes could be described as Ritualist, and a further one as moderate High Church. On the face of things, then, this was precisely the kind of area, urban and suburban, in which contemporaries assumed Tractarianism and Ritualism were embedding themselves. An anti-Ritualist tract at the beginning of the twentieth century claimed, for example, that the energetic Ritualist curates 'found greater scope for work

---

53   Details in this paragraph are taken from J. N. Morris, *Religion and Urban Change: Croydon 1840–1914*, pp. 21–2 & 37–71.

in large and crowded populations; there was a disinclination on their part to vegetate in quiet country parishes' – a sentiment that, as we have seen, Yates's work has challenged.[54] It is significant, then, that the growth of the High Church in this part of south London occurred largely in spite of powerful opposition from local clergy, including successive vicars of Croydon until the 1880s, with their powers of patronage, and Archbishops of Canterbury.

Anglican church extension in the Croydon area was extremely piecemeal, and not at all like the systematic, planned kind that Hook was able to execute in Leeds. The eight High Church parishes that were in existence by the end of the century formed in effect three clusters, the churches within them being partly linked by ties of patronage. In and around the centre of Croydon were St James', St Andrew's, St Saviour's, and St Michael's and All Angels, the last one springing from the first two; to the north, at Upper Norwood and South Norwood, were St John the Evangelist and its daughter parish of St Albans; south of the town centre were St Peter's and St Augustine's. The eight fall broadly into two different groups, namely those where Tractarian or Ritualist views came to hold sway as a result of clergymen being appointed to existing non-Tractarian churches (and here local controversy was usually most intense), and the establishment of new churches explicitly on Tractarian or Ritualist lines.

Only two churches really fall into the first group, existing churches subsequently 'Tractarianised'. St Peter's, in South Croydon, was formed directly out of the old parish of Croydon to cater for a growing suburban population; made into a separate parish in 1853, the patronage of the benefice remained in the hands of the vicar of Croydon.[55] Nothing in its early years suggests that it was anything other than conservative High Church at most; its second vicar, John White, appointed in 1854, seemed happy to continue the established pattern of Morning and Evening Prayer, with monthly communion.[56] Sometime in the late 1870s, however, he began to adopt more overtly Ritualistic practices, increasing the frequency of communion, adopting altar lights and a crucifix, and even fitting up a cubicle similar to a confessional at the door of the church, all of which in 1878 prompted the resignation of his churchwardens and the usual letters in the local press from 'Anti-Rome' and others.[57] The vicar of

54 L. Heitland, *Ritualism in Town and Country: A Volume of Evidence*, p. 3.
55 Anon., *St Peter's, Croydon: The First Hundred Years*.
56 Service details in this and the following paragraphs are mostly taken from advertisements in *Gray's Commercial and General Directory for Croydon* (annually, 1851–61), and its successors, *Warren's Directory* (1865–9) and *Ward's Directory* (1874–1914).
57 *Croydon Chronicle*, 30 March 1878.

Croydon, as patron, was unable to control what happened at St Peter's. His power effectively stopped at the appointment itself; he had not appointed a known Tractarian or Ritualist priest, and White's views began to change, so far as one can tell, at a time when powerful lay opposition to Ritualism – despite the actions of his churchwardens – had begun to ebb.

Even more controversial, and far more complex, was the case of St Saviour's church, built in 1865 east of the town centre as a chapel of ease to St James' church. Here the conservative High Church vicar of St James appointed as incumbent-designate William Cameron, a moderate Tractarian who fell ill within two years and appointed one Richard Hoare as his curate.[58] Hoare was to occupy a pivotal role in the High Church revival in this part of South London, and his Ritualist sympathies became apparent very quickly. Here the story parts company with the seeming parallel of St Peter's; Hoare seems to have attracted a large congregation and sympathetic churchwardens, so that, as Cameron lay dying in early 1869, they memorialised the patron, the vicar of St James, and also the vicar of Croydon and the Archbishop of Canterbury, to appoint Hoare as Cameron's successor.[59] The subsequent correspondence, both private and in the local press, is too complex to summarize here; the gist of the conflict was that the patron refused to appoint Hoare and gave only limited guarantees about preserving the character of the services at St Saviour's.[60]

The controversy at St Saviour's provides an appropriate bridge to the second group of churches, namely those founded explicitly on Tractarian or Ritualist lines, because the result of the controversy was to prompt a group of influential, wealthy laity to press for the establishment of a new church for Richard Hoare.[61] This they were able to achieve, despite the opposition of the vicar of Croydon – from whose parish the new district and, ultimately, parish would be taken – by appeal to Archbishop Tait and the use of Peel's Church Building Act of 1843.[62] As Tait is reported to have said, 'The matter is in your own hands, gentlemen. You have only to provide the money and a new parish can be

---

58   Anon. (ed.), *Memorials and Correspondence respecting the recent appointment of an Incumbent for St Saviour's Church, Croydon*, p. 5.

59   Anon, *Memorials and Correspondence*, pp. 8–11.

60   Anon, *Memorials and Correspondence*, p. 24.

61   F. N. Heazell, *The History of St Michael's Church, Croydon: A Chapter in the Oxford Movement*, pp. 4–9.

62   This allowed the establishment of new churches in existing parishes even at the cost of the entrenched interests of the incumbent and patron; Best called this willingness to override established interests a 'moral revolution in establishment principles': G. F. A. Best, *Temporal Pillars: Queen Anne's Bounty, the Ecclesiastical Commissioners and the Church of England*, p. 400.

formed.'[63] The parish of St Michael and All Angels was formed by Order in Council in July 1871, and the patronage vested in five lay trustees, as yet without any building or even a site for one. The church of St Michael's as eventually built, described by Cherry and Pevsner as 'one of [J. L.] Pearson's finest', became a highly visible centre for Ritualism in the area, and the host church for the Croydon branch of the English Church Union.[64] Richard Hoare was incumbent for almost fifty years, occupying a position of some national influence in Anglo-Catholicism, especially as Warden of the CBS.[65] This pattern of establishing a church using lay patronage under the Church Building Act was repeated in the foundation of St John the Evangelist in Upper Norwood, another Pearson church, and paralleled to some extent by the earlier establishment of St Andrew's as a Tractarian church in South Croydon under the patronage (and with the financial aid) of a rural Tractarian clergyman.[66] Two other churches in this group were uncontroversial in foundation, since they were daughter churches of existing Tractarian or Ritualist parishes – St Alban's in South Norwood, and St Augustine's in South Croydon.[67]

What do these patterns of Tractarian and Ritualist growth suggest about the nature of the High Church revival? Clearly in an area such as South London, urban growth provided the underlying justification for church extension, and the opportunity for the establishment of churches along distinct doctrinal or party lines. That was true, however, for all shades of Anglicanism, including Evangelicalism.[68] Two observations are appropriate. First, the characteristic devices by which the Church of England sought to make its parochial machinery more flexible and responsive to demographic change in the nineteenth century could weaken, rather than strengthen, the control that incumbents of existing parishes exercised over church affairs in urbanizing districts. Despite the apparent 'mildness' of Peel's 1843 Act, in particular, its consequences were far-reaching in the context of party divisions.[69] Churches of one 'party' could be intruded into the parish of another, provided there was sufficient demon-

---

63   Heazell, *History of St Michael's*, p. 7.

64   B. Cherry & N. Pevsner, *The Buildings of England: London 2: the South*, p. 210.

65   *Croydon Chronicle*, 21 September 1878.

66   H. W. Bateman, *A Short History of the Church of St John the Evangelist, Upper Norwood 1871–1937*; see also W. F. La Trobe-Bateman, *Memories Grave and Gay* (London, 1927); Anonymous, *St Andrew's Church for the Poor*.

67   Bateman, *Short History of St John the Evangelist*, chapter 2, 'Expansion and Consolidation'; J. H. White, *A Short History of the Foundation and Progress of the Church of St Augustine, South Croydon*.

68   Morris, *Religion and Urban Change*, pp. 52–3.

69   Cf. Best, *Temporal Pillars*, pp. 356–8.

strated need and sufficient local support and money. Furthermore, the failure of Parliament to institute even a moderate reform of the patronage system before 1898 meant that it was relatively easy for church parties to perpetuate their influence in parishes they had established, through the use of patronage trusts. Initial Tractarian and Ritualist suspicion of such trusts, presumably of a piece with their overall suspicion of private patronage, had receded by the 1870s; by this period, as M. J. D. Roberts has suggested, the Ecclesiastical Commissioners and many bishops had 'come to regard trust patronage as "normal" in new urban parishes'.[70] The use of patronage to advance High Church views is well attested in numerous local cases: Yates, for instances, cited the establishment of St Barnabas's church in Tunbridge Wells, with its patronage vested in the Warden, Council and Scholars of Keble College Oxford, despite opposition from the rural dean, the Evangelical vicar of Holy Trinity, who asserted: 'I can scarcely imagine a body of men less fitted for the appointment of a parochial clergyman.'[71] Other cases that Yates mentioned include churches in Frome and Bovey Tracy.[72] Patronage could also be used the other way round, to resist Tractarianism. Yates again described how, in large parts of Wales, episcopal control of most patronage severely contained the growth of Tractarianism.[73] Cobb has demonstrated similarly how the Evangelical Bristol Church Trustees were able to do so in Bristol.[74]

Linked to the question of the patronage system is a second observation, and that is the important role of lay supporters and patrons. The significance of aristocratic and gentry patrons is widely acknowledged – Lord Halifax and his relations in Leeds and surrounding areas, for example, the Beresford Hopes in various Kentish and London churches, the Thynnes in Cornwall and at Wells Theological College, and the Baths at Frome.[75] But the South London cases I have described suggest that there was a humbler and yet still significant class of lay patrons and other supporters, for whom the patronage trust was a useful way of combining to support High Church views. These were middle class, professional people, relatively wealthy but not outstandingly so, who were prepared to take offices and responsibilities in Tractarian churches and socie-

---

70   M. J. D. Roberts, 'Private Patronage and the Church of England, 1800–1900', p. 213.

71   W. N. Yates, *Kent and the Oxford Movement*, p. 98.

72   Yates, 'Bells and Smells', pp. 130 & 132.

73   W. N. Yates, 'The Parochial Impact of the Oxford Movement in South West Wales', p. 223.

74   Cobb, *Oxford Movement*, p. 31.

75   Yates, *Leeds and the Oxford Movement*, pp. 12, 40 & 43; idem, *Kent and the Oxford Movement*, 7; Brown, *Catholic Revival in Cornish Anglicanism*, p. 66; W. M. Jacob, 'The Diffusion of Tractarianism: Wells Theological College 1840–49', p. 134.

ties – men such as William Drummond, solicitor, chairman of the Local Board of Health, and active layman at St Saviour's.[76]

Transformation and Consolidation: Two Telling Examples

The contrasting urban contexts of Leeds and Croydon present illuminating studies of the ways in which rapidly-growing urban areas in the nineteenth century could offer opportunities for distinct ecclesiastical movements to embed themselves. But the new trends in High Church opinion were not confined to new churches and new parishes. There were many instances of existing parishes and churches being 'Tractarianised', but once again a close study of some of these instances brings to light interesting contrasts and local complications. Just two London examples will be presented here, both of them notorious in their own way – the early eighteenth century church designed by Nicholas Hawksmoor, St George-in-the-East, in Stepney, and what came to be the flamboyant Gothic West End church designed by William Butterfield, All Saints, Margaret Street.

St George-in-the-East became, briefly, a byword for popular opposition to Tractarianism when a series of riots occurred against the Ritualistic innovations of the incumbent, Bryan King (1811–1895), for over a year from May 1859, leading eventually to the breaking down of King's health, intervention by the Bishop of London, Archibald Campbell Tait, and in 1863 King's removal from the parish altogether through an exchange of livings with the vicar of Avebury, in Wiltshire. For a short time, the church was the *cause célèbre* of anti-Catholic feeling in east London, attracting the unwelcome attentions of the local mob, discussion in Parliament, and agonised letters to the national newspapers. King was not new to the parish, however, having gone there in 1842, already as a known sympathizer with the Tractarians. Although his High Church views had gradually led to a deterioration in relations with local inhabitants, there was little forewarning of what was to come in 1859. What went wrong?

The riots were a particularly complex series of events, and there are many different ways of reading them. It is certainly possible to see them as an expression of popular Protestantism, coupled with intense anxieties around ideas of 'Englishness' or 'Britishness' and even 'manliness'.[77] The ritual and ceremonial innovations of Bryan King could be seen as threatening traditional values,

---

76   Morris, *Religion and Urban Change*, p. 112; Anon., *Memorials and Correspondence*, p. 10.

77   See e.g. David Kent, 'High Church Rituals and Rituals of Protest: The 'Riots' at St George-in-the-East, 1859–1860'.

provoking a thoroughly traditional response, namely uproar and mayhem. King himself, and his supporters, naturally considered the riots to be nothing more than the irrational, prejudiced thuggery of a desperate mob. But that is presumably not how the rioters themselves saw things: they, instead, saw this as part of a wider struggle against the corruption and idolatry of Rome, which threatened to worm its way even into the English Church. One of the many anonymous messages King received told him to 'Shut up the church ... We will never, never rest until St. George's-in-the-East is stripped of all drapery, crosses, candles, choristers, intoning, preaching in the surplice, or any one thing tending to Popery and Puseyism.'[78] Sentiments such as this were typical of the virulent anti-Catholicism which still ran through elements of British society in the mid-nineteenth century. Yet the presenting cause, or 'trigger', for the riots was not so much conflicting ideas – though those certainly mattered – as changes in what historians often call 'material culture', namely the way that ideas are embodied and expressed in very concrete artefacts and practices. That opens up a rich – and as yet largely unexplored – vein of possibilities about contrasting ideas of the place of art, music, and movement in religious experience.[79]

King was probably never anything but a moderate Tractarian, who had been profoundly influenced by Pusey's university sermons when he was a student at Oxford; Pusey took part in his ordination. It is most unlikely that King was unaware of the development of Pusey's thought on the eucharist in the 1840s. King could echo Pusey's view, in emphasizing too 'the deep doctrine of the Holy Eucharist and the place which that Sacrament holds in the economy of Christian grace as the one great act of Worship and Sacrifice offered by the Church to Almighty God' – indeed, for him, it was precisely to re-establish that truth and convince congregations of it that the 'external adjuncts of ritual' such as vestments and altar lights were necessary.[80] Writing long after he had left St George's, he noted how the very same Ritualist priests who all too often were obstructed by their bishops were 'endeavouring to rescue the one great act of Divine service, the one great Christian sacrifice of the Church, from the neglect and degradation to which it has been consigned for more than three centuries'.[81] But there was irony in this, because it was Bishop Blomfield's

78   W. Crouch, *Bryan King and the Riots at St. George's-in-the-East*, p. 54.
79   Though I note an interesting contribution in D. Janes, *Victorian Reformation: The Fight over Idolatry in the Church of England, 1840–1860*.
80   B. King, *Sacrilege and its Encouragement, being an Account of the St George's Riots and of their Successes, in a Letter of Remonstrance to the Lord Bishop of London*, pp. 11–12.
81   B. King, *Disestablishment the Present Hope of the Church: An Appeal to his Brother Churchmen*, p. 22.

instructions about proper observation of the rubrics which had led to King's use of the surplice on his first appointment to St George's, and hence to local unhappiness about his policy from the very beginning.[82] From then on, his relations with most of his parishioners were unhappy and difficult. His ritual innovations were relatively modest, at least in comparison with what was adopted at many other churches. But popular unease was manifest in mid-century, with disturbances at the beginning of the 1850s at St Barnabas, Pimlico, and the lasting irritation of 'Papal aggression', namely the restoration of the Roman Catholic episcopal hierarchy in 1850, seemingly exacerbated by the continuing stream of conversions to Rome. In 1856 King adopted eucharistic vestments – chiefly chasubles – but it was the election of a virulently anti-Catholic lecturer, Hugh Allen, in April 1859 which provoked the rioting.

Like a number of East London parishes, the vestry of St George's had a traditional right to elect a Sunday afternoon lecturer. The weekly 'lecture' Allen was due to deliver was really a sermon, delivered in the course of worship on a Sunday afternoon. Since it was sandwiched between services led by King himself, the afternoon lecture gave King's opponents the perfect opportunity to stoke themselves up and then hang on into the early evening, disrupting King's evening service. Complaints about disruption of the evening service first surfaced in late May 1859, and then snowballed into the equivalent of a weekly riot, made worse by King's futile attempts to clear the church and to prevent Allen from entering it. The police were drawn in, and yet hampered from action by a long-neglected statute from Mary's reign which deemed disturbance inside a church to be a matter of ecclesiastical, rather than civil, law.[83] The disturbances carried on for months, despite many attempts by the civil and religious authorities to suppress them. At some point – presumably quite early on – they widened into a celebration of mayhem. As Chadwick put it, Sunday afternoons at St George's for almost a year (apart from six weeks when Tait secured closure of the church) were 'the zoo and horror and coconut-shy of London'.[84] The riots only came to an end when King gave up, exhausted, and left London in July 1860, some months after Tait had forced his hand anyway and instructed the churchwardens (who, elected by the vestry, were happy to oblige) to remove altar hangings, choir stalls and the altar cross.[85]

---

82   Crouch, *Bryan King*, pp. 32–3.

83   P. T. Smith, 'The London Police and the Holy War: Ritualism and St.George's-in-the-East, London, 1859–1860', pp. 112–13.

84   W. O. Chadwick, *The Victorian Church*, Vol. 1, p. 499.

85   Smith, 'London Police', p. 118.

Such is the better-known aspect of the trouble at St George's. What is perhaps less well-known is that in fact St George's did not revert to 'Low Church' worship, in capitulation to the rioters, but rather settled into a moderate High Churchmanship, despite continuing grumblings from local residents led by disgruntled Nonconformist churchwardens, for many years. The incumbent appointed to succeed King reinstated the choir stalls and a surpliced choir, and by the late 1880s, long after controversy had faded, congregations had climbed to over two hundred in the morning and over four hundred in the evening.[86] Several of King's curates – including Charles Lowder and Alexander Mackonochie – went on to become famous Anglo-Catholic 'slum priests' in the East End. The disturbances did not, then, altogether impede the growth of High Church opinion even in this part of London, despite the strength of local feeling. It was possible, though difficult, to make headway even against the grain of popular anti-Catholicism.

Nevertheless the 'Tractarianizing' of established parishes was complicated by the very Church-State link which many High Churchmen (though not King) still strenuously defended. King was to become a strong advocate of the disestablishment of the Church of England. Later in life, he even wrote a pamphlet on it, *Disestablishment the Present Hope of the Church* (1882). It is not difficult to see why he should have become so sceptical of the Church-State link. His difficulties started long before the riots, when he found the parish vestry organised against him. The vestry, before local government reform of the late-nineteenth century, was in effect a meeting of all of the resident male householders in the parish, irrespective of their actual church affiliation or belief. It was responsible for a great many functions of civil government, as well as for the overall maintenance of the parish church, and the appointment of churchwardens. There was nothing to stop the vestry from electing Dissenters, or atheists even, as churchwardens. Elsewhere in Britain, and particularly in the towns, the vestry became a focal point of Dissenting opposition to Anglicanism. King himself, and his defenders, tended to see the riots as fomented by disgruntled owners of sweat shops in the area, and brothel-keepers, but they also talked of the rioters being led by the churchwardens and by the vestrymen. In established parish churches, such as St George's, it was often remarkably difficult for the incumbent to change the style of service substantially without provoking the irritation of parishioners who would have a means of organizing opposition to him through the vestry meeting. But the parishioners concerned need not even be regular, or occasional, members of the congregation. Thus, the vestry

---

86   Crouch, *Bryan King*, p. 122; *The Religious Census of London. Reprinted from the British Weekly*, p. 22.

could give a powerful voice to parishioners seeking to defend the Protestant character of the Established Church against Ritual innovation.

To King, this represented an absurd contradiction in parish Anglicanism. Again and again, he emphasised the support of the regular members of his congregation for his ritual innovations. But to others this simply looked sectarian and inward-looking, catering only for a small proportion of his parish. Tait certainly thought so. For him the Church of England, as the national Church, gloried in its ability to comprehend widely different doctrinal views. The problem with Ritualism, he thought, was that it narrowed the appeal of the Church of England, and catered for just one small part of it – and that one which veered dangerously close to Rome. It is in that spirit he urged King to give up the vestments: 'I do beg you to give up the matters complained of ... In carrying out the simple Scriptural system of our own Church, you will receive, I assure you, all sympathy and assistance from me.'[87] Tait's willingness to accept the complaints of the petitioners against King stemmed, not from spinelessness or indecisiveness, but from his conviction that the national Church was duty-bound to reflect the popular Protestantism of the petitioners – to stay close, as it were, to the founding formularies of the Church of England, and to reflect its Protestant identity closely in its worship and practice.[88]

By way of contrast to the events at St. George-in-the-East, the evolution of the Margaret Street chapel into what became the ultra-Ritualist All Saints was relatively uncontroversial. Why was this so? Whereas at St George's the historic parish structure had given King's opponents the means to resist his ritual innovations, at Margaret Street the chapel was outside the legal constraints of the parish system, as it was a proprietary chapel. A chapel had existed in what subsequently became Margaret Street since the mid-eighteenth century, as a private chapel, originally serving a small Deistic congregation.[89] It passed through a variety of forms of opinion ('its history was a kind of type of the variations of Protestantism') into Low Church Anglicanism in the early nineteenth century.[90] An accident of religious change marked its transition to High Churchmanship. The chapel attracted the appointment of William Dodsworth, an Evangelical increasingly drawn to the sacramental views of the premillennialist preacher Edward Irving, in 1829; Dodsworth rapidly moved through

87   R. T. Davidson & W. Benham, *Life of Archibald Campbell Tait: Archbishop of Canterbury,* Vol. 1, p. 235.

88   A useful study of Tait's attempt to implement these views in the face of mounting challenges is P. T. Marsh, *The Victorian Church in Decline.*

89   T. F. Bumpus, *London Churches Ancient and Modern,* Vol. 2, p. 239.

90   F. Oakeley, *Historical Notes on the Tractarian Movement,* p. 60.

Irvingism to embrace the principles of Tractarianism by the mid-1830s.[91] From Dodsworth, who left in 1838, via the brief ministry of a Mr Thornton, the chapel passed to Frederick Oakeley in 1839, former Fellow of Balliol and already an 'advanced' Tractarian.

Oakeley transformed the worship and ethos of the chapel in six years there, before his reception into the Roman Catholic Church in 1845. A 'complete paragon of ugliness' in his view when he took it over, the interior of the chapel was radically altered along familiar Tractarian lines: the three-decker pulpit, galleries and high-backed pews were removed; an altar was installed in place of a communion table; altar frontals and candles came into use.[92] A surpliced choir was formed, and although Oakeley's reform of worship was constrained by the obligation to use the *Book of Common Prayer*, the liturgy was enhanced considerably by music. There were some obstructions, including a reluctant clerk and the cats he allowed into the chapel during services.[93] But in general terms hostility was slight. This may have been helped by the relatively affluent setting of the chapel, though there were certainly pockets of poverty nearby. The congregation swelled, however. By the mid-1840s, alongside many members of the aristocracy and gentry, it included people such as the lawyer Edward Bellasis, William Gladstone, and Alexander Beresford Hope.[94]

Oakeley's success at Margaret Street later led him to conclude, writing as a Roman Catholic, that even the deficiencies of Anglican worship could not altogether occlude 'the natural attractiveness of Catholic principles and Catholic practices', and that the advance of Tractarianism in London was assisted by the exercise of a certain reserve and flexibility ('moderation and forbearance') on the part of its advocates, who 'wisely let things take their course, as if diffident of their own right to put obstacles in the way of what might be God's own method of effecting His own purposes'.[95] Oakeley may have been right to suggest that the failure to act as a concerted party or pressure-group in London paradoxically helped Tractarianism to embed itself in the capital, but his experience at Margaret Street was perhaps not the best vantage-point from which to make such a claim, given the altogether contrasting, favourable circumstances in which the chapel found itself, in comparison with St George-in-the-East, where a great deal of moderation and forbearance was also

---

91   S. E. Young, 'William Dodsworth', *ODNB*.

92   Oakeley, *Historical Notes*, pp. 62–3; Oakeley, *Personal Reminiscences of the 'Oxford Movement'*, p. 11.

93   Oakeley, *Historical Notes*, p. 64.

94   Oakeley, *Historical Notes*, p. 65; P. Galloway, 'Frederick Oakeley', *ODNB*.

95   Oakeley, *Historical Notes*, pp. 61–2 & 70.

employed, but to no effect. But despite the almost inevitable conversions from Margaret Street, including Oakeley himself, the chapel was on the way to becoming one of the leading Anglo-Catholic churches in London. Rebuilt in the 1850s principally through the energy and fortune of Alexander Beresford-Hope, All Saints, as the new church was to be dedicated, was designed by William Butterfield as the 'model church' of the Ecclesiological Society. Hope also paid half of the stipend of the new priest, Upton Richards.[96]

It was not, then, a simple question of whether or not popular resistance to High Church principles and practice was sufficient to overcome a policy of 'Tractarianizing' these two London churches. If we broaden out into a generalisation, many other factors have to be taken into account in considering High Church 'advance' in the nineteenth century, including the social composition of particular localities, the presence or absence of sympathetic and influential lay leaders, the availability of financial support, local religious traditions including the strength of Dissent, and the situation of a church in or out of the traditional legal structure of the parish system. It is broadly true that it was usually easier to form new Ritualist or Anglo-Catholic churches than to 'Catholicize' existing parishes, but the growth of High Churchmanship in the countryside as well as in established urban parishes disproves the suggestion that this was a decisive factor.

Conclusion

This discussion of various aspects of the local dynamics of the High Church revival perhaps risks a certain untidiness and complexity, but that is in the nature of the case. Religious movements *are* complex, and their patterns of growth and decline depend upon the operation of a great number of variables that resist reduction to a simple formula. Local religious destinies varied immensely and have to be studied in depth, in particular localities, along the lines pioneered by Yates in his studies of Leeds, for example, before much sense can be made of them. Even in this chapter I have had to simplify to some extent, taking little account, for example, of episcopal policy or of the reform of theological education. Far from being clearly a 'London, Brighton and South Coast' phenomenon, existing local studies demonstrate at the very least that the regional pattern of High Church growth was diverse. However, in summary several tentative conclusions can be drawn.

---

96   P. Thompson, 'All Saints' Church, Margaret Street, Reconsidered', p. 74.

First, areas of urban development do seem to have provided special opportunities for the High Church revival. Growing areas demanded more churches, and, given the nature of the patronage system, both individual patrons (clerical or lay) and corporate patrons were much less likely to be able to resist the establishment of new Ritualist or Anglo-Catholic churches in urban areas than they obviously could (through the refusal to appoint) elsewhere. Moreover, as the Croydon examples demonstrated, the very mechanisms by which new churches could be established tended to limit the degree of control hostile clergymen could exercise over an area. This conclusion surely applies as much to small but expanding market towns as it does to large urban conglomerates. Even so, again the exercise of the power of appointment by a sympathetic patron could, even in settled market towns or rural parishes, eventually override local unhappiness at High Church innovations – perhaps the best-known example of that would be Thaxted, under the ministry of the radical Anglo-Catholic Conrad Noel (1869–1942), appointed through the patronage of the socialist Countess of Warwick.[97] Nonetheless, in urban areas the possibility of choosing between different churches undoubtedly assisted the development of distinctively Tractarian and Ritualist congregations.

Second, High Churchmen were often able to seize the opportunities thus presented to them because High Churchmanship did attract a substratum of genuine lay support, ranging from wealthy aristocratic patrons through middle-class professionals to humbler worshippers, many of whom could be organised into voluntary associations of communicants. Plainly, the revival did not amount to a mass movement; nevertheless it did represent a genuinely popular church movement in the sense that it attracted considerable lay support. To say this is not to prejudge many other questions, such as to what extent it was a movement of lay women rather than men, or how active the majority of High Church attenders really were, and so on.

Finally, resistance to the High Church revival was generally ineffective not just in the courts, but in the localities as well. On the clerical side, church structures and procedures provided plenty of opportunities for High Church clergy to resist attempts to discipline or control them. Popular hostility in the end was of little avail, either; it was rarer than sometimes assumed, and seems to have begun to wither in the 1860s and 1870s. The changing public profile of Establishment almost certainly assisted this, along with the reform and redefinition of church government; particularly relevant was the reduction in the

97   K. Leech, 'Conrad Le Despenser Roden Noel', ODNB; cf. also R. A. Burns, 'Beyond the "Red Vicar": Community and Christian Socialism in Thaxted, Essex, 1910–84'.

role of the vestry meeting at the end of the nineteenth century, and the eventual emergence of alternative agencies, especially communicants' guilds (to be discussed in chapter 3) and the voluntary church councils, a precursor of the parochial church councils eventually created nationwide in 1919.

Sacramental Renewal and Popular Religion

Introduction

The High Church revival in Anglicanism was nothing if not fundamentally eucharistic in its primary liturgical development. As such, it was part of a wider European movement of piety. A glance at the religious history of Roman Catholic Europe helps to set the background. The Revolutionary attack on the Church, following as it did currents of fashionable, 'Enlightened' religious opinion that shunned many of the traditional features of Roman Catholic devotion proved limited in its effects. The eucharist became one of the central means by which religious revival was achieved in Catholic Europe after 1815. The revival of processions, the foundation of lay associations and confraternities, the promotion of the Roman rite as a vehicle for a reinvigorated Papal Catholicism, parish missions, these were some of the signs of a new-found relevance for this most ancient of Christian forms of worship. Nor was sacramental revival confined to Roman Catholicism alone for, as we have seen, one can trace parallel movements in Anglicanism, but also in Lutheranism, and also in a more restricted way in the Reformed churches. The very prominence of eucharistic worship in all these traditions demonstrated the response of Europe's ancient Christian traditions to the destructive, anomic effects of the political and economic individualism running through European society in the early nineteenth century. Through successive waves of church reform and liturgical renewal, the perception that the eucharist represented, not just an incidental if important aspect of Christian piety, but rather the focal, paradigmatic form of it became implanted in the minds of church leaders and theologians in Western Christianity in the nineteenth and on into the twentieth centuries.[1]

For this reason, study of the eucharist as a social symbol potentially opens up a rich field of analysis for historians of religion in the nineteenth and twentieth centuries. Hitherto – unlike colleagues in medieval studies – modern church historians have rarely used specific practices as a lens through which to

---

1   Cf. Henri de Lubac's formula: 'the Church produces the Eucharist, but the Eucharist also produces the Church': idem, *The Splendour of the Church*, p. 92, a formula indebted to a long tradition of Catholic theological reflection, including J. A. Möhler and Dom Prosper Guéranger in the nineteenth century.

look at a whole religious way of life. Amongst medieval studies, one could cite, for example, Miri Rubin's study of the cult of Corpus Christi, John Bossy's exploration of the mass as a social institution, and above all Eamon Duffy's hugely influential study of late medieval devotion, *The Stripping of the Altars* (1992).[2] Some modern examples have attempted a similar breadth, including studies of Marian devotion by Ruth Harris and David Blackbourn.[3] But these are relatively rare, perhaps because of academic specialisation: liturgical history, ecclesiastical history and social history rarely speak to each other, and the result is a somewhat fragmented understanding of the role that particular devotional practices have played in Europe's modern history.

What is not asserted here is that a trans-historical concept of the eucharist can be deployed as a heuristic device for reading social history effectively. There was no real, existent unity around the eucharist anywhere in Europe in the nineteenth and early twentieth centuries. Denominational and confessional divisions were replicated in and through the celebration of the eucharist. Communities were divided between churchgoers and non-churchgoers, in any case. Particular traditions were divided between advocates of eucharistic devotion, and those indifferent to it, or frankly opposed. Clerical elites were divided amongst themselves on this, as on other questions. The eucharist symbolised and effected Europe's religious divisions just as much as it sought to realize the unity of the Church. To explore all of these divisions, in all their different dimensions, would require much more space than is possible in a single chapter, and in any case here my focus remains fixed firmly on sacramental renewal within Anglicanism.

Underlying this chapter is the proposal that interpreting the eucharist as social symbol helps to illuminate the religious experience of High Church Anglicanism. As I shall indicate, from around the mid-nineteenth century until the early twentieth century High Churchmen, in pursuit of a programme of renewal and evangelisation that they hoped would revive the fortunes of traditional Anglicanism, evolved a model of parish management which was premised on the reception of communion as the central ritual act of the Church. This model, which I describe here as 'eucharistic community', integrated liturgical practice and parish organisation with eucharistic theology

2 J. Bossy, 'The Mass as a Social Institution', pp. 29–61; M. Rubin, *Corpus Christi: The Eucharist in Late Medieval Culture*; E. Duffy, *The Stripping of the Altars: Traditional Religion in England 1400–1580*.

3 R. Harris, *Lourdes: Body and Spirit in the Secular Age*, and D. Blackbourn, *The Marpingen Visions: Nationalism, Religion and the Rise of Modern Germany*. On a rather more general scale, another model study is D. M. Thompson, *Baptism, Church and Society in Modern Britain*.

and an understanding of church order and membership based on the doctrine of apostolic succession and on eucharistic participation. Like all models of management, its application was often selective, imperfect, contested and unsuccessful. It was never formulated or presented as a *model* as such in its day, but rather it was an implicit mode of organisation which presupposed that the moral and doctrinal principles articulated by High Church clergy in their preaching would find expression not only in particular codes of personal behaviour, but also in forms of association amongst their people. Why was it not held up explicitly as a model of parish management, and why has it there-fore slipped under the radar of many church historians? The answer perhaps lies in the very intellectual processes by which the historian seeks to extract significant elements of past religious practice and to highlight their signifi-cance, for by implication this move itself implies a separation of concept and practice which no one would have accepted at the time. Indeed, the High Church conviction that theology is a moral imperative and requires life and that life in turn bespeaks theology is exactly why one would not expect to find what I am discussing announced as a model or a technique, since that would have presupposed a set of practices with a quite different and probably instru-mental justification from the theological preconceptions of High Churchmen.[4] Thus, 'eucharistic community' is best thought of as an interpretative device by which I describe particular patterns of association (and these were as much moral and theological patterns as practical ones), rather than a self-consciously propagated management style or concept. Nevertheless, granted all these elu-sive dimensions of the concept, in the late nineteenth century its influence appeared to be increasing. But to some extent it was liturgically and devotion-ally premature: its theological basis included a theory of church membership defined by eucharistic participation which was not matched by the actual practice of many Anglican congregations. As liturgical historians have long recognised, not until the emergence of the 'Parish Communion' in the middle years of the twentieth century could Anglican eucharistic practice – at least, in many parishes – really be said to reflect adequately the sacramental doctrine of the High Church revival.[5] As a consequence, when discussion took place

---

4   'The whole system of the Church, its disciplines and ritual, are all in their origin the spontane-ous and exuberant fruit of the real principle of spiritual religion in the hearts of its members': J. H. Newman, *Parochial and Plain Sermons*, Vol. 5, p. 41.

5   The principal authorities are A. G. Herbert, *Liturgy and Society;* idem (ed.), *The Parish Communion;* D. Gray, *Earth and Altar: The Evolution of the Parish Communion in the Church of England to 1945;* and J. Fenwick, and B. Spinks, *Worship in Transition: The Twentieth Century Liturgical Movement.*

about the basis on which the franchise for a fully national, mandatory system of church representation should rest, initial support for the High Church conception melted away in the face of a much broader, looser understanding. This was a significant, largely forgotten and yet early defeat for the movement.

Evidence for the emergence of 'eucharistic community' will be explored under three headings briefly – frequency of communion, ritual, and the theory of parish work – before we turn to consider at greater length the growth of guilds and confraternities. Through these features it is possible to discern in the late-nineteenth century a definite trajectory, the development of which amounted to a new basis for Anglican parish organisation, and which found concrete expression in particular parishes to a greater or lesser extent. The High Church revival, with the eucharistic renewal which it promoted, was focused on a particular view of the priestly office, and propagated a view of society in which the Church, hierarchically ordered, sought to effect a reordering of society through ritual and sacrament. Thus the changes described here implied a particular programme of pastoral and liturgical reform on the part of clergy. But the movement was not exclusively clerical: it drew on currents of lay devotion, and so a more substantial section will follow discussing the organisations used to promote *lay* eucharistic piety. The programme could be accepted or rejected, however. Just as it is important to consider the organisation and promotion of lay eucharistic piety, so it is also necessary to acknowledge the limits of this programme of renewal, and that means, finally, turning to consider how it was ignored or resisted by those who were the target of its strategies of renewal.

The Eucharist as Social Symbol in Nineteenth-century England

Before turning to the specific question of the place of the eucharist in the High Church revival in England, some comment on the method of interpretation adopted here may be useful. Much has of course been written already on Anglican eucharistic theology and practice. But conventional approaches to liturgical history concentrate on the triangular relationship between liturgical texts, theology or doctrine, and liturgical experts. The wider history of the Church often passes out of view this way, however, and the complexity of the process of liturgical change is flattened into an ordered narrative that does not do justice to the complex situations in which liturgical change occured.[6] In

---

6 Cf. J. A. Jungmann, *The Mass of the Roman Rite: Its Origins and Development*; E. B. Koenker, *The Liturgical Renaissance in the Roman Catholic Church*.

this approach, the eucharistic symbol, with its texts and its official subtexts, is separated from much of its social and ecclesial context. Liturgical text is read as symbolizing (and realizing) doctrine, and therefore as a social symbol, since it sought to represent (and effect) a theological understanding of the social, but it is not read as symbolizing the social order in which it was *actually* located.

The Roman Catholic theologian Philippe Gerbet described the eucharist as the 'generative dogma' of Catholic piety, and that seems apt for High Church views too: the eucharist does not merely symbolize the heavenly order, but actually creates it (generates it) in the body of the worshipping community. Gerbet, whose work was profoundly influenced by Johann Adam Möhler and in turn exercised a significant influence on Prosper Guéranger, could thus write of the eucharist that it was 'the union with God raised ... to the highest degree that can be attained within the limits of the present order; beyond this is heaven'.[7]

What does this imply for the eucharist as social symbol, in the religious world of the nineteenth and early twentieth centuries? It opens up a wide range of possible approaches to the history of the eucharist, and I cannot elaborate this comprehensively here. Adapting John Bossy's explanation of the way in which the late medieval community was symbolised in the Mass, we might look to the eucharistic rites and practice of the main Christian traditions to discern their vision of community. The separation of men and women on different sides of the church in some traditions, the reservation of seats for gentry, indeed the widespread practice of renting or 'owning' seats that were then spatially allocated according to rank and station, the educational differentiation of clergy and laity, all these and more bespoke a particular kind of society in transition in the nineteenth and early twentieth centuries. The French clerical traveller in England, M. Robert, visiting a village church near 'Barkley' [presumably Berkeley] in 1840, was delighted to find the faithful sitting on a gender alignment, with men on one side, and women on the other, even though no one was telling them where to sit; evidently impressed by this sign of piety, he concluded it was a pity that they were not Roman Catholic.[8] Since Robert was interested particularly in Tractarian parishes, this may well have been a church recently 'Tractarianised'. Bossy described the Mass in terms of the movement from sacrifice to sacrament: as a sacrifice, the Mass tended 'to represent its social universe as a concatenation of distinct parts', whereas as a

7   P. Gerbet, *Considerations on the Eucharist, viewed as the Generative Dogma of Catholic Piety*, p. 52.
8   Jean-François Robert, *Souvenirs d'Angleterre et considérations sur l'église Anglicane*, pp. 87–8.

sacrament 'it represented and embodied unity and wholeness'.[9] But in this sense the unity of the sacrament was a projection of the clerical mind. It is no accident that liturgical reform often went hand in hand with a certain social radicalism: reformers often sought to abolish social distinctions through the freeing-up of pews, and the rearrangement of church interiors, and yet in doing so they unconsciously echoed the social assumptions of a society in which progress and 'advanced' opinion were the preserve of a privileged, educated elite.[10] The liturgical movement in its early manifestations was thus scarcely democratic: it imposed 'progressive' reform on often unwilling parishioners, and so followed centralised, hierarchical models of authority that were a fusion of theological principle and secular precedent.

Another approach would be to apply Mary Douglas's discussion of the mass as meal.[11] The Mass unifies and sacralizes a human experience of eating which stretches across past, present and future: again, the Mass *effects* what it also symbolizes. The shared meal is thus such a central aspect of human behaviour that it actually generates particular representations of it in particular societies, so that there is a relationship between the ritual of eucharist and the ritual of the shared meal in society at large. (This is, after all, what Paul specifically alludes to in the Corinthian Christian community, as in 1 Corinthians 11.) It is surely no accident that, in the nineteenth century, one would often encounter eucharistic separation occurring again and again – first the gentry receiving communion, then the 'middling sort', then the poor (if they were there at all, for their exclusion or non-attendance was itself a symbolic display of their social situation). After all, all these classes would not actually *eat* together. A transposition of so-called 'secular' eating rituals to the context of the eucharist lies behind what is one of the best-known Victorian horror stories about the lax religiosity of an earlier age, Francis Kilvert's anecdotes about early nineteenth century Fordington:

> Then the Vicar of Fordington told us of the state of things in his parish when he first came to it a half century ago. No man had ever been known to receive the Holy Communion except the parson, the clerk and the sexton. There were 16 women communicants and most of them went away

9   Bossy, 'The Mass as a Social Institution', pp. 34–5.
10   One of the more controversial aspects of this was sacred music, where clergy-led initiatives suppressed lay-led, 'folk' forms of music, such as the church band. Cf. V. Gammon, 'Babylonian Performances: the Rise and Suppression of Popular Church Music, 1660–1870'.
11   M. Douglas, *Natural Symbols: Explorations in Cosmology*.

when he refused to pay them for coming. They had been accustomed there at some place in the neighbourhood to pass the cup to each other with a nod of the head.

At one church there were two male communicants. When the cup was given to the first he touched his forelock and said, 'Here's to your good health, Sir'. The other said, 'Here's to the good health of our Lord Jesus Christ'.[12]

Superficially this is a story of simple rural ignorance and confusion. But there may have been more going on here, and Kilvert's story merits exploration. The reference to the poor refusing to attend if they were not paid is probably based on the practice of taking a collection at celebrations of communion (the 'sacrament money'), which could then be given to the poor. Registers or accounts of 'sacrament money', noting either collections taken or sums awarded, were very common indeed.[13] The parish records of St Mary's, Chatham, for example, include an account of sacrament money given by the incumbent and church-wardens to named recipients over several decades from 1827.[14] One specific example occurs in the diary of William Holland, parish priest of the benefices of Over Stowey and Monckton Farley in the Diocese of Bath and Wells: '[George Adams] is 86 ... weak and with a long beard. I gave him some of the sacrament money. God bless you he said I have no one but you and madam [Holland's wife] to look after me.'[15] The practice at Fordington may not have been all that unusual. What made it noteworthy, in all probability, was not that it happened, but rather that the new vicar reacted the way he did, noting the story for posterity. He was almost certainly Henry Moule (1801–1880), the Evangelical vicar of Fordington from 1829 until his death, and father of the Evangelical scholar Handley Moule (1841–1920). Henry Moule's earnest piety, learned under the influence of Charles Simeon at Cambridge, jarred with the sensibilities of his parishioners at both ends of the social scale. Handley wrote of the 'great contempt' of religion at Fordington:

---

12   F. Kilvert, *Diary*, Vol. 2, p. 442.

13   There is no study as yet of the 'sacrament money'. The latest reference I have found to it dates from a report on the Easter vestry of St Mary's, Broughton Hall, in Cheshire: *Cheshire Observer*, 27 April 1895. Some context – though not specific comments as such – can be deduced from J. Broad, 'Parish Economies of Welfare, 1650–1834'.

14   Medway Archives & Record Centre, Rochester: Chatham St Mary, 1568–1974, P085 01 018.

15   J. Ayres (ed.), *Paupers and Pig Killers: The diary of William Holland, a Somerset parson 1799–1818*, p. 272.

[When] the young Vicar was found to be a 'Methodist', that is to say ... the preacher of a Gospel of definite and personal change of heart and conse-quent devotion of life, he had much to bear in the way of opposition and even of personal insult. Careless groups at the churchyard gates reviled the worshippers as they passed in. My elder brothers still remember the cries that followed them as 'the *passons* lambs'.[16]

Handley's *Memories of a Vicarage* also records, fleetingly, the spate of rick burnings in that part of Dorset in 1831, as part of what later came to be called the 'Swing' riots.[17] So social tensions ran through the area in the 1820s and 1830s, and his father's parish reform, in some ways matching High Church ini-tiatives, represented a 'modernising' programme that set the clergy at odds with more customary mores and forms of leisure.[18] The very telling of the story, as it was handed down to Kilvert, probably reflected, not so much the oddity of eucharistic practice in Fordington, as the incomprehension of a clergyman encountering a traditional feature of parish worship and welfare.

Close study of the eucharist as a social practice, then, can open up a com-plex world of contemporary associations and meanings. Careful work is required here. However much there was immense variety in the forms and shapes of medieval piety, still a certain unity did inhere in the very notion of Christendom. By 1800, that could hardly be said of Western Europe as a whole: Europe's religious divisions ran through class, locality and nation. A study of the eucharist as social symbol in the modern era must be alert to the fact that its subject matter is irredeemably pluralist, complex and multi-dimensional in character. It requires not merely an account differentiated according to doc-trine, denomination and tradition, nor to social class, but also according to the complexity of popular belief. Churchgoing depended in the past, as now, on a fusion of several different motives, some of which might never in any case have come to conscious recognition. And yet to reach down even just a little way below the surface is to bring to light hints of such a variety of views. In receiv-ing and exploring the significance of the eucharist as a social symbol, such a variety can never be far from our mind.

---

16 H. C. G. Moule, *Memories of a Vicarage*, pp. 54–5.

17 Moule, *Memories of a Vicarage*, p. 67.

18 There is a large literature on this theme of middle-class suppression or redirection of popular leisure: cf. for example A. P. Donajgrodski (ed.), *Social Control in Nineteenth-Cen-tury Britain*; also R. W. Bushaway, *By Rite: Custom, Ceremony and Community 1700–1880*.

The Eucharist in the High Church Revival

That brief survey of the theme of the eucharist as social symbol could only sketch a way of approaching this subject. But I shall draw on it as I turn to consider more specifically the place of the eucharist in the High Church revival. Though the subject of this book, and more specifically this chapter, is the Church of England, the sacramental revival in England had significant continental connections, and by the 1840s and 1850s British and overseas commentators alike were perfectly capable of seeing this. The young F. D. Maurice, for example, in a work that touched on Tractarianism, could write of its setting in 'that great Catholic movement which all parts of Europe have experienced'.[19] But it was a movement with its own theological consistency and coherence, nevertheless. As the Tractarian 'supercharged' emphasis on apostolic succession worked its way through the various levels of Anglican polity, it reawakened interest in sacramentalism *per se*, and especially in the doctrine of the eucharist.[20]

This mutation in High Church argument was hardly unexpected. The early *Tracts for the Times*, and associated sermons, pamphlets and other works, were motivated first and foremost by the desire to defend the Church of England from the depredations of a 'Whig' reformism aided and abetted by Nonconformists and 'non-dogmatic' Anglicans, including Evangelicals. Apostolic succession came to represent a central principle not only for the Tractarians, but for other High Churchmen initially or critically supportive of Tractarian teaching, such as William Palmer of Worcester College, whose mighty *Treatise on the Church of Christ* (1838) was to stand as the 'classic' or most systematic defence of the so-called 'branch' theory of the Church, uniting Anglicans, Orthodox and Roman Catholics around the continuity of episcopal office. Apostolic succession was vital because it demonstrated that the authority of the Church did not depend on the State or on the will of the people, but on the Church's own history, and in particular on its foundation by Christ. Church authority, therefore, was in a sense self-authenticating, and High Churchmanship, as it was influenced by Tractarianism and came to expression in belief and practice more commonly called 'Anglo-Catholic', thus eventually acquired a quite different, more radical character than was typical of an earlier generation, sceptical as it was of the constitutional conventions of the religious Establishment. Following this basic assertion of spiritual authority, much of

---

19   F. D. Maurice, *Three Letters to the Revd William Palmer*, pp. 23–4.
20   P. B. Nockles, *The Oxford Movement in Context: Anglican High Churchmanship 1760–1857*, pp. 146–52.

the early work of the Tractarians and their supporters was devoted to establishing as much as they could the content of authoritative teaching and practice, and for that they returned to the evidence of the Early Church.

Developments in Tractarian sacramental theology thus largely followed on from the initial preoccupation with ecclesiology. It was Pusey's tracts on baptism – tracts 67 to 69 – which first marked a decisive turn towards sacramental theory, invoking a defence of an 'objective' view of baptism as a saving ordinance, effecting regeneration. Pusey's controversial interpretation, whilst compatible with older High Church views, cemented High Church affiliation to the baptismal service of the Prayer Book.[21] That was to prove crucial in reactions to the Gorham judgement at mid-century, when the Judicial Committee of the Privy Council – a civil court – upheld the right of an Evangelical incumbent in the diocese of Exeter to deny the doctrine of baptismal regeneration as it seemed to be taught in the Prayer Book, and triggered a further round of secessions, including that of Henry Manning. But consideration of the eucharist followed closely, given its intrinsic connection to ordination and succession. Härdelin, in the most thorough survey of Tractarian eucharistic theology published to date, saw the publication of Robert Wilberforce's *Doctrine of the Holy Eucharist* (1853) as particularly important, as the first book to subject the question of real presence to 'a full theological and systematic analysis'.[22] In Wilberforce's hands, initial tentative conceptions by Newman and others were developed into a full belief 'in a real presence connected with the elements'.[23] The increasing emphasis that the Tractarians came to place on the eucharist was evident well before the publication of Wilberforce's book, however. Pusey, again, had already produced his Tract 81, containing a *catena* of Patristic quotations in support of the doctrine of eucharistic sacrifice, in 1837, and he courted controversy – including an inhibition from preaching in Oxford before the University for two years – with his controversial sermon of 1843, *The Holy Eucharist a Comfort to the Penitent*. Doctrines both of real presence and of eucharistic sacrifice were strongly defended by Pusey, not least in his sermon of 1853, *The Presence of Christ in the Holy Eucharist*. Alexander Penrose Forbes, Bishop of Brechin, raised controversy in England as well as Scotland over the real presence in his 1857 *Primary charge delivered to the clergy of his diocese*.[24]

---

21   Cf. Thompson, *Baptism, Church and Society*, pp. 65–80.

22   A. Härdelin, *The Tractarian Understanding of the Eucharist*, p. 141.

23   Härdelin, *Tractarian Understanding of the Eucharist*, p. 147.

24   Cf. B. Douglas, *A Companion to Anglican Eucharistic Theology, 1: The Reformation to the Nineteenth Century*, pp. 490–1; also, Anon., *Remarks on the Primary Charge of the Bishop of Brechin*.

Keble likewise raised a storm in the same year with his sermon *On eucharistical adoration*. Both authors wrote in the aftermath of the Denison judgement in which the holding of a doctrine of real presence in the Church of England had apparently been rejected, only for the judgement to be overturned on a technical point of law. *Pace* Härdelin, Wilberforce's systematic treatment no more than focused and intensified a theological development already under way well before Newman's conversion. In essence, the position adopted by 'advanced' High Churchmen, including the Tractarians, was one described by Brian Douglas as 'moderate realism': Christ's body and blood were objectively present in the consecrated bread and wine without the 'natural substance' of the bread and wine being obliterated.[25] This view was virtually indistinguishable from the Lutheran doctrine of consubstantiation, though that was a word that English High Churchmen generally avoided. The evidence was there, for example, in what Walter Hook wrote about the eucharist. As a sometime sympathiser with Tractarianism, yet one also unafraid of the term 'Protestant' and a staunch defender of the Reformation, he was commonly taken as an 'orthodox' or 'traditional' High Churchman. Yet he too defended real presence (though without explicitly using the term) and sacrifice in a sermon of 1846, *The Eucharist a sacrament and a sacrifice*: even the English Reformers, he asserted, had not wished to deny the reality of presence, but only the obliteration of the natural substances of bread and wine implied in the Roman Catholic doctrine of transubstantiation.[26] Another example is George Selwyn, sometimes described as 'Tractarian', but who in general is also better considered as a 'traditional' High Churchman. In an unpublished sermon preached in Auckland, New Zealand in 1848 Selwyn asserted that the natural elements remained after consecration, but 'by Christ's appointment' they were 'part of a sacrament of which the inward part and thing signified is the Body and Blood of Christ'.[27]

For our purposes, leaving systematic theology to one side, the recovered or revitalised assertion of eucharistic doctrine was central to the devotional and ceremonial development of High Anglicanism in the nineteenth century. Practice matched theology: the ritual 'six points' were all essentially about the eucharist, and mostly implied a doctrine of real presence in the consecrated elements, and a concept of eucharistic sacrifice – vestments, the eastward

---

25   Douglas, *Companion*, I, p. 533.

26   W. F. Hook, *The Eucharist a sacrament and a sacrifice*, p. 15.

27   Cited in Wilson, 'G. A. Selwyn, the colonial episcopate and the formation of the Anglican Communion', p. 54; Selwyn's sermon notes are in the archives of Selwyn College, Cambridge.

position, unleavened bread, altar lights (lit candles), mixing of water and wine, and incense. As Brilioth acknowledged, 'The re-birth of eucharistic piety is the most active of all the forms of fermentation which the Oxford Movement set working in the spiritual life of England.'[28]

If Brilioth was correct, one would expect to see this rebirth of eucharistic piety working itself out in manifest changes in religious practice. And that is what we do find. The first, and most telling, aspect is the evidence of growing frequency of communion throughout the second half of the nineteenth century. This was not necessarily an indication of Anglo-Catholic sympathies. More frequent celebration of Holy Communion was initially an Evangelical concern.[29] The old High Churchmen shared it, as Peter Nockles has suggested.[30] The ex-Evangelical Frederick Faber, on his rapid journey towards Roman Catholicism, noted approvingly the case for daily eucharist whilst travelling in Europe in 1841.[31] W. J. E. Bennett, the first vicar of St Paul's, Knightsbridge, was even arguing in favour of a daily eucharist long before he became associated with the Tractarians.[32] Evidently, the recovery of a greater role for the communion service in the Church of England was not a one-party issue: it was perceived to be an intrinsic aspect of the early Victorian reform and recovery of public worship throughout the Church. Yet undoubtedly it also received particular impetus from High Churchmen, and especially Tractarianism, and by the 1850s it was almost a *sine qua non* for Tractarian clergy and their sympathisers.

Its theological rationale was mainly located in the process of sanctification. In his sermon on 'Increased Communions', preached 'to remove misgivings where Weekly Communion had been restored', Pusey dwelt on the tension between the fear of receiving communion, which he traced to a legitimate sense of awe in the presence of God, and the evident growth in holiness which a faithful heart drew from frequent communion.[33] God, Pusey suggested, in past days may have withdrawn communions from the Church, in case they would be damaging to those of weak faith, but now he is calling his followers 'to new degrees of devotedness, devotion, love ... He is setting a higher measure

---

28   Y. Brilioth, *Eucharistic Faith and Practice*, p. 215.

29   C. J. Cocksworth, *Evangelical Eucharistic Thought in the Church of England*, p. 74.

30   Nockles, *Oxford Movement in Context*, p. 216.

31   F. Faber, *Sights and Thoughts in foreign churches and among foreign peoples*, p. 307.

32   In his *The Eucharist, its History, Doctrine, and Practice* (1837), and cited in F. Bennett, *The Story of W. J. E. Bennett*, p. 35.

33   E. B. Pusey, 'Increased Communions', *Parochial Sermons*, Vol. I, *For the Season from Advent to Whitsuntide*, p. 309.

of Grace before us'.[34] Weekly communion, in its union of the faithful believer with God, would become 'the very Centre, as it is the Fulness of your life'.[35] J. H. Blunt (1823–1884) called the eucharist the 'climax of all sacraments', for in it all other rites 'look up to this one ... the grace of each of them finds its complement in the grace bestowed at the Altar'.[36] But there were other, more indirect theological reasons for the practice, too. The Tractarians' acceptance of the common Catholic argument that the exclusive authority of the priest to preside at communion derived from his episcopal ordination was almost *bound* to lead to a renewed emphasis on the frequent exercise of that authority.[37] That priestly role was defined by sacramental function, in baptism, absolution, and communion. As Paul Bradshaw has pointed out, the Tractarians believed that their case rested on the Ordinal, and the Ordinal appeared to connect the function of dispensing the sacraments with the laying on of hands, and then reinforced this with the giving of authority 'to minister the sacraments' at the donation of the Bible: 'Receive the Holy Ghost for the Office and Work of a Priest in the Church of God, now committed unto thee by the Imposition of our hands ... And be thou a faithful Dispenser of the Word of God, and of his holy Sacraments.'[38] So, even when the more frequent celebration of communion did not actually lead to a more frequent reception of communion by the faithful, its theological rationale was secure, since it was implicit in the very understanding of the character and exercise of priestly ministry itself. Bad priests neglected communion.

The trajectory of the rising frequency of communion in the parishes is fairly well established. Chadwick suggested that the change was already evident in many places through the 1840s and 1850s.[39] The argument for increased communion as an aspect of revived worship was already won in High Church circles by then. Hook, for example, had introduced weekly communion at Leeds parish church soon after his appointment in 1837.[40] Edward Denison, an 'orthodox' High Church bishop of Salisbury, though with some Whig sympathies, oversaw a doubling of the number of parishes in his diocese in which communion was celebrated monthly in the fifteen years from 1836 to 1851, from

---

34   Pusey, 'Increased Communions', p. 322.

35   Pusey, 'Increased Communions', p. 324.

36   J. H. Blunt, *The Sacraments and Sacramental Ordinances of the Church: Being a plain exposition of their history, meaning, and effects*, p. 106.

37   Cf. Nockles, *Oxford Movement in Context*, chapter 3, 'Ecclesiology: The apostolic paradigm'.

38   P. F. Bradshaw, *The Anglican Ordinal*, pp. 113–4.

39   W. O. Chadwick, *The Victorian Church*, Vol. I, p. 514.

40   W. N. Yates, *Leeds and the Oxford Movement*, p. 14.

35 to 81.[41] By about the 1870s, this trend was definitely observable in 'low' as well as 'high' parishes. Reed cites Charles Mackeson's *Guide to the Churches of London and its Suburbs* to support the contention that, between 1869 and 1884, the proportion of London churches with weekly celebrations of communion rose from 26 per cent to 58 per cent – an astonishing rate of change.[42] By the 1900s, it was rare to encounter an Anglican parish at which Holy Communion was not celebrated at least once on Sundays, even though the predominant pattern of Sunday worship retained late morning Mattins and afternoon Evensong as the best-attended services. As Green has pointed out for Halifax and its environs – with perhaps just a trace of exaggeration – the idea of restoring the celebration of the eucharist as the central act of Sunday worship 'was almost universal at this time amongst local Anglican clergymen'.[43]

It is worth pausing to reflect on what the implications of this increasing frequency of communion were for the local ecclesiology of Anglicanism. As indicated above, frequent communion did not automatically reflect the direct adoption of Tractarian, Ritualist or 'Anglo-Catholic' sacramental theology, though Cocksworth admits that Evangelical enthusiasm was generally muted in practice.[44] Certainly strictly theological or devotional motivation may have varied from place to place and from person to person. But any change in liturgical practice required an implicit justification, and this particular change implied at least the elevation of regular eucharistic participation into an important element of the worship of the parish church, even if, formally, some clergy from the Evangelical and 'Broad' wings continued to regard communion as not strictly necessary for Christian discipleship. The movement for eucharistic restoration that Green characterised helpfully in the three distinctive concepts of 'liturgical separation', 'ritual elaboration', and 'ceremonial intensification' perhaps inevitably influenced the ways in which incumbents thought about the identity and organisation of worshipping congregations.[45] Thus, if the rising frequency of communion does not on its own provide direct evidence of a definite model of 'eucharistic community' as the basis of parish practice, it is an important element.

---

41 J. Cardell-Oliver, 'George Anthony Denison (1805–1896): A Georgian High Churchman in Victorian times', unpublished PhD Thesis, Murdoch University, 2015, p. 102.
42 J. S. Reed, *Glorious Battle: The Cultural Politics of Victorian Anglo-Catholicism*, p. 267.
43 S. J. D. Green, *Religion in the Age of Decline: Organisation and Experience in Industrial Yorkshire 1870–1920*, p. 310.
44 Cocksworth, *Evangelical Eucharistic Thought*, pp. 87 & 96.
45 Green, *Religion in the Age of Decline*, p. 310.

All the more significant, against that background, is the changing religious
ritual and ceremonial of High Churchmanship in this period. Again, here the
really significant changes were under way by the 1840s and 1850s. The general
outlines of this process are familiar enough to historians, including the apparent paradox of widespread, gradual adoption of certain 'High Church' practices
alongside continued, sharp controversy over particular ritual. At least two
lines of interpretation of High Church influence in the mid to late nineteenth
century are possible. One is the 'minimalist' view, which concentrates on the
'six points' – the eastward position, eucharistic vestments, mixed chalice, altar
lights, wafer bread, and incense – and suggests a very small constituency
indeed. Nigel Yates, following the first edition of the *Tourist's Church Guide* of
1874, found some 136 churches using lighted candles and having 'at the very
minimum' a weekly communion, with a further 67 parishes with incumbents
who were members at that date of the Society of the Holy Cross, giving a total
of 203 'Ritualist' churches in all.[46] But this way of counting simply demonstrates the limitations of relying on a handful of measurable practices, since it
significantly underestimates the number of churches where High Church
innovation of one kind or another was under way by then. The other is a 'maxi-
malist' view, which includes features such as the adoption of a surpliced choir
and the use of *Hymns Ancient and Modern* to suggest a much more widespread
and diffuse pattern of influence. Both lines are plausible, and by no means
incompatible. What is easily forgotten, however, is that many of the new ritual
and ceremonial practices were linked, more or less directly, to eucharistic theology, and especially to the sacramental theology of the Tractarians and their
successors.[47] The 'orthodox' High Churchman George Denison saw the connection perfectly well, and grasped that attacks on ritual innovation were also,
by implication, attacks on High Church eucharistic doctrine.[48] Ritual, in other
words, was not a marginal, superficial or merely 'fashionable' feature of late-
nineteenth century Anglo-Catholicism: it was integral to its identity and
practice.[49] Inasmuch as some of that ritual was adopted more widely than in

---

46   W. N. Yates, *Anglican Ritualism in Victorian Britain*, pp. 386–414.

47   Of recent historians of Anglo-Catholicism, the one who has most firmly grasped this con-
      nection is Reed, *Glorious Battle*, pp. 68–72; Reed's attention at this point to eucharistic
      doctrine stands in some contrast to Yates' work (see below).

48   Cardell-Oliver, 'George Anthony Denison', p. 326.

49   Keble's view has been taken as typical of the main Tractarian leaders – 'the inward wor-
      ship ... is the main point in question; the posture and mode are secondary and variable'
      – but this is taken from a text notorious for encouraging ritual development, and cannot
      be taken to suggest that ritual forms were simply arbitrary: J. Keble, *On Eucharistical Ado-
      ration*, p. 1.

parishes which can be clearly identified as 'Anglo-Catholic', again it is a sign of a renewed emphasis on the importance of communion in the worship of the local church.

As I showed in chapter two, historians of Ritualism have sometimes been prone to depict the late-nineteenth century's reconstruction of Anglo-Catholic religious ceremonial as a phenomenon that is to all intents and purposes detachable from the practical, pastoral strategies of High Church clergy. But the biographies of Tractarian and Ritualist churchmen make it very clear that such a separation would not have been readily comprehensible to them. T. T. Carter's *Life and Letters*, for example, contains much more information about his development of pastoral agencies such as the House of Mercy and his contribution to the development of the penitentiary movement than it does about ritual.[50] Ellsworth's account of Charles Lowder's ministry in East London demonstrates the clear connection that Lowder made between his liturgical preferences and his pastoral practice.[51] Evidently the adoption of surpliced choirs, chanted psalms, candles, the restoration of a church on 'ecclesiological' lines, and many other such changes might have occurred in some parishes in which little accompanying change in pastoral practice was put in place, but this seems *prima facie* unlikely in most cases. For one thing, nearly all of these changes had definite implications for the liturgical organisation, servicing and management of public worship, which in turn required new forms of parish organisation. For another, the rationale offered for liturgical change and innovation was often evangelistic, as is commonly recognised, even if its results ultimately fell far short of its practitioners' ambitions.

So far I have considered two areas of evidence which provide a basic context for the emergence of a model of eucharistic community as the basis of parish practice in this period. Adoption of any of these specific changes did not necessarily imply a deliberate intention to put the celebration and reception of communion at the very centre of parish life. But in many parishes it undoubtedly did. To take one example alone at this stage: at St Andrew's, South Croydon, the adoption of regular weekly communion came some eight years after the church's foundation in 1857, though the institution of an extra communion service on the third Sunday of the month (that is, in addition to the original monthly celebration on the first Sunday) within six months of the church's opening illustrated a desire to make this, 'the highest and most solemn and

---

50   W. H. Hutchings, *Life and Letters of Thomas Thellusson Carter*, passim.

51   Cf. L. Ellsworth, *Charles Lowder and the Ritualist Movement*, especially chapters 5, 'Vast and Neglected Populations', and 6, 'Principles of a Pastoral Experiment'.

significant part of the Church service', a central feature of the church's life.[52]
At St Andrew's, a pamphlet on the church published anonymously but from
internal evidence written by its first priest-in-charge, H. R. Reynolds, explicitly
described those who were regular communicants as 'full members of the
Church' and, estimating that only a fifth of the congregation at this stage were
such, argued that 'all ought to be so; and none who are not so, can be considered in a healthy or happy condition, as regards their state in God's sight'.[53] But
in other churches the rationale for change was probably much more piecemeal
and practical, though it is often difficult to find explicit evidence in this regard.
Even so, it seems *prima facie* unlikely that such a profound change in the liturgical provision of Anglican churches across the spectrum of church opinion
would have been possible without *any* corresponding change in the understanding of the place of communion in forming the identity and character of a
local church.

Renewal of eucharistic faith and practice was certainly also reflected in the
way High Church clergy conceived of their parish work. One of the most influential High Church pastoral manuals, the *Directorium Pastorale* (1864), written
by J. H. Blunt, called the sacraments of baptism and eucharist 'essential parts
of the pastoral system'.[54] Blunt regarded a parish's communicants as the natural or appropriate group whom a priest might want to draw into regular
association for promoting more frequent church attendance and more frequent communion, private prayer, and practical work; such an association
could effectively supersede 'in a great degree ... the necessity of any other for
Church work'.[55] Here, then, in essence was the rationale which underlay the
development of communicants' guilds and other lay associations. But it is
worth emphasizing that, for Blunt, as for other High Church clergy, such associations were not to be seen simply as an occasional or 'leisure' pursuit: they
were integral to the vision of community clergy such as Blunt was promoting,
and that vision was exemplified in the celebration of the eucharist itself. This
is evident from Blunt's description of the order of reception: first a celebrant
would communicate himself; then he would deliver the 'Body and Blood of
Christ' to any bishops, priests or deacons who were 'officially present'; then 'in

---

52   Anon, *St Andrew's Church for the Poor*, p. 22. The first evidence for weekly communion is
      supplied by service details in *Warren's Commercial and General Directory for Croydon*,
      1865.

53   *St Andrew's Church for the Poor*, pp. 23–4.

54   J. H. Blunt, *Directorium Pastorale. Principles and Practice of Pastoral Work in the Church of
      England*, p. 158.

55   Blunt, *Directorium Pastorale*, p. 359.

well-regulated churches' the other communicants present would receive in successive order, first the choir as 'subordinate ministers' in the service, then the men, and lastly the women.[56] This was on any view a hierarchical or sacerdotal vision of a worshipping community, with a notion of separation and recombination which harks back to my earlier discussion of Bossy and Douglas. Worthy of note too is the clear implication of gender separation at communion, though it is difficult to establish how widely this practice was actually followed. But at the same time it must also be borne in mind that Blunt, like many other High Church writers in the mid-nineteenth century, also assumed that the worshipping community or congregation essentially recognised no distinctions before God, and that financial or property differences ought to make no difference to the status of the communicant – hence the campaign against pew rents, for example. Blunt condemned, in the *Directorium*, the tendency of clergy to associate especially with the rich and congenial: 'In such a case the Church becomes almost avowedly the Church of a sect ... Thus there comes into play a sort of "pew system", in the pastor's work of spiritual oversight'.[57] For Blunt, as for other High Church clergy, the spiritual ordering of church and society did not automatically validate social hierarchies.

An even sharper conception of the significance of being a regular communicant can be found later in the century, in the work of Vernon Staley (1852–1933), another prolific writer of popular religious and pastoral manuals in the 'advanced' Anglo-Catholic tradition. For Staley, 'no one could be considered a genuine Christian who failed to take part' in the celebration of the eucharist 'with regularity'.[58] Once again sanctification was described as the immediate and direct benefit of receiving communion: 'In Communion Christ enters into us through the higher part of our nature, pervading us hiddenly [sic] and silently, cleansing our souls from the stain of sin, subduing in us what is evil, and quickening in us what is good.'[59] For Staley, as for Blunt forty years earlier, regular communion was the centre of a web of practical, pastoral and devotional life, fanning out into religious communities, guilds and other active societies, all part of a 'fuller and more perfect devotional system' which could be traced back to the influence of the Oxford revival.[60] Another High Church writer, Clement Rogers (1866–1949), in his manual of pastoral theology, also

---

56   J. H. Blunt, *A Key to the Knowledge of the Book of Common Prayer*, p. 65.

57   Blunt, *Directorium Pastorale*, p. 90.

58   V. Staley, *Christian Duty: A Plain Guide to the Knowledge and Practice of Religion*, p. 179.

59   V. Staley, *The Catholic Religion: A Manual of Instruction for members of the Anglican Church*, p. 271.

60   V. Staley, *The Practical Religion*, p. vii.

placed the reception of communion at the very centre of his understanding of the Church, and on that basis argued for a franchise for the church's representative system based on being a communicant: 'Churchmanship does not consist in a voluntary association between men, but in being admitted into a Divine Society founded by Christ.'[61] High Church theologians were thus pressing on their readers from mid-century on, if not earlier, the importance of proper, faithful attendance at communion services, and likewise the importance of moving from being a non-communicating baptised member of the congregation, through confirmation, to being a regular communicant.

How far was this devotional programme – ritually and liturgically the very heart of the High Church revival – actually pursued in practice? In the next section I shall explore a number of examples of the widespread phenomenon of communicants' guilds and lay associations, which gave practical expression to this emergent ideal of eucharistic community. Before leaving the discussion of clerical conceptualizing of eucharistic renewal and community, it is worth looking briefly at some tantalizingly rich evidence of a practical programme of eucharistic renewal. This comes from the little market town of Axbridge in Somerset, and indicates a consistent clerical programme of incorporating – or converting – parishioners into regular eucharistic practice. In the 1870s and early 1880s either the incumbent or the curate kept a register of all the households in the main street and square in the centre of town, noting their residents' names, occupations and likelihood of becoming communicants – for example:

> No. 22 John G Day & wife, both communicants. The ss teacher. A large family …
> No. 23 … Eliz.th Stokes. an industrious widow, communicant, and, other side, Mr & Mrs James Coomes, old people, might be confirmed, and become communicants.
> No. 24 Styles & wife, he bell-ringer, she makes boxes
> [later] Edward [?O]ffer & wife. One boy Ed[ward]. Nat Sch, another and a daughter, at work. – church, when anywhere he subject to rheumatism. Robert and Eliza ready for confirmation next year.[62]

The likelihood is that the record-keeper was the curate, Philip Willis, who served at Axbridge from 1875 to 1883 and had been trained at Wells Theological

---

61   C. F. Rogers, *Principles of Parish Work: An Essay in Pastoral Theology*, pp. 30–1.
62   Communicants' registers with some personal notes, Axbridge parish records, Somerset Record Office [SRO], Taunton, D\P\ax/2/6/3.

College, after St John's College, Oxford.[63] Willis – if it was him – also kept, at the back of the same book, a tabular record of communicants over an eight-year period, registering what appear to have been wildly varying rates of communion, and, for a small Somerset parish, a remarkable turnover in people. In the course of 1880, for example, we can count some 65 communicants' names, but 12 of them (a fifth) are struck out, including Mr & Mrs John Day, mentioned above, suggesting that they left the parish at some point in the year.[64] But less than two-thirds communicated on Easter Day, and only 17 people communicated monthly in the course of the year. To my mind, these are sobering observations for those who lean heavily on church statistics. So extensive are the comments on Axbridge residents and their status as communicants in the household enumeration, that it seems clear that the perspective of the record-keeper was shaped by envisaging the local community as a eucharistic community in potential at least.[65] The systematic survey of a single parish in this way yields conflicting data, of course – both the ambition (and some success) of drawing parishioners closer into the circle of regular communicants, and at the same time the clear falling short of the High Church ideal that *all* ought to be communicants.

Communicants' Guilds and Lay Confraternities

If it was the clergy who were the principal instigators and encouragers of eucharistic renewal in the Church of England, nevertheless the laity were not passive bystanders, simply coralled or put upon. On the contrary, as we saw in chapter 2, just as there were local notables and others who were not ordained who were instrumental in the establishment and running of High Church parishes in the nineteenth century, so too there were local or parochial organisations which were formed for their benefit and which served as vehicles of eucharistic devotion. Foremost amongst these were the communicants' guilds which sprang up under the influence particularly of Tractarian and Ritualist thought from mid-century onwards. These have been largely ignored by historians, but they were very widespread and numerous. Although relatively short-lived, such was

---

63 *Crockford's Clerical Directory*, passim.
64 Communicants' registers with some personal notes, Axbridge parish records, SRO, Taunton, D\P\ax\2/6/3.
65 The Axbridge material is very rich; I am working on a detailed study. There is some useful material in V. Castle & S. Castle, *Richard Trew 1793–1874, Mayor of Axbridge: A History of Axbridge in the Nineteenth Century.*

their ubiquity, by the end of the nineteenth century, that they were evidently a vital element in local sacramental renewal in the period.

The guilds were essentially local, parish-based voluntary associations usually formed around the principle of gathering together regular communicants to support the work of the local church and to deepen lay devotion. They partly echoed the remarkable growth of *confraternités* in post-Restoration France.[66] They also existed in British Roman Catholicism well into the twentieth century.[67] Precisely how much the Anglican guilds owed to Roman Catholic precedent is not clear, however, and it is likely that their creation at least in part also owed something to the renewed Victorian interest in all things medieval, and that in that sense they were an attempt to recreate the parish guilds of the Middle Ages. The earliest such lay associations – not necessarily at first specifically for communicants – were created in the wake of the Oxford Movement, as with (for example) the formation of the Guild of St Mary the Virgin at Oxford in 1844 under Pusey's guidance, for the study of ecclesiastical art and architecture, and the Guild of St Alban the Martyr founded at Birmingham in 1851 to assist the clergy in 'maintaining and extending the Catholic Faith and to spread a true knowledge of the doctrines of the Church'.[68] But the model was quickly adapted into one that suited parish work, and particularly the renewed emphasis that High Churchmen were placing on the eucharist by mid-century. Direct testimony from guild members is rare, but a glimpse into their local significance comes from the life of the Catholic Modernist George Tyrrell (1861–1901), who was brought up in Ireland as an Anglican and attended All Saints' Church, Grangegorman in Dublin. All Saints was High Church, though not Ritualist, and under the instruction of its incumbent, Dr Maturin, in 1876 Tyrrell committed himself 'yet more deeply to the life of Grangegorman Church by joining the Guild'.[69] Maturin asked Tyrrell to leave the Guild in 1879 when he learnt that he had begun to attend Mass at the Roman Catholic church in Gardiner Street.[70]

Even as associations for communicants, and for encouraging eucharistic devotion, in some parishes guilds arose originally as local branches of national associations. By far the most important of these was the Confraternity of the

66   Cf. M. Agulhon, *Pénitents et francs-maçons de l'ancienne Provence*.
67   A. Archer, *The Two Catholics Churches: A Study in Oppression*, p. 93; see also M. Heimann, *Catholic Devotion in Victorian England*, pp. 125–36.
68   Reed, *Glorious Battle*, p. 50, citing P. F. Anson, *The Call of the Cloister*.
69   N. Sagovsky, *On God's Side: A Life of George Tyrrell*, p. 8.
70   M. Petre (ed.), *Autobiography and Life of George Tyrrell*, Vol. I, p. 138.

Blessed Sacrament (CBS), which was founded at St Mary's, Soho in February 1857 as a brotherhood of priests to promote 'more frequent celebration of the Holy Sacrifice, and that due Honor [sic] and Adoration which belong to our Blessed Lord therein present'.[71] The original founders envisaged the formation of local wards, each headed by an elected Superior, but in fact only two wards came into existence – the 'Western', based in Soho, and the 'Eastern', based at St Bartholomew's, Cripplegate – before the CBS foundered at the end of the year after most of its leading figures seceded to Rome.[72] Under the leadership of T. T. Carter, it was refounded as a lay as well as clerical association in 1862. The 'Objects' and 'Rules' of the refounded CBS are worth stating here in full, as they bear comparison with the rules often adopted by local communicants' guilds that were not ostensibly connected with the CBS:

> Objects.
> The Honour due to the Person of our Lord Jesus Christ in the Blessed Sacrament of His Body and Blood.
> Mutual and special Intercessions at the time of and in union with the Eucharistic Sacrifice.
> The promotion of the observance of the Catholic and primitive Law of receiving the Holy Communion fasting.
>
> Rules.
> To Communicate, or at least to be present, on Sundays and the greater Festivals and other Holy-days, when the Holy Eucharist is Celebrated, unless prevented by sickness or other urgent cause.
> To promote, by all legitimate means, frequent and reverent Celebrations of the Holy Eucharist, as the Chief Act of Divine Service.
> To make such special Intercessions as shall be from time to time directed.[73]

The CBS thus made membership dependent on being confirmed and on being an active communicant, and aimed at binding clergy and laity together

---

71 LPL, CBS, Minute Book 1857–62, Ms 2889.

72 LPL, CBS, Minute Book 1857–62, Ms. 2889. The account contained in Walter Walsh's hostile *The Secret History of the Oxford Movement*, pp. 210–11, which sees 1862 as the foundation of the CBS and which is generally followed by other historians, such as Reed, *Glorious Battle*, p. 89, needs to be modified in the light of this early evidence on the origins of the CBS.

73 *Manual of the Confraternity of the Blessed Sacrament.*

in a common commitment to eucharistic renewal, and especially fasting communion.

By the 1880s, the CBS had developed into a nationwide organisation with branches in many local parishes. Hard evidence of these local branches is hard to come by, as many of the CBS's records appear to have been destroyed or lost, but local records do yield an insight into its regional diffusion. The parish of St Clement's, Cambridge, for example, in the 1880s and 1890s had a local branch of the CBS, operating under the title 'The St Thomas Aquinas Cambridge Ward'.[74] Walter Walsh, the hostile ultra-Protestant critic of Ritualism, noted that the CBS's 1894 report claimed it had 1,682 clerical and 13,444 lay members.[75] A glimpse into the ethos of the CBS as it may have been experienced by local members comes from the record of a series of addresses, delivered in Advent 1876, and from internal evidence to members of a local branch, the whereabouts unknown. The giver of the addresses is also unknown to us, but the transcript gives a vivid portrait of the eucharistic spirituality that he was promoting, as can be caught from his opening sentences on 'Preparation':

> As we try more especially now to realize our great responsibilities as communicants, & so see more of what the life ought to be, let us think what it is, – what it ought to be, to be a communicant! a human being who feeds on the body & blood of Christ himself – those hands that take It – the mouth that eats It – the body that is nourished by It – What ought those hands, that mouth, that body to be, wh. are so filled with that precious food? This life is of a three-fold nature – one of constant preparation – of perpetual thanksgiving – & of a perpetual advance – a communicant ought always to be going forward – not backward.[76]

This was a spirituality in which communion was intimately bound up with attentive pursuit of holiness of life. Self-examination and confession were an integral part of regular preparation for receiving communion, and the life of the believer in return was to be one of thanksgiving: 'The general life of a Communicant ought to be a Eucharistic life – one of constant Thanksgiving'.[77]

---

74 St Clement's Register of Services, Cambridge Record Office [Cambs RO]: P27/1.
75 Walsh, *Secret History*, p. 210.
76 LPL, CBS, Minute Book 1857–62, Ms 2889; note that the text of this address is appended to a minute book catalogued for an earlier date range.
77 LPL, CBS, Minute Book 1857–62, Ms 2889.

The timescale of the growth of local communicants' guilds is hard to establish without a synoptic survey of all the surviving local records, but we do know that they were springing up across the country by the 1850s and 1860s. Yates, for example, found that at St Saviour's, Leeds, the parish guild was *reconstituted* in 1868 and that three other guilds were established around then.[78] Where surviving records enable us to do so, we can reconstruct something of the organisation and life of these local associations. Time and again, the constitutions and rules seem to have predicated their existence on regular reception of communion, and sought to instil practices of private devotion and preparation for communion, and even 'rules of life' for laity as well as clergy. Only regular communicants could become members of the Guild of the Ascension, the parish guild of St Modwen's, Burton-on-Trent, for example, with 'regular' here defined as 'at least once a month at the Burton parish church'.[79] The Guild had a card with rules of life, headed 'All should strive, God helping them to be: pure in body and mind, watchful in conversation, truthful in word and deed', and so on. The rules of the guild included saying of the daily offices, attendance at church twice on Sundays, receiving communion at least once a month at an early celebration (i.e. fasting), and promoting order and reverence in church.[80] The parish guild of All Saints', Cambridge, revived by J. Armitage Robinson in 1889, required members to be communicants who would receive communion corporately on specified festivals, and who would make preparation (the words 'some special' were struck out of a printed circular) for holy communion.[81] They were also to use the special prayer of the Guild at least once a week, and to read daily the second evening lesson appointed in the lectionary. A number of 'Recommendations' went further, suggesting that the 'Rules' established only minimum conditions, and that the real goal of the Guild was to instil a deeper devotional life; they included having regular and fixed times for private daily devotion, with a record kept, exercising self-discipline during Lent, setting apart a portion of income for 'pious and charitable purposes', and offering a short prayer for the Parish on hearing the church bell ring when unable to be present.[82]

These were fairly typical rules, and could be replicated from dozens of other examples. In the vast majority of instances confirmation and regular com-

78   Yates, *Leeds and the Oxford Movement*, p. 39.
79   Rules and Office of the Guild of the Ascension, St Modwen's, Burton-on-Trent (c. 1891): I am grateful to Dr Ian Atherton for supplying this information.
80   Rules and Office of the Guild of the Ascension, St Modwen's, Burton-on-Trent: Staffs RO, D4379/1/14.
81   Minute Book, Guild of All Saints', Cambridge: CambsRO, P20/24/2.
82   Minute Book, Guild of All Saints', Cambridge: CambsRO, P20/24/2.

munion were conditions of membership, though the definition of 'regular' varied somewhat. The guilds sought to encourage, in turn, the wider and more rigorous observance of those very conditions. But they had a further aim of strengthening the commitment of active members of the congregation, and in this sense the predetermination of the definition of 'active member' virtually by reference to frequent and regular communion is significant. In this respect, Green is right to describe the guilds as a means by which Sunday Scholars were induced 'to assume the duties of adult worship', though they were evidently much more than that.[83] Even Stewart Headlam's Guild of St Matthew, so often described by historians exclusively in terms of Headlam's then notorious social theology, illustrated the primacy of sacramental theology in his thinking perfectly, and in fact in origin was simply the parish guild of St Matthew's, Bethnal Green. Its objects included to 'promote frequent and reverent worship in the Holy Communion, and a better observance of the teaching of the Church of England, as set forth in the Book of Common Prayer'.[84] As Headlam's biographer commented, its parochial character 'it soon shed, but its sacramental basis was to remain to the end'.[85]

Surviving minute books in places can give a sense of what happened at the meetings of the local guilds. In many cases, they met regularly to hear addresses (usually from clergy) on particular spiritual and devotional matters, inevitably often in connection with the subject of the eucharist. At All Saints', Cambridge, for example, in the first year of its existence the communicant women's Guild of St Agnes heard addresses from its Warden (the Vicar) on 'Perseverance in grace', 'Winning the hearts of their companions to Jesus Christ', 'Communion with God', 'Holy Communion as a bond of union', 'Friendship', 'Recreation', 'The Holy Catholic Church, the Communion of Saints' and 'The lessons of Advent applied to daily life'.[86] In some instances, too, the principle of securing the active commitment of laity through an association defined by eucharistic participation was extended into practical matters of parochial organisation. At All Saints', Cambridge, again, the Guild of All Saints was actually sub-divided into four branches overseeing practical matters concerning the liturgical preparation and maintenance of the church: the Branch of St Agnes attended to the ornaments of the sanctuary, and vestments, St Gabriel to regular assistance in

83 S. J. D. Green, 'Religion and the Rise of the Common Man: Mutual Improvement Societies, Religious Associations and Popular Education in Three Industrial Towns in the West Riding of Yorkshire c. 1850–1900', p. 31.

84 F. G. Bettany, *Stewart Headlam*, p. 80.

85 Bettany, *Headlam*, p. 79.

86 Minute Book, Guild of St Agnes, All Saints', Cambridge: CambsRO, P20/24/1.

daily worship, St Radegund to parish visiting and school teaching, and St Stephen to the support of foreign missions.[87] In other places the guilds effectively became elementary parish councils, and a means for clergy to consult lay opinion. At St Augustine's, Croydon, in 1886 the matters discussed included the foundation of a Band of Hope, the formation of a Men's Institute in the parish, and resolutions and petitions on the education question.[88]

At Bathwick in Somerset the Guild of St Mary's affiliated itself to the English Church Union, and encouraged even non-members of the guild (that is, members of the congregation who were not members of the Guild) to pay a subscription through the guild to the ECU. As one speaker argued of the ECU:

> Defence and defiance and unbound charity [h]as been the motto, he spoke of the high power of Prayer and the great power of Grace also of the necessity of each member saying the E.C.U Collect daily, by the increasing of the Union they would have a worldly power in the House of Commons upon all church affairs.[89]

Here at Bathwick the minutes hint at an impressive level of lay participation, with nearly 100 attending the annual meeting in 1888, and with lay members of the congregation taking an active role in supporting specific motions and in speaking on specific matters. The Guild was run by a Council with apparently equal representation for lay men and women. How far the impression of active lay participation really ran is very hard to establish, however. Bathwick was a relatively affluent suburb, with local notables of the kind we saw in action in the founding of Anglo-Catholic churches in Croydon in chapter 2, for example. Assessment of actual numbers of members is usually hazardous, given the absence of membership rolls, but sometimes minute books can help to substantiate the impression that the guilds were genuinely capable of mobilising significant lay support.

In many other cases, it is clear that the guilds depended entirely on clerical zeal for their existence. In the Cambridgeshire village of Barrington, for example, a parish guild was 'revived' by the local parish priest, Edward Conybeare, in 1888. Conybeare saw it as a way of binding the parish church back into village life, with a somewhat romantic glance backwards to medieval England:

---

87   Minute Book, Guild of All Saints', Cambridge: CambsRO, P20/24/2.

88   J. N. Morris, *Religion and Urban Change: Croydon 1840–1914*, p. 67.

89   Entry for 22 March 1888 in the minute book of the Guild of St Mary, Bathwick, SRO, Taunton, D\P\bath.m/2/9/5.

> I believe the time has now come to revive one of the oldest institutions of
> this Parish. For 700 years, from the days of King Alfred to the year 1548,
> the Church Guild existed here. It was composed of Members of the
> Church, who used to meet together from time to time under the direction
> of the Parish Priest, for special services and mutual edification and for
> Love Feasts ... All [its] property was made away with in the unhappy reign
> of King Edward VI by those who called themselves Protestants.[90]

In fact the guild was not much more than what would today be called a social
club, meeting to hold teas, dances and excursions for church members. Its
members had to endure entertainment provided almost exclusively by the
Vicar himself and his family. The minute book entry for the Christmas Church
Tea on 30 December 1891 was thus typical: lecture by Mr James Conybeare on
his journey to Italy and Switzerland, songs by Miss Conybeare.[91] Barrington
was a poor parish, with a high proportion of labourers in the cement and brick-
making industries. Minuted explanations for low guild attendance included
'owing to sickness and the pecuniary distress caused by the recent stoppage of
the Cement works' and 'owing to the unexampled distress through the collapse
of all local industries'.[92]

The growth of these associations in some ways mirrored that of ritual innovation. By the 1870s, a twofold pattern of development was under way: guilds
were spreading to churches whose clergy were closer to central or Broad
Churchmanship than had been the case twenty years before, and in High
Church parish churches they were spawning a host of sub-guilds, as at All
Saints', Cambridge. The historic parish church of Croydon, St John the Baptist,
had a parish guild by 1885, for example, yet could hardly be described as anything other than moderately 'High'; the same could be said of Holy Trinity,
Selhurst, which also had a guild by 1889.[93] Yet at the Ritualist parish of St John
the Evangelist, Upper Norwood, by 1900 no less than six guilds were in existence, the guild model having been extended from communicants to other
identifiable groups in the church (women in service, and church watchers,
amongst others).[94] Visitation records covering the deanery of Cambridge in
1896 – generally a city of Evangelical strength, given the influence of the

90   Barrington Parish Records, P8/24 1. Minute Book of Church Guild, CambsRO, Printed
      notice, 'To the Members of the Church, All Saints, Barrington'.
91   Barrington Parish Records, Minute Book of Church Guild, entry for 30 December 1891.
92   Barrington Parish Records, entries for St Mark's Day, 1890, and 1 January 1997.
93   Morris, *Religion and Urban Change*, p. 66.
94   Morris, *Religion and Urban Change*, loc. cit.

Simeon Trust – give a good indication of the state of play at that time. Of sixteen city churches, seven had guilds, though these clearly varied enormously in size and character. St Andrew the less, on the Newmarket Road, for example, had a membership of 288 in its communicants' guild, and a voluntary parish council of twelve; by contrast, the moderately High Church St Giles had two guilds, one for church workers, with about 50 members, and the other the Guild of the Good Shepherd for young university fellows; a communicants' guild was restarted two years later, but foundered after a few meetings. Even some moderate Evangelical churches were adopting the term 'guild': St Barnabas on Mill Road, for example, had a Young Persons' Guild of 40 members, though it is unlikely that this was actually a communicants' guild, but it also had a voluntary parish council of 24, and though definite information is lacking, the likelihood is that it was composed of communicants.[95]

Thus, in many High Church or Anglo-Catholic parishes, by the end of the nineteenth century not only had liturgical practice been reorganised in order to express a profound reorientation of traditional Anglican worship towards the reinstatement of holy communion as the central liturgical rite of the Church, but participation in that rite had become the means through which significant local, parish associations were organised, and even in some cases local representative bodies formed. Implicitly, this suggests that the practice of these parishes was redefining active church membership in such a way as to illustrate and enforce the centrality of eucharistic theology to the late-nineteenth century, High Church understanding of the Christian Church. Yet this process had definite limits. Although some of the membership figures quoted in the surviving records do look impressive, nonetheless for the most part these seem to have been relatively short-lived organisations. Time and again they had to be refounded, possibly after meetings had lapsed when an incumbent moved on to another post, or when numbers slumped. Explanations for this are inevitably speculative. It is hard to avoid the thought that creating a lively network of local lay associations based on eucharistic spirituality and practice was a step too far for many congregations. The insistence of High Church clergy on fasting communion in particular seems to have put a glass ceiling in the way of mass eucharistic participation. That insistence is palpable in virtually all the late-nineteenth century High Church commentary on communion. Vernon Staley, for example, urged clergy to impress on their communicants the 'ancient duty' of fasting before communion.[96] Fasting went

95   Ely Diocesan Records, CUL, Visitation returns, C3/36.
96   V. Staley, *The Holy Communion: Addresses and Instruction Doctrinal, Practical, and Ceremonial concerning the Sacrament of the Body and Blood of Christ*, p. 36.

hand in hand with self-examination and contrition as preparation for receiving the holy mysteries. Even Gabriel Hebert, who was to do so much to modify the Victorian practice of non-receiving communions through his advocacy of the parish communion, regarded fasting before communion as obligatory.[97] Yet this symbolised an ascetic view of spiritual growth and preparation, however perfunctory, that seems to have had little appeal to many congregation members, and associations based on eucharistic participation and which emphasised fasting communion were hindered accordingly. The Bathwick evidence perhaps hints at some of the difficulties. At the annual meeting in 1888 the Vicar gave a brief resumé of the growth of the guild:

> [T]he Rector in a few opening remarks said that the Guild was first formed on March 6th 1878, it had since then, year by year increased, (in numbers) in many ways but there was still more to be done, he urged members to keep to the Rules namely, to always say Guild collect daily, attend Guild office, all meetings, and to make their early [i.e. fasting] monthly corporate communion.[98]

If they needed urging, then surely – to his eyes – they were falling behind.

Conclusion: Renewal and Resistance

Thus the harmonious social world summoned up by the advocates of sacramental renewal in Anglicanism – a world of devotion and discipline, of tradition and social conscience, of religious hierarchy and secular responsibility – did not really exist, except in the minds of its clerical proponents and their elite lay supporters. There is impressive evidence of a systematic programme of church renewal at local level pursued by High Church clergy and based on eucharistic participation. Yet this seemed to bump up against powerful counter-currents in popular piety. Evidence of the eucharist as a failing social symbol, a symbol of division, or even a symbol of religious rejection, is not hard to come by. Just as clergy, and religiously active laity, both generated a vision of eucharistic community and also drew it out of their social world, so others perceived such a vision as threat. We have already seen, in chapter two,

---

97   A. G. Hebert, 'A Note on the Fast before Communion', in idem, *The Parish Communion*, pp. 23–29; this advice was still being reprinted in 1954.

98   Entry for 3 February 1888 in the minute book of the Guild of St Mary, Bathwick, SRO, Taunton, D\P\bath.m/2/9/5.

one of the more notorious instances of popular opposition to sacramental renewal, namely the riots at St. George's-in-the-East, in the East End of London. Popular Protestantism, here as elsewhere, may have been on the wane by the end of the century, but its residual presence nevertheless inhibited High Church activity.

But popular resistance to High Churchmanship did not necessarily come in explicitly anti-Catholic form. It could be more inchoate, or indifferent. Admittedly refusal in the sense of absolute rejection of Christianity in all its manifestations was rare in British society. Edward Royle's persuasive study of secularists bears this out. Although the National Secular Society had achieved an impressive network of local branches by the 1880s, nevertheless its members were never very numerous on the ground, and by the end of the nineteenth century ironically it too, like the very churches it spent so much time criticizing, was in decline.[99] By the end of the century, secularism, or 'freethinking' to use the more usual term, often went hand in hand with socialism. McLeod cited the example of an Ancoats family, most of whose members were freethinkers: 'Pa Holt was what was then called a Determinist, he believed that people were what their heredity and environment made them. He denied "free will" and held that actions followed from a balance of desires.'[100] More common, however, was a tenacious but indistinct popular Christianity, which was ethical and non-dogmatic in its orientation, and overlapped with the religion of the churches largely in relation to the rites of passage. For this reason, the religious ceremonies that continued to engage most of the population, and continued to bring them within the orbit of the clergy, were baptism (and its associated rites such as the churching of women after childbirth), marriage and funerals. Communion hardly featured in this world. The elaborate ceremonial, the music and colour of Anglo-Catholic worship were widely held by Anglo-Catholic clergy to be an important element of popular appeal, and undoubtedly that was so for some. That is why a much more variegated understanding of popular piety, and of reasons for churchgoing, is vital if we are to understand the relation of Church and society aright. Nevertheless, by any standard, the broad mass of the non-Roman Catholic labouring classes were not much interested in going to communion. Church rites – including communion – might well be regarded as sources of good fortune. But there is little evidence that people actually attended communion services, rather than go to any other service, specifically in order to procure good luck – again presumably testimony to the powerful, long-lasting effect of centuries of relative neglect of

99   E. Royle, *Radicals, Secularists and republicans: Popular freethought in Britain, 1866–1915*.
100   D. H. McLeod, *Religion and Society in England, 1850–1914*, pp. 50–1.

communion services. The one exception to this is the First World War, when, as Sarah Williams points out, study of the religion of men in the trenches disclosed 'a superstitious attachment to the ritual of communion'. Participation in communion just before combat 'was believed to be sufficient to ensure divine protection' – as one man said, 'They believe that having taken communion they will be safe'.[101]

The evidence is as mixed in the countryside as it is in the towns. Obelkevich's study of religion in South Lincolnshire argued that there was a near-fundamental clash between the values of the clergy and gentry, and those of the labouring poor when it came to matters of sacramental ritual. The clergy hoped that the eucharist would be 'the focus and expression of a reconstituted community of worshippers, in which all villagers, labourers as well as squires, should take part', but 'at every stage they came into conflict with the prejudice and preference of laymen in a class-divided society in which privacy and convenience ranked above law and communal sentiment.'[102] In the countryside, as in the towns, many clergy increasingly saw the eucharist as a test of church commitment, and the energy with which they sought to renew it along those lines reflected 'an impressive shift' in clerical opinion, but one which risked alienating the majority of their own parishioners.[103] In Obelkevich's Lincolnshire the situation was complicated by the presence of significant numbers of Dissenters. Close study of three villages, South Ormsby, Driby and Panton concluded that the young rarely received communion, and neither did servants; that farmers were more likely to receive communion than labourers; and that communion was in fact mostly for the elite; even ordinary churchgoers generally stayed away from it, and clung to the Anglican 'staple' of Morning and Evening Prayer.[104] Yates's work on Kent – another county with significant Nonconformist minorities – reinforced this picture. Conventionally, historians especially favourable to Anglo-Catholicism have been prone to cite rising numbers of communicants as direct evidence of the success of the mission strategies adopted by Anglo-Catholic clergy. Such statistics, stated baldly, do indeed convey the impression of remarkable success. Yet they are rarely quite what they seem. They rely on the registration of numbers of those actually receiving communion, and what is striking, time and again, is how small this number was in relation to overall attendances and to the population of the parish. In Kent, increased provision of communion services appears to have

---

101   S. C. Williams, *Religious Belief and Popular Culture in Southwark, c. 1880–1939*, p. 93.

102   J. Obelkevich, *Religion and Rural Society: South Lindsey 1825–1875*, p. 127.

103   Obelkevich, *Religion and Rural Society*, p. 138.

104   Obelkevich, *Religion and Rural Society*, pp. 140–2, & 243.

been matched by a rising number of communicants at the major festivals. But the numbers nevertheless remained small overall. At Holy Trinity, Maidstone, for example, in 1865, when communion was celebrated monthly, there were 235 Easter communicants, and 43 Christmas communicants. By 1905, with weekly communion, plus two or three celebrations during the week, the respective numbers had risen to 358 and 261 – a substantial increase, or at least one that looks remarkable on the surface. But the parish population was over 4,900, and other attendance figures suggest that, after at least forty years' emphasis on the importance of communion, still the numbers of those who actually received even at the major festivals were relatively small. At the small village of Rolvenden, over the same period Easter communicants increased from 48 to 112, and Christmas communicants from 25 to 61, but again this was in a population of over 1,000, and – moreover – against a backdrop of falling numbers of attenders at non-communion festival services: the numbers of those receiving communion remained steady at about 25 per cent of overall attenders.[105]

Once again, social realities were reflected in, and influenced by, sacramental renewal. Such a view is likely to have been replicated across rural Britain. A recent study of the church in Norfolk, for example, emphasised the controversial, divisive nature of the Anglican Catholic revival in the countryside. Ritualism was 'especially loathed' by rural trade unionists, most of whom were active Dissenters.[106] Again, popular anti-Catholicism had a part in this: the *English Labourer's Chronicle* 'even produced a special supplement on the subject [of Ritualism], entitled 'Christianity and Priestcraft'.[107] The poor often continued to go to church in some numbers. But evidence suggests that they rarely contributed much to the restoration of their local churches, something that was part of a wider cultural interest in heritage in the Victorian period, but which was particularly required by the changing liturgical and ceremonial perspectives of Catholic Anglicanism. In many parishes, church restoration was 'clearly an elite project', with no more than a handful of people in many cases raising the bulk of the money required.[108] Even so, the evidence of rural disaf-

---

105   W. N. Yates, R. Hume & P. Hastings, *Religion and Society in Kent, 1640–1914*, p. 73. As Yates says, the increase in communicants 'did not indicate any general increase in churchgoing, but simply a greater willingness to receive the sacrament, rather than just attending the services of Morning and Evening Prayer': ibid., p. 72. Anglo-Catholic clergy must have felt like Sisyphus, heaving up a hill the great boulder of their parishioners' reluctance to change the ingrained devotional habits of generations.

106   R. Lee, *Rural Society and the Anglican Clergy, 1815–1914: Encountering and Managing the Poor*, p. 3.

107   Lee, *Rural Society and the Anglican Clergy*, p. 3.

108   Lee, *Rural Society and the Anglican Clergy*, p. 51.

fection with the Established Church should not be exaggerated. There were plenty of churchgoing labourers. Rather, the evidence suggests the extent to which the social vision of High Church clergy, and in particular that associated with revived sacramentalism, simply did not overlap all that much with the religious preoccupations and social world of the poor.

For much of the nineteenth century, ironically, both High Churchmen and their Evangelical opponents claimed to be faithful to the true spirit of the Anglican liturgy, the *Book of Common Prayer*. There was no direct English equivalent to the struggles in France between Gallican and Roman rites. When liturgical revision in Anglicanism finally began in earnest in the early twentieth century, it proved to be enormously controversial.[109] But sacramental revival in Anglicanism had already provoked competing visions of ecclesial identity, and these in turn reflected and encouraged different understandings of community. High Churchmen, and especially Anglo-Catholics, articulated an idealised view of eucharistic community, a reconstituted hierarchical medievalism that simply failed to match several dimensions of popular belief. Within the Church of England it seemed to go from strength to strength, but its appeal was never deeply rooted in the enduring patterns of devotion of the population at large. There were genuine contrasting visions of what society was like, what role the Church could play in society, and above all what the eucharist signified in relation to society. The 'snapshots' I have presented can only give a hint of this. Even High Churchmen themselves were divided: for some of them eucharistic participation was an austere and demanding discipline, implying a faithful remnant called out of Israel; for others, the eucharist was a radical paradigm of social justice, calling the broken and marginalised together around the one altar of Christ.[110] But this was surely symptomatic of the history of the eucharist in Western Europe altogether. In each place, in each era, in each religious tradition, liturgical renewal attracted and provoked different readings of the existing social order, different aspirations towards its rejuvenation.

That is a conclusion drawn out of methodology and general history. But this study also tends, however, to more specific conclusions on the theme of sacramental renewal. On the one hand it suggests that the view presented by some historians of Anglican liturgical renewal that English developments were

---

109   Cf. Donald Gray, *The 1927–28 Prayer Book Crisis*; 2 vols; Vol. 1, *Ritual, Royal Commissions, and reply to royal letters of business*; Vol. 2, *The Cul-de-sac of the* Deposited Book ... *until further order be taken*.

110   Contrast, for example the eucharistic theologies of Vernon Staley (e.g. in *The Catholic Religion*) and Stuart Headlam (e.g. in *The Meaning of the Mass: Five lectures*, 1905).

largely unrelated to what was happening on the continent is profoundly misleading. It at least requires considerable finessing by reference to the influence of continental models of devotional community, the reading and translation of devotional and liturgical manuals, cross-channel currents of theological influence, and even the very intense level of interest sustained by English, French and German church people in what was happening in each other's churches when they travelled, in order to provide what I would argue is a much more rounded, and more satisfactory perspective from which to view Anglican history in the nineteenth and early twentieth centuries. But on the other hand it also suggests that, even if Anglo-Catholics in particular were influenced by a vision of Catholic renewal that drew much from continental precedent, nevertheless their efforts to create an integrated, harmonious religious community, symbolised in and effected by the Eucharist, conflicted with deep currents of popular belief and practice, varying in nature and intensity from place to place. I have of course said little here of intra-Anglican conflict on the eucharist, and nothing on contrasting notions across the free churches and the Roman Catholic Church. But even without that added dimension of denominational difference, popular perceptions of communion were sufficiently fragmented and complex so as to render sacramental renewal in Anglicanism if not stillborn, nevertheless cramped, awkward and badly fitting to many aspects of traditional Anglican practice. The eucharist was a powerful symbol, but more than that, a powerfully divisive symbol in practice.

PART 2

Continental Perspectives

∴

CHAPTER 4

Outside Influences: Continental Church Tourism

If close examination of the High Church Revival discloses deep roots in a complex array of local factors affecting church development and growth, this does not mean that it can be studied without reference to influences stemming from outside Britain. In this chapter and the following one I shall explore two sets of interactions which open up largely unexamined themes in the Revival. In this chapter we see High Churchmen going out to observe continental churches, and in the next, a continental church encountering and commenting on Anglicans. Both cast an unfamiliar light on English church history. It was long a scholarly commonplace that the British churches in the early nineteenth century stood aloof from continental developments. Separated by water, language, distinct economic and social development, and a cultural suspicion of all things foreign that prefigured the 'splendid isolation' of British foreign policy in the second half of the century, British Christians apparently showed little interest in the Continent, stoutly resisting many of the intellectual influences stemming from theologians there.[1] The conservatism of British Biblical criticism was often cited as evidence.[2] So too was the strong current of popular anti-Catholic opinion.[3] The theory of separate development was often implied rather than openly stated, however, simply through a failure to consider continental influences as they may have borne in on British churchmen.[4] The result of this long neglect of continental comparisons was a tendency by

---

1 Cf. S. Neill, *The Interpretation of the New Testament 1861–1961*, p. 1; also A. R. Vidler, *The Church in an Age of Revolution*, p. 33.

2 'Germany entered this phase in the history of ideas nearly half a century earlier than England': W. O. Chadwick, *The Victorian Church*, Vol. 1, p. 530; cf. also David Hempton's assertion about Francis Watts, professor of theology at Spring Hill College in Birmingham in the 1840s, that he was one 'of the few Englishmen aware of the issues raised by German higher criticism of the Bible': idem, *Evangelical Disenchantment: Nine Portraits of Faith and Doubt*, p. 32.

3 Cf. E. R. Norman, *Roman Catholicism in England*, pp. 62–73; but this is part of a much wider current of controversy over the connection between national identity and religious belief, for which see T. Claydon and I. McBride (eds), *Protestantism and National Identity: Britain and Ireland, c. 1650–c. 1850*.

4 Cf. F. W. Cornish, *The English Church in the Nineteenth Century*; S. C. Carpenter, *Church and People 1789–1889: A History of the Church of England from William Wilberforce to 'Lux Mundi'*; Vidler, *Church in an Age of Revolution*; Chadwick, *Victorian Church*; B. M. G. Reardon, *Religious Thought in the Victorian Age*.

© KONINKLIJKE BRILL NV, LEIDEN, 2016 | DOI 10.1163/9789004326804_005

historians to see movements in British church history as largely *sui generis*, either unaffected directly by what was happening across the Channel or, if affected, largely so in reaction *against* developments in continental Protestantism as well as Roman Catholicism. This was true even for historians of the High Church revival in Anglicanism, for whom the temptation was often (as much for apologetic reasons as strictly historical ones) to view High Church Anglicanism as the central strand of an 'English religious tradition' that could be expressed and understood largely on its own terms.[5]

This argument, which is still common enough, certainly receives some support from a close examination of the opinions of nineteenth-century churchmen themselves, many of whom can be shown to have expressed critical or hostile views of continental churches at times. Naturally, these opinions can often be differentiated along denominational and church party lines. Protestant Nonconformists and Scottish Presbyterians were especially critical of Roman Catholicism, and naturally tended to identify with the North European churches of the Reformation, both Lutheran and Reformed.[6] So too did Anglican Evangelicals, though usually not without some adjustment in favour of the distinctiveness and providential history of the English religious settlement. 'Broad Church' Anglicans were a little harder to predict: although some of them demonstrated a particular interest in the theology and example of Luther, and could be accused of helping to reshape Luther's reputation in a way particularly congenial to English churchmen, they too could often display remarkable antipathy to Roman Catholicism. They were also no less prone to cheap nationalistic jibes about other nations than other churchmen were. High Churchmen of various hues were also frequently critical of Roman Catholicism, but their desire to justify the *via media* of the English Church also led them sometimes to disparage the continental Reformation. The *locus classicus* of High Church ambiguity about, or hostility to, continental Protestantism was the joint Jerusalem bishopric scheme of 1841, the proposal to establish an alternating Anglican-Prussian bishopric in the Middle East to cater for Anglican and German Protestant congregations which unleashed a pamphlet war between the Tractarians and many other Anglicans.[7] Of the major Christian denominations, only Roman Catholics – for obvious reasons – could be said to have had a strongly European focus, and yet even then there were British

---

5   Cf. G. Rowell (ed.), *The English religious tradition and the Genius of Anglicanism*.

6   On this and the following point, cf. various contributions in P. Nockles & V. Westbrook (eds.), *Reinventing the Reformation in the Nineteenth Century: A Cultural History*.

7   Cf. R. W. Greaves, 'The Jerusalem Bishopric, 1841'; also P. B. Nockles, *The Oxford Movement in Context: Anglican High Churchmanship 1760–1857*, pp. 157–64.

Roman Catholics who were keen to stress that Catholicism could satisfactorily be adapted to an English idiom quite different from that of much of continental Europe. Putting all these diverse impressions together, it is not difficult to construct an account of British church opinion which emphasizes the concern of churchmen to distance themselves from continental church life.

Reassessment has been under way for some time. Building on the pioneering work of W. R. Ward, who reawakened interest in the continental roots of the Evangelical Revival, historians have begun to rediscover contacts between British Evangelicals and the continental Reformed and Lutheran churches.[8] The formation of the Evangelical Alliance in 1846 and the network of continental contacts it drew together have been studied by Nicholas Railton; others have drawn attention to the work of the Bible Societies.[9] Study of the influence of German Biblical criticism, theology and philosophy on British theologians has begun to add to the litany of names whose acquaintance with German theology was already well known – Coleridge, Marsh, Pusey, Hare, Mansel, amongst others.[10] In relation to High Churchmanship specifically, revision of the 'separate development' view has also begun. Connections between the Oxford Movement and French Catholicism have sometimes been noted, if rarely explored in depth until recently.[11] The use made by Pusey and others of French devotional manuals again is noted by a number of historians, and R. W. Franklin has shown how influence was exerted by the Catholic Tübingen school of Drey, Moehler and Hirscher on the liturgical theology and practice of Prosper Guéranger, and on the Oxford Movement.[12] These are disparate strands, but they suggest that the presumed 'splendid isolation' of British church history is not quite what it seems. However distinct Britain may have been, British church life was open to developments on the Continent of Europe at many different levels.

---

8   W. R. Ward, *The Protestant Evangelical Awakening*.

9   N. Railton, *No North Sea: The Anglo-German Evangelical Network in the Middle of the Nineteenth Century*, and idem, *Transnational Evangelicalism: The Case of Friedrich Bialloblotzky, 1799–1869*; T. C. F. Stunt, *From Awakening to Secession: Radical evangelicals in Switzerland and Britain, 1815–35*.

10   See Neill, *Interpretation*, pp. 1–32 for an account of most of the common connections.

11   L. Allen (ed.), *John Henry Newman and the Abbé Jager: A Controversy on Scripture and Tradition (1834–1836)*; W. G. Roe, *Lamennais and England: The Reception of Lamennais's Religious Ideas in England in the Nineteenth Century*; J. N. Morris, '"Separated Brethren": French Catholics and the Oxford Movement', (an earlier version of this chapter).

12   R. W. Franklin, *Nineteenth-century Churches: The history of a new Catholicism in Württemberg, England, and France*.

By implication, many aspects of the High Church revival in Anglicanism cannot readily be understood without some consideration of the broader continental context. That is the contention of this chapter, which examines a neglected source of evidence, namely the many accounts Anglicans left of their travels on the Continent. A few were published separately and were once sufficiently well known to have drawn the attention of some biographers. Edmund Purcell, the biographer of Henry Manning, noted in particular the published accounts by Thomas Allies and Frederick Faber, both of whom subsequently converted.[13] Allies and Faber were not unique, however. Driven partly by the Tractarians' refocusing of interest on Roman Catholicism and Eastern Orthodoxy via the 'apostolic paradigm', in Paul Avis's phrase, other High Churchmen were also travelling the Continent, touring churches, making contacts with church leaders, and attempting to interpret what they found.[14] Christopher Wordsworth's *Diary in France* (1845) was another example, as was his later *Notes at Paris* (1854).[15] So too was Arthur Perceval's *Results of an Ecclesiastical Tour in Holland and Northern Germany* (1846).[16] A little later, Malcolm MacColl wrote at length of his visit to Oberammergau in Bavaria to see the passion play; so too did Henry Scott Holland.[17] J. M. Neale's *Notes, Ecclesiological and Picturesque* (1861) drew on a visit to the Balkans in 1860 accompanied by Joseph Oldknow, himself another published traveller and church observer.[18] Benjamin Webb, another leading Ecclesiologist, like Neale a leading light of the Camden Society, was instrumental in refocusing the Society's interests on continental examples of church architecture.[19]

Alongside these accounts published by the authors themselves, there are also the letters and travel diaries of British churchmen as published posthumously in memoirs. Mostly more selective and more diffuse, nevertheless they are more numerous than the published volumes mentioned above. The British

---

13   For Purcell, the descriptions of continental Catholicism by various travellers such as Faber and Allies came 'as a revelation' to the Tractarians: E. S. Purcell, *Life and Letters of Ambrose Phillipps de Lisle*, Vol. I, p. 116; cf. T. W Allies, *Journal in France*; F. Faber, *Sights and Thoughts in Foreign Churches and among Foreign Peoples*.

14   P. D. L. Avis, *Anglicanism and the Christian Church*, p. xvii.

15   Christopher Wordsworth, *Diary in France, mainly on topics concerning Education and the Church*; idem, *Notes at Paris, particularly on the State and Prospects of Religion*.

16   A. P. Perceval, *Results of an Ecclesiastical Tour in Holland and Northern Germany*.

17   M. MacColl, *The Ammergau Passion Play*; [H. S. Holland], *Impressions of the Ammergau Passion Play, by an Oxonian*.

18   J. Oldknow, *A Month in Portugal*; Neale was Oldknow's companion on this journey too.

19   B. Webb, *Sketches of Continental Ecclesiology, or Church Notes in Belgium, Germany, and Italy*.

upper middle classes were indefatigable travellers in the Victorian period, and the invention of the steamboat and steam train made the business of continental travel both cheaper and easier than it had been in the great age of the 'Grand Tour'. Given the relative affluence of the upper ranks of the Victorian clergy, it comes as no surprise that many of them also toured the Continent.[20] The young Henry Liddon, later Canon of St Paul's, toured extensively on the Continent in late 1851, keeping extensive travel diaries, and visiting churches, for everywhere, his biographer observed, 'he notes with interest the Church life'.[21] Later journeys took him back to France (many times), Italy and Switzerland, Russia, Bavaria (he was there to see the Oberammergau passion play at the same time as MacColl and Holland), Bonn for the reunion conferences with the Old Catholics, the Balkans, and the Low Countries, as well as the Middle East.[22] A typical six-week tour in 1865 took in Brussels, Trèves, Freihof, Nuremberg, Munich, Salzburg, Gölling, Radstadt, Villach, Trieste, Venice, Padua, Verona, Brescia, Bellagio, Lugano, Lucerne, Basle, and Paris.[23] That was his second overseas trip that year: an earlier one had taken him to Pau, via Paris, Poitiers and Bordeaux, in order to give the Holy Week addresses to the English congregation.[24] Few English churchmen can have been as well informed about French church affairs as was Liddon. Breaking into conversation with an abbé he met on the train to Bordeaux, for example, he noted the abbé 'argued that there was no much difference between the 2 churches, & that all would be reunited in no distant time. He thought that the attacks of infidelity would help to produce this result.'[25]

Another frequent traveller was R. W. Church, Dean of St Paul's, who spent most of his early youth on the Continent, especially in Italy.[26] Trips mentioned in the *Life* include a long vacation in Belgium and Germany in 1839 with Frederick Faber and A. P. Stanley, a few weeks in Brittany in 1844 with Frederic Rogers, almost a whole year abroad in Greece and Italy in 1847 and early 1848

20 According to Piers Brendon, Bulwer Lytton reckoned that the income of those travelling on Cook's continental tours would usually have been between £300 and £600 a year: P. Brendon, *Thomas Cook: 150 Years of Popular Tourism*, p. 85.
21 J. O. Johnston, *Life and Letters of Henry Parry Liddon*, p. 15; the account of this journey occupies pp. 15–27.
22 Johnston, *Liddon*, pp. 64, 92, 98, 100–10, 137–9, 150–1, 183–90, 201–2 (letter on attending services abroad), 206–13, 300, & 318–28.
23 H. P. Liddon, mss diary entries for 2 August to 14 September 1865; Pusey House archives.
24 H. P. Liddon, mss diary entries for 31 March to 20 April 1865; Pusey House archives.
25 H. P. Liddon, mss diary entry for 4 April 1865; Pusey House archives.
26 According to his daughter, Florence to him 'always seemed a home': M. C. Church, *Life and Letters of Dean Church*, p. 7.

(some 69 pages are devoted to it), a summer in France in 1862, almost annual
Alpine holidays from 1866, a trip to Italy in 1875, and again to Italy as well as
Germany and Austria in 1883, and again to Italy in 1885.[27]

These are just a few indicative examples of the scale of continental tourism
undertaken by many High Churchmen in the nineteenth century. There are
many more – indeed so many, that the non-travelling senior Anglican clergyman was a rarity.[28] Certainly, other Anglicans than High Churchmen were also
touring the continent and writing about their experiences, including William
Whewell, Master of Trinity College, Cambridge, and the Evangelical Henry
Alford, Dean of Canterbury.[29] Alford's *Life* records numerous trips abroad.[30]
His 1862 tour, for example, was to at least 22 different European cities.[31] Arthur
Stanley, Dean of Westminster and a Broad or Liberal Churchman, was an
equally ardent traveller: a long summer tour was an almost annual occurrence
with him, his interests being driven as much by political and social matters as
by church affairs.[32] Another travelling Broad Churchman was George Ridding,
the first bishop of Southwell and a man blessed with a large private income.
Though the biography by his wife makes little of them, the manuscript addenda
to her interleaved copy in the Bodleian Library lists no less than 31 trips abroad
in the fifty years from 1852 to 1902.[33]

This chapter naturally concentrates on travelling High Churchmen, and
especially on their reactions to continental Catholicism, which attracted by far

---

27   Ibid., pp. 24, 47–51, 64–133, 158–66, 173–5, 250–1, 277–8, 308–17, & 317–20.

28   One example seems to have been W. F. Hook. On an apparently unique trip to Paris, he
      wrote to his curate, 'I am heartily sick of Paris; hate France, and think Frenchmen the
      most detestable of human beings. In three weeks I hope to be in dear old England, and
      never shall I wish again to quit her shores': W. R. W. Stephens, *Life and Letters of Hook*, Vol.
      I, p. 203.

29   W. Whewell, *Architectural Notes on German Churches: With notes written during an archi-
      tectural tour in Picardy and Normandy*; H. Alford, *Letters from Abroad*.

30   *Life and Letters of Henry Alford, DD, Late Dean of Canterbury, Edited by his Widow*, pp. 110–
      1, 134–5, 147–8, 156–62, 246–55, 259, 274–280, 302–34, 345–7, 350–2, 365–77, 380–1, 409–12,
      422–9, & 444–5.

31   *Life and Letters of Alford*, p. 350–6.

32   Stanley and Benjamin Jowett visited Paris in the spring of 1848 to see for themselves the
      impact of the revolution of that year: J. Witheridge, *Excellent Dr Stanley: The Life of Dean
      Stanley of Westminster*, pp. 147–8; there are also many references in R. E. Prothero, *The Life
      and Correspondence of Arthur Penrhyn Stanley*.

33   Bodleian Library, interleaved copy of Laura Ridding, *George Ridding, Schoolmaster and
      Bishop* (1908), GB 0161 MSS Eng.hist. d. 185–6; vol. I., 50B-50C; for a reassessment, see J. N.
      Morris, 'George Ridding and the Diocese of Southwell: a Study in the National Church
      Ideal'.

the most of their attention. It uses mostly the more extensive published accounts, yet draws wherever appropriate on wider material available in biographies and private papers. First, however, it may be helpful to discuss what kind of literature is at issue, including questions of genre and motivation, since there has been so little study of this material before now.

The Literature of Continental Church Tourism

The very extensive but piecemeal nature of much of the evidence to be discussed raises some difficulties of interpretation. One concerns the question of motivation. Continental travel could be undertaken by clergy for a variety of different reasons. Some were sent abroad for health reasons, which were not always distinguishable from a more general desire to be thrilled by mountain scenery. The pervasive nature of Romantic aesthetics, with its appreciation of the sublimity and terror of extremes of contrast in nature, is very striking in many letters and journals, as was the frequent assumption that such experience was cathartic, restorative, and morally improving.[34] Frederick Faber even dedicated his *Sights and Thoughts in Foreign Churches* to the poet William Wordsworth, with gratitude for 'much personal kindness, and many thoughtful conversations on the rites, prerogatives, and doctrines, of the Holy Church'.[35] Many clergy seem to have travelled as much as anything to interrupt the tedium or the exhausting routine of ministerial responsibility. Clerical 'burn out', as it was to be described by later generations, was a widespread phenomenon in the nineteenth century, and travel gave some respite. The High Churchman and church musician J. B. Dykes, in his last illness, which was partly brought on by the stress of his controversy with the Bishop of Durham over Ritualism, was sent to France and on to Switzerland to recuperate, for example.[36] Another, earlier example was Hugh James Rose, who spent a year from 1824 travelling in Bavaria, Austria and Italy in an attempt to shore up his failing health.[37] For many clergy, travel offered the opportunity to complete a classical education. Rome, for that reason, was an inevitable magnet, and travel diaries and letters

---

34 The editors of a recent collection of essays on the history of British tourism have even claimed that the very idea of tourism in the modern sense, with its element of 'temporary escape from the everyday', had its most immediate roots 'in romantic travel': H. Berghoff, B. Korte, R. Schneider & C. Harvie (eds), *The Making of Modern Tourism: The Cultural History of the British Experience, 1600–2000*, p. 5.

35 Faber, *Sights*, p. v.

36 J. T. Fowler, *Life and Letters of John Bacchus Dykes*, p. 221.

37 P. B. Nockles, 'Hugh James Rose', ODNB.

were often littered with extensive discussion of ancient ruins. For many, too, there was a complementary motive in the desire to study a foreign language or culture, or to consult continental scholars. Bishop Colenso (a Broad Churchman), for example, seized the chance of a rare visit to England from South Africa in 1863 to spend some time in Leiden, meeting Professor Abraham Kuenen (1828–1891), whose work on the Old Testament he had already seen, and other scholars.[38] Julius Hare and Edward Pusey are perhaps better known examples. None of these motives placed 'church tourism' in the foreground as a reason for travelling, though even when abroad for other reasons, clergy often visited churches, attended services on Sundays, and recorded their impressions.

Clergy who travelled primarily to study church life were relatively few, though the number rises somewhat if those who went to study architecture and historic buildings are included. J. M. Neale straddled both groups: as a member of the Camden Society, he travelled extensively on the Continent studying Gothic church architecture, but he also undertook several tours specifically to examine the religious life of overseas churches, including research trips to the Netherlands and to Scandinavia.[39] Of course, in quarrying the architecture of the Continent for models which could be applied to the design or restoration of buildings in Britain, the Victorians were merely following a well-worn practice going back several centuries. But we should be wary of supposing that most of these continental church tourists went with an entirely open mind about what they would find. There is some evidence, to be explored later, that some clergy did indeed change their minds about the religious life of the continent, and their experiences may have been a significant influence in the development of their religious outlook. Even so, in almost all cases the evidence suggests that they took with them, not just a general inclination to read other churches' beliefs and practices in a certain way, but quite specific convictions or hypotheses which they sought to test in the light of continental evidence. Whewell, for example, made his 'rapid tour' through German churches in order to test his theory that the adoption of the pointed arch was a consequence of developments in vaulting, and in particular of the need to have arches of a similar height but with different widths.[40] William Palmer (of Magdalen College), whose extensive notes of his travels in Russia in the early

---

38   G. W. Cox, *The Life of John William Colenso, Bishop of Natal*, Vol. I, p. 221.

39   The chief source is J. M. Neale, *Letters, Edited by his Daughter*, but there are also some unpublished letters and diaries in Lambeth Palace Library, though the diaries are only available as copies and for a few years, the originals having gone missing many years ago.

40   Whewell, *Architectural Notes*, pp. 17 & 19.

1840s were not published until long afterwards, after his death, went to Russia specifically with the goal of seeking to establish communion with the Russian Church.[41]

This has a bearing on the question of theology. Anglican clergy of all shades of opinion travelled, and their reactions could not always be predicted from their existing convictions. High Churchmen in particular displayed two conflicting sets of opinions, an inclination to recognize and value an affinity with the practices of the ancient Catholic churches of the continent, and yet a common suspicion of the superstition of Rome. Again, clergy of all doctrinal opinion seem to have been willing to attend Roman Catholic churches from time to time. Edward Bickersteth, the Evangelical rector of Watton, was appalled by the 'popish superstition' he witnessed inside Milan's 'beautiful cathedral'.[42] In cases such as this, evidently the desire to travel, to see new sights and to 'collect' culture and history overrode qualms about setting foot inside Catholic churches, but nevertheless had little impact on long-settled opinion. In general terms, however, two distinct sets of party opinion influenced particular patterns of church tourism. By far the largest group of travellers consisted of High Churchmen who were interested particularly in observing the churches of the two 'branches' of Catholic Christianity with which, through the apostolic succession of the ministry, they considered the Church of England to be aligned, Roman Catholicism and Eastern Orthodoxy.[43] Where they encountered continental Protestantism, in most cases – though not all – they were critical, not to say dismissive. By contrast, much the smaller group of church tourists with a specific interest in continental affairs was composed of Evangelicals, whose interests gravitated naturally towards Protestantism, and particularly towards the Reformed churches. The operation of the Bible Societies in parts of Europe, the creation of the Evangelical Alliance in 1846, and the Basle mission, all provided Evangelical Anglicans with valuable networks of contacts in Europe. Henry Alford, for example, attended the Berlin conference of the Evangelical Alliance in September 1857, where some 150 English Christians of different denominations worshipped with their continental co-religionists; a service of joint communion at the Hôtel de Russie, at which there was no liturgical form

---

41   W. Palmer, *Notes of a Visit to the Russian Church in the Years 1840, 1841, selected and arranged by Cardinal Newman*, pp. vii & 1–14.

42   T. R. Birks, *Memoir of the Rev. Edward Bickersteth, late Rector of Watton, Herts*, p. 402.

43   The influence of William Palmer's *Treatise on the Church of Christ* (1838), with its systematic exposition of the 'branch' theory on travelling High Churchmen should not be underestimated. It was one of the books that the other William Palmer, for example, took to Russia to convince the Orthodox of the Catholicity of the English Church: Palmer, *Notes of a Visit to the Russian Church*, p. 364.

except the reading of the words of institution ('a thing I should imagine with-out parallel in the history of the Church'), provoked fierce criticism in High Church circles back home.[44] Alford felt obliged to write a private memoran-dum justifying his participation in the service, arguing that it had been doubly important 'seeing that the [German] high Lutheran party kept aloof from, and denounced the Conference on the ground of their own peculiar sacramental views'.[45] Bickersteth's interest in the Bible Societies was exemplified in his translation of D'Aubigné's *A Voice from the Alps* (1838).[46]

Motives for observing and commenting on continental church affairs var-ied, then, from the intense to the more occasional, from the deliberate and theologically-informed wish to identify with particular streams of European Christianity, or to criticize them, to the passing curiosity of travellers who were as much interested in landscape, culture and architecture as they were in over-seas church life. It is possible, bearing this in mind, to differentiate a number of distinct, if overlapping, genres of writing.

First are publications specifically devoted to recording impressions of con-tinental churches, their worship and their theological currents. This is a relatively small group, but one rich in detail. It includes the works, already mentioned, by Allies, Faber, MacColl, Perceval, Whewell, and Wordsworth, but also others by members of the Camden Society which focused particularly on architecture but often had passing references to church life too.[47] Neale's *Notes, Ecclesiological and Picturesque* certainly included comments on church life. With the exception of Whewell's book, which had almost nothing to say about contemporary church life and theology, these books were evidently pub-lished in order to use information about continental churches to influence discussion within the Church of England. They were mostly written by High Churchmen, and may have been influenced by the poet Thomas Moore's *Travels of an Irish Gentleman in Search of a Religion* (1833), a popular work

---

44   *Life and Letters of Henry Alford*, p. 277. Another English churchman present was W. H. Fremantle who, while disavowing theological agreement with the 'narrowness' of the Evangelicalism of the founders of the Alliance, claimed the conference was 'of a more general character and was felt in Germany as an emancipation from the old Church and State views of the old Lutherans': W. H. Draper, *Recollections of Dean Fremantle, Chiefly by Himself*, pp. 57–8.

45   *Life and Letters of Henry Alford*, pp. 279–80. The memorandum was addressed to George Moberly, Headmaster of Winchester College and later Bishop of Salisbury.

46   J. H. Merle d'Aubigné, ed. E. Bickersteth, *A Voice from the Alps: Or, a Brief Account of the Evangelical Societies of Paris and Geneva*.

47   Foremost amongst these were Webb, *Sketches of Continental Ecclesiology*, and Neale, *Notes, Ecclesiological and Picturesque*.

which combined religious polemic, theological history and travel to explore the deficiencies of Protestantism and the attraction of the ancient Irish faith.[48]

A second group of publications, also small, includes books which can better be described as general accounts of travel, in which nevertheless there are comments on church matters. Alford's *Letters from Abroad* (1865), which drew on his continental travels in 1863 and 1864, falls within this category, as does his *Riviera: Pen and Pencil Sketches from Cannes to Genoa* (1870), and Thomas Arnold's *Travelling Journals* (1852). Stanley's description of his travels in the Holy Land, *Sinai and Palestine* (1856), could also fall into this category, though its scope of course lay outside continental Europe. Another example was the nephew of Hugh James Rose, also called (confusingly) Hugh James Rose (1840–1878), a Church of England clergyman, who travelled widely in Spain, living with the peasants and learning their dialect, and publishing two widely acclaimed volumes on his experiences.[49] These works and others like them shared many characteristics with the increasingly popular genre of travel writing combined with social and political commentary, and built on clear precedents, such as Arthur Young's *Travels in France* (1787), or William Hazlitt's *Notes of a Journey through France and Italy* (1826).[50] They tended to include lengthy passages of topographical description, as well as comments on art and architecture, and observations on more general cultural mores. They were crafted self-consciously as literature, whether by the author himself, as in the case of Alford, or by the editor, as in the case of Stanley acting as Arnold's amanuensis.

Much more numerous are the works in a third category, namely letters and diaries written originally for private use, but which found their way eventually into print through biographies and memoirs. The fact that in most cases these were not at first intended for publication may give them a degree of spontaneity missing in the more crafted or polished books of travel, but on the other hand many of these letters and diaries were probably edited or tidied up for eventual publication, often by adoring wives or children. Letter-writing was cultivated as a rather self-conscious practice in its own right, with its own conventions and models, and journals could be written to be shared with friends or loved ones.[51] J. M. Neale's early diaries – though not those covering his expe-

---

48   T. Moore, *Travels of an Irish Gentleman in Search of a Religion*.

49   H. J. Rose, *Untrodden Spain, and her Black Country;* idem, *Among the Spanish People*.

50   See C. Chard, *Pleasures and Guilt on the Grand Tour: Travel Writing and Imaginative Geography, 1600–1830*.

51   For a history covering an earlier period, see James How, *Epistolary Spaces: English letter-writing from the foundation of the Post Office to Richardson's Clarissa*.

riences in Madeira, discussed below – were written to be read by his sister
Mary.[52] The limitations of this kind of evidence are clear. When published,
they were often edited or cut, and possibly rewritten, in order to fit them into
the narrative followed by the biographer, apparently to illustrate especially
interesting or worthy features of their subject's personality – his cultural
breadth, his energy, the knowledge and wisdom with which his judgements
about ecclesiastical matters were formed, and so on. Whatever the limitations
of this kind of source material, its quantity and density make it an invaluable
resource in assessing the impact of foreign travel on English churchmen.
Among the richest and fullest of the diaries covering foreign travel were those
kept by Henry Manning during his visit to Rome in 1847–8, and by Henry
Liddon for much of his adult life. Neither have been published in full, but substantial extracts from Manning's diary found their way into Purcell's biography,
and some passages from Liddon's diaries have appeared in print, both separately and in Johnston's biography.[53]

A fourth genre is useful largely as an additional way of highlighting English
churchmen's interest in continental church affairs. It is the works of theology
or history published by English churchmen on the continental churches, and
the texts translated by them or edited by them, which were written partly as a
result of travel, but which did not explicitly refer to travel itself. This group
includes, for example, Neale's *Voices from the East: Documents on the present
state and working of the oriental church* (1859), his uncompleted *History of the
Holy Eastern Church* (1847–50), and his *History of the So-called Jansenist Church
of Holland* (1858); Stanley's *Lectures on the History of the Eastern Church* (1861);
Palmer of Magdalen's *Dissertations on Subjects relating to the 'Orthodox' or
'Eastern-Catholic' Communion* (1853), and his *Replies of the Humble Nicon: By
the mercy of God Patriarch, against the questions of the Boyar Simeon Streshneff*
(1871); and Liddon's edition of Rosmini's *Of the Five Wounds of the Holy Church*
(1883).

The diverse and even disparate nature of the modes of expression through
which continental church experiences were eventually made available to the
reading public militates against easy generalisations, both about the reactions
of English churchmen to what they saw, and about the impact of their experiences back in England. Nevertheless, their scope is a sign that the continental

---

52   See MSS 4779 & 4780, Lambeth Palace Library [LPL], transcript edited by L. Litvack of
      Neale's diaries 1836–38.

53   H. S. Purcell, *Life of Cardinal Manning, Archbishop of Westminster*, Vol. I, pp. 348–76, &
      386–411; Johnston, *Liddon*, supra; M. N. Cohen (ed.), *The Russian Journal – II: A record kept
      by Henry Parry Liddon of a tour taken with C. L. Dodgson in the summer of 1867*.

context or background of church life was never as remote from discussion of English church affairs as is sometimes thought. The accounts to be examined here were, for the most part, written by senior clergymen. Their experiences and observations unquestionably helped to shape English church matters.

High Church Travellers and Roman Catholicism

Prejudice about the practice and doctrine of Roman Catholicism on the continent of Europe was central to the controversies surrounding Anglo-Catholicism, from early in the Tractarian revival to the liturgical and ritual innovations of the movement in mid and late century. As Sheridan Gilley, Peter Nockles and others have demonstrated, the doctrinal basis of Newman's conversion lay as much in eschatology, and in particular his eventual reversal of a long and deeply-held conviction that the Church of Rome was the Antichrist of Revelation, as it did in ecclesiology.[54] The evidence which seemed to confirm Newman's conviction – as for that of many others hostile to Roman Catholicism – lay in the corruption he discerned in popular Roman practice. Tractarians, following the 'branch' ecclesiology epitomised by Palmer's *Treatise*, could acknowledge the Roman church's essential, or theoretical, apostolicity, but frequently pointed out its apparent dilution or even abandonment of the Patristic *regulum fidei* in the latitude it permitted to popular devotion, as well as in its doctrinal and organisational embellishments, including the Papal primacy of jurisdiction, infallibility, and the Marian dogmas. Ironically then, Tractarians, and indeed Anglo-Catholics in general, in considering Roman Catholicism, often fell back on a distinction between theory and practice which mirrored the distinction they themselves frequently made between the theory of Anglicanism they endorsed, and the practice that they perceived to be lacking in it. This was a perspective which sprang up time and again when they encountered continental Roman Catholicism, and which raised obvious criticisms from their Roman Catholic critics. When they accused Rome of allowing too much elaboration and speculation in popular devotion – as when, for example, they charged Roman Catholics with giving devotion to Mary that was due to Jesus instead – they were handicapped by the obvious riposte that Anglicanism too failed to put into practice the 'Catholic' devotional system that Anglo-Catholics believed to be embedded in the Prayer Book. The charge against 'popular Catholicism' could be mirrored by that against 'popular Protestantism', suggesting a need to carve out space for the *via media,* and this

---

54   S. Gilley, *Newman and his Age*, p. 190; Nockles, *Oxford Movement in Context*, pp. 177–8.

was a nuance which some who could not be described justly as Tractarians nevertheless implicitly accepted – such as F. D. Maurice, whose criticisms of the distortions of popular Evangelicalism were to get him into such difficulties over eschatology in 1853. Newman, as is well known, came to accept the accusation that Anglican Catholicism (or 'Anglicanism' as he had tried to interpret it) was but a 'paper' theory. Tractarian arguments, then, whether apologetic or critical, often relied on the presumption of a certain elasticity between teaching and popular devotion, and consequently opened up a wide range of differing reactions to the experience of encountering continental Catholicism in practice.

Most of the accounts to be explored here date from the late 1830s and 1840s, when the Tractarian controversy was at its height. Perhaps the best known journey of all is that of Newman himself, with Hurrell Froude and his father, Archdeacon Froude, through the Mediterranean in December 1832 to mid-1833. Newman especially appears to have left England with an acute sense of coming crisis about the Church of England: his experience of overseas travel was bound to lead him to reflect on the state of Anglican worship in comparison with continental Catholicism. As he wrote to his mother, his vacation was to be 'a preparation and strengthening time for future toil'.[55] All this indicates a certain suggestibility on Newman's and Froude's part about what they might encounter of continental Catholicism. But it does not significantly alter the fact that their observations were a by-product of their travel, and not the main purpose of it.

Three substantial, published accounts were precisely that – those of Allies, Faber, and Wordsworth. Allies' *Journal in France* (1849) was a composite volume which contained material from three separate visits, in 1845, 1847, and 1848, which drew on both diaries and letters, and which included testimony from Charles Marriott, who had travelled with Allies in 1845.[56] Unlike conventional travel writing it had little topographical description. Its audience was plainly a theologically-informed or clerical one: Allies' aim was to correct the 'prodigious ignorance' of each other's churches, and to see things 'as they are' in the Roman system out of an assumption that Anglicans and Roman Catholics

---

55   I. Ker & T. Gornall (eds), *The Letters and Diaries of John Henry Newman*, Vol. 3: *New Bearings, January 1832 to June 1833*, p. 123.

56   The entry on Allies in the ODNB is inaccurate in putting the year of publication of the *Journal in France* as 1848 rather than 1849, in assuming that J. H. Pollen travelled with Allies in 1845 and 1847, whereas he did in 1847 and 1848, and in making no mention of Marriott at all, nor of J. H. Wynne, who also travelled with Allies and Pollen in 1847: W. B. Owen, 'Allies, Thomas William (1813–1903)', ODNB.

differed very rarely 'in principle, though sometimes in facts'.[57] His interest in France was partly stimulated, he said, by its tyrannical separation of Church and State during the Revolution; France served in effect as a sort of experiment, where the Church of God was so externally oppressed 'that nothing but the irrepressible life of the Gospel could penetrate and leaven society under such conditions'.[58] In the light of Allies' conversion to Rome in 1850 after the Gorham judgement, these terms are telling, and the book for the most part reads like judicious, sometimes critical and yet generally admiring reportage on the whole condition of the French Church, with brief excursions into northern Italy. Allies travelled widely in France, visited many churches, built up contacts with leading Roman Catholic scholars and educationalists, and particularly concerned himself with the life of the religious orders and with Roman Catholic educational institutions. He noted carefully details of daily routines in religious houses and schools, the course of conversations with Roman Catholic clergy, and his impressions of all he saw. Over a hundred pages are devoted simply to a month's intensive travel in 1845. When he returned to France in 1847 he renewed some of his Roman Catholic acquaintance, before travelling south to northern Italy in the company of John Hungerford Pollen and J. H. Wynne, also subsequently converts. Here, after meeting Manzoni in Milan, they visited two Italian Tyrolese women stigmatics, Maria Domenica Lazzari, or the 'Addolorata', and Maria Mörl (more conventionally 'Marie de Moerl'), or the 'Ecstatica', who experienced recurrent states of ecstasy.[59] Allies went back to Paris again in July 1848 in Pollen's company, and stayed for nearly six weeks, resuming his round of visits, conversations, and church attendance, and noting much of this in his journal.

Faber's earlier *Sights and Thoughts in Foreign Churches and among Foreign Peoples* (1842), by contrast, reads largely as a literary travelogue. Inviting the reader to travel with him 'as one from the Middle Ages', the author traces a journey down France, through Amiens, Paris, Chartres, Orléans, Lyons and Avignon, and then on via Provence to northern Italy and Venice, and eventually to Greece and the Aegean.[60] The book combines topographical description

---

57   Allies, *Journal*, pp. 2–4.

58   Allies, *Journal*, pp. 4–5.

59   Allies was not alone in his interest. In 1842, the eminent Roman Catholic layman John Talbot, Sixteenth Earl of Shrewsbury, had published a *Letter ... to Ambrose Lisle Phillipps, Esq.: Descriptive of the Estatica of Caldaro and the Addolorata of Capriano*. It seems likely Allies was well aware of this publication. On Pollen, see A. Pollen, *John Hungerford Pollen 1820–1902*, which also has many references to Wynne, including (pp. 223–4) a brief account of Wynne's conversion in 1851.

60   Faber, *Sights*, p. 5.

with extensive quotations from continental writers and with commentary on
the state of religion on the continent. It was based on a six-month journey
taken in 1841 with the son of a friend, Matthew Harrison, for whom he was acting as tutor, through France and Italy, on to Greece and Constantinople, and
back through central Europe and Germany.[61] But fact and fantasy are somewhat blurred through the literary device of a ghostlike, medieval figure who
accompanies the author at various points of his journey and challenges him
about his Anglican convictions. Faber converted in 1845, just after Newman,
but his continental travels were evidently significant steps in his disillusionment with the Church of England. By the point in the book at which he has
reached the Certosa outside Pavia, he can admit that the appearance of the
'man of the Middle Ages' felt to him 'not unfrequently ... as a weight upon my
spirit', and from then on the conversations recounted feel more and more one-
sided, as the author is forced to make concession after concession to his ghostly
interlocutor.[62] In Venice, the stranger's tone has become almost polemical:
'You are not a fasting Church; yet every other Church has been so from the
earliest times.'[63] And it is with the stranger's words that the book comes nearly
to an end, when he disavows the intention of making Faber leave the Church
of England, but aims merely to make him feel that 'there is a catholic body
above and beyond particular churches, which is capable of being realised'.[64]
In all this, Faber's observation of the Roman Catholic churches that he encounters are threaded through with admiration, as he gradually uncovers authentic
elements of the spirit of the Middle Ages.

Nothing could be further from the spirit of Christopher Wordsworth's *Diary
in France* (1845). Almost all of Wordsworth's month-long stay was in Paris.
Like its successor volume, the *Notes at Paris* (1854), the *Diary* as published was
just that – a series of journal entries, covering visits to churches and schools,
and meetings with individuals. Originally private letters for the 'interest and
amusement' of a female friend, however, it was only drawn up as a diary for
publication.[65] A strong current of contempt for recent French history and
culture runs through both books, as does great suspicion of Ultramontane
Catholicism. Wordsworth claimed that the turbulence of recent French history had left an indelible mark on its culture and politics: there seemed to be a

61   J. E. Bowden, *The Life and Letters of Frederick William Faber DD*, p. 85.

62   Faber, *Sights*, pp. 200 & 202.

63   Faber, *Sights*, p. 363.

64   Faber, *Sights*, p. 417.

65   Wordsworth, *Diary*, p. v.

'natural disposition in the French people to be soon weary of their toys'.[66] He criticised the double-standards of the French clergy on authority, the social exclusiveness of city congregations, the faulty logic of Roman Catholic preaching, superstitions surrounding relics, and the empty show and magnificence of the Mass.[67] He met a number of leaders of the French church and commentators on French religious affairs, including Jules Gondon, Prosper Guéranger, and the Abbés Migne, Bautain and Jager. But his encounters were as much an opportunity to defend the Church of England (especially for the benefit of his readers) as to learn about the French church. This was even more evident in the *Notes*, where Wordsworth's suspicion of the extreme elements of Anglo-Catholicism was even more to the fore. A conversation with a 'learned friend' in Paris raised the example of Robert Wilberforce's recently-published *On the Doctrine of the Holy Eucharist* (1853); intersplicing quotations from the book with passages from various French texts, Wordsworth implied that Wilberforce's understanding of objective presence and eucharistic sacrifice was identical to that of Ultramontane Catholicism.[68] Whilst not without some positive appreciation of French Catholicism, both of Wordsworth's books in effect presented travel largely as a pretext for ecclesiastical apologetic, rather than as an opportunity for sympathetic study of another religious tradition.

Church Tourism and Religious Change

The accounts of Allies, Faber and Wordsworth represent the most extensive published repertoire of High Church or Tractarian reactions to continental Catholicism, but they varied considerably in form and content. This makes it difficult to summarize their impressions easily – a difficulty certainly increased when other accounts, published and unpublished, such as those of Neale, Liddon, Church, Manning and MacColl, are added to the reckoning. Webb's *Sketches of Continental Ecclesiology* (1848) is another: intended to be a 'book of reference', containing detailed church descriptions from several journeys in Belgium, Germany and Italy in the 1840s, it also contained some observations on church life.[69] In order to help sift and analyze the wide range of impressions this literature represents, three questions seem pertinent. First, was there a difference between the impressions of those High Churchmen who subsequently

---

66   Wordsworth, *Diary*, p. 66.
67   Wordsworth, *Diary*, pp. 24–5, 55–6, 87, 98, & 119.
68   Wordsworth, *Notes*, pp. 64–72.
69   Webb, *Sketches of Continental Ecclesiology*, p. xi.

converted to Rome, and those who did not? Second, in the case of those who did subsequently convert, what evidence is there that travel was instrumental in the process of conversion? Third, did continental church tourism, and travel in a more general sense, help to shape the views of these High Anglicans on theology, ritual and liturgy?

The first question looks at first sight the easiest to answer. After all, both Allies and Faber converted to Rome, and both men published travelogues which presumed a purpose or disposition essentially favourable to much of the Roman line, unlike Wordsworth, who did not convert. Right at the very beginning of his volume, in the introduction, Allies claimed that the reunion of the English Church with the Church of Rome would be an 'incalculable blessing'.[70] This was unlikely to endear him to many Anglican readers, except perhaps those on the extreme fringe of Tractarianism, and it was but a year before his conversion. Faber's inclination towards the Roman position is also very evident in his work: at Avignon, for example, he was prompted to exclaim that the unshakeable allegiance of distant nations was evidence of the 'inherent vitality (*one might almost rise to higher words*) of the papacy'.[71] Like Allies, Faber peppered his book with comments critical of the Church of England. Faber had toured Belgium and Rhenish Germany with Arthur Stanley and Richard Church in 1839, a visit which is also mentioned briefly in Church's biography.[72] Faber mentions this trip in *Sights and Thoughts* only to draw a parallel between the beautiful procession he had seen in Bruges and the 'entire tumult of holyday' he saw in Genoa, on the Feast of the Annunciation, when the churches were thronged, the bells ringing, and the streets filled with flowers.[73] If one were to follow this account, already in 1839, then, his reaction to Catholic piety had been one of admiration; two years later this had become an instinctive sympathy. The picture is more complex, however. Bowden included a letter to J. B. Morris, written from Cologne in August 1839, in which Faber was scathing about the 'careless irreverence, the noise, the going out and in, the spitting of the priests on the Altar steps, the distressing representations of our Blessed Lord' he had witnessed.[74] This was despite his efforts to accustom himself to Roman devotions, via a breviary he had bought in Mechlin.[75] The change in his views in just two years is evident, and Faber's resultant inner turmoil about his

---

70   Allies, *Journal*, p. 8.

71   Faber, *Sights*, p. 48; my italics.

72   Church, *Life and Letters*, p. 24; Bowden, *Faber*, pp. 71 & 77–8.

73   Faber, *Sights*, pp. 145–6.

74   Bowden, *Faber*, p. 78.

75   Bowden, *Faber*, p. 77.

religious identity was evident again another two years on, in 1843, when he visited Rome again and witnessed the devotion and seriousness of Roman Catholic piety.[76] Wordsworth, by contrast, remained steadfastly critical of great swathes of continental Catholic life and teaching, even as he expressed admiration for the devotional spirit of some of the congregations he witnessed. He found the congregation at vespers at Nôtre Dame des Victoires, for example, 'very attentive and devout', so that 'on the whole the service ... presented one of the happiest specimens of social fervent worship', and he was especially admiring of the French Church's emphasis on catechizing.[77] Nevertheless, even when he returned to Paris in 1853, he found that 'public display' and ostentation were an important aspect of French Catholicism, and so severe was his judgement on the Marian images decorating Parisian churches, quite overwhelming the images of Jesus, that he could exclaim 'How near Romanism sometimes approaches to Socinianism!'[78] Likewise, Richard Church's admiration of aspects of continental Catholicism was almost always tempered by criticism too. A long and full description of the procession celebrating St Paul in Valetta in 1847 dwelt on the 'shouting and skirmishing' of the boys witnessing it, and concluded, 'But of course all displays of popular religion, however, imposing, must be grotesque also. Certainly this was.'[79]

It is scarcely surprising that High Churchmen who did subsequently convert to Roman Catholicism voiced admiration for elements of continental Catholicism. But even the accounts of Allies and Faber do contain significant critical comments. Marian doctrine and devotion came in for attack from both authors. Allies, for example, was alarmed by the extremism of the Marian litanies he encountered in Paris in 1845, and taxed M. Noirlieu, curé of St Jacques, with his objection that repeated invocations of Mary under various titles 'threw the Godhead into the shade'.[80] Marriott (a non-convert) went even further, though the publication of his comments in Allies' book presumably suggested the author's approval: 'The system of devotion to the Blessed Virgin, as it now stands, wants some foundation beyond all they tell me of when I ask them to give an account of it.'[81] Faber claimed that the Catholic revival in France was being thrown on to devotion to Mary without 'even refining

76 Bowden, *Faber*, pp. 186–200.
77 Wordsworth, *Diary*, pp. 200–1.
78 Wordsworth, *Notes*, pp. 24 & 60.
79 Church, *Life and Letters*, p. 74.
80 Allies, *Journal*, p. 48.
81 Allies, *Journal*, p. 63.

any of its grossness and dishonourable excess'.[82] He was particularly critical of French Catholic approaches to baptism, which in his view almost completely subsumed it under the eucharist: 'One Sacrament is made to obscure, if not eclipse, the other'.[83] This opinion was based largely on a reading of the Abbé Genoude's *Exposition du Dogme Catholique* (1840), which Faber regarded as 'very poor' and in which the word 'regenerate' was constantly used, Faber alleged, in reference to the eucharist rather than baptism, which it barely mentioned: in this respect, he claimed, Roman Catholicism was nearer to the spirit of Puritanism.[84]

Just as the future converts could be, at times, critical of Roman Catholicism, so the non-converts could be positive and appreciative, as we have seen in the cases of Wordsworth and Church. An early example was Edward Copleston, later Bishop of Llandaff. Confounding the usual claims that English people could not visit the continent until after Waterloo, Copleston travelled extensively through Europe in 1813 and 1814 (including some days in Paris even before the fall of Napoleon), and again in 1816.[85] He seems to have encountered Roman Catholicism with a genuinely open, if sometimes surprised, mind. Describing the monastery of Great St Bernard, for example, he wrote to a friend that the prior was 'just what a monk ought to be, that is, just the opposite of what they are represented to be in all books – mild, well-bred, well acquainted with what is going on in the world, and, though very temperate himself, pressing his hospitality as far as decorum will allow'.[86] He was very impressed with the piety of people in Flanders in 1816. He was surprised by the well-marshalled processions he observed, with figures of Christ and the Virgin Mary, and women and children singing with the appearance of sincere piety: 'I was not aware that the people took so warm a part in the performance of religious offices, it being one of the commonest objections to popery, that it leaves all to the priests, while the people are merely passive.'[87]

Another non-convert who recorded many favourable impressions of Roman Catholicism was Henry Liddon. Of High Mass in Ghent Cathedral in 1851, for example, he could say 'The Service was very imposing; the people uniformly

---

82   *Faber, Sights*, p. 118.

83   Faber, *Sights*, p. 120.

84   Faber, *Sights*, pp. 119–20.

85   W. J. Copleston, *Memoir of Edward Copleston, DD, Bishop of Llandaff*, pp. 50–60 & 69–83. He was thus a visitor to Paris before the better-known traveller John Scott, whose *Visit to Paris in 1814: Being a review of the moral, political, intellectual and social condition of the French capital* was published in 1815.

86   Copleston, *Memoir*, p. 53.

87   Copleston, *Memoir*, p. 78.

devotional ... it had about it a winning awe, which was distinct from poetry; it must have conveyed to the most uninitiated a semblance of the Supernatural.'[88] At Auxonne, for example, in June 1864 he visited a large church – presumably Nôtre-Dame – in the evening, finding several worshippers there 'kneeling before the Blessed Sacrament. How ones [sic] heart was with them! The mischief of separation in the Ch [sic] came home to me today most powerfully my heart ached: if we are strong in other formuli [?] in this we English are assuredly weak.'[89] Liddon was courted by Roman Catholic clergy eager to secure his conversion, but there is no evidence that he was ever seriously tempted.[90] However, his positive comments on continental Roman Catholic liturgy and devotion in his diaries are so frequent that one can understand the effort. Liddon's practice was often to say the office in Roman Catholic churches he visited, as well as attending mass on occasions.[91] For balance's sake, it should be noted that he sometimes also recorded aspects of Lutheran, Reformed or simply 'low' church worship favourably: at Baveno, for example, again in 1864 he attended the English service at the Pension, noting 'the H.C. administered, but very irreverently', before proceeding, 'Still the sermon contained some beautiful passages on Providence.'[92] Again, exactly three years later, he admired the 'earnestness and devoutness' of the Lutheran congregation at the (Lutheran) Petruskirche in Berlin.[93] Liddon's openness, incidentally, contrasts favourably with Benjamin Webb's criticism of Lutheran churches in terms reminiscent of the way that High Churchmen commonly saw Dissent: at Nassau, for example, he noted 'a most miserable pued [sic] and galleried preaching-room for Lutheran worship'.[94]

From later in the century, Malcolm MacColl provides another example of a non-convert. Attending High Mass in the village church at Oberammergau, he noted, evidently with approval, that much of the service (the greeting, the

---

88   Johnston, *Liddon*, pp. 15–6; the whereabouts of the mss of Liddon's travel journal for 1851 is unknown.

89   H. P. Liddon, mss diary entry for 13 June 1864; Pusey House archives.

90   The most serious attempt was in October 1852, during his first visit to Rome: Johnston, *Liddon*, p. 25.

91   A typical entry from his stay in Berlin in 1867 whilst travelling with Charles Dodgson runs: 'Went to early mass at St. Hedwig's Cath Ch, & said office', but the entry immediately proceeds to describe a visit after breakfast the same day to the (Lutheran) Dom Kirche: 'abendmahl, sermon, licentiate turned towards people except at consecration': H. P. Liddon, mss diary entry for 21 July 1867; Pusey House archives.

92   H. P. Liddon, mss diary entry for 17 July 1864; Pusey House archives.

93   H. P. Liddon, mss diary entry for 17 July 1867; Pusey House archives.

94   Webb, *Sketches of Continental Ecclesiology*, p. 77.

sermon, the creed, the Lord's Prayer, the litany) was in the vernacular, and that the service was very well attended; he had never seen a more devout congregation.[95] Liddon was equally impressed by their devotion, noting of the passion play that it was 'unequally sustained but on the whole was an astonishing product of the faith and love of the village'.[96] Brooke Foss Westcott, hardly a High Churchman in any party-specific sense, visited the Marian shrine of La Salette near Grenoble in 1865 in the company of J. B. Lightfoot and E. W. Benson, and prepared an appreciative article on it, which Lightfoot managed to persuade him not to publish for fear it would damage his reputation.[97] As David Thompson has pointed out, Westcott's concern was not so much with Marian doctrine *per se*, as with the sign represented by the miracles taking place at La Salette that the 'age of faith' was returning.[98] La Salette nevertheless drew from Liddon a particularly sharp criticism: 'a miracle like that of La Salette, and many of which it is a sample, is discredited by its typical character, and still more by the insufficiency of the producible proof that it ever occurred.'[99] Nevertheless, the point still stands that Anglican church tourists could not be divided into pro- and anti-Roman Catholic witnesses simply on the grounds of whether they converted or not.

The effusiveness of some of the comments of Faber and Allies nevertheless leaves in place the suggestion that travel was instrumental in their conversion. Was this indeed the case? This is difficult to prove with any certainty. Allies, late in life, thought it had been. In his autobiography he noted how he had drawn contrasts 'in the exuberance of my strength as an Anglican' between the richness and vitality of the worship he observed in France, and the poverty of Anglican church life.[100] So, in addition to the example of the Fathers and his parish experience, he now had a 'third force' propelling him towards conversion, namely 'the actual sight of the Church abroad', struck as he was by all the evidence of its revival.[101] Faber's book certainly implied that continental Catholicism was a strong influence on him. It mapped a journey in three dimensions – geographically, through France and down into the Mediterranean,

95   MacColl, *The Ammergau Passion Play*, p. 44.

96   H. P. Liddon, mss diary entry for 24 July 1870; Pusey House archives.

97   See the brief account in D. M. Thompson, *Cambridge Theology in the Nineteenth Century: Enquiry, controversy and truth*, pp. 117–8; cf. also the account given by the convert to Roman Catholicism, J. S. Northcote, *Pilgrimage to La Salette, or, a Critical Examination of all the facts*.

98   Thompson, *Cambridge Theology*, p. 117.

99   H. P. Liddon, *Clerical Life and Work*, p. 256.

100   T. W. Allies, *A Life's Decision*, p. 36.

101   Allies, *A Life's Decision*, p. 38.

historically, into the Middle Ages, and theologically, into the catholicity and apostolicity of the Roman Church. In all three senses, this was a journey away from Anglicanism. Having noted, at Avignon, the vitality of the Papacy, he could go on to criticize its bondage to the French State in the years of Papal exile in Avignon, and then to criticize Gallicanism itself, for, as he said, what 'high-hearted man' could sympathize with it or (significantly) with 'any other *national* Church system'?[102] Another touchstone of his changing sympathies was clerical celibacy. His ghostly companion offered no less than nineteen reasons in favour of celibacy, which left Faber apparently unconvinced, except that he remained sitting on the beach 'with a very vacant mind' and threw pebbles into the Mediterranean.[103] Commenting on the Mass that he observed in Genoa, he claimed to have been repulsed by it at first, and yet at the same time said that the Roman liturgies were

> so beautiful, so solemn, so reverently bold, so full of Catholic teaching, so fitted to the deepest devotional cravings of which we are capable ... that we return almost with a feeling of disappointment and sense of lowering to our own formularies, forgetting that ... the Catholic richness of the Common Prayer is far above our actual condition and practice.[104]

Faber's book was published more than three years before his conversion, but it is impossible to avoid the conclusion that, by the time he had completed it, his resistance to Roman Catholicism was all but gone.

Another convert for whom travel was significant was Henry Manning. His travel diaries were not published in his lifetime; only extracts from them appeared in Purcell's *Life*. On his first visit to Rome, in 1838, his reactions were negative: he deplored the secular nature of church music there, and found Roman devotions and practices 'actually repugnant'.[105] But extensive travel ten years later, following a near-fatal illness (and long after the death of his wife) found him much more receptive. At Malines, for example, he was unsettled at finding his claim to the title 'Catholic' challenged by simple monks, observed the *Salut* and exposition in the cathedral with admiration, and noted, of the relics deposited in the seminary, 'I could not but feel that the effect of such objects is to awaken and keep alive a high standard of personal devotion.'[106]

---

102   Faber, *Sights*, pp. 66 &114; italics original.
103   Faber, *Sights*, p. 132.
104   Faber, *Sights*, p. 155.
105   Purcell, *Manning*, Vol. I, p. 153.
106   Purcell, *Manning*, Vol. I., pp. 347 & 349–50.

When he reached Rome, in November 1847 (he stayed until early May 1848, and naturally was interested in the turbulent events of that year), his reactions were quite different from nine years earlier. Though he spent much time in the company of expatriate Anglicans, he attended the English Protestant Church outside the walls 'but very occasionally'.[107] He met Newman and Ambrose St John, before their return to England in December 1847, visited Roman Catholic churches, attended mass and observed Catholic ceremonial, and carefully recorded what he saw. At the Quirinal in early December, for example, he attended a mass in the Papal Chapel: 'It was a splendid sight. The Pope in white and gold, and gold mitre, on a throne of white and gold.'[108] He was there again in March 1848: 'The Pope gave the benediction [from the palace balcony] with a mixture of majesty, love, and supplication I never saw. It was a sight beyond words. A man near me said with emotion: *"Non é un uomo, é un angelo"*.'[109] It seems very unlikely that an Anglican of Manning's strength of character, already wavering in his Anglican convictions and recording such impressions as this, was not influenced by travel in favour of his eventual conversion.

If travel was an important and possibly decisive influence on those Anglican High Churchmen who converted to Roman Catholicism, nevertheless did it have any long-term influence on the views and practices of non-converts? This was not a question that most of them appear to have faced in quite that form, which is something entirely understandable given both the reluctance of High Churchmen to tamper with the Anglican formularies and popular sensitivity over Romanism. Benjamin Webb is an exception here. Despite concentrating mostly on architecture in his ecclesiological sketches, in the Preface he professed that the more his observation of continental Catholicism confirmed him in his 'hearty allegiance' to the Church of England, the more confidently he was able

> not only to seek for points of unity and sympathy, rather than those of difference, between his own and foreign Churches; but also occasionally to point out and recommend for thoughtful consideration among English Churchmen, anything in the practical religious system of the Roman Catholic body, which – if adopted by competent authority – might seem likely to be beneficial to ourselves.[110]

---

107   Purcell, *Manning*, Vol. I, p. 362.
108   Purcell, *Manning*, Vol. I, p. 365.
109   Purcell, *Manning*, Vol. I, p. 372.
110   Webb, *Sketches of Continental Ecclesiology*, p. xiii.

On the very first page of his travelogue he noted how the light cast from the windows of ss Peter and Paul church at Ostend, from the lamp before the Blessed Sacrament, 'seemed to take off all feelings of loneliness, such as sometimes our own churches produce: it made one feel as if the church was tenanted'.[111] Most of Webb's descriptions of Roman Catholic services are matter-of-fact, as if deliberately stepping back from risky comment, but here and there approbation appears – the 'grouping and general ministration' of the twenty-one clergy that he observed engaged in the liturgy at Ratisbon cathedral in 1844, for example, he found 'most beautiful'.[112] If anything, Webb's friend J. M. Neale surpassed his profound interest in strands of continental Roman Catholicism and extended it to embrace Eastern Orthodoxy, though in his published account of his Balkan tour in 1861 comments on church life and worship are relatively spare. They are, nonetheless, revealing. Echoing – as we shall see – Liddon, Neale appears to have had no qualms about participating in services to the fullest extent possible for an Anglican priest, though naturally stopping short of receiving communion. In Graz, for example, he was most impressed by a visit to an infirmary and dispensary run by the Barmherzige Brüder: 'We made some little offering to the House, – on which the Prior took us in to pray before the Blessed Sacrament, in a small distinct oratory. These brethren quite took my heart.'[113]

The example of Henry Liddon is particularly telling, given his personal acquaintance with the some of the circle of 'Liberal Catholics' out of whom liturgical reform in the Church of England was eventually to come. According to his biographer, Liddon was restrained in ritual matters.[114] But Johnston chose not to publish entries from Liddon's diaries which show another side of him. At Pau in 1865, for example, on Good Friday, he slipped out to St Jacques, the local Roman Catholic church, for the Mass of the Pre-Sanctified, 'at which I had never assisted before. I went up to the altar & kissed the cross.'[115] In the same year, Liddon was one of the signatories to a petition to the Archbishop Canterbury requesting that any revision of the Prayer Book be undertaken in conformity with the arrangements and contents of the First Prayer Book of

---

111   Webb, *Sketches of Continental Ecclesiology*, p. 1.

112   Webb, *Sketches of Continental Ecclesiology*, p. 120.

113   Neale, *Notes, Ecclesiological and Picturesque*, p. 34.

114   '[He] felt ... the absolute necessity for loyal self-restraint within the limits of the legitimate interpretation of the Prayer-book': Johnston, *Liddon*, p. 177.

115   H. P. Liddon, mss diary entry for 14 April; Pusey House archives. I have been unable to ascertain what 'assisted' meant here. It is scarcely likely that Liddon acted as an assistant or officiant.

King Edward VI, a touchstone for Anglo-Catholic ritual and liturgical matters.[116] When he was admitted as a Canon of St Paul's in 1870, Liddon noted in his diary that it was 'according to the Sarum use', probably the first time such a thing had happened at the cathedral since the early sixteenth century.[117]

Conclusion

Given the piecemeal and diverse nature of the evidence for continental church tourism, its impact on High Churchmen is difficult to assess comprehensively. Unquestionably travel was an important influence on the outlook of many leading High Churchmen, helping to propel some towards conversion to Rome. But the precise contours of any broader influence on the liturgical and devotional life of the Church of England are harder to describe, especially when other factors such as the translation of theological and devotional texts, the study of Patristic and medieval sources, and scholarship on English liturgical history, are taken into account. Further work is needed to test the range and scope of continental church tourism, taking into consideration both High Church reactions to Eastern Orthodoxy and to the Protestant traditions, and the observations that other Anglicans made on the whole range of Christian practice across Europe. The cumulative evidence assembled in this chapter suggests that links between the ritual controversies in the Church of England in the second half of the century and observation of ritual practices on the Continent of Europe are plausible, indeed likely, and there are striking cases in which High Churchmen who did play a considerable part in promoting ritual and liturgical reform were influenced by their experience of travel as well as their theological and liturgical scholarship. The continental context supplies a new dimension to our understanding of the changing character of High Churchmanship in this period.

It is tempting to extend these admittedly cautious and provisional conclusions to the history of subsequent liturgical change too. Donald Gray, in a widely-appreciated study of the theological roots of modern Anglican liturgical reform, implied that it was largely *sui generis*, and in particular the product of a fusion of Tractarian sacramentalism with the social theology of F. D. Maurice and his ilk.[118] Without questioning the general outline of Gray's

---

116   Circular folded into the mss diary for 1865; Pusey House achives.

117   H. P. Liddon, mss diary entry for 27 April 1870; Pusey House archives.

118   D. Gray, *Earth and Altar: The Evolution of the Parish Communion in the Church of England to 1945.*

account, continental church travel in the nineteenth century does at least imply that the steady erosion of popular hostility to ritual practices and eucharistic renewal experienced by High Churchmen by the early twentieth century owed something to wider cultural trends, and in particular to a growing appreciation of elements of continuity between their vision of Anglicanism and their observation of continental Roman Catholicism. As we have seen, in the early and mid-nineteenth century, Anglican church travellers on the Continent of Europe were often struck by the piety and devotion of the Roman Catholic congregations that they observed, and by many of the ritual and ceremonial practices, at times seeking to draw out implications for the practice of the Church of England. We can at least posit an amplification, amongst leading High Churchmen, of the practical content of their understanding of Roman Catholicism's devotional practice, enriched as it was by contact with the continental churches.

It seems ironic, then, that the chief authors of the proposals for liturgical change in early twentieth-century Anglicanism, including Charles Gore, Armitage Robinson, and Walter Frere, were not likely to have been influenced much, at least directly and personally, by continental models. To judge from their biographies, they were not great travellers, and indeed the decline of the kind of church tourism that I have described here towards the end of the nineteenth century is itself a phenomenon requiring explanation. Their work was shaped particularly by historical scholarship, and the study of the English liturgy, and also by the emergence in the late nineteenth century of the division in Anglo-Catholicism between advocates of the Roman or 'Papal' style and the more common neo-Gothic 'English' or Prayer-Book style.[119] Yet even here things may not be quite as they seem. Both Frere and Gore were founders of the Community of the Resurrection, and certainly well acquainted with Liddon and with the cultural and intellectual world of Tractarianism. Charles Lindley Wood, 2nd Viscount Halifax, for long President of the English Church Union and probably, after Gladstone, the most influential Anglo-Catholic layman in the late nineteenth century, was profoundly influenced by Liddon, and himself a frequent traveller on the Continent; his outlook was also far from insular.[120] Halifax, with Frere, Robinson and Gore, was a participant in the informal Malines conversations with Belgian Roman Catholics on reunion which took place from 1921 to 1926, and although by then the impetus for Prayer Book revision was well under way, Frere's own account of the conversations gives no hint

---

119   Cf. V. Staley, *Ceremonial of the English Church.*
120   J. G. Lockhart, *Charles Lindley Viscount Halifax*, Vol. I, pp. 245–52.

of unease or strong disagreement over liturgical matters.[121] When the modern Anglican equivalent of the continental Liturgical Movement got under way in the 1920s and 1930s, particularly under the influence of the liturgist Gabriel Hebert, the influence of continental trends was readily acknowledged.[122] All this is not to suggest that close parallels and patterns of influence can be found consistently between Anglicanism and church traditions on the Continent of Europe; but it is to suggest that there are far richer seams of influence to be studied here than previously thought.

---

121   W. Frere, *Recollections of Malines: A Contribution to the Cause of Christian Reunion.*

122   A. G. Hebert, *Liturgy and Society*; see pp. 125–38 on the Liturgical Movement.

CHAPTER 5

High Churchmanship and French Catholics

If High Churchmen were touring the Continent of Europe in ever-increasing numbers in the early and mid-nineteenth century, and noting aspects of church life there, we should hardly be surprised that the current of interest ran the other way as well. According to the Roman Catholic biographer, Edmund Purcell, 'In those stirring and eager days of the revival of religion ... an extraordinary interest was taken by foreign Catholics in the Oxford Movement'.[1] Purcell had lived in Germany from 1837 to 1844, and may have drawn on his own memory in saying this, though it is equally likely that he was influenced by his friend Ambrose Phillipps de Lisle.[2] And yet the cross-currents of mutual curiosity and regard have rarely been studied in any depth. Most historians have simply not followed Purcell's suggestion and considered at length what continental Roman Catholics might have made of Tractarianism. Gordon Roe's study of Lamennais and England is perhaps an exception, but as Roe himself acknowledged, it was really a study of Lamennais' reception in England, and not of Lamennais' views of England.[3] Louis Allen's editing of Newman's replies to the Abbé Jager was rare in its acknowledgement of the scale of continental interest in Tractarianism: he listed various links, including the visits of Gladstone and Monckton Milnes to France, the attention spent by French newspapers on the Oxford Movement, and the taking of French journals by various Tractarians. But his purpose was merely to provide some background to the correspondence between Jager, Benjamin Harrison and Newman, and he did not study these links at any length.[4]

The history of Anglo-French ecclesiastical relations was a complicated one, made more complicated perhaps by the political and military rivalry of these two nations in the eighteenth and early nineteenth centuries. France's status

---

1   E. S. Purcell, *Life and Letters of Ambrose Phillipps de Lisle*, Vol. 1, p. 137.
2   S. Gilley, 'Purcell, Edmund Sheridan (1823–1899)', ODNB; on Phillipps, see also M. Pawley, *Faith and Family: The life and circle of Ambrose Phillipps de Lisle*, and idem,'Lisle, Ambrose Lisle March Phillipps de (1809–1878)', ODNB. Phillipps's name is rendered in different ways by different authors; here I have followed the convention simply of using his family name, Phillipps, though he made 'de Lisle' his surname in 1862 after his father's death.
3   W. G. Roe, *Lamennais and England: The Reception of Lamennais's Religious Ideas in England in the Nineteenth Century*, p. v.
4   L. Allen, *Newman and the Abbé Jager: A Controversy on Scripture and Tradition (1834–1836)*, pp. 2–3.

© KONINKLIJKE BRILL NV, LEIDEN, 2016 | DOI 10.1163/9789004326804_006

as the major continental Catholic power by the late seventeenth century might have been expected to play into the hands of a Papacy keen to exert whatever pressure it could in favour of efforts to return Britain to the Roman Catholic Church. Despite their willingness to provide refuge for the exiled Catholic Stuarts after 1688, in general French monarchs were not willing to play anyone's game but their own, however, and religious considerations rarely featured consistently in their diplomatic machinations. After the expulsion of the Huguenots, following the revocation of the Edict of Nantes in 1685, the cultivation of a state of semi-independence for the French Church, based on the Gallican Articles of 1682, effectively marginalised the Counter-Reformation agenda of the reconversion of England: State and dynastic considerations took precedence. There were even some tentative, early ecumenical conversations between English and French ecclesiastics in the early eighteenth century, notably Archbishop William Wake and the Abbé Le Courayer, and Drs. L. E. Du Pin and Piers Girardin of the Sorbonne.[5] But these did not lead to active or constructive relations, and the intensity of popular anti-Catholicism in Britain, and anxiety about the Jacobite connection, quite apart from significant theological differences, almost certainly acted as an effective barrier. Things were to change somewhat, of necessity, during the French Revolution, when thousands of Catholic clergy fled France in the wake of Pius VI's refusal to allow them to subscribe the oath to the new constitution. Some 7,000 settled in Britain during the 1790s, returning to France in stages after the 1801 Concordat, and again after the fall of the Bonapartist regime in 1814–15.[6] Although the exiled clergy were scattered around Britain, there were concentrations of them in the Channel Islands, along the south coast of England, and in major cities. Senior clergy in exile in particular settled in London.[7] Inevitably this brought with it greater contact between Anglican and French Catholic clergy. By the 1820s, however, the vast majority of the exiled clergy had long returned to France – with the exception of some 1,000 or so who had died in exile.

As the previous chapter showed, there is some evidence to suggest that French Catholicism exercised a hitherto unacknowledged influence over Tractarianism. Purcell, again, claimed that the descriptions of continental Catholicism by various travellers such as Frederick Faber and Thomas Allies

5 See N. Sykes, *Old Priest and New Presbyter: Episcopacy and Presbyterianism since the Reformation*, pp. 196–208; also J. H. Lupton, *Archbishop Wake and the Project of Union (1717–1720) between the Gallican and Anglican Churches*.

6 [Dom] A. Bellenger, *The French Exiled Clergy in the British Isles after 1789: A Historical Introduction and Working List*, p. 3.

7 Bellenger, *French Exiled Clergy*, p. 4.

came 'as a revelation' to the Tractarians.[8] But the purpose of this chapter is to observe and evaluate the reactions of French Catholics (and some Belgian figures) to the Oxford Movement, the form in which High Churchmanship effectively presented itself to French Catholics in the mid-nineteenth century as something novel and interesting. After setting out the main lines of French Catholic attitudes to Anglicanism, both before and during the Oxford Movement itself, the views of three representative groups will be explored. These are, first, the so-called 'Mennaisian' or 'Liberal Catholic' circle, that is former followers of Felicité de Lamennais, including the lay theologian and politician Charles de Montalembert, and Jean-Baptiste Henri Lacordaire, the re-founder of the Dominican order in France; second, the 'extreme Ultramontane' circle of Louis Veuillot, editor of *L'Univers*, probably the most influential Catholic newspaper of the century; and third, one of the most influential Gallican organs, the newspaper *L'Ami de la Religion*, which by the early 1840s was under the influence of Félix Dupanloup, later Bishop of Orléans and one of the leaders of the 'Inopportunists' at the first Vatican Council.

Many scholars have pointed out the inadequacy of the typology of Gallicans, Liberal Catholics and extreme Ultramontanes, given the substantial differences within as well as between these groups, and certainly many Roman Catholics straddled these divisions awkwardly.[9] Dupanloup, for example, could be classed with the so-called 'Mennaisian school' (a particularly weak designation), or with the Gallicans: neither seems wholly apposite.[10] Whatever their differences, however, they were mostly of a common mind when they commented on developments in the Church of England. Only in the case of some of Montalembert's circle was there a significant departure from central elements of this shared view.

---

8   Purcell, *Phillipps*, Vol. 1, p. 116. Purcell could have added the Tractarian-sympathizer Christopher Wordsworth's *Diary in France* and his *Notes at Paris*, though unlike Allies and Faber, Wordsworth did not convert.

9   See A. R. May's strictures on the conventional classification, in idem, '"The Falloux Law, the Catholic Press, and the Bishops: Crisis of Authority in the French Church'; and Norman Ravitch's alternative typology contrasting a 'Catholicism of order' ('bourgeois Catholicism') and a 'Catholicism of change', in idem, *The Catholic Church and the French Nation 1589–1989*, pp. 60–6.

10   Philip Spencer, for example, saw him as a Liberal Catholic, whereas Austin Gough marked him as a Gallican: P. Spencer, *Politics of Belief in Nineteenth-Century France: Lacordaire, Michon, Veuillot*, p. 134; A. Gough, *Paris and Rome: The Gallican Church and the Ultramontane Campaign 1848–1853*, p. 58.

The Scope and Nature of French Catholic Literature on Anglicanism

A fairly extensive French literature commenting on English church affairs existed even before the religious revival of the 1830s, and it was a subset of the much larger body of writing commenting on English affairs and conditions produced by French travellers in Britain.[11] The relative sophistication of this writing varied enormously, however, ranging as it did at one end of the spectrum from informed, considered scholarly works such as those by Trévern, Montalembert, Brajeul and Jager, touched on below, to much cruder, more populist works at the other end. Many appreciative things were said about the Church of England at the more sophisticated end of the spectrum, which was not the case naturally with the more polemical approach adopted by the populist writers, who were plainly influenced by historic Anglo-French rivalry and simple chauvinism. What is striking when reading these works today, nevertheless, is a basic underlying agreement about the weaknesses of Anglicanism as a religious system. Some eight common characteristics can be drawn out.

First, and most obviously, there was a basic readiness amongst these writers to assert the Papal primacy as a central, defining element of Catholicity, and to criticize Anglicanism accordingly for its repudiation of Papal authority. Thomas Allies, touring France with Charles Marriott in 1845, found the Papal primacy advanced as the first point of Roman Catholic controversy with Anglicans again and again: 'this is universally the *first* thing with them – to be in communion with Rome.'[12] Naturally there were differences between Roman Catholic writers themselves – at least in the first half of the century, well before the first Vatican Council – as to how the authority of the Papacy was to be construed. But all agreed that communion with the see of Rome, and obedience to the authority of the Pope, were vital. Granted that, the differences among French Catholics on the question of papal infallibility were not very significant in determining their views of Anglicanism. The Gallican bishop and exile Le Pappe Trévern, on whom more in a moment, argued that the right of teaching and interpreting revelation authoritatively had been entrusted exclusively to the episcopate, but nevertheless was effective only in concert with the Pope; he had no difficulty, he said, in asserting the infallibility of a

---

11   For a recent anthology, see J. Gury (ed.), *Le voyage Outre-Manche: Anthologie de voyageurs français de Voltaire à Mac Orlan du XVIIIe au XXe siècle.*

12   T. W. Allies, *Journal in France in 1845 and 1848, with Letters from Italy in 1847, of Things and Persons concerning the Church and Education*, p. 43; italics original.

majority of the episcopate when united to the Pope.[13] This 'Gallican' position was to be repudiated by Ultramontanism, and decisively defeated at the first Vatican Council, but in practical terms it was just as critical a platform from which to view Anglicanism as was the Ultramontane position itself. The Abbé Bautain, of the seminary at Juilly, told Christopher Wordsworth in 1844 that the English Church presented to the world 'the anomalous sight of a body without a head' and that it had, therefore 'no spiritual authority' to which it could defer.[14] An anonymous writer, probably clerical, 'Joseph F. P.', who reflected in broad terms the Ultramontane point of view, in a polemical, populist guide to Protestantism published in 1842 singled out the Papal primacy as a point requiring special attention:

> Let the sovereign Pontiff be considered infallible on his own, or let him not; I leave to others the task of settling ['trancher'] this controversial question. Let his conduct itself be edifying or not, he is no less the rightful successor of St Peter; he has his authority over all the Church, and we can recall Protestants on that point to the words of the Gospel.[15]

As to England, he said it was like a 'pilotless boat' when it had thrown off the link to Rome.[16] This was an image that recurred frequently. The abbé J.-B. Abbeloos, professor at Malines, used it nearly thirty years later, in another polemical work which crowed over the disestablishment of the Irish Church, predicting the imminent demise of the Established Church in England; like a boat without steering or a pilot, he said, the Anglican Church had thrown Christian truth overboard.[17] Even Montalembert could say with Manzoni against Protestants, that if the main point was denied, even the smallest deviation was a 'damnable heresy', and that the main point was the infallibility of the Church, 'or rather the Pope'.[18]

---

13   J. F. M. Trévern, *Discussion amicale sur l'eglise Anglicane, et en générale sur la Réformation, dediée au clergé de toutes les communions Protestants*, Vol. 1, p. 226.

14   C. Wordsworth, *Diary in France, mainly on topics concerning Education and the Church*, p. 138.

15   Joseph F. P., *Du Protestantisme suivi d'une dissertation sur le casuel et d'une abrégé de la religion Anglicane*, pp. 58–9. Translations of French texts in this chapter are my own.

16   Joseph, *Du Protestantisme*, p. 249.

17   J.-B. Abbeloos, *La crise du Protestantisme en Angleterre*, p. 17.

18   Le Comte de Montalembert, *A Letter addressed to a Rev. Member of the Camden Society, on the Subject of Catholic Literary Societies, on the Architectural, Artistical, and Archaeological Movements of the Puseyites*, p. 10.

If Anglicans had thrown over the Papal primacy, under what authority did their Church stand? This led to the second point. Roman Catholic writers almost to a man were agreed in seeing Anglicanism essentially as a State church, tyrannized over by the State, or the monarch, and in turn tyrannizing over its subjects. Baron de Grovestins suggested that the Anglican church was 'tired and humiliated' by the spiritual supremacy of the Crown; Anglicans could not get away with pretending that this was merely a political supremacy, and not a religious one.[19] Shorn of its political privileges, as it was after the constitutional changes of 1828–1832, it was facing a desperate struggle, fearing for its very life ['réduite à trembler pour elle-même'].[20] Again, 'Joseph F. P.' opined that it was strange that a woman, the queen, who was 'radically incapable of exercising the least of sacerdotal functions', should be head of the Church.[21] Christopher Wordsworth encountered the same view in Paris in 1853, when a 'Roman Catholic friend' told him that the Church of England was 'subject in all matters of doctrine to the civil power', deriving its '*Creed* from the *State*', so that it was 'like a vessel tossed on the sea'.[22] The Abbé Robert, admiring St Paul's Cathedral, nevertheless dismissed Anglicanism as a religion of the State, and was shocked to see how the house of God was profaned with the presence of unbelieving politicians who had abjured the faith.[23] If the near ubiquity of such criticism is a little surprising, given the relative strength of Gallican opinion at this period in France and the fact that English writers in turn tended to interpret the Concordatory settlement as a subjugation of the French Church to the State, it should be seen against the background of the experience of revolution.[24] To French Catholics, the English religious settlement smacked, not of Louis XIV and the Gallican Articles, but of the Civil Constitution of the Clergy, of State attempts to interfere in and reform the affairs of the Church, and even of the failed attempts at devising a Rousseauist 'civil religion' hard on the heels of the suppression of Catholicism in the mid-

---

19   Le Baron Sirtema de Grovestins, *Considérations sur l'église Anglicane et l'église Catholique, à l'occasion de la création de l'évêché Anglican de Jérusalem et du rétablissement de la hiérarchie catholique en Angleterre*, p. 67.

20   Grovestins, *Considérations*, p. 5.

21   Joseph, *Du Protestantisme*, p. 254.

22   C. Wordsworth, *Notes at Paris, particularly on the State and Prospects of Religion*, p. 39.

23   Jean-François Robert, *Souvenirs d'Angleterre et considérations sur l'église Anglicane*, p. 41.

24   In taking this view, English commentators almost certainly tended to include the practical operation of the unilaterally-imposed Organic Articles along with the Napoleonic Concordat itself, and these Articles remained in place, though varying in practical import, all through the nineteenth century. On the operation of the Concordatory regime, see ch. 2, 'Gallicanism under the Concordat', of Gough, *Paris and Rome*.

1790s. Whatever their disagreements over the nature and scope of Papal authority, French Catholics were united in seeing the State as an organ whose authority could only be mischievous in the religious sphere unless it was tempered and held in check by the Papacy.

In abandoning Rome, Protestants had rejected the authority of the one, visible Church of Christ, and were then, almost by definition, heretics. But – the third point – Protestantism was not just a constitutional heresy, or a heresy of order; it was a developmental and moral heresy, which brought in its train the evils of rationalism, liberalism, socialism, moral decay and ultimately atheism. It cannot be emphasised enough how much the Roman Catholic case against Anglicanism, and indeed against all forms of Protestantism, rested on the readiness of Roman Catholic writers to perceive the most extreme moral perils as following naturally from rejection of Rome. This clearly came as a shock to some Anglicans who had hoped to find kindred spirits in France. As Christopher Wordsworth put it, describing his meeting with the Abbé Bautain at Juilly:

> His frankness of language showed me the feeling with which the Church of England is regarded by Romish theologians; and however much they may wish for advances in their direction from England, certain, I think, it is that they are wholly indisposed to make any approaches whatever towards us, simply because in their minds we are not only heretics but are unworthy of the name of *Christians*.[25]

Jules Gondon, dividing the world simply into rationalists and Catholics, could describe Protestantism as leaning on rationalism.[26] Particularly in the more polemical literature, these comments were – to modern eyes – absurdly exaggerated. Abbeloos claimed, long after hopes about the imminent conversion of England had subsided, that Anglicanism was utterly unable to resist the growing tide of unbelief, and once it had disappeared (which he clearly expected to be very soon), it would leave the field of conflict free to the supreme struggle between unbelief and Jesus Christ.[27] The Abbé Robert's *Souvenirs d'Angleterre*

---

25 Wordsworth, *Diary*, p. 139.

26 Jules Gondon, *Motifs de conversion de dix ministres Anglicans, exposés par eux-mêmes, et rétraction du Réverend J. H. Newman*, p. ix.

27 Abbeloos, *La crise du Protestantisme*, p. 4. Such views were not restricted to French Catholics, however. Many English Roman Catholics themselves used similar kinds of language. Henry Manning, for example, refused to agree with Newman that their former church could be regarded as 'a serviceable breakwater against errors more fundamental than its own' (Newman's words towards the end of his *Apologia*), saying 'I am unable to consider the Church of England to be ... the great bulwark against infidelity in this land': H.

is a particularly illuminating scrapbook of this kind of comment. He was unable to find any Anglicans of the stature of Bossuet and Fénelon; Anglicanism was condemned, he thought, to a 'sort of intellectual and moral sterility'.[28] The Owenite sect, by which he seems to have meant the followers of Robert Owen, were cited for their rejection of conventional marriage; they had made, he claimed, 'terrible progress in England amongst the lower classes'.[29] The Owenites were hardly an offspring of Anglicanism, of course, but the very fact that Robert assumed they were, and could use their case this way, shows just how eager he was to pin all the things he found shocking in Britain on Anglicanism. For him, as for others, the moral corruption of Anglicanism was evident in its wealth, which (Roman Catholics assumed) must have been one of the main motives for Anglican reluctance to convert to Rome. Time and again, French writers raised the wealth of the Church of England, and claimed that it was the richest church in Europe.[30] Baron de Grovestins, a Dutch layman who settled in Paris and wrote extensively on diplomatic matters, cited a *Daily News* report as proof that the revenues of the 25 Church of England bishops were, at 200,000 livres p. a., more than four times those of the 49 French bishops.[31] Almost certainly this impression was fed by the feverish and often inaccurate way in which the British press itself reported the controversies over Church reform from the 1820s on, since the French Catholic press seems to have combed British papers avidly for news that it could reproduce and was evidently delighted to publicize the woes of the Church of England. Even the Oxford Fellows whom Robert met, whom he was at pains in one breath to describe as a personally estimable body of men, in another he was ready to

---

E. Manning, *The Workings of the Holy Spirit in the Church of England* (1864), cited in D. Newsome, *Convert Cardinals: Newman and Manning*, p. 255. Manning had even called London 'the capital of the most anti-Christian power of the nominally Christian world and the head of its anti-Christian spirit': ibid., p. 252.

28   Robert, *Souvenirs d'Angleterre*, p. 148. Robert (1797–1885) was an honorary canon of Tours. The fact that this work was republished three times is perhaps an indication of the popularity of his Anglophobia, as well as a sign of continuing public interest in Anglicanism.

29   Robert, *Souvenirs d'Angleterre*, pp. 125–6.

30   If the testimony of one Anglican witness is to be believed, it was not only in France and amongst Roman Catholics that these things were said: according to John Hamilton Gray, German Protestants, influenced by their contacts with English Dissenters, regarded the Church of England as 'a wealthy harvest field, where a golden crop was to be reaped, not of souls ... but of guineas to the purse of a Right Reverend political jobber, or Reverend foxhunter': J. H. Gray, *Letter to the Rt Hon. and Rev. the Lord Bishops of London, on the State of the Anglican Congregations in Germany*, p. 5.

31   Grovestins, *Considérations*, p. 58.

describe as seduced by a comfortable life.[32] Comfort and rationalism were grounded, so many Roman Catholic writers believed, on State support. Even the English Sunday, which again he praised for its seriousness, ultimately rested only on the foundation of civil law, and was therefore simply a means of comforting the nation in its voluptuousness and moral flabbiness ['mollesse'].[33] But this was hardly surprising since, for Robert, at root there was precious little true piety in Anglicanism: it was 'pure deism', acting as a veil for 'hideous atheism'.[34] In asserting all this, Robert was trading explicitly on an almost unquestioned connection that Roman Catholics tended to make between the doctrine of *sola scriptura*, the exercise of private judgement, and moral decay.[35]

Furthermore, Protestantism was inherently divisive, a fourth but closely-related point: it provoked disagreement and disunity. Allies again found that one of his hosts in France was convinced that the Church of England was 'simply a mass of heresy and schism'.[36] The lay Catholic engineer and journalist Count Achille de Jouffroy, looking back on a visit to England in a long satirical poem, *Adieux à l'Angleterre* (1832), could claim that he knew a hundred dissenting chapels in England where one could change one's faith four times a week – a deliberately ridiculous exaggeration, to be sure, but telling in its dependence on Roman Catholic views of Protestant sectarianism.[37]

The chain of association described so far was powerful enough to affect even the more measured and sophisticated writers. The Abbe Brajeul, curé of Saint-Saveur in Dinan, and formerly professor of rhetoric at Dinan's *petit séminaire*, conducted a correspondence with an unnamed Anglican (whom he claims to have converted) sometime in the late 1830s.[38] Only his side of the correspondence was published – if indeed the other side ever existed, which of course is certainly an open question given French Catholics' penchant for using the epistolary form as a vehicle for polemic – and its spirit is, for this genre of Catholic-Anglican controversy, remarkably eirenic. Brajeul was no narrow and ill-informed polemicist: not only did he demonstrate familiarity with some English texts it is at first glance surprising to find a Breton Catholic priest reading, such as Joseph Blanco White's *The Poor Man's Preservative against Popery* (1825) and Sir James Mackintosh's *History of England* (1830), but

---

32   Robert, *Souvenirs d'Angleterre*, p. 107.

33   Robert, *Souvenirs d'Angleterre*, p. 126.

34   Robert, *Souvenirs d'Angleterre*, p. 155.

35   Robert, *Souvenirs d'Angleterre*, p. 155.

36   Allies, *Journal in France*, p. 43.

37   Count Achille de Jouffroy, *Adieux à l'Angleterre*, p. 24.

38   M. Brajeul, *Lettres d'un Catholique à un Protestant de l'église Anglicane*.

he also attempted to meet his opponent on his own ground, quoting at various points the *Book of Common Prayer* and the *King James Bible* against him.[39] He was at pains to stress, for example, the tolerance and openness of Roman Catholics as to the question of the spiritual status of unbaptized children and unbelieving adults who had died, summoning on his side the authority of Monseigneur Denis-Antoine-Luc Frayssinous, titular bishop of Hermopolis, who had argued in public lectures in Paris that baptized adults sincerely mistaken in their religious views nevertheless belonged to the Catholic Church.[40] He could admit and regret, with some warmth, the travails of the Papacy in the Middle Ages, and even continuing abuses of the Church.[41] Nevertheless Brajeul did lay a great deal of emphasis on the absolute necessity of unity, and he quoted with glee Mackintosh on the void which the Reformation had left in the question of ultimate authority in the Church.[42] There was no middle way: one must be 'either Roman Catholic, or nothing at all'.[43] Protestantism's claim to represent a middle way was unfounded, and created a vacuum into which division (and by implication sectarianism) flooded. To Catholics, the existence of a bewildering variety of dissenting sects in Britain was decisive proof of Protestantism's corruption, as was also the zeal with which Protestants seemed to want to intrude their doctrines into Catholic Europe via the Bible societies. London was, in Gondon's words, the arsenal whence the champions of Protestantism drew the weapons with which venal souls ['âmes vénales'] had triumphed.[44]

---

39   On Blanco White, see Brajeul, *Lettres*, p. 93, where unfortunately the title of Blanco White's book is rendered *The poor man's preservative against papers*, and on Mackintosh, pp. 137 & 187. Quotations from the *Book of Common Prayer* and the *King James Bible* are frequent, but mostly take the form of footnotes providing an English translation of a quote made in French in the text. Charles-Auguste Brajeul was a non-juring priest, who almost certainly was forced into exile after the Civil Constitution of the Clergy. He does not appear in the list of exiled clergy in Britain compiled by A. Bellenger, but his knowledge of English works suggests that that is where he was.

40   Brajeul, *Lettres*, p. 14. Frayssinous (1765–1841) was a controversial figure, who had hidden in the mountains of Rouergue during the Revolution, and on his return to Paris had been appointed as Professor of Dogmatic Theology at the newly re-established seminary of Saint Sulpice, and whose dialogical lectures on Christianity and truth had been suppressed by Napoleon in 1809. Later, under the Restoration, he had become grand-master of the University, and Minister of Ecclesiastical Affairs. Details from J. Balteau at al., *Dictionnaire de Biographie Française*.

41   Brajeul, *Lettres*, pp. 104–6.

42   Brajeul, *Lettres*, p. 189.

43   Brajeul, *Lettres*, p. 194.

44   Gondon, *Motifs de conversion*, p. vii.

On these first four points, some French Catholics subsequently shifted ground, as we shall see. They did not dissent substantially, however, from the remaining four. Fifth, then, French Catholics' strongly critical view of Protestantism was contextualised by a sense not of the *vulnerability* of the Roman Catholic Church, but rather of its astonishing revival in the early nineteenth century. Catholic writers spoke freely, by the 1830s, of the utterly changed religious situation in Europe since the fall of Bonaparte, noting the extraordinary growth in religious orders, and the revival of parish life, as well as a sea-change in the intellectual atmosphere. Lacordaire, for example, could write to a correspondent of how it was a marvellous thing that the destiny of Europe could depend on a Pope, Gregory XVI: all had changed since 1815.[45]

Sixth, more specifically, all of these writers shared a fascination with the – to their eyes – miraculous revival of Catholicism in Britain, and a common assumption that the reconversion of Britain to Catholicism was imminent. Many adverted to the common description of Catholic England before the Reformation as the 'Isle of Saints'.[46] The anonymous polemical writer 'Joseph F. P.' claimed that this title had been abandoned by England, through its people's inconstancy and the bad example of its notables ['grands'].[47] The Abbé Robert, seeing the dreariness of Protestant worship in England, was depressed to think that this was once called the 'Isle of Saints'.[48] The Dominican Chéry, twenty years later, also spoke of the 'sweet and glorious [name] of the Isle of Saints'.[49] Given this glorious Catholic heritage, Roman Catholics were understandably immensely excited at the possibility of the national reconversion that could follow from the collapse of Anglicanism. Gondon could write of the 'last gasp' ['la dernière pulsation'] of Anglicanism.[50] Lacordaire could claim – in 1840 – that England should be counted amongst the Catholic powers of Europe, because in 50 or 60 years 'it will be ours'.[51] If this was a shared assumption, nevertheless in time some divisions opened up on strategic lines: how best could this goal be achieved?

---

45   *Correspondence du R. P. Lacordaire et de Madame Swetchine, publiée par le Cte de Falloux*, p. 241: Lacordaire to Swetchine, 24.7.1840.

46   This is a quite distinct usage from the also very common application of the term to Ireland, for which see Louis Gougaud and Maud Joynt, 'The Isle of Saints'.

47   Joseph F. P., *Du Protestantisme*, p. 236.

48   Robert, *Souvenirs d'Angleterre*, p. 123.

49   Le R. P. M. Chéry, *Appel à l'Église Russe et à l'Église Anglicane*, p. 76.

50   Jules Gondon, *Du Mouvement Religieux en Angleterre, ou Les Progrès du Catholicisme et le Retour de l'Église Anglicane à l'Unité; par un Catholique*, p. xix.

51   *Correspondence du R. P. Lacordaire et de Madame Swetchine*, loc. cit.

Seventh, glee at Catholic revival and imminent national reconversion in Britain ran alongside a more paradoxical view of the true state of British society. In a way eerily reminiscent of the arguments used by the cause of the American South in *antebellum* America, many French Catholics made a ready identification of the perils of industrialisation, mass poverty, and urbanisation with the very individualism of British society that had ostensibly produced the anti-slavery campaign, and then made the further connection, predictably, to the pervasive influence of Protestantism.[52] Hailing the restoration of the hierarchy in England, Veuillot could write that this was a country in which the influence of Protestant barbarity over 300 years had created the widest possible gulf between rich and poor, a country of all countries in which the rich least knew their soul, and the people were most despised, and whose capital had more prostitutes than any other city in Europe.[53] Le Comte de Jouffroy naturally made the most of this theme: he had gone to examine this utopia, where 'sweet liberty reigns in peace', but found instead a land where the poor were left a simple choice between prison and starvation for, he said, here 'gold alone is sacred'.[54] The Abbé Robert, visiting England in the spring of 1840, at first saw signs of oppression at every turn (a view hard to reconcile with his equally vehement claim that Protestantism was founded on an absolute right of each person to make their own religion).[55] At Dover, he saw no poor people on the streets, and speculated they were not allowed to beg in public.[56] In Canterbury, he saw lots of police, and concluded that a people who needed so many police could not be as free as they thought.[57]

Finally, all these points were brought together and epitomised in Roman Catholic views of Ireland. French Catholic writers almost universally saw Ireland as the great flaw in the British governmental system – a practical, political and religious despotism. The French press carried frequent reports on Irish affairs. Daniel O'Connell was hailed as a hero of Catholicism, not nationalism. Veuillot typified widely shared views: before O'Connell, he wrote, Ireland was a slave, more imprisoned by the Anglican despotism than by the seas around it;

---

52   Cf. E. Fox-Genovese & E. D. Genovese, *The Mind of the Master Class: History and Faith in the Southern Slaveholders' Worldview*, passim;

53   L. Veuillot, 'Le Pape et l'Angleterre (rétablissement de la hiérarchie)', dated 12.11.1850, originally published in *L'Univers*, reprinted in idem, *Mélanges religieux, historiques, politiques et littéraires (1842–1856)*, Vol. VI, p. 17.

54   Jouffroy, *Adieux à l'Angleterre*, pp. 9 & 18.

55   Robert, *Souvenirs d'Angleterre*, p. 101 for this view of Protestantism.

56   Robert, *Souvenirs d'Angleterre*, p. 13. On this point, Robert was of course basically right, writing as he was after the reform of the Poor Law, though he makes no reference to that.

57   Robert, *Souvenirs d'Angleterre*, p. 17.

but now, due to this great citizen of the world, whose country was Rome ['Rome était sa patrie en effet'], she was free.[58] For the Abbé Robert, the insults Anglicans had thrown at O'Connell were proof of their bad faith.[59] The Abbé Bautain told Wordsworth that Ireland felt keenly 'the oppression which it has suffered from England in the interests which affect it most nearly – those of its Religion and its Church'.[60] Eugène Burnouf, later a distinguished French Orientalist and lay Roman Catholic who toured England in his youth and met Pusey, amongst others, at Oxford, made no bones of telling his remarkably forbearing host, William Cureton, that 'all honest people' in France thought the religious system in Ireland absurd.[61] Ireland also played a central role in the Baron de Grovestins' interpretation of the difficulties of Anglicanism. He began with an unusually favourable view of William III as a pragmatist who had sought to ameliorate the sufferings of Irish Catholics, but was blocked by the Anglican hierarchy and the Tories.[62] Quoting Sydney Smith on the Irish establishment, he labelled it a 'permanent insult' to the Irish people, built as it was on wealth and property stolen from their national religion, Catholicism.[63] It was Catholic emancipation which had forced parliamentary reform on the English, and now the whole rotten structure of a State religion in Britain and Ireland was tottering, marked above all by the success of O'Connell.[64] Montalembert was another admirer of Ireland, which he toured for the first time in 1830, seeing it as 'the ideal country of his dreams, the place where the causes of Catholicism and liberty were wedded'.[65] He met O'Connell on various occasions in London and France, even if his admiration was not without some nuance, finding a speech of O'Connell's to the House of Commons in 1839, for example, 'quite mediocre'.[66]

Despite the shared nature of these assumptions about the world, there were of course significant differences between the various elements of the French Church on issues directly affecting it, such as the liturgy, education, the French monarchy, and above all the scope and nature of the Papal primacy. But French

58   L. Veuillot, 'Mort de M. O'Connell', dated 27.5.1847, originally published in *L'Univers*, reprinted in *Mélanges*, Vol. III, p. 552.

59   Robert, *Souvenirs d'Angleterre*, p. 103.

60   Wordsworth, *Diary*, p. 139.

61   [E. Burnouf], *Choix de lettres d'Eugène Burnouf 1825–1852*, p. 204.

62   Grovestins, *Considérations*, p. 6.

63   Grovestins, *Considérations*, pp. 9–10.

64   Grovestins, *Considérations*, pp. 26–30, & 53–4.

65   Guillaume de Berthier de Sauvigny, 'The young Montalembert: Liberal, Catholic, and Romantic', p. 487.

66   Charles de Montalembert, *Journal intime inédit*, Vol. III, p. 409.

reactions to the Oxford Movement demonstrated the tenacity and ubiquity of French suspicion of Britain. Just as one could encounter surprisingly critical views of the British monarchy amongst French monarchists – as when the Comte d'Artois, the future Charles X, claimed that he would rather earn his living as a wood-cutter than be King of England[67] – so too in Gallican ecclesiastical circles (as opposed to *civil* Gallicanism) generally speaking there was very little sympathy for the constitutional position of the established Church of England.[68] Gallicans and Ultramontanes alike simply wrote it off as Erastian.[69]

Rarely were French commentators on English religious affairs entirely negative. Even amongst the populist and polemical writers, here and there admiring observations emerged. The Abbé Robert, for example, attending a church or chapel in Gloucestershire, encountered none of the distracting noise usually found in French churches when people moved the chairs around, and was also 'very struck' with the religious bearing of the clergyman's daughters.[70] Like others, he was also impressed with the seriousness of the English Sunday, noting how work stopped, shops were closed, and there was no public transport, and he wished similar legislation could be enacted in France.[71] But comments like this were usually spiced with regret and further criticism for the failure of Anglicanism to adhere to the true faith, or for the superficiality or formalism of English religion. 'Joseph F. P.', for example, perhaps influenced by the arguments of the Tractarians, also approved of the way in which the Church of England had preserved church discipline with regard to festivals, Lent, fasting, and ember days, but no sooner had he noted this, than he went on to claim that the 'Protestant spirit' had removed the cult of the saints, Purgatory, and clerical celibacy.[72]

Another, rather more eminent French critic of Anglicanism, J. F. M. Trévern, later Bishop of Strasbourg, displayed what in the circumstances was a remarkable degree of appreciation of Anglicanism, even though, like so many others,

67   A. Cobban, *A History of Modern France. Vol. 2: 1799–1871*, p. 73.
68   On the distinction between civil and ecclesiastical Gallicanism, see Gough, *Paris and Rome*, pp. 22–33.
69   See *L'Ami de la Religion* on the corruption, nepotism, and subjection of the Church of England, drawing probably on John Wade's *Extraordinary Black Book*: idem, 'Sur L'état de l'église Anglicane et des communions dissidents en l'Angleterre', 11 October 1831, and a shorter report in idem, 6 September 1831.
70   Robert, *Souvenirs d'Angleterre*, p. 87.
71   Robert, *Souvenirs d'Angleterre*, p. 122.
72   Joseph, *Du Protestantisme*, p. 253.

he was also struck with the extraordinary variety of sects in England.[73] He had spent some years in exile in England during the Revolution, and made great play of his experiences there: even when he lived 'among you', he had groaned ['gémi'] inwardly over the state of Anglicanism.[74] He is described by a modern historian of the diocese of Strasbourg as a bishop of the Ancien Régime, legitimist and Gallican, and it is almost certain that both traits were reinforced by his emigré experience.[75] Trévern's *Discussion Amicale sur l'Église Anglicane* (1817) is worth considering at some length, as it was written well before the Oxford Movement, and can stand as a useful, and typical, example of the kinds of arguments that Roman Catholic theologians raised against Anglicans even before the Oxford Movement intensified mutual interest. It was reprinted several times in the course of the century and was almost certainly used by French clergy as a major source of knowledge of Anglican teaching. It was an enormous work, by far the largest of the genre, stretching in its second edition of 1824 to two volumes of over 400 pages each, with a further *Défense de la Discussion Amicale*, itself over 360 pages, added in 1829 in response to a volume of criticism by the Anglican clergyman George Stanley Faber.[76] It is perhaps no wonder that a collective biography of the nineteenth century French bishops has claimed that Trévern's involvement in controversial writing impeded his

---

73   Trévern, *Discussion amicale*. Trévern (1754–1842) studied at the Collège du Plessis in Paris, then at the seminary of Saint-Magloire, refused to take the oath required by the Civil Constitution of the Clergy in 1791, and after years in exile in England and Austria returned to France in 1818, becoming bishop of Aire in 1823, before being translated to Strasbourg in 1827. According to Baunard's *Episcopat Français depuis le Concordat jusqu'à la Séparation* ('ouvrage publié sous la Direction de la Société Bibliographique ... et une introduction par Mgr. Baunard'), p. 606, the conversion of Protestants was a special interest of his. Biographical details of Trévern are from this work.

74   Trévern, *Discussion Amicale*, Vol. I, p. 15.

75   F. Rapp (ed.), *Le Diocèse de Strasbourg*, p. 204. There is as yet no comprehensive study of the experience of the emigré French clergy. Jacques-Olivier Boudon, historian of the French episcopate in the nineteenth century, touches on it in a few pages in his magisterial *L'Épiscopat Français à l'Époque Concordataire (1802–1905)*, pp. 161–6, and concludes that whether they opted for exile abroad, or for a life of concealment in France, bishops who had been émigrés had almost certainly suffered such privations that many of them had aged prematurely, and were all the more receptive to the values of the Counter-Revolution, making them more inclined to seek a return to the situation of the Church before the Revolution: ibid., p. 166.

76   See G. S. Spencer, *The Testimony of Primitive Antiquity against the peculiarities of the Latin Church: Being a supplement to the Difficulties of Romanism: In reply to an Answer to the Difficulties of Romanism, by J. F. M. Trévern, Bishop of Strasbourg*.

management of his first diocese, Aire.[77] But there was substance, as well as
scale, in his scholarship,. His breadth of reference was striking, encompassing
the Fathers, Gallican authorities such as Bossuet and Fénélon, and then an
impressive array of Anglican authorities, including John Jewel, George Bull,
John Pearson, Samuel Parker, and Robert South, as well as various other English
authorities such as Francis Bacon and Conyers Middleton. The tone, moreover
was calm, measured, and sympathetic at points, if ultimately critical: it was, as
the title indicated, an amicable argument. His strategy was to advance a proposition on which both churches could agree, almost as if it were a matter of
common sense, and then explicate the Roman argument in such a manner
that it appeared a perfectly logical development from what was held in common. So, for example, his exposition of the invocation of saints began from the
observation that when in England he had been struck by the way he had heard
English people commending each other to prayer, and inviting him to pray for
them; this was surely a matter of common courtesy and generosity; but he was
a poor sinner, and his prayers on behalf of others could not therefore carry
anything like the force of the great saints, whose sanctity was recognised by the
whole Church.[78] His work was peppered with comments displaying respect for
the Church of England. And yet his general view of the English Church was
profoundly negative. The Reformation had destroyed the unity of the Church
in England, and led to the relentless and unending development of different
sects. The English, he opined, respected the civil law, yet left divine law in the
hands of anyone who wanted to set up their own religion.[79] Thus, altar was
raised against altar, with the result that 'one no longer knows to whom to listen,
one no longer knows what to believe, what to think, what to do' – a situation
comparable, he thought, to that of paganism before the coming of Christianity.[80]
Quoting Francis Bacon, he claimed that sectarianism led directly to atheism.[81]
The divisions of Protestantism merely proved the need for an infallible authority, and yet the English Church had in effect taught its followers to despise the
authority of the Church.[82] But we can be assured, he said, that Christ would
not have left his Church without the means of being able to fulfil his great com-
mandment; the need for a supreme, infallible authority in the Church was thus
proven by our own inability individually to perform this role, since our own

77 *Episcopat Français depuis le Concordat jusqu'à la Séparation*, p. 6.
78 Trévern, *Discussion amicale*, Vol. II, pp. 265–6.
79 Trévern, *Discussion amicale*, Vol. I, p. 16.
80 Trévern, *Discussion amicale*, Vol. I, p. 17, with the discussion of paganism on pp. 18–20.
81 Trévern, *Discussion amicale*, Vol. I, pp. 32–3.
82 Trévern, *Discussion amicale*, Vol. I, p. 163.

individual judgement could be so erroneous.[83] Without such an infallible authority, anyone could declare themselves competent to judge theological questions.[84]

The question of authority thus proved to be the decisive point of Trévern's attack on Anglicanism. He did not dispute the wisdom of many of its scholars, or the sincerity of many of its church leaders and clergy, and indeed could speak approvingly of how English Sabbath observance shamed Catholic countries.[85] But Anglicanism rested, like the systems of the continental Reformers, on the insecure base of an exclusive appeal to Scripture: although there were Anglican writers who valued tradition, others – and Conyers Middleton was particularly handy here – disputed the need to defend it.[86] All the early witnesses, Trévern argued, showed the necessity of an authoritative ministry as interpreters (not masters) of Scripture, and this in turn implied the existence of an infallible authority amongst a clear majority of the bishops.[87] Trévern even went some way in recognizing that Anglicans did stand by early doctrines of the Church; but they had failed to recognize the truth of 'that most august of sacraments', the eucharist.[88] He spent nearly 300 pages in all defending the Roman Catholic doctrine of the eucharist, and showing how it accorded with the double deposit of Scripture and tradition, before turning finally to disagreement over doctrines such as confession, satisfaction, indulgences, and the invocation of saints.[89] But it was Anglicanism's weak authority to which he returned, and with which he ended. Now that the protection of Establishment was under threat, what was to stop even more of its members passing out of its body, for after all, the Methodists had done so, and in London it was common knowledge that floods of people were leaving the Anglican Church for Dissenting chapels?[90] Surely the day was not far off when the Anglican bishops and clergy would be all alone in their great churches, their congregations gone? This tendency to divide and separate was endemic in Protestantism, and

83   Trévern, *Discussion amicale*, Vol. I, pp. 102–3.

84   Trévern, *Discussion amicale*, Vol. I, p. 155.

85   Trévern, *Discussion amicale*, Vol. I, pp. 176–7.

86   Trévern, *Discussion amicale*, Vol. I, pp. 206–9.

87   Trévern, *Discussion amicale*, Vol. I, p. 226.

88   Trévern, *Discussion amicale*, Vol. I, p. 236.

89   On the eucharist, Trévern, *Discussion amicale*, Vols I, pp. 233–467, and II, pp. 1–137.

90   Trévern, *Discussion amicale*, Vol. II, 410. It is difficult to know what Trévern is specifically referring to at this point – perhaps to early reports of the Irvingites, since the early 1820s were the time that Edward Irving's impact in London was at its greatest: see S. Gilley, 'Edward Irving: Prophet of the Millennium'.

showed just how Anglicanism, despite its best efforts, could not ultimately shake off the fragility of its origins.[91]

Trévern's long and elegant, if ultimately rather uneven work encapsulates neatly the substance of French Catholic views of Anglicanism in the years before the Oxford Movement. Even the assistance given to French Catholic exiles during the Revolutionary and Napoleonic era could not shift fundamentally the critical eye they cast on the Anglicanism they encountered. It should not be forgotten that criticism of English religion was not the exclusive possession of French Catholics, however: both Evangelicals and Anglo-Catholics advanced their respective positions by contrasting true religion with the lethargy and worldliness that they thought they observed in the Georgian Church of England. It is possible, then, that French criticism of Anglicanism was influenced as much by what Anglicans were saying about themselves as it was by traditional or long-standing Roman Catholic opinion of English Protestantism. Nevertheless, the general consistency showed by French Catholic writers' views of Anglicanism before, during and after the Oxford Movement is striking.

Charles de Montalembert and the 'Liberal Catholics'

The most significant shift away from this framework occurred amongst the so-called 'Mennaisian' or 'Liberal Catholic' school, which generally showed the warmest French Catholic reaction to the Oxford Movement. It was not a particularly large group, and its influence on the French Church has perhaps been exaggerated. It was composed, at its core, of those who embraced Lamennais's intoxicating mixture of political liberalism and Ultramontanism, and yet distanced themselves from Lamennais and submitted to the judgement and discipline of the Church after Gregory XVI's encyclical *Mirari Vos* (1832).[92] Admiration for British political and religious liberty predisposed many of this group towards sympathy with Anglicans. Yet papal condemnation of Lamennais, as well as French ecclesiastical politics, made this a highly sensitive matter.

This is evident in Charles de Montalembert's *Letter to a Rev. Member of the Camden Society on ... the Puseyites* (1844), published in English by a Roman Catholic publishing house based in Liverpool. Montalembert was an ardent

---

91   Trévern, *Discussion amicale*, Vol. II, pp. 414–5.

92   The most useful discussion in English probably remains A. R. Vidler, *Prophecy and Papacy: A study of Lamennais, the Church, and the Revolution*, but see also B. M. G. Reardon, *Liberalism and Tradition: Aspects of Catholic thought in nineteenth-century France*.

Anglophile.[93] He had been born there to an English mother, during his father's exile in England in the First Empire, and was brought up largely by his maternal grandfather, whom he continued to regard as the person to whom he owed all he had and was.[94] The recent publication of a critical edition of Montalembert's private diaries at last enables us to gauge something of the complexity and sophistication both of his knowledge of British society, and of his continuing experience of it long after he had married and settled back in France.[95] Even as an occasional visitor, his education, wealth and social standing meant that he had an impressive network of friends and acquaintances with whom he could consort when he was in Britain, including William Gladstone, Richard Monckton Milnes, and Ambrose Phillipps de Lisle, on whom more later. Moving in these social circles, it would have been very difficult for him to have sustained the prejudices one could encounter in more chauvinistic French descriptions of Britain and of Anglicanism. During the second of his two extended stays in Britain in 1839, for example, occasioned by his mother's illness and death, he had dinner with Milnes one evening, was delighted to be introduced to the poet Thomas Moore, and met a certain Mr Monteil, whom he described as belonging to the 'zealous and traditional' class of Anglicans, 'like Gladstone ... which I noted with pleasure'.[96] Earlier that year, on a visit to Westminster Abbey, like many French visitors he admired the monuments there, but unlike so many he also admired the 'admirable chanting of the Anglican liturgy'.[97] He was better placed to discern what was happening in Oxford more sympathetically than many French oberservers. Yet his *Letter* was provoked by the Camden Society's making him an honorary member without consulting him – something that could have played badly in France. J. M. Neale, whom Montalembert had met at Madeira in 1843, was the likeliest addressee of the *Letter*, as is made clear by Montalembert's private diary for 1844, in which he mentions writing to Neale on the errors in his novel *Ayton Priory*, and recounts his pleasure at the good effect his letter 'against the Puseyites' has had on the *Tablet* and the *Dublin Review*.[98] The letter's general tone therefore was

---

93   The most recent biography is B. Cattanéo, *Montalembert: Un catholique en politique*; there is also a relevant older study, É. Lecanuet, *Montalembert: Sa jeunesse (1810–1836)*.

94   See his tribute to his grandfather, in his *Journal intime inédit*, Vol. III, p. 412.

95   Seven volumes have appeared so far of Montalembert's *Journal intime inédit*.

96   Montalembert, *Journal intime inédit*, Vol. III, p. 426. I have not been able to establish the identity of Mr Monteil.

97   Montalembert, *Journal intime inédit*, Vol. III, p. 415.

98   Montalembert, *Journal intime inédit*, Vol. IV, pp. 32 & 140. Michael Chandler mentions Montalembert's honorary membership of the Camden Society in his biography of Neale; Neale thought Montalembert was privately delighted, but Chandler does not connect the

hostile.[99] Montalembert and the Society alike idolised the art and architecture of the Middle Ages, and he might have been expected, then, to be in sympathy with its basic aims.[100] But instead he took a strongly critical line. The Camden Society posed as a scientific society, he argued, but in fact aimed at identifying the Catholic Church of the Middle Ages with the 'Anglican schism'.[101] The Church of England had stolen the term 'Catholic'; not even the 'debased' Russian Church recognised Anglicans as Catholic.[102] To dig out 'a small channel of your own ... wherein the living truth will run ... will no more be granted to you, than it has been to the Arians, the Nestorians, the Donatists, or any other triumphant heresy'.[103] The great luminaries of the medieval English Church would be horrified to see married priests and English prayers in the now 'desecrated edifices' they had built.[104] In a passage which he must have regretted subsequently, Montalembert claimed that the Anglican Church surpassed even continental Protestantism in its subservience to the State: 'Was there ever a Church, except perhaps the Greco-Russian since Peter I, which has so basely acknowledged the supreme right of secular power'?[105] The pretensions of the Puseyites to resurrect Catholic art and teaching within the Church of England were misplaced; even if they succeeded, they would not have taken

honorary membership directly with the *Letter* and does not seem aware of the public embarrassment that the Society's action would have caused Montalembert in France: M. Chandler, *The Life and Work of John Mason Neale, 1818–1866*, pp. 20–1 & 128.

99 The only English pamphlet (to my knowledge) to reply directly to Montalembert's was by an Evangelical who thanked him for his candour about Romanism and used it to criticize the 'moral dishonesty' of the Tractarians: [Anon.] 'An Enquirer', *A re-print of a letter addressed to a Revd Member of the Cambridge Camden Society ... with a few remarks and queries*, p. 3.

100 Visiting Fountains with Phillipps in June 1839, for example, he wondered at its beauty, and called it one of the most perfect and admirable ruins in Europe; the two men kissed the yew trees which were said to have been growing there before the Dissolution, because they had seen 'men and centuries so much better than our own': Montalembert, *Journal intime inédit*, Vol. III, p. 429.

101 Montalembert, *Letter*, p. 3.

102 Montalembert, *Letter*, p. 4.

103 Montalembert, *Letter*, loc. cit.

104 Montalembert, *Letter*, p. 5.

105 Montalembert, *Letter*, p. 8. Comparison of royal domination of the Anglican and Russian Orthodox churches was a common trope of Catholic polemic; see for example *Le Guide des Curés*, as quoted by Christopher Wordsworth: 'Ce n'est qu'à Petersbourg et à Londres qu'un autocrate qui est Roi-pontife et qu'une femme à la fois Reine et Papesse peuvent s'ériger, en régulateurs du culte et en juges du Clergé, des sects grecques et protestantes': Wordsworth, *Diary*, p. 164.

a step nearer to true unity, and would have severed their church from the rest
of Protestantism, as Newman himself implied.[106]

If these views were sincere – and by then Montalembert was relatively well-
informed about the Oxford Movement – the intensity of his criticism nevertheless contrasts with the position he had adopted by the mid-1850s. In a work
which attracted some notoriety on both sides of the Channel, *The Political
Future of England* (first published as articles in *Le Correspondant* in 1855),
we find an altogether different reading.[107] This book's main focus was political, endorsing British constitutionalism in almost extravagant terms.[108] But
Montalembert also reviewed the condition of both the Roman Catholic and
Anglican churches in England. He still had harsh things to say about Anglican
'greedy pride' in usurping the magnificent buildings of medieval England.[109]
And yet a more cautious note was present in his assessment of the Christian
character of Britain. Though disfigured, Christianity in England had force and
energy, and Roman Catholics should not seek to import a foreign Catholic culture into England, but to trust the Catholic Church's ability to adapt itself to
national customs and traditions, including liberty.[110] Montalembert's French
target was obvious. But far from disparaging Anglicanism by comparison with
continental Protestantism, he now suggested that it had more vitality and
strength: it was a 'positive, substantial religion, incomplete as it is and sover-
eignly illogic [sic]'.[111] He praised the faith and the influence of Anglican laymen
and ministers, and admitted there had been a 'revival of religious feeling in
England amongst Anglicans as well as amongst the Catholics'.[112] This had
produced a general improvement in morality and public religious feeling.[113]

---

106   Montalembert, *Letter*, p. 10. Montalembert referred to a passage in Newman's sermon on
       the 'Connexion between personal and public improvement' in *Sermons on Subjects of the
       Day*, pp. 149–50, where he warned against severing personal, spiritual unity from the
       external unity of the Church: 'We cannot hope for the recovery of dissenting bodies, while
       we are ourselves alienated from the great body of Christendom ... Break unity in one
       point, and the fault runs through the whole body', p. 150.

107   Charles de Montalembert, *The Political Future of England*.

108   For example, 'England alone has created and for centuries maintained a system which
       oppresses and humiliates no one, and permits every Englishman to walk erect, and to say
       for himself, as well as the King [sic], *Dieu et mon droit!*': Montalembert, *Political Future of
       England*, p. 95.

109   Montalembert, *Political Future of England*, pp. 166–7.

110   Montalembert, *Political Future of England*, pp. 176–8.

111   Montalembert, *Political Future of England*, p. 193.

112   Montalembert, *Political Future of England*, p. 194.

113   Montalembert, *Political Future of England*, p. 195.

Montalembert described the Anglican clergy as a branch of the aristocracy, and, an aristocrat himself, he had a very high view of aristocracy.[114] The overthrow of the Anglican Church would not be a triumph for Catholicism, but would simply enlarge the ranks of Rationalists and Socinians.[115] The Puseyites had opened the door to the serious study of ecclesiastical antiquity, and put many on the road to the unity of the Church; they had engendered 'a profound respect for religious traditions, and consequently for Catholic authority'.[116] They had restored and built hundreds of churches, freed up pew sittings, and made efforts to throw off the yoke of temporal power, including reviving Convocation.[117] In sum, the Anglican Church had a vital, though not exclusive, role to play in the struggle against the social difficulties which threatened England.[118]

Why had Montalembert changed his mind? Even in the 1840s, there was a certain ambiguity in his views of English religion, arising from his admiration for English political institutions, for he could not but recognize that these institutions in part arose from and protected the role and place of religion, even as they supported a schismatic church. When Thomas Allies met him at a reception in Paris in July 1848, he declared that it would be almost miraculous if England, having resisted revolution and Napoleon, could survive the crisis it was then facing (by which he meant presumably not the Chartist movement, which by then had largely fizzled out, but rather the general risk of being drawn into the wave of revolutions affecting the Continent), because this was the 'struggle of paganism against religion'.[119] He admitted that England was more religious than most other parts of Europe, and yet it was a rather thin religion, and there were very few English people who held 'an integral Catholicism'.[120] By the mid-1850s Montalembert was thoroughly disillusioned with the Second Empire, however, and a gulf had opened up between him and Veuillot on the relations of Church and State in France, marked by his praise of political liberty in *Les intérêts catholiques au XIXe siècle* (1852). *The Political Future of England* had a French audience in view: Montalembert was reminding the French of what they were lacking, and idealised English society

114   Montalembert, *Political Future of England*, p. 197.
115   Montalembert, *Political Future of England*, p. 200.
116   Montalembert, *Political Future of England*, p. 201.
117   Montalembert, *Political Future of England*, pp. 202–3.
118   Montalembert, *Political Future of England*, p. 205.
119   Allies, *Journal in France*, p. 232.
120   Allies, *Journal in France*, p. 233.

accordingly.[121] But he was also perhaps influenced by others in his circle of contacts, including the Liberal Catholic Ambrose Phillipps de Lisle. Phillipps (as he is usually described) was a frequent correspondent of Montalembert's. In 1840, for example, he wrote to Montalembert that the 'great mass of the English people are profoundly religious though heretical'.[122] Writing again, in 1841 he expressed a view on the Oxford Movement that casts more light on Montalembert's later change of heart:

'I am fully persuaded', Phillipps affirmed,

> that there is no point of the globe at the present moment in which a more important work is going on for the glory of the Catholick Church, than that which is in progress in Oxford ... you can have no idea, excepting from personal intercourse, of the immense advance towards Catholicism, which these good men have made. In fact they are in every respect much more Catholick [sic] than half of those who have been born and bred Catholick.[123]

Phillipps was out on a limb amongst English Catholics on this; in the same letter he even accused his co-religionists of being 'stupidly perverse' for their sneers against the Tractarians.[124] Though his views echoed to some extent those of Nicholas Wiseman – a man himself of incalculable influence in interpreting Tractarianism to the wider Catholic world – they were expressed with much less discretion and realism. Montalembert too never went as far as Phillipps, either in his appreciation of the Tractarians, or in Phillipps's apparent extension of a notion of partial Catholicity to include Anglicans.[125] Phillipps's role in the Association of Universal Prayer for the uniting of the Anglican and Catholic churches is well known, as is the fact that his Association for the Promotion of Christian Unity was effectively condemned by the Vatican in 1864.[126] He was a risky associate. And yet his ceaseless networking drew Montalembert and his friends into the fringes of the Tractarian circle. The

121   On this, see Roger Aubert (ed.), *Correspondance entre Charles de Montalembert et Adolphe Dechamps 1838–1870*, pp. 5–12.

122   L. Allen, 'Letters of Phillipps de Lisle to Montalembert', p. 59.

123   Allen, 'Letters', p. 62.

124   Allen, 'Letters', loc. cit.

125   '[T]he Roman Church is (to use the expression of the creed of P. Pius IV) the Mother and Mistress of ALL Churches, but She is only an integral though the principal part of the Church Catholick': Allen, 'Letters', p. 60.

126   M. Chapman, 'The Fantasy of Reunion: The Rise and Fall of the Association for the Promotion of the Unity of Christendom'; on Spencer, see J. V. Bussche, *Ignatius (George) Spen-*

warmth of Montalembert's feelings for Phillipps is evident from the former's private diaries. They met in London in 1839, when Phillipps was introduced as the translator of Montalembert's *Life of Saint Elizabeth*; within a matter of weeks Montalembert had gone to stay with Phillipps at Grâce-Dieu, his country estate in Leicestershire.[127] It was then that the two men went on a hectic tour north and east, visiting new Catholic institutions, and some of the great medieval cathedrals.[128] It was during a conversation at Ripon that Phillipps seemed to have alerted Montalembert to the *Tracts for the Times*.[129] After that, they were fairly frequent correspondents. In 1841 Phillipps was enthusing to J. R. Bloxam about the prospect of introducing to the Tractarian leaders 'some foreign Theologians, who ... thoroughly appreciate the Catholic movement [at Oxford]', and this must surely have included Montalembert.[130]

Lacordaire apparently shifted ground on the Oxford Movement much as Montalembert did. In July 1845, Thomas Allies and Charles Marriott counted themselves blessed to meet this 'veritable monk' in Paris, 'a St Bernard as it were, returned again in the vigour of manhood'.[131] But his conversation was distressing. He pronounced the 'deadness' of Protestantism evident in its failure to produce monastic institutions, and implied that the Oxford leaders, who clearly were men of intellect and learning, were presumably unable to convert to Catholicism (this was before Newman's conversion) through a corruption of will, however subtle.[132] The two Anglicans vainly tried to convince him that a man might conscientiously believe in all sincerity and after much hard study that the Church of England was part of the true Church of Christ, but, Allies commented sadly, he 'did not seem acquainted with the peculiarities of our position.'[133] By contrast, Allies and Marriott found the Abbé Guéranger 'more indulgent' towards the Anglican position, and prepared to admit that a sincere and conscientious Anglican must be presumed to belong to the Catholic Church.[134] Yet when Allies met Lacordaire again, in 1848, a somewhat warmer

---

cer, Passionist (1799–1864), Crusader of Prayer for England and pioneer of ecumenical prayer.

127 Montalembert, *Journal intime inédit*, Vol. III, p. 427; see also Allen, 'Letters', pp. 53–4.
128 Montalembert, *Journal intime inédit*, Vol. III, pp. 427–32: their tour encompassed Sheffield, Barnsley, Wakefield, Leeds, Kirkstall Abbey, Ripon, Fountains, Rievaulx, York, Lincoln, Newark and Southwell.
129 'Curious conversation about the progress of popery in a collection of tracts': Montalembert, *Journal intime inédit*, Vol. III, p. 429.
130 Purcell, *Phillipps*, Vol. I, p. 203; in the event, the meeting did not take place.
131 Allies, *Journal in France*, p. 72.
132 Allies, *Journal in France*, p. 74.
133 Allies, *Journal in France*, p. 77.
134 Allies, *Journal in France*, p. 77.

tone prevailed. Lacordaire apparently acknowledged that the English Church had preserved much that the Lutherans and Calvinists had not, and although the 'full life' of Catholicism remained in the Catholic Church, Protestants nevertheless had a portion of the truth: 'What you have of good is ours, is Catholic.'[135] There is further evidence yet of movement on Lacordaire's part. In 1852 he was a guest at Grâce-Dieu, from whence he made a brief detour to Oxford. His description to another associate, Madame de Swetchine, was almost rhapsodic: 'I do not remember having seen anything which has produced such a delightful impression ['aussi douce impression'] on me.'[136] The Comte De Falloux, another associate, described Oxford in the 1830s similarly: 'It is a city crowded ['toute peuplée'] with catholic monuments and preserved by protestants, like a sort of national Pompei. The monasteries have become colleges where the teaching of Christian science is maintained.'[137] Lacordaire described religious revival in England in terms similar to those of Phillipps himself: 'one feels throughout this country that the era of religious liberty has here begun its reign and is producing its due effects: they are building, founding, creating an art for the Church.'[138] He explicitly repudiated the characteristic view of Protestantism encountered amongst French Catholics: Protestantism had its weaknesses, and did lead some people out of Christianity, but this was not its general effect. England had been Protestant for 300 years, but was hardly a pagan country. The Bible, taught by the clergy, encouraged Christian notions in the population at large, and a supernatural life properly so-called in many souls of good faith, in whom the Holy Spirit worked through grace and salvation.[139] If there are echoes there of Phillipps, there are surely also some of Newman himself, or at least of his admission that the National Church was a 'serviceable breakwater' against doctrinal error.[140]

Ultramontanism: The Veuillot Circle

Lacordaire's striking appreciation of the merits of Anglicanism would not have found much sympathy with Louis Veuillot (1813–1883), the self-made journalistic genius of the 'extreme Ultramontane' party, and editor of L'Univers.

135   Allies, Journal in France, p. 263.
136   Correspondence du R. P. Lacordaire et de Madame Swetchine, p. 507.
137   Comte de Falloux, Mémoires d'un royaliste, 1, p. 115.
138   Correspondence du R. P. Lacordaire et de Madame Swetchine, p. 508.
139   Correspondence du R. P. Lacordaire et de Madame Swetchine, p. 518, letter dated 21 September 1852.
140   J. H. Newman, Apologia Pro Vita Sua, p. 362,

Montalembert had been a major shareholder in the paper in the late 1830s, but by 1842 Veuillot had taken over completely, and turned it in a direction which 'openly disdained moderation and restraint'.[141] Yet commercially his policy was a success. The paper's circulation increased fourfold in just five years alone.[142] It outsold all the other religious journals, and parish clergy snapped it up. Christopher Wordsworth, visiting Paris in 1844, found it 'now the principal organ of the church party in France'.[143] As Austin Gough put it, Veuillot in effect 're-educated the parish clergy, giving them a daily course in simplified theology and political doctrine, supported by a highly tendentious précis of Church history'.[144] Though welcoming English conversions, it was hardly likely that Veuillot would take a generous view of the Oxford Movement as a movement within Anglicanism: Anglicanism was simply another form of the general heresy of Protestantism, with all its dire effects.[145]

Nevertheless *L'Univers* was an essential medium for those who wanted to communicate what was happening in England to a continental audience, and even those much out of sympathy with Veuillot – Phillipps, for example – used it.[146] Though he did not write all that much himself on England, Veuillot was an astute judge of what his readership wanted, and made a point of employing a specialist writer on English church matters, Jules Gondon.[147] Gondon himself occupied a mediating position between Veuillot and, for example, Montalembert; he was on good terms with the latter, and with Phillipps, and Veuillot himself doubted that 'he was really one of us'.[148] It was Gondon, for

---

141   J. N. Moody, 'The French Catholic Press in the Education Conflict of the 1840s', p. 398.

142   Moody, 'French Catholic Press', loc. cit.

143   Wordsworth, *Diary*, p. 13.

144   Gough, *Paris and Rome*, p. 96.

145   See his judgement on the Gorham case: 'There are bishops in England who call themselves Christian and who tolerate the fact that one of their colleagues has been obliged to give to part of his flock a pastor who denies baptismal regeneration; and this bishop, after having vainly protested against this impiety, simply accepted it; that's what we call barbarousness': Veuillot, *Mélanges*, Vol. VI, p. 18.

146   Phillipps's letter to Bloxam, quoted above, referred to *L'Univers*'s approval of his letter to the *Tablet* rebutting its crude criticism of the Tractarians: Purcell, *Phillipps*, Vol. I, p. 203; this was before Veuillot became editor-in-chief. Gondon claimed that *L'Univers* was the only paper to keep continental readers informed of the progress of Catholicism in England, and of the Anglican Church; this, however, was patently untrue, as a review of the contents of *L'Ami de la Religion* demonstrates (see below); but then Gondon was hardly an impartial witness.

147   Apart from his writing on English church affairs, Gondon was probably best known for his pamphlets on Italian politics, including *De l'état des choses à Naples en Italie*.

148   Allen, 'Letters', p. 61; E. Veuillot, *Louis Veuillot*, Vol. 2, p. 429, as cited in Gough, *Paris and Rome*, p. 99.

example, who took Thomas Allies along to Montalembert's Paris reception in July 1848.[149] Gondon's writing on Tractarianism and in particular on the motives of converts to Roman Catholicism is extensive and worthy of a study in itself.[150] Here I shall concentrate on the work which most directly addressed the Oxford Movement, *On the Religious Movement in England, or, The progress of Catholicism and the return of the Anglican Church to Unity* [my translation] (published in Paris in 1844), complementing it with his introduction to an anthology of translations from writings of converts.[151]

On the Religious Movement in England is a substantial work, constructed from Gondon's contributions to *L'Univers*, and based on firsthand acquaintance with the Oxford leaders. Gondon made three visits to England between 1838 and 1844, and in 1842 met Pusey, Newman and others in Oxford.[152] Drawing on Cobbett's *History of the Protestant 'Reformation'* (1824–7), he claimed that the strength of the English constitution derived, not from its Protestantism, but from its origins at the hands of Catholic kings.[153] He devoted seven chapters to the Church of England, identifying three parties – the Evangelicals, the 'political' High Churchmen (who corresponded somewhat to Froude's Zs, the so-called 'High and Dry' school, or the High Church 'Orthodox', in Peter Nockles's terminology), and the Puseyites, or Anglo-Catholics.[154] The latter re-emphasised the Catholic roots of Anglicanism, and rejected state interference in the Church; in this, the sincerity of Pusey, Newman and others could not be doubted.[155] They had no desire to be leaders as such: 'they limit themselves to engendering ['à féconder'] by their genius and their talent the marvellous renaissance of which Oxford was now the heart.'[156] They were not innovators;

149 Allies, *Journal in France*, p. 232.

150 See also Gondon, *Conversion de soixante ministres Anglicans*, and *Notice biographique sur le R. P. Newman.*

151 Gondon, *Mouvement*; idem, *Motifs.*

152 Gondon refers to these meetings, in *Mouvement*, p. viii. The introductory letter he brought with him from Fr. James Jauch, a Catholic chaplain in London, is preserved amongst Newman's papers, and includes an interesting warning to Newman about Gondon, who was 'a good young man of sound catholic principles, but still rather belonging as yet more to this world ... You will wisely measure Your word, because redactors of newspapers take hold of every one fit to create sensation': F. J. McGrath (ed.), *The Letters and Papers of John Henry Newman*, Vol. 9, pp. 101–2, & 115. Christopher Wordsworth met Gondon in Paris in 1844; his *Diary* contains an extensive account of their conversations.

153 Gondon, *Mouvement*, p. 33.

154 Gondon, *Mouvement*, pp. 224–6; see also P. B. Nockles, *The Oxford Movement in Context: Anglican High Churchmanship 1760–1857*, pp. 25–43.

155 Gondon, *Mouvement*, p. 227.

156 Gondon, *Mouvement*, p. 232.

they merely sought to restore doctrines lost to the Anglican Church; 'in a word, the Catholic spirit is being rekindled ['l'esprit catholique se rallume'] gradually within the Anglican Church.'[157] On another occasion, to Thomas Allies in Paris, Gondon could admit the many good things he had heard of other High Churchmen, including the colonial bishops Broughton and Selwyn.[158] Catholics should welcome this renewal, and encourage individual conversions, so that in time the whole Anglican Church might be drawn towards the centre of Catholic unity, Rome.[159]

This sounds not dissimilar to the views of Montalembert and Lacordaire, but whilst Gondon certainly showed a great deal of sympathy for the Tractarians, he conceded very little to their claims of Catholicity.[160] He strongly denied that unity with Rome would be gained more quickly if Roman Catholics in England and Ireland rectified their own abuses – there were none.[161] There was no salvation outside the Roman communion.[162] There was nothing intrinsically Catholic about the Oxford Movement; all hung on its value as a means for leading people to Rome. His understanding of Protestantism savoured strongly of the degenerative view; in England, he said, all possible forms of Protestantism were to be found, and they were all breaking up, piece by piece.[163] He could the hail the Roman Catholic Church as mother of true religious liberty – on liberty he came near to Montalembert, and one can see why Veuillot was a little ambivalent about him – but there was nothing intrinsically valuable about Anglicanism.[164] Moreover, Gondon's cast of mind shared with Veuillot's a predilection for sharply defined contrasts and oppositions. The world was divided simply into rationalists and Catholics; Protestants were in effect a subset of rationalism.[165] Anglicanism had lost its light and life, and so its sons walked in darkness, their spiritual life extinguished.[166] Even when he considered the temperance movement, he could only see that the efforts of the Protestant associations were sterile; only the approach of the Roman Catholic

---

157   Gondon, *Mouvement*, pp.233–4.

158   Allies, *Journal in France*, p. 222.

159   Gondon, *Mouvement*, pp. 235–6.

160   This was reflected in Christopher Wordsworth's response: *Letters to M. Gondon, author of 'Mouvement religieux en Angleterre'*, a strongly-worded rebuttal of Gondon's arguments.

161   Gondon, *Mouvement*, pp. 331–3.

162   Gondon, *Mouvement*, p. 335.

163   Gondon, *Mouvement*, p. xiv.

164   Gondon, *Mouvement*, p. xii.

165   Gondon, *Motifs*, p. ix.

166   Gondon, *Motifs*, p. vii.

agencies, and the influence of Fr Matthews, were fruitful.[167] Thus, Gondon's position overall had some elements of the constructive approach favoured by the Montalembert circle, and yet it also shared much with the polarised view of Veuillot himself.

Gallicanism: *L'Ami de la Religion*

Despite the Gallican loathing of Veuillot, Gallican reactions to the Oxford Movement were much the same as his. Here, there is space only for a brief consideration of what was, by the 1830s, the most influential Gallican paper, *L'Ami de la Religion*. *L'Ami* never had the circulation of *L'Univers*; appearing three times a week, rather than daily, its influence lay in its popularity with the ecclesiastical hierarchy. Founded in 1796 and frequently suppressed under the Directorate and the Empire, by the 1830s it was moderately legitimist.[168] Later it was purchased by Félix Dupanloup, though its editorial policy did not change substantially.[169]

In contrast to *L'Univers*, *L'Ami* was moderate in tone and rather stuffy. It was a perplexing mixture of periodical and newspaper, carrying a handful of long articles along with columns of news. Its coverage was international: ransacking the foreign press for titbits of information, it maintained a consistently high level of interest in religious and political news about France's most powerful neighbours in particular. Almost every issue carried news and articles about England. Naturally news specifically about Roman Catholicism predominated, especially when, from the late 1820s, the paper began to comment on the remarkable efflorescence of Roman Catholicism in Britain. Reports drawing on the *Laity's Directory* and other sources frequently enumerated new churches built, new monasteries opened, and conversions made.[170] But Anglicanism featured too, and with increasing frequency in the late 1830s and early 1840s. In 1841, for example, *L'Ami* carried 17 separate articles on Tractarianism; in 1842, 16; in 1843, no less than 20; often these were substantial articles, including long extracts from translations of Tractarian works.

---

167   Gondon, *Mouvement*, pp. 210–9.

168   Moody, 'French Catholic Press', p. 397. Moody's assertion that, by the 1840s the paper had moved to a 'rigid ultramontanism' makes little sense, in the light of Dupanloup's involvement.

169   May, 'The Falloux Law', p. 84.

170   See, for example, in 1832 alone: 21 February, 28 July, and 20 October.

L'Ami's editorial outlook on Tractarianism differed little from the main lines of the Ultramontanes' view. It shared with other French Catholics abhorrence for the English tyranny in Ireland, and for the missionary work of the Bible societies.[171] Its references to Protestantism were always negative: Protestantism's existence was 'the most striking witness to the infirmity of human reason, which wraps itself up ['qui s'isole'] in its own pride'.[172] Anglicanism was a 'parliamentary religion', and certainly not a sister church to Rome.[173] *L'Ami* could not resist quoting with approval the Abbé Genoude's letters on England, originally published in the *Gazette de France*: 'The English are all mad when they speak of religion. You have just been speaking with a man you have found perfectly reasonable – but you discover he won't even go to Rome; like Luther, he would rather see the devil than the Pope.'[174] Placing the characteristic prejudices about Protestantism alongside suspicion of British colonial policy enabled French Catholics to see Anglicanism as the handmaid of tyranny. Not only in Ireland, but in India, Africa and, back on the doorstep of Europe, Gibraltar were all evidence of the English establishment's oppression of Catholics – the word almost always used for the Gibraltar government, for example, was 'junta'. On the Oxford Movement, the paper's line was not all that different from Gondon and Veuillot (and indeed Gondon almost certainly wrote for it as well as for *L'Univers* from time to time).[175] The movement was to be welcomed as a rejection of Protestantism and for its recovery of elements of Catholic devotion and doctrine, but only because it assisted the movement of converts to Rome. So eager was *L'Ami* to see this goal fulfilled, that it was frankly credulous. Several times in the early 1840s it carried without question wildly exaggerated claims about the numbers of Anglican clergy who were Puseyites – 5,000 on one informed estimate, or half of the total, on another.[176] It quoted and apparently accepted a report from *The Examiner* that even Queen Victoria was tending to Puseyism, and a Puseyite was to be private tutor to the Prince of Wales.[177]

---

171   See, for example, *L'Ami de la Religion*, 'Sur la réforme de l'église anglicane en Irlande', 12 March 1833, and the implied approval of Count Achille de Jouffroy's criticism of the Bible societies, in idem, 22 December 1832.

172   *L'Ami de la Religion*, 8 October 1840.

173   *L'Ami de la Religion*, 'De la reaction qui s'opère en Angleterre, dans le sens catholique', 30 July 1842, and 'Sur le Puseysme (1)', 19 September 1843.

174   *L'Ami de la Religion*, 9 February 1841.

175   An item on the divisions of Anglicanism in 1844, for example, was couched in terms closely matching those of Gondon's *Mouvement*: *L'Ami de la Religion*, 9 March 1844.

176   *L'Ami de la Religion*, 29 July 1843, and 31 October 1843.

177   *L'Ami de la Religion*, 8 October 1842.

L'Ami's naïveté about such things is telling: by the early 1840s, the Catholic press in France was working within a hermeneutic of imminent national conversion. Stories about Tractarianism, however flimsy, were instantly seized on as proof of what Catholics thought was about to happen in England. But over the course of the 'twelve years', the coverage of the paper varied considerably. A narrative of the Oxford Movement from *L'Ami* alone would look oddly misshapen. Apart from some passing references, the first article directly on Tractarianism did not appear until June 1835, when the paper covered the Abbé Jager's literary exchange with Benjamin Harrison and Newman.[178] There were several articles in the early and mid-1830s on the activity of the Catholic convert, George [Ignatius] Spencer.[179] Not until 1838, however, was there a substantial assessment of the English movement. This was an article that drew heavily on Wiseman and which for the first time placed Pusey before the paper's readership.[180] For the next five years, it was his name that dominated *L'Ami*'s coverage, and the terms 'Puséyste' and 'Puséysme' became the most common designations in French journalism to describe the movement. Much of the conventional narrative of the movement was scarcely touched on, if noticed at all, by *L'Ami*, until 1843. The controversies over Hampden's chair, Froude's *Remains*, the Jerusalem bishopric, even Tract 90, were largely ignored as they occurred. General descriptions of the movement's progress abounded, however. But all that changed in the early 1840s. The swelling number and scale of articles on Tractarianism marked a new phase in *L'Ami*'s coverage. A substantial article on Newman's retraction in April 1843 began a shift in emphasis away from Pusey.[181] Thereafter, the paper's coverage tracked the conventional narrative of the movement much more closely: Newman's resignation from St Mary's, Littlemore, Pusey's sermon and his inhibition from preaching, Ward's *Ideal* – these and other events were extensively reported and discussed, leading up to Newman's conversion. The paper's reporting of that event captured perfectly its impression of the movement's value and limitations: the news would rejoice all truly Catholic hearts; Newman's reception had taken place in the chapel attached to the monastery he had built; some years ago Pusey had begun to lose the best part of his influence; his most enlightened disciples, and those most faithful to the principles he had adopted, had chosen another master, and now that master is one of our brothers; this, of all the graces God

---

178   *L'Ami de la Religion*, 27 June 1835.

179   Cf. *L'Ami de la Religion*, 4 June 1836.

180   *L'Ami de la Religion*, 'Rapport sur l'état actuel du protestantisme en Angleterre (1)', 13 January 1838.

181   *L'Ami de la Religion*, 'Sur M. Newman, l'un des chefs des Puséystes', 4 April 1843.

has given recently to English Catholics, is the most illustrious and the one likely to lead to the most abundant fruit.[182]

Conclusion

The readership of *L'Ami*, *L'Univers*, and other French Catholic papers and journals were gradually tutored to read the Oxford Movement, not so much for what it told them about the Church of England and the religious condition of England, as about the post-Napoleonic resurgence of the Roman Catholic Church, and above all the imminent conversion of England. Their expectations were unrealistically high. But it is easy to understand why. It was hardly surprising that French Catholics tended to read Tractarianism in terms of their own preoccupations and struggles.[183] The revolutions of 1830 and 1848 were in different ways catastrophes for the French Church and book-ended a period of deep tension between Church and State. The growing internal struggle of ecclesiastical Gallicans and Ultramontanes over education and the Roman rite ran through a period that otherwise looked like one of remarkable revival for the Church. French Catholics identified readily with Roman Catholics in England – whom they almost never differentiated into Irish and English constituents – when they saw them growing remarkably in numbers and struggling with the political and social challenges thrown at them by the State Church. Furthermore, apart from the practice of shadowing the English press, information about the Oxford Movement mostly came from a small group of people, some of whom were hardly likely to furnish impartial evidence. There were some Anglicans who did not convert, and were never likely to, who travelled in France and clearly acted as a source of information for the French – men such as Christopher Wordsworth, whose published *Diary in France*, as the previous chapter showed, itemised extensive conversations with a variety of French Catholics, including Gondon, in August 1844. But French commentators also did treat as trustworthy a number of converts who were not reliable sources at all.[184] The ensuing distortion of perspective gradually unravelled

---

182 *L'Ami de la Religion*, 18 October 1845.

183 They were, of course, not alone in this: the Italian Catholic patriot and writer, Manzoni, is said to have 'envisaged a nationwide conversion of the English as an event which by force of example might lead to a renaissance of Catholicism in Italy': J. Lindon, 'Alessandro Manzoni and the Oxford Movement: His Politics and Conversion in a New English Source', p. 298.

184 One was Francis Diedrich Wackerbath, who, while still an Anglican, confided to a French contact that if O'Connell had secured the appointment of a Puseyite bishop during the

after Newman's conversion, though not instantly: it was sustained by the restoration of the hierarchy in 1850, but the hostile popular reaction to that in England almost certainly disillusioned many of those who had swallowed the idea that large swathes of the Church of England were only waiting for the opportune moment to cross over to the Church of Rome.

This discussion of French Catholic reactions to the Oxford Movement opens up some glimpses into deeper issues in Catholic ecclesiology and ecumenism. The clue is there in the terminology. Stephen Sykes observed that the word 'Anglicanism' referred at first only to the ecclesiological system advocated by Tractarianism.[185] Yet French writers used the term in the 1830s in the modern sense, for the whole Anglican 'system', as it was a handy enough derivation from 'l'église Anglicane' and summarised a system of belief and practice distinct from Catholicism. But that raised a difficulty of description when dealing with Anglican claims to Catholicity, and especially with the terms 'Anglo-Catholic' and 'separated brethren'. Gondon, for example, did use the term 'Anglo-Catholic', but explained to his readers that he did not intend any concession to Anglican claims of Catholicity in doing so: in fact, he said, linking the words Anglican and Catholic 'implied a contradiction', but it was useful because it 'expressed perfectly the abnormal position ['la position anormale'] of the Church of England'.[186] Yet Gondon's view was evidently not quite the same as that of Lacordaire, for example, and the later Montalembert, for whom there did seem to be a sense in which it was not absolutely a contradiction to see some Catholic identity in the Church of England. What about the phrase 'separated brethren', however? It was a fairly common expression in Roman Catholic discourse, and again did not necessarily concede anything to Protestant claims; it could be used in a heavily ironic way, with the emphasis on the 'separated'. More commonly, French observers used the phrase 'misled' or 'misguided', or even 'lost' brethren – 'frères égarés'.[187] Yet increasingly the term 'frères separés' also came into use to describe the Tractarians, particularly in the hands of people like Spencer and Phillipps, when their letters and articles were translated into French.[188]

Whig ministry, that bishop could have gone to Rome and secured the reunification of the Anglican and Catholic churches, and the Queen would not have been troubled about renouncing the Royal Supremacy: *L'Ami*, 5 October 1841.

185   S. W. Sykes, *Unashamed Anglicanism*, p. xiv.

186   Gondon, *Mouvement*, p. vii.

187   For example, *L'Ami*, 1 June 1844.

188   Cf. *L'Ami de la Religion*, 12 August 1841, citing a letter from George Spencer to *L'Univers*.

That terminological shift differentiated two different reactions to Tractarianism. One was strategic appreciation: from Gallican circles to extreme Ultramontanes, mostly French Catholics watched the Oxford Movement with growing excitement, as they contemplated the overthrow of a State Protestant Church and the reconversion of England. The Church of England could not in any sense be called Catholic; but the so-called Catholic movement within it could well bring, not just thousands of individuals, but a whole nation back to the See of Peter. To the extent that it was likely to do so, the movement could be welcomed, and the hand of friendship extended to its followers. Here, then, the Oxford Movement both affirmed religious revival in England, and at the same time masked the strength of the wider High Church movement of which it was a part. But among a small, if influential, minority a more subtle appreciation of the merits of the movement gained ground. Montalembert, Lacordaire and their circle shared a more positive evaluation both of the English constitutional settlement and of Anglicanism as a religious tradition. Implicitly, they recognised a certain substantial, if attenuated, Catholicity within it. Their brothers were 'separated', but not thereby 'lost' altogether. Is it altogether fanciful to see a distant connection between their appreciation of their 'separated brethren' and the ecclesiology of 'separated brethren' in *Unitatis Redintegratio*?

By the 1850s, French Catholics' interest in the Oxford Movement was certainly on the wane. The restoration of the Roman Catholic hierarchy in England and Wales, and in time the growing prominence of English Catholic leaders such as Henry Manning, probably drew attention away from the Catholicizing elements of the Church of England. The excitement of the early 1840s evaporated rapidly, once the wave of mid-century conversions had subsided. Nevertheless, interest could flare up again from time to time. Pusey's *Eirenicon* of 1865, which suggested that Anglicans and Roman Catholics could be reconciled by a patient exposition of their teaching, but which also (counter-productively) concentrated attention on what Pusey took to be the doctrinal innovations or popular distortions of Roman Catholicism, was certainly one stimulus to further commentary.[189] The Dominican Marcelin Chéry, for example, in an *Appeal to the Russian Church and to the English Church* (1866), reiterated many of the points made by French Catholics against the Anglicans twenty or thirty years before. He wrote effusively of Pusey – 'the honour of England' and one of the most loyal and beautiful of souls – but he recognised that he was but the head of a 'small faction' of the Anglican clergy.[190] Overall, he claimed, amongst 'our cous-

---

189   E. B. Pusey, *The Church of England a portion of Christ's one holy Catholic Church, and a means of restoring visible unity: An eirenicon, in a letter to the author of 'The Christian Year'.*

190   Chéry, *Appel*, pp. 6 & 61.

ins' across the Channel, Christianity was dying, faith being extinguished, and Anglicanism passing into pure rationalism.[191] The 'Isle of the Saints' had been lost over three hundred years ago; the churches in England were 'decomposing' into numerous sects, or passing over to Rome.[192] This was all very familiar rhetoric, and Chéry referred to other French Dominicans, including Jacques Marie-Louis Monsabré and Marie-Dominique Souaillard, who had argued along the same lines.[193] A few years later, the Belgian Jean-Baptiste Abbeloos, in response to the controversy over Gladstone's disestablishment of the Church of Ireland, surveyed the state of the Church of England for the *Revue Catholique*.[194] Many of the same points were made: national and sectarian religion was dying and 'decomposing'; the Protestant churches were being killed by private judgement and individualism; Anglicanism had preserved some Catholic forms on the surface, but lacked the power to 'animate the body'; Anglican wealth concealed moral instability ('moralement désétabli'); only Catholicism could survive.[195] It is ironic that these views remained so powerful, at a time when the Church of England was undergoing what some observers then, and historians since, have called a time of institutional revival – when more churches were being built than ever before, when enormous resources were being poured into charitable and educational work, and when, though scarcely overtaking it, nevertheless Anglican churchgoing, at least in England itself, was keeping pace with population growth. But, as in a reflection in a mirror, the same could have been said of Anglican views of French Catholicism in the first half of the century. Doctrinal difference was a forceful mould for shaping mutual perceptions of church life on both sides of the Channel.

---

191   Chéry, *Appel*, p. 73.

192   Chéry, *Appel*, pp. 76 & 101.

193   Chéry, *Appel*, p. vi.

194   Subsequently published separately as Abbeloos, *La Crise du Protestantisme en Angleterre*.

195   Abbeloos, *La Crise du Protestantisme en Angleterre*, pp. 1, 2, 4 (quotation), & 5.

PART 3

Theological Identity and Difference

∵

CHAPTER 6

Preaching the Oxford Movement

Introduction

In earlier chapters I sought to demonstrate the integration of the High Church revival with other aspects of British social and religious history, and also its situation in a broader religious context on the Continent of Europe. In a book which seeks to open up new perspectives and arguments, in the very nature of the case the approach could not be other than piecemeal, taking particular aspects or themes as a way of exploring unfamiliar territory. In this third part, the analysis is extended into more familiar ways of reading theological history, looking at a number of neglected themes which confirm the broad-ranging nature of the revival. In this chapter the focus is on the specific subject of Tractarian preaching, though its conclusions could be extended to cover much High Church preaching more generally.

From its very beginning, the Oxford Movement courted controversy. If it was a movement seeking to renew the theology, devotional life and liturgical practice of the Church of England, at the same time, like the Evangelical Revival, it also raised time and again points of critical challenge against the Church. Its style seemed to many contemporaries polemical, harsh, sectarian, clerical and exclusive. In its early years, its most notable publications were the *Tracts for the Times*, which asserted distinct points of controversy, and lent to the movement one of its names, 'Tractarianism'. Other names, however, carried much the same overtone of *odium clericum*, especially 'Puseyite' and 'Newmanite'.[1] It propagated its views through house journals, above all the *British Critic*.[2] It produced treatises of original but controversial divinity, which spared no one in their readiness to criticize the theological positions of opponents. Beginning with a suspicion of the Whig government's 1833 proposals to reform the Irish Church widely shared amongst High Churchmen, its trajectory has commonly been seen as one of ever deepening isolation, until the catastrophic year of 1845, when Newman finally converted to Rome.

---

1 P. B. Nockles, *The Oxford Movement in Context: Anglican High Churchmanship 1760–1857*, pp. 33–43.

2 There has as yet been no comprehensive study of the Tractarians' use of this journal, but there is a telling analysis of Newman's editorship in S. A. Skinner, *Tractarians and the 'Condition of England': The Social and Political Thought of the Oxford Movement*, pp. 33–64.

© KONINKLIJKE BRILL NV, LEIDEN, 2016 | DOI 10.1163/9789004326804_007

Yet it is often forgotten that the Oxford Movement was not so much written as *preached*. It was not merely or even predominantly an academic movement, but one which rapidly sought to embed itself in the parishes and to promote a reform of the Church's teaching and pastoral practice. With a few significant exceptions, most of its leading figures were at one time or another parish priests whose staple means of expression was the weekly sermon. Richard Hurrell Froude died young and Edward Pusey remained an Oxford professor for most of his life, but throughout the 'twelve years' (1833–1845) characterised by Dean Church, Keble was Vicar of a country parish, and Newman himself both incumbent of St Mary's, Oxford, and also priest-in-charge of the hamlet of Littlemore.[3] Almost all of the other Tractarians occupied pastoral positions for long stretches of their ministry. For this, the principal vehicle was naturally the sermon. According to Francis Paget (1806–1882), preaching formed, with catechizing, 'the most efficient of all machinery for the purposes of Christian instruction'.[4] And yet even contemporaries frequently overlooked this fact. The conventional impression of the Oxford Movement's attitude to preaching was summed up by Dean Goulburn's biographer, who claimed that its reaction against the 'sermon-loving proclivities of the old Evangelical school' unduly depreciated sermons altogether 'as having robbed liturgical observances of much of their proper honour'.[5] Isaac Williams (1802–1865), in Tract 87, was often assumed to have played down the significance of preaching ('it may be necessary in a weak and languishing state'), but as we shall see, in practice Williams was far from derogating it.[6]

Such a perception of Tractarianism as motivated by a critical reaction against the dominant religious trends of the age (and therefore, depending on whether one was an opponent or a sympathizer, as a distortion or a recovery of the essential spirit of the Church of England) has coloured its reception amongst scholars. There is no need to repeat here the summary of that reception I offered in the first chapter. Suffice it to say that the difficulties in the historiography I described there are naturally reflected in the scope of this chapter. Whether or not there was ever something so characteristic and distinctive as a 'Tractarian sermon', there was certainly a distinct set of pre-

---

3   R. W. Church, *The Oxford Movement: Twelve Years 1833–1845.*

4   F. E. Paget, *The Parish and the Priest: Colloquies on the Pastoral Care, and Parochial Institutions of a Country Village*, p. 77.

5   B. Compton, *Edward Meyrick Goulburn, D. D., D. C. L., Dean of Norwich. A Memoir*, p. 31.

6   I. Williams, Tract 87, 'On Reserve in Communicating Religious Knowledge (continued)', in *Tracts for the Times*, Vol. 5, p. 408; Williams' words are quoted by J. H. Blunt as an example of an extreme, 'party' objection to preaching, but Blunt misattributes the quotation to Tract 89: J. H. Blunt, *Directorium Pastorale*, p. 99.

occupations commonly shared by those who followed the Oxford Movement. The preaching of Tractarian clergy is therefore an important lens through which to view the Movement's identity. The richness of Tractarian parochial sermons in particular has perhaps still to be exploited to the full by historians. Almost every volume yields myriad insights into the characteristic theological and devotional themes of the Oxford Movement. This chapter will thus not confine itself to considering the sermons of the handful of leaders, but will also encompass the preaching of some of the more minor Tractarian clergy, and its time-frame is broadly the middle quarters of the century.

Influences

As part of its professed revival of a historic, Catholic Anglicanism, the Oxford Movement naturally leant much upon the teaching and practice of the Early Church, as well as upon that of seventeenth-century churchmen. Patristic influences included the sermons of St Ambrose, St Augustine and St Chrysostom. These were not usually present in explicit reference or quotation, but rather in the doctrinal content of Tractarian sermons, and perhaps also in the very conception the Oxford Movement sponsored of a Church whose liturgy, devotional practice and sacramental discipline were of a piece with its teaching. The Patristic model, exemplified above all in St Augustine, of a priest or bishop teaching doctrine through pastoral engagement, and so adjusting their mode of preaching to suit a congregation, but never in the process compromising Church teaching, was echoed in the importance Tractarians attached to the sermon. Pusey even edited for the *Library of the Fathers* a collection of St Augustine's sermons on the New Testament.[7] The much-vaunted principle of 'reserve', which the Tractarians traced back to Patristic sources, was in evidence here. As Isaac Williams put it in Tract 80, 'On Reserve in Communicating Religious Knowledge', 'the important practical conclusion' was that, if God at once concealed himself from human beings so that they should not speak lightly of him or obscure their faith in him by vanity and self-preoccupation, 'all the means of grace faithfully cherished will lead us, as it were, step by step, into all these treasures, inexhaustible in their nature'; in other words, proper teaching adjusted religious truth to the capabilities of those to whom it was addressed.[8] A similar conception was present in Tractarian emphases on

---

7   E. B. Pusey (ed.), *Sermons on Selected Lessons of the New Testament, by S. Augustine*.

8   I. Williams, Tract 80, 'On Reserve in Communicating Religious Knowledge', in *Tracts for the Times*, Vol. 4, p. 82.

'adaptation'. William Gresley (1801–1876), parish priest near Lichfield in the 1830s, who wrote an early Tractarian handbook on preaching, placed great importance on this principle: 'it is essential to the force ... of a sermon ... that [it] should be specially adapted to the character, capacity, circumstances, the habits, prejudices, mode of thinking, and degree of knowledge of the hearers.'[9] Whilst regretting excessive Evangelical emphasis on the preaching of the Word, to the neglect of the Sacrament and public prayer, the Tractarians highly valued the sermon, and sought to exploit it as a means of teaching 'Church Principles' along lines they considered to have been laid down in the Early Church.

Yet the Tractarians were heirs of Evangelicalism, nonetheless – many of them had passed through an Evangelical phase – and their conviction of the importance of preaching cannot but have been influenced by Evangelical models. Particular attention was paid to J. B. Sumner's *Apostolical Preaching* – it was specifically commended by Gresley – and many would have been influenced too by John Wesley's sermons, and Charles Simeon's sermon outlines.[10] The readiness of Tractarian clergy to criticize Evangelicals for their emotionalism, and for their alleged elevation of 'private judgement' in interpreting Scripture above the authority of the Church, masks this debt. But grudging admiration was often present alongside condemnation. Francis Paget feared the degradation of the clergy if they aped 'the profane ribaldry of a Spurgeon', and yet he acknowledged that Spurgeon too would serve the Church of England well if he roused the younger clergy to learn the art of public speaking.[11] He distrusted arguments drawn from the state of religious feelings: 'Religion does not consist in excitement, but in action.'[12] But, as Yngve Brilioth acknowledged, the experiential elements of Evangelicalism were central to the religious sensibility of Tractarianism.[13] Gresley criticised 'modern Evangelicalism' for its lack of a spirit of Christian unity, but he shared many of its convictions, such as its emphases on the inward spirit ('It is the presence of Christian motive which sanctifies every faculty'), on conversion as well as regeneration as the proper

9   W. Gresley, *Ecclesiastes Anglicanus: Being a Treatise on the Art of Preaching, as a adapted to a Church of England Congregation*, p. 5.

10   J. B. Sumner, *Apostolical Preaching considered in an Examination of St Paul's Epistles*, referenced in Gresley, *Ecclesiastes Anglicanus*, p. 13; cf. J. Wesley, *Standard Sermons: Consisting of Forty-Four Discourses*, & C. S. Simeon, *Horae Homilecticae or, Discourses (principally in the form of skeletons) now first digested into one continued series and forming a commentary upon every book of the Old and New Testament.*

11   Paget, *The Parish and the Priest*, pp. 82–3.

12   F. E. Paget, *Sermons on Duties of Daily Life*, p. 56.

13   Y. Brilioth, *The Anglican Revival: Studies in the Oxford Movement*, pp. 42–3.

task of the Church, and on the heart as the true seat of Christian character.[14] Pusey too stressed the heartfelt assent necessary to faith in asking that characteristic Evangelical question, 'Who or what is a Christian?', and in replying 'He who believes in Christ, who loves Christ, hopes in Him, and obeys Him; and ... with all his mind and soul and strength, owning no other Lord, but only Christ', for whoever 'wilfully falls short of this, in faith, or love, or obedience, is *not* a Christian, is hanging on only to Christianity'.[15] Evangelical hearers of Tractarian sermons were likely, then, to detect a common mood, and a common sensibility.

Conventional High Church (or 'Orthodox') preaching was another influence. Gresley, like Newman in the *Apologia*, professed a deep obligation to the teaching of Charles Lloyd at Oxford, who urged his students to write their own sermons, rather than rely on the printed sermons of others (a common practice in the early nineteenth century).[16] Yet time and again the Tractarians appeared to denigrate the preaching of the 'Orthodox'. Pusey claimed that, for all its earnestness, respectability, and loyalty in faith, the High Church school, though antagonistic to Calvinism, was 'sadly wanting in depth and warmth'.[17] According to Liddon, in the early 1830s 'Orthodox' sermons of the day 'were wanting in that affectionate devotion to our Divine Lord which was inculcated by the earlier Evangelicals', so that Walter Kerr Hamilton, though brought up 'High and Dry' and later regarded as a 'Tractarian' Bishop of Salisbury, found in Evangelical teaching 'a warmth which was then sought in vain elsewhere'.[18] Francis Paget evidently had the 'Orthodox High Church' in mind when he contrasted the weaknesses of those who had made 'outward forms, and their trust in Church privileges, a substitute for inward piety' with Evangelicals whose 'boast of Bible knowledge' and 'self-confident reliance on their own private judgment' had led them away from 'Scripture-truth, and Scripture holiness'.[19] Yet others brought up in the High Church tradition, including Keble and Froude, even as they criticised the formalism of the 'High and Dry', at the same time proclaimed their loyalty to the ordinances of the Church of England and their trust in devotional habit. 'It is too plain', as Keble asserted in 1833, 'that

14   W. Gresley, *The Necessity of Zeal and Moderation: The Present Circumstances of the Church, enforced and illustrated in five sermons preached before the University of Oxford*, pp. iv, 21 (quotation) & 100; idem, *Practical Sermons*, p. 86.

15   E. B. Pusey, *Lenten Sermons, preached chiefly to young men at the Universities*, p. 55.

16   Gresley, *Ecclesiastes Anglicanus*, pp. 1–2.

17   E. B. Pusey, *Sermons during the Season from Advent to Whitsuntide*, p. vii.

18   H. P. Liddon, *Walter Kerr Hamilton, Bishop of Salisbury: A Sketch, reprinted, with additions and corrections, from 'The Guardian'*, p. 11.

19   Paget, *Duties of Daily Life*, pp. 237–8.

those who pray least regularly have least devotion when they pray.'[20] One of his earliest sermons, long predating the Oxford Movement, claimed in a manner quite characteristic of the Keble of twenty years later, that the doctrine of sanctification implied there could never be an excess of virtue or holiness.[21]

A third possible area of influence is harder to assess, and that is the homiletic practice of Roman Catholicism overseas. As we have seen in an earlier chapter, when they travelled, Tractarians often took advantage of the opportunity to hear sermons in Catholic churches. In all his trips abroad, Henry Manning, for example, frequently attended sermons and, according to his biographer, kept copious notes on them.[22] So did Henry Liddon, rather later, noting for example in detail the subject and main heads of argument of a sermon he heard at St Sulpice in June 1864.[23] But Liddon always took pains to attend services and summarize the preaching in his diary when he travelled. Thomas Allies, visiting Paris with Charles Marriott in July 1845, noted the Abbé D'Alzon's preaching without notes and his animated action (quite in contrast to 'our quiet manner'), and reflected that his people would find preaching from a prepared text quite insupportable.[24] What struck Tractarians, then, was a quite different preaching style from that common in England – extempore preaching (which of course was common enough with Evangelical preachers) married to a dramatic manner as a means for communicating Catholic theology, an approach sometimes characterised as 'Sulpician', from the great French seminary at St Sulpice in Paris. Summing up his experiences of Roman Catholic preachers on the Continent, Allies noted again that they usually preached without a text, that their sermons were much more rhetorical than English ones, and appealed to the feelings 'rather than the understanding', but that, notwithstanding this, English clergy should try this approach.[25] Paget was another who affirmed himself not averse to extempore preaching, since 'an address delivered without book seems ... to come more freshly from the heart than a written discourse'.[26] Keble, Pusey noted, late in his ministry made a practice of preaching extempore.[27] Significantly the more traditional-minded

20 J. Keble, *Sermons, Occasional and Parochial*, p. 308.
21 Keble, *Sermons, Occasional and Parochial*, p. 8.
22 H. S. Purcell, *Life of Cardinal Manning, Archbishop of Westminster,* Vol. I, p. 346.
23 Liddon, Diary for 1864, entry dated 12 June written on blank pages near the beginning of the Lett's printed journal he used; archives of Pusey House, Oxford.
24 Allies, *Journal in France*, p. 61.
25 Allies, *Journal in France*, pp. 344–5.
26 Paget, *The Parish and the Priest*, p. 81.
27 E. B. Pusey, 'Advertisement', to J. Keble, *Sermons for the Christian Year: Sermons for Lent to Passiontide*, p. v.

Christopher Wordsworth, perhaps more an 'Orthodox' High Churchman than strictly a Tractarian, was critical of the continental practice of extempore preaching, which, he feared, could expose the preacher to 'the utterance of language in the pulpit, in the heat of a discourse, which he may afterwards regret in his calmer moments'.[28] However, against this has to be set the example of the moderate High Churchman, J. H. Blunt, who regarded extempore preaching, properly done, as the best practice on all occasions.[29]

Preaching Doctrine

The sheer notoriety of some of the best-known examples has perhaps obscured the fact that the vast majority of surviving Tractarian sermons were aimed at ordinary parish congregations, and did not so much seek to assert long-lost doctrinal truths or to comment pointedly on particular questions of ecclesiastical governance and identity, as simply to build up the Christian character of their hearers. Though it is not a distinction which can be sustained in every case, nevertheless this suggests that a survey of Tractarian preaching has to reckon with two rather different categories of sermon. One was aimed at propagating for a wider audience the doctrinal principles central to the Oxford Movement. The other – to be covered in the next section – might be called 'pastoral' or devotional sermons, no less theological in content in that they built on, and articulated, a coherent set of doctrinal principles, but nevertheless produced in the main for ordinary parish congregations or for particular pastoral contexts. The former would naturally include Keble's 'Assize Sermon' which Newman hailed later as the start of the Oxford Movement, a number of Newman's own sermons, and particularly some of those subsequently included in his *Oxford University Sermons* (1843) such as that on 'The Theory of Developments in Religious Doctrine'.[30] It could also include the most controversial of all, Pusey's 1843 sermon *The Holy Eucharist a Comfort to the Penitent* which, through its advocacy of the doctrine of the Real Presence, led to his condemnation by a committee appointed by the Oxford Heads of Houses and a two-year suspension from preaching, although the sermon itself, as Liddon pointed out, was practical and not intentionally controversial, having as its aim 'not the formal statement of disputed or forgotten truth, but the

---

28   C. Wordsworth, *Notes at Paris, particularly on the State and Prospects of Religion*, p. 55.
29   Blunt, *Directorium Pastorale*, p. 152.
30   J. H. Newman, *Fifteen Sermons preached before the University of Oxford* (Oxford, 1843).

encouragement of a certain class of souls'.[31] But these are only the best-known of what is after all a quite extensive literature of ecclesiastical controversy. Other examples might include, for example, William Gresley's sermons at St Paul's, Brighton, on *The Present State of the Controversy with Rome* (1855), or William Bennett's two sermons on the Gorham judgement, or again Bennett's 1842 course of sermons on the errors of Romanism.[32] Whether these sermons can be said to have contributed to development of the art of preaching itself is doubtful, since in almost every case reportage and publication for a wider readership was perhaps the primary goal from the very beginning. But they certainly reflected the Tractarian concern not only to reassert a set of doctrinal principles they were convinced had been neglected by the Church of England, but also to promote and effect the reform of the Church along Tractarian lines. The Tractarians were in two minds about religious controversy, since they both deplored it and – frankly – indulged in it with gusto. Paget could even claim that 'controversy is a sign of life' and yet at the same time admit that those who loved controversy for its own sake were 'hateful characters'.[33] Like Evangelicals, a sense of urgency runs through these sermons on disputed Church matters, as if the time was propitious for asserting Church principles because the Church was in dire straits without them. Dwelling on the trials of the Church, Paget, for example, could suggest that 'Churchmen' should 'keep close to the Catholic Faith, maintaining *that* whole and undefiled'.[34] For Pusey, the proper response to the time of trial which the Church was undergoing was not to trust to any human project of chastisement, but to 'commit ourselves into the Hands of God, to chasten, correct, wound, heal, sift, cleanse, as He wills'.[35] Nor did many of them flinch from the divisive implications. Amongst the fiercest was the apparently mild-mannered Keble, for whom love of Christ required honouring friends and 'discountenancing and shrinking from His enemies'.[36]

The sermon was thus a valued weapon in ecclesiastical combat, and as such was exploited to the full by the Tractarians. Their leaders' prominence in Oxford gave them access to an influential audience, assisted by sympathetic

---

31   Cf. H. P. Liddon, *Life of Edward Bouverie Pusey*, Vol.II, p. 308. The whole of the chapter from which this quotation comes deals with the sermon and its condemnation: idem, pp. 306–69.

32   W. Gresley, *The Present State of the Controversy with Rome: Three Sermons preached in S. Paul's Church, Brighton*; W. J. E. Bennett, *The Church, the Crown, and the State: Their junction or their separation*; idem, *Distinctive Errors of Romanism: A series of lecture-sermons*.

33   Paget, *Duties of Daily Life*, p. 111.

34   Paget, *Duties of Daily Life*, p. 204.

35   Pusey, *Sermons from Advent to Whitsuntide*, p. 95.

36   Keble, *Sermons, Occasional and Parochial*, p. 319.

publishers such as Rivington's and Parker's.[37] In these sermons, a particular theme could be expounded at greater length than would have been appropriate for a village context, with a supporting arsenal of authors and quotations.

The redoubtable Pusey is perhaps the example that springs most readily to mind. His bibliography includes many examples of sermons which were preached for a wider audience than that of their immediate congregation.[38] Especially in the years after Newman's secession to Rome in 1845, and after the furore caused by his own 1843 sermon on the eucharist, the suspicion which followed Pusey around meant that he attracted significant publicity for the causes he espoused. Not only the 1843 sermon, but others such as *This is my Body*, preached before the University in 1871, thus were almost guaranteed to attract a wide audience, if not always a sympathetic one.[39] Pusey himself disavowed any controversial intention ('he endeavoured, with deep conscientiousness, to avoid the bitterness of controversy'), but his position as Professor of Hebrew and Canon of Christ Church in the University of Oxford inevitably gave him a platform from which to address the Church as a whole, especially after Newman's conversion, when his name came to the fore as leader of those Tractarians who remained in the Church of England.[40] The very fact that many of his sermons were addressed to congregations of undergraduates and Fellows, whether at Christ Church or at St Mary's, the University church, blurs the distinction between 'controversial' and pastoral sermons: this was Pusey's pastoral context, after all. But the educated nature of the congregations surely gave full rein to Pusey's inclination to set forth complex and weighty argument and crushing evidential support. As published, *The Holy Eucharist a Comfort to the Penitent* was almost 8,000 words long, and would have taken almost an hour and a half to deliver. But this was not unusual for Pusey. His two sermons on 'The Church the Converter of the Heathen', preached for the SPG at Melcombe Regis in 1838 in the morning and afternoon of one day, amounted to almost 20,000 words, if the published texts are anything to go by.[41] Each one must have taken almost two hours to preach. The course of sermons he envisaged at St Saviour's, Leeds on its consecration in 1845 included no less than ten preached in a single week by various preachers, and although these

---

37   On Rivington's, see B. L. Fitzpatrick, 'The Rivington family', *ODNB*; also R. Riddell, 'John Henry Parker', *ODNB*.

38   Cf. the bibliography published in Liddon, *Pusey*, Vol. IV, pp. 395–446.

39   E. B. Pusey, *This is my Body: A Sermon preached before the University at St Mary's*.

40   Church, *The Oxford Movement*, p. 222.

41   E. B. Pusey, *The Church the Converter of the Heathen: Two Sermons preached in conformity with the Queen's Letter on behalf of the Society for the Propagation of the Gospel*. Many thousands of words more were added by way of notes and appendices.

were ostensibly aimed, not so much at clergy, but at ordinary churchgoers, they indicated the high and demanding standard of attention Pusey demanded of his hearers; his own contribution of three in that week amounted to almost 15,000 words.[42]

Even the apparently self-effacing Keble, however, was capable of delivering sermons sharply angled towards a particular point of controversy, or with a wider audience in mind. The best-known of these, of course, was his sermon on 'National Apostasy', preached at St Mary's in Oxford to mark the start of the county assizes, and called by one biographer 'perhaps the most famous sermon in the history of English ecclesiastical writing'.[43] The conventional connection that historians have made is to the Whig government's proposals to reduce the number of Irish bishoprics – in this again they have largely followed Richard Church's lead – and undoubtedly this was one of Keble's targets, but it is not explicitly mentioned in the sermon, which dwells more generally on the danger of the State abandoning the Church.[44] Given the date of the sermon – 14 July – Keble surely cannot but have borne in mind the (for him) terrible example of Revolutionary France and its persecution of the Church. Parts read like a warning to the Church of England that it could face the same danger if it did not defend its spiritual integrity and authority, if necessary by separation from the State, fearing that it could 'happen ... that the Apostolical Church should be forsaken, degraded, nay trampled on and despoiled by the State and people of England'.[45] This was deliberately provocative language. The sermon was rushed into print, advertisements for it appearing within three weeks in various national newspapers such as the *Standard*, and the *Morning Post*.[46] Whatever the merits of Newman's judgement about the significance of the sermon, Keble certainly intended it to make a mark, and aimed at a national readership.[47] But far from shrinking altogether from national controversy

---

42   E. B. Pusey (ed.), *A Course of Sermons on Solemn Subjects chiefly bearing on Repentance and Amendment of Life, preached at St Saviour's, Leeds, during the week of its Consecration.*

43   J. R. Griffin, *John Keble: Saint of Anglicanism*, p. 82. In fact, such was the controversy following Newman's conversion to Roman Catholicism in October 1845 that only two of Pusey's guest preachers turned up in person, and apart from reading out seven other sermons by invited preachers, Pusey had to preach the remaining ten planned sermons himself; see W. N. Yates, *The Oxford Movement and Parish Life: St Saviour's, Leeds, 1839–1929*, p. 5.

44   Church, *The Oxford Movement*, p. 68. Newman, in the *Apologia*, despite hailing the sermon as the start of the Oxford Movement, in fact said next to nothing about its content: ibid., p. 36.

45   J. Keble, *National Apostasy Considered*, p. 21.

46   Cf. The *Standard*, 2 August 1833; *Morning Post*, 5 August 1833.

47   Keble's biographers have cast little light either on the formulation or on the reception of the sermon, however: cf. J. T. Coleridge, *A Memoir of the Rev. John Keble*, pp. 209–11;

thereafter, Keble from time to time repeated this foray into it. Another example was his 1836 sermon, *Primitive Tradition recognised in Holy Scripture*. As published, this ran to over 12,000 words; since it was preached at a visitation, its congregation would have consisted mostly of clergy, and its content was proportionately more demanding than his parish sermons, with, for example, a detailed exposition of the Greek word παρακαταθηκη, or 'trust'.[48]

A Pastoral Vision

For all the attention that these controversial sermons have attracted, they are a misleading guide to the general tenor of Tractarian preaching. For that, we must turn instead to sermons aimed largely at ordinary congregations. The dominant concern of Tractarian preaching was essentially pastoral, expressing Christian doctrine so as to continue the work of conversion, building up the believer in Christian faith and life. This was articulated time and again in the reasons Tractarian clergy gave for publishing their sermons, but perhaps nowhere more definitively than in the 'Advertisement' that Isaac Williams drafted for the series of *Plain Sermons* that he collected and published from 1839.[49] His aim in persuading Newman, Keble and others to contribute was to steady the Movement, by showing that its principles were not set forth 'as themes for disputation', but as 'truths of immediate and essential importance, bearing more or less directly on our every day behaviour, means of continual resource and consolation in life, and of calm and sure hope in death'.[50] Williams feared that the Movement was being distracted by those who had adopted Church principles superficially, and who were all the more 'noisy and voluble' as a result without feeling these principles to be deeply founded 'in divine and eternal truth'.[51] Even these sermons, plain and practical as they were, therefore were not without a wider programmatic intent. They demonstrated a characteristically Tractarian determination to transform the life and worship of the Church of England in the parishes as much as in the universities and bishop's palaces.

---

48   J. Keble, *Primitive Tradition recognised in the Holy Scriptures: A Sermon, preached in the Cathedral Church of Winchester*, pp. 14–16.

49   Williams attests that though he wrote the advertisement, it was 'so altered … by [Henry] Jeffreys and others, as to have been quite spoilt': I. Williams, *Autobiography*, p. 97. The *Plain Sermons* were eventually to stretch to a ten-volume series, published from 1839 to 1848.

50   'Advertisement', to *Plain Sermons by Contributors to the 'Tracts for the Times'*, Vol. I, p. 2.

51   *Plain Sermons*, p. 1.

This required, or rather dictated, an approach to preaching which was eminently practical and adaptive, recognizing the difficulties of particular pastoral situations and calibrating the teaching of Church principles accordingly. William Gresley's manual on preaching took its cue in this respect from Aristotle's *Rhetoric*, adumbrating 'general rules of the art of persuasion' which could be applied in many different contexts, since they were founded on human nature.[52] He emphasised the preacher's need to adapt his discourse to 'the peculiarities of those whom he addresses'; the 'varying circumstances' of readers were the justification for the continuous publication of new volumes of sermons.[53] The Tractarian system of divinity, for all its importance as a reassertion of Church principles, needed 'reasoning and analogy' to work out its implications in parishes.[54] For Gresley, the parish system was as much of divine institution as was episcopacy.[55] Along with it went the value of pastoral visiting, something which Paget, for example, held to be crucial for a willingness for a people to listen to the preaching of their priest, for where 'the Parson sees little of his people, and knows little of their spiritual condition, he has no right to complain if he finds the post which he has deserted occupied by another'.[56] Edward Monro (1815–1866) was another whose vision of Church principles was wholly infused with a conviction of the integrated and interdependent character of all pastoral work. Preaching, along with teaching, was a vital means by which the people of a parish could be induced to take more seriously the sacramental provision through which their personal salvation and their pursuit of holiness could be assured: there could be 'no appreciation of sacraments or Church discipline until the people became alive to the need of personal religion'.[57]

Such a vision of the place of preaching in parish life was reflected in the welter of pastoral sermons published by Tractarian clergy. If the *Plain Sermons* compiled by Isaac Williams could be seen as a model, nevertheless almost all the Tractarians published volumes of 'plain', or 'practical', or 'parochial' sermons. The plainness was reflected in simplicity of language, economy of construction, and relative brevity. In commending the sermons of his friend Robert Suckling, Williams appealed to their 'eminently plain, and practical,

---

52   Gresley, *Ecclesiastes Anglicanus*, p. 12.

53   Gresley, *Practical Sermons*, pp. v-vi.

54   Gresley, *Zeal and Moderation*, pp. vi-vii.

55   Gresley, *Zeal and Moderation*, p. 72.

56   Paget, *The Parish and the Priest*, p. 89.

57   E. Monro, *Parochial Work*, p. 89. On Monro, see P. Davie, *Raising up a Faithful People*, pp. 9–12.

and full of life' character, which made them 'well suited for parochial use and edification'.[58] Pusey commended Keble's 'simple, earnest style', which aimed, following the pattern of St Frances de Sales, to send the hearer home saying, 'God be merciful to me, a sinner'.[59] But even many of Pusey's own sermons attempted to emulate this ideal. Plainness or simplicity did not only mean short sentences and simple style, however: it also denoted a certain directness, a readiness to go straight to the point without getting distracted by speculative indulgence and rhetorical flight. As Gresley commented, there was no place for 'cutting sarcasm, nor fierce invective, nor cool and dignified irony', for all those 'spirit-stirring' devices should be avoided, in order to confine oneself to 'the plain words of soberness and truth'.[60] In line with this commendation, most Tractarian pastoral sermons were not littered with references to the Fathers, but were intensely and almost exclusively scriptural, indeed almost severely so. Perhaps the most famous and influential of all these sermons, Newman's *Parochial and Plain Sermons*, were an outstanding example of this biblical concentration. In this, Tractarian preaching owed much to Evangelical expository homiletics. But, true to Tractarian instincts, the reading of Scripture assumed by preachers was one steered by the Church. As was hardly surprising from those who vaunted 'Church principles', Tractarian sermons took the calendar and liturgy as the framework within which Scripture would be interpreted, as shown again and again in sermon series to be read in concert with the believer's progress through the Church year. Keble's eleven-volume series *Sermons for the Christian Year* is a case in point.[61] But Pusey also published different volumes of sermons for Advent to Whitsuntide, and later for Lent, Isaac Williams a volume tied specifically to the Book of Common Prayer Sunday lections, and J. M Neale sermons for the Church's year, to name but a few examples.[62]

The frequency with which Tractarian preachers insisted that sermons should be *practical* as well as 'plain' showed a concern to achieve a definite change in the religious life of the believer. The temptations that surrounded the Christian could be kept at bay by the proper cultivation of regular and

---

58   I. Williams (ed.), *Sermons, Plain and Practical, by the late Rev. R. A. Suckling*, p. iii.

59   Pusey, 'Advertisement', to Keble, *Sermons for Lent to Passiontide*, p. vii.

60   Gresley, *Ecclesiastes Anglicanus*, p. 25.

61   The entire series was published posthumously as *Sermons for the Christian Year* in eleven volumes, but it consisted of individual volumes including many sermons published separately during Keble's lifetime.

62   E. B. Pusey, *Sermons from Advent to Whitsuntide*, and *Lenten Sermons*; I. Williams, *A Series of Sermons on the Epistle and Gospel for each Sunday in the Year*; J. M. Neale, *Sermons for the Church Year*.

frequent habits of prayer and contemplation. For Pusey, nothing but 'a continued active habit of directing our actions to God, such as results from offering them to God, morning by morning, for the day, and then renewing that direction often through the day, by some brief prayer ... will rescue some fragments of our acts from the unclean contact of those spiritual harpies, our besetting faults'.[63] Gresley commended daily reading of the Bible, 'our familiar companion and friend'.[64] His list of practices for cultivating the Christian life included 'self-examination, self-discipline, regard to conscience, frequent prayer, devout communion, holy observance, and habitual watchfulness': all these things were necessary to cultivate 'that heavenly principle of faith which is the essence of the life of God in the heart of man'.[65] For Pusey, again, prayer, alms and fasting formed 'one holy band, for which our Blessed Lord gives rules together, and which draw up the soul to Him'.[66] Keble even emphasised the importance of punctuality in prayer.[67] For him, nothing less than Church principles, drawn above all from the Prayer Book, could save Church people, as otherwise 'we shall become heretics, or worse, before we are aware'.[68] He was also a strong advocate of fasts as 'special helps' to bring the believer nearer to Christ, for by following Christ's own example in the wilderness even the poor might learn not to be tempted by their sense of need.[69] The vision of the devotional life which emerges from consideration of these sermons is one in which the earnestness of Evangelical 'heart' religion has been translated into a no less earnest and attentive series of daily practices, guided by reflection on the Church's year, and designed to deepen the believer's understanding of, and dependence on, the Christian gospel.

But a precondition for a deepening of the spiritual life was a corresponding willingness to let go of many of the pleasures of contemporary life. Tractarian sermons accordingly displayed a startling austerity. Paget called his contemporaries 'a luxuriant, pampered, self-indulgent people, who have altogether got out of the way of bodily mortification and self-denial'.[70] Pusey warned his Oxford hearers that 'the world is the enemy of the Gospel, in faith as well as in life.'[71] Keble even lamented that the 'whole Christian world is fallen and

---

63   Pusey, *Lenten Sermons*, p. 100.

64   Gresley, *Practical Sermons*, p. 8.

65   Gresley, *Practical Sermons*, p. 56.

66   Pusey, *Sermons from Advent to Whitsuntide*, p. 189.

67   Keble, *Sermons, Occasional and Parochial*, p. 307.

68   Keble, *Sermons, Occasional and Parochial*, p. 367.

69   Keble, *Sermons for Lent to Passiontide*, p. 48–9.

70   Paget, *Duties of Daily Life*, p. 291.

71   Pusey, *Lenten Sermons*, p. 56.

decayed' and that God 'has more or less withdrawn His grace and presence from us'.[72] Tractarian sermons, no less than those of Evangelical clergy, were intended to sharpen up the believer's sense of urgency and dread, to the point at which a renewed commitment in faith would be produced. Again, it was Keble who urged his congregation to 'pray to God, day after day, that we may fear Him more and more', for if they did not seek continually to improve, they were, in practice, 'sure to go back'.[73] And so the parochial sermons of Tractarian clergy mostly give the lie to the charge, sometimes made by Evangelicals, that they neglected or downplayed the significance of sin.[74] Charles Marriott, for example, warned the congregation of St Saviour's, Leeds, against precisely that danger: 'A little sin may be made great by indulging such unholy weakness.'[75]

Devotional practice was not commended without an eye on wider doctrinal implications, however. Though the Tractarians' emphasis on a disciplined spiritual life, public prayer, and the sacraments could lead to Evangelical accusations of an undue emphasis on 'works', it was always situated within a broader theological perspective which modified Protestant teaching on justification through faith alone as traditionally understood, and attempted to emphasize the place of sanctification in the life of the believer.[76] This was most famously expressed in Newman's controversial *Lectures on Justification* (1838), which Brilioth called 'the most important attempt to find the theological expression of [the Oxford Movement's] piety'.[77] Here, Newman argued for a *via media* between what he took to be the Lutheran interpretation of justification by faith, and the 'Roman' position of justification by obedience, and asserted, on Patristic (especially Augustinian) grounds in effect a doctrine of justification through baptismal regeneration. Justification, Newman said, 'comes *through* the Sacraments; is received *by* faith; *consists* in God's inward presence, and *lives* in obedience'.[78] Newman may have laid especial emphasis on obedience, but in a more general sense sanctification constituted the core doctrinal principle of the Tractarian system of devotion, and it was reflected and advocated forcefully in Tractarian sermons. It was depicted time and again as a neces-

---

72   Keble, *Sermons for Lent to Passiontide*, p. 89.

73   Keble, *Sermons for Lent to Passiontide*, p. 131.

74   See, for example, Daniel Wilson's claim that the Tractarians lacked a deep sense of sin, lowliness, and prostration of soul, as cited in Pereiro, *'Ethos' and the Oxford Movement*, p. 65, referring to D. Wilson, *Revival of Spiritual Religion the Only Effectual Remedy for the Dangers which now Threaten the Church of England* (1851).

75   C. Marriott, in Pusey (ed.), *A Course of Sermons on Solemn Subjects*, p. 27.

76   Cf. Nockles, *The Oxford Movement in Context*, p. 262–9.

77   Brilioth, *Anglican Revival*, p. 282.

78   J. H. Newman, *Lectures on Justification*, pp. 316–7.

sary complement to justification. For Gresley, for example, 'the one would be incomplete without the other'.[79] There was a fine line between emphasizing the importance of sanctification, with appropriate devotional and ascetic practice, and claiming 'merit' for works rather than faith, and Tractarians were well aware of this. Francis Paget, for example, strove to maintain with equal strength the double proposition that salvation came from Christ alone, and that human beings would be judged for their deeds.[80]

Evangelical suspicion of Tractarian devotional practice was validated, in part at least, by the prominence given to the sacraments, and to sacramentalism more broadly, in Tractarian preaching. Salvation, as the Oxford leaders iterated, was mediated to the believer through the sacramental life of the Church. There was, then, an intrinsic link between justification and the Church, which was not merely a gathered body of believers, but the means whereby Christ's presence on earth was made real, not only in a general sense but also in the very particular sense of his presence in and through each of his followers. Pusey emphasised the unity of the gift of grace: the features or aspects of truth might appear to be manifold, but the one gift underlying them all was the incarnate Christ himself.[81] Christ himself was sanctification to us, and the sacraments were the 'channels whereby, through Union with Him, He conveys these Exceeding Gifts to us'.[82] Tractarian sacramentalism was thus disposed to a practical or devotional mysticism, in which the presence of the eternal life of God, itself in a sense beyond all human capacity for definition or comprehension, was made real and tangible for believers through the material means of the sacraments. Accordingly, the frequency with which Tractarian preachers spoke about the sacraments reflected not just – as some might have expected – a preoccupation with the authority of the ministry, but also, and perhaps more significantly, a concern for salvation. Tractarian sacramentalism was exactly coterminous with Tractarian soteriology.

This was particularly in evidence in the very great prominence given to baptism in Tractarian preaching. The salvation of the individual, in the Tractarian understanding, was achieved not merely through a conversion of the heart and soul of the believer, but through the medium of the Church. Here the Tractarians could draw, so they thought, on significant support from the baptismal liturgy of the Prayer Book, in which the regeneration of the child followed directly from his or her baptism: '[s]eeing now, dearly beloved brethren, that

79   Gresley, *Practical Sermons*, p. 32.
80   Paget, *Duties of Daily Life*, pp. 4–11.
81   Pusey, *Sermons from Advent to Whitsuntide*, p. 219.
82   Pusey, *Sermons from Advent to Whitsuntide*, p. 220.

this child is regenerate, and grafted into the body of Christ's Church'.[83] It was a matter of grave importance that the child (or baptised adult) subsequently lived up to their baptismal promises. An austere theology of baptismal regeneration thus ran through Tractarian sermons. The most notorious expression of this point of view was Pusey's three *Tracts for the Times* on baptism, which propounded such a severe understanding of post-baptismal sin that they caused F. D. Maurice to break off his association with the Tractarians.[84] But Paget, for example, was equally fierce, asserting that, since in Baptism human beings received 'the gift of an in-dwelling grace to enable [them] to serve and please God', they were 'without excuse' if they forgot him.[85] Baptism was especially prominent in Isaac Williams' sermons: it signified 'the unspeakable gift of the Holy Spirit imparted to you', and yet, as heaven opened at Jesus's baptism, so in ours we become heirs of the heavenly country, so that we then 'have nothing at all to do here but to fit and prepare ourselves for it'.[86] Keble was another for whom post-baptismal sin was a matter of the utmost gravity. He compared the behaviour of those who flouted their baptismal commitments to the nine lepers who failed to give thanks for their healing, for baptism, as a 'thorough spiritual cleansing', was the equivalent of physical healing.[87]

Whilst there is too little space here to give a full account of the sacramental system encountered in Tractarian sermons, it is important to note the essential unity and coherence of the attention given to the place of sacraments in the life of the Church, following on from this conception of baptism. As we have seen, Tractarian preaching – like High Church preaching generally – strongly emphasised the importance of frequent reception of communion as a vital means of deepening and sustaining the believer's faith. Again, the seriousness with which Tractarians viewed post-baptismal sin merely served to highlight the importance of regular confession, and the sacramental nature of penance and absolution by a priest even though the Thirty-Nine Articles ruled out treating penance as a sacrament in the same sense as baptism and the eucharist. Gresley, like many Tractarians, used the exhortations in the service of Holy Communion to argue that the Prayer Book in fact commended private confession; this was different from the compulsory, periodical confession required of Roman Catholics.[88] Pusey's advocacy of private ('auricular') confession is

---

83   Cf. D. M. Thompson, *Baptism, Church and Society in Modern Britain*, pp. 67–91.

84   F. Maurice, *Life of F. D. Maurice*, Vol. I, p. 186.

85   Paget, *Duties of Daily Life*, p. 38.

86   I. Williams, *Plain Sermons on the Catechism*, pp. 38 & 46.

87   Keble, *Sermons, Occasional and Parochial*, p. 351.

88   Gresley, *Practical Sermons*, pp. 103–8.

well-known, and was deeply controversial, but Keble was no less vehement in his profession of the need for all Christians to make their confession regularly, and if need be in private. Even children had need of penitence, he said, and he too cited the Prayer Book in justification of the practice of regular confession.[89]

In addition to the sacraments, and corresponding to the importance of confession, Tractarian preachers also directed the attention of their hearers inwards, to a constant, prayerful examination of interior motives and states of mind. This was also a corollary of the renewed emphasis on sanctification. If justification brought with it union with God, and the presence of the indwelling Spirit, so that the life of the earnest believer would be marked by the development of an obedient heart, and of a life of devotion and discipline in accordance with the teaching and ordinances of the Church, it followed that the believer ought to be concerned above all with purity of motive, with humility and an eye ever alert to temptation. Tractarian sermons displayed a constant awareness of the condition of danger in which the soul might find itself. 'Listen we then to every whisper of our conscience', Pusey urged his hearers, for '[it] is Jesus Who, within, is speaking to us by His Spirit'; and again, 'We may know His Presence by the deep, breathless stirrings of our hearts.'[90] Constant attention to the inward state of one's soul was needed. Keble especially emphasised the importance of 'consideration' in prayer.[91] As Pusey commented, Keble's Lenten sermons were marked by a sense of sin as the 'malice of an unseen enemy', and aimed to 'unveil his hearers' hearts to themselves', so that they might turn to God in penitence and with renewed zeal.[92] Again, as Pusey said, 'Dare, my brother, to look into thyself; dare to see what that is in you, which still holds thee back from God'.[93] This attention to the cultivation of one's spiritual state, supported by the Tractarian conception of the priest as confessor, promoted the practice of what later came to be called spiritual direction, by which a priest would seek to give regular guidance to those who came to them for advice. Both Pusey and Keble were to have collections of their letters of spiritual advice published posthumously.[94]

Anchoring Tractarian conceptions of interior contemplation and the spiritual life, and preventing their dissolution into subjectivism, was the strong emphasis preachers placed on the authority of the Church. As Keble argued,

89   Keble, *Sermons for Lent to Passiontide*, pp. 63 & 66.
90   Pusey, *Sermons from Advent to Whitsuntide*, p. 285.
91   Keble, *Sermons, Occasional and Parochial*, p. 309.
92   Pusey, 'Advertisement', to Keble, *Sermons for Lent to Passiontide*, p. vi.
93   Pusey, *Lenten Sermons*, p. 87.
94   J. Keble, *Letters of Spiritual Guidance and Counsel*; E. B. Pusey, *Spiritual Letters*.

the Church, with its clergy and sacramental provision, was the safeguard appointed by God 'from the beginning' to defend us against new and false doctrine.[95] The whole course of the world's history, he claimed, with regard to the Church 'is a scheme ordered by Almighty God to bring lost souls back into saving communion with Him'.[96] Without the authority of the Church to direct and shape Christian discipleship, society itself was at risk. Gresley illustrated perfectly the conviction that the 'private judgment' of Scripture was the root of religious disunity and social disharmony, asserting that 'the want of sound views on church authority' underlay the present ills of the nation.[97] God had provided both Scripture and the Church, together, as safeguards against error.[98] Keble, again, taught his village congregation the importance of the apostolic authority of the Church: the presence of Christ's clergy, spiritually commissioned by their bishops, was not merely an external blessing, but an inward one too, 'a true token to faithful men of our exceeding nearness to Christ'.[99]

Newman

The sermons of John Henry Newman stand in a class of their own, despite sharing many of the characteristics described above. Newman's notoriety – in Protestant circles – after 1845 seems not to have dented the popularity of his published sermons, especially the *Parochial and Plain Sermons*, which continued to appear in considerable numbers throughout his lifetime. Probably they attracted a new, predominantly Roman Catholic readership after his conversion, though almost certainly they continued to attract Anglican and other Protestant readers too. Ian Ker has called them 'one of the great classics of Christian spirituality'.[100] But he is not alone in his estimation of them. According to Yngve Brilioth, they represented a 'literary master-work belonging to the best productions of English prose', and were perhaps the best single introduction to Tractarian piety.[101] It is surely true that, great English stylist as Newman was, the readers of these sermons would have found in them not only a characteristically Tractarian scheme of doctrine and devotion, but also a

---

95   Keble, *Sermons, Occasional and Parochial*, p. 328.
96   Keble, *Sermons, Occasional and Parochial*, p. 334.
97   Gresley, *Zeal and Moderation*, p. 9.
98   Gresley, *Practical Sermons*, p. 7.
99   J. Keble, *Sermons for the Christian Year*, p. 191.
100   Ker, *Newman*, p. 90.
101   Brilioth, *The Anglican Revival*, p. 212.

remarkably penetrating analysis of elements of religious experience. Time after time, Newman combined psychological realism with a demanding standard of devotion, as when he asserted that 'to pray attentively is a habit', for 'No one begins with having his heart thoroughly in [prayers]; but by trying, he is enabled to attend more and more, and at length, after many trials and a long schooling of himself, to fix his mind steadily on them.'[102] Or again, preaching on the 'difficulty of realizing sacred privileges', he could suggest that 'Every act of obedience has a tendency to strengthen our convictions about heaven ... This is a use, too, of the observance of sacred seasons; they wean us from this world, they impress upon us the reality of the world which we see not.'[103] Many of the characteristic features of Newman's preaching are present here: the relative simplicity of language, the emphasis on obedience, the pervasive sense of human frailty, the boldness of assertion, the sacramental or mystical awareness of the dependence of the world of sense on that of spiritual reality. When placed in the context of Newman's quite explicit endorsement of the whole range of Tractarian doctrinal and devotional teaching, the popularity and penetration of these sermons in High Church circles perhaps comes as no surprise. But that depended also on an exceptional clarity of theological vision, which Ker argues was secured above all by Newman's conception of the indwelling Spirit, a doctrinal but also spiritual and pastoral *locus* which cohered his very practical understanding of the spiritual life along with his sacramentalism.[104] 'The whole system of the Church, its discipline and ritual', he claimed, 'are all in their origin the spontaneous and exuberant fruit of the real principle of spiritual religion in the hearts of its members. The invisible Church has developed itself into the Church visible, and its outward rites and forms are nourished and animated by the living power which dwells within it. Thus every part of it is real, down to the minutest details.'[105] Even though so much of Newman's homiletic strategy appeared to be to stress the significance of obedience and discipline, from the human side, the persuasive power of his preaching surely lay in his articulation of human dependence on God, and so on the transfiguration of human religious activity by the love of God, for as he said memorably, 'Grace ever outstrips prayer.'[106]

But Newman was also perfectly comfortable with controversial preaching of a kind which was not demonstrably 'plain' or 'parochial'. His *University Sermons,*

---

102   J. H. Newman, *Parochial and Plain Sermons*, Vol. I, p. 142.

103   Newman, *Parochial and Plain Sermons*, Vol. VI, p. 100.

104   I. Ker, *John Henry Newman. A Biography*, p. 91.

105   Newman, *Parochial and Plain Sermons*, Vol. V, p. 41.

106   Newman, *Parochial and Plain Sermons*, Vol. V, p. 351.

published with numbered paragraphs, though addressing in some respects similar congregations (university ones) to those of his parochial sermons (for his parish was, after all, that of the University church, St Mary's), nevertheless showed a quite different conception of what preaching was for. He used them to assert or rediscover teaching which had been neglected in the Church of England, or to propose an idea which might seem needlessly speculative for a pastoral context, but which merited exploration. Sermons of this type were amongst his most famous, including those which helped to lay the foundations for his later work, such as 'The Nature of Faith in relation to Reason', preached in 1839 and anticipating aspects of *The Grammar of Assent* (1870), and 'The Theory of Developments in Religious Doctrine', preached in 1843 as Newman was already beginning work on what would become his *Essay on the Development of Christian Doctrine* (1845), the work which facilitated his conversion to Rome. The style of these sermons is clear and has moments of poetry, but in general it is detached and analytical, much more akin to that of a lecture. Just a brief example may suffice. Preaching on 'Implicit and Explicit Reason' in 1840, he could say of the 'science' of interpretation that 'in considering the imperfections and defects incident to such scientific exercises, we must carefully exempt from our remarks all instances of them which have been vouchsafed to us from above, and therefore have a divine sanction; and that such instances do exist, is the most direct and satisfactory answer to any doubts which religious persons may entertain, of the lawfulness of employing science in the province of Faith.'[107] This is the formal register of the treatise or the lecture-hall. It is – even in comparison with Pusey and Keble – still relatively uncluttered, and marked with many of those epigrammatic moments which also clinch the style of the parochial sermons, and yet it is unafraid of careful distinctions and philosophical vocabulary. The sermon, in Newman's hands, was an effective, sharp foray into theological controversy.

There can be no question about the lasting impact of Newman's preaching. Brilioth, shadowing Wilfrid Ward, notes how a significant number of undergraduates were seduced by it, and references testimony from R. W. Church, always an admirer, and J. A. Froude, an admirer turned sceptic as to its power.[108] But many others have done the same. Perhaps the most famous testimony was that of Matthew Arnold who, as an undergraduate at Balliol in the early 1840s, heard Newman at St Mary's:

---

107   J. H. Newman, *University Sermons*, p. 265.
108   Brilioth, *The Anglican Revival*, p. 212.

Who could resist the charm of that spiritual apparition, gliding in the dim afternoon light through the aisles of St. Mary's, rising into the pulpit, and then, in the most entrancing of voices, breaking the silence with words and thoughts which were a religious music, – subtle, sweet, mournful? ... I seem to hear him still, saying: 'After the fever of life, after wearinesses and sicknesses, fightings and despondings, languor and fretfulness, struggling and succeeding; after all the changes and chances of this troubled, unhealthy state, – at length comes death, at length the white throne of God, at length the beatific vision'.[109]

But in the end it was not the sermons as heard, but as *read* that influenced subsequent generations of High Churchmen, and read almost certainly through the lens of the post-1864 view of Newman, when his controversy with Kingsley and his *Apologia* transformed his popular reputation from that of suspicion to one of growing appreciation.

Postscript: Liddon

If Newman's sermons were to prove the enduring literary monument of Tractarian homiletics, as a preacher the Oxford Movement's greatest heir was Henry Parry Liddon. Liddon was born in 1829, the year that Peter Nockles claims as the real beginning of the Oxford Movement, and he was not an undergraduate until after Newman's conversion. Yet he entirely imbibed the Movement's theological and spiritual ideals, and in a life centred on Oxford and St Paul's, London, placed them at the very centre of his ministry.

There is more than an echo of Liddon's own estimate of the value of the sermon in his description of bishop Hamilton's preaching, which became 'ever more fervent than before, and ... was attended with larger results in the increased devotion of his people and in the conversion of sinners to earnest and living Christianity'.[110] The importance of adequate teaching and preaching was underlined in Liddon's approval of the Italian Catholic Rosmini's analysis of the lack of sympathy between clergy and people, the 'Wound of the Left Hand of the Crucified', according to Rosmini, which was due above all to 'the want of adequate Christian teaching'.[111] We have already seen Liddon's intense interest in the preaching he heard whenever he travelled abroad.

---

109 M. Arnold, 'Emerson', in *Discourses in America*, in vol. 4 of idem, *Works*, p. 350.
110 Liddon, *Walter Kerr Hamilton*, p. 14.
111 H. P. Liddon (ed.), *A. Rosmini, Of the Five Wounds of the Holy Church*, p. xviii.

It is in Liddon's *Clerical Life and Work*, a collection of sermons and essays delivered over 30 years from 1856, that we see probably the most coherent, rounded interpretation of the place of preaching in the Tractarian conception of ministry. It is not a systematic description of clerical tasks, but it contains many references to the task of preaching, and above all helps to situate Liddon's conception of preaching in the context of his view of the clergyman's spiritual vocation. His chapter on 'The Priest in his inner life', for example, closely linked the saying of the daily offices of Morning and Evening Prayer to the practice of preaching, since the saying of the offices – along with the whole life of the clergyman – would reflect the pattern of personal devotion; conversely, for Liddon extempore preaching divorced from the recitation of the office would be disastrous.[112] Likewise, the daily, pastoral round of parish life inevitably would help to prepare a priest for preaching.[113] A preacher had to stand 'inside' the spiritual life: his sermons would be of a piece with his praying and his whole mode of life.[114] Preaching was thus an integral aspect of what Liddon called the 'moral value of a mission from Christ', for so enormous and responsible was the task, that it could only be undertaken on the basis of a belief in the reality of the Divine call and mission.[115] The aim of preaching was to assist in the work of conversion and sanctification; Liddon's models included St Augustine, St Francis Xavier and, perhaps more surprisingly, Henry Martyn.[116]

All this was surely reflected in the seriousness with which Liddon himself took the responsibility for preaching. Like his great mentor, Pusey, at times Liddon's sermons were immense. One on 'Fatalism and the Living God', preached at an ordination in Salisbury Cathedral in 1866, was almost 12,000 words long in its printed form, for example, though the published version was likely to have been longer than that actually delivered during the service itself, since Liddon's practice seems to have been to preach from fairly extensive notes.[117] It was common for him to preach for an hour at St Paul's. The crowds he drew were such that the doors were opened fifteen minutes earlier than usual when he was in residence, though even then it was often difficult to hear him – despite the strength of his voice – unless one was standing under or around the central dome.[118]

112   H. P. Liddon, *Clerical Life and Work: A Collection of Sermons*, pp. 18–19.
113   Liddon, *Clerical Life and Work*, p. 43.
114   Liddon, *Clerical Life and Work*, p. 129.
115   Liddon, *Clerical Life and Work*, p. 218.
116   Liddon, *Clerical Life and Work*, pp. 99–100 & 117.
117   Liddon, *Clerical Life and Work*, pp. 172–206; Johnston, *Liddon*, pp. 53–4.
118   G. L. Prestige, *St Paul's in its Glory: A Candid History of the Cathedral 1831–1911*, p. 101.

Edward Benson (1829–1896), the future archbishop, heard Liddon preach at St Paul's in 1876, and testified not just to his technical skills, but to the moral force that his preaching exemplified and which seemed to proceed from an almost painful sense of the dispossession of the self:

> I have been hearing Liddon at St. Paul's. Very beautiful and very eloquent – yet the art part of it does not seem so unattainable. But he unites many charms. His beautiful look and penetrating voice are powerful over one – and then his reasoning is very persuasive ... But all his physical and intellectual structure is quite swallowed up in spiritual earnestness, and he is different to other preachers in that one feels that his preaching is itself a self-sacrifice to him – not a vanity nor a gain; I do not mean that one feels others' preaching to be these, but with him one is conscious that it is the opposite. He does not look as if he were in pain, yet you can't help thinking of it.[119]

Liddon can stand as a thread of connection from the Oxford Movement down to the late Victorian Church, and on into the twentieth century. He died in 1890, revered for the quality of his preaching. Although by then he was increasingly associated in the popular mind with tenacious resistance to the critical concessions of liberal Catholicism, his coherence of spiritual, pastoral and doctrinal vision remained influential. It was Liddon above all who helped to ensure that the legacy of the Oxford Movement was not to be defined by suspicion of the preached Word, but by a commitment to effective teaching as well as sacramental practice.

---

119   A. C. Benson, *Edward White Benson*, pp. 152–3.

CHAPTER 7

Ecclesiology and Contested Identities: The Parting of the Ways

Although it formed a distinct movement within Anglicanism, as we saw in earlier chapters, the High Church revival nevertheless crossed many borders and interacted in complicated ways with other streams of Anglican thought and life. Pietro Corsi once described the Church of England in the early nineteenth century as 'a federation of parishes and dioceses'.[1] This implies complicated internal contrasts and relationships. Yet the tendency of some scholars of Anglicanism has been to emphasize idiosyncrasy in High Churchmanship at the cost of overlap, counter-distinction and internal differentiation. In this and the following chapter, whilst following a more conventional methodology – concentrating particularly on the thought of leading theologians and church leaders – I aim to explore some of the 'borders' of High Churchmanship in the nineteenth century, both internal and external, demonstrating their fluidity and porousness.

High Churchmen professed pride in their fidelity to the unchanging deposit of Church doctrine and tradition, and yet High Church opinion mutated constantly in the course of the century, responding to changing external, institutional pressures, to intellectual challenges from within Christian theology as well as from outside it, and to shifts within the movement itself. In earlier chapters, attention was paid to ritual transformation, to the emergence of new forms of popular devotion, and to the attempt to embed Anglo-Catholic concepts of the eucharistic community in local church life. The High Churchmanship of the 1830s looked very different from that of the 1860s or the 1890s: the diffusion of 'advanced' ritual, disagreements over ritual style, the growing professional and institutional force of the movement through the new theological colleges, and through the new representative systems, theological disagreements over historical and biblical criticism, all these and other features in one way or another changed the way that High Churchmen saw themselves and their church. In this chapter I examine the source, and the difficulties, of the fusion of two quite different kinds of argument that were common in High Church circles, which came together later in the century in the growing interest in 'sacramental socialism', in the ecclesiology of the 'liberal Catholic' circle

---

1   P. Corsi, *Science and Religion: Baden Powell and the Anglican debate 1800–1860*, p. 19.

© KONINKLIJKE BRILL NV, LEIDEN, 2016 | DOI 10.1163/9789004326804_008

associated with Charles Gore and others, and which persisted well into the twentieth century in the thought of Michael Ramsey.

Both F. D. Maurice and J. H. Newman were profoundly influential and yet controversial figures for late nineteenth-century High Churchmanship, the one because he repudiated the theology of Tractarianism yet defended in essence and outline a High Church ecclesiology, and the other because he converted to Roman Catholicism after leaving a body of theology which continued to shape Anglo-Catholic arguments even as he claimed to have demonstrated their practical inefficacy. Both were assumed to have conceived of an ecumenical Anglicanism that was finely poised as a *via media* or 'bridge' between other Christian traditions, as well as providing, through Maurice, a concept of Christian socialism that proved to be compatible with Anglo-Catholicism.

It is not necessarily easy to place F. D. Maurice and J. H. Newman side by side in comparative perspective, though it has been tried from time to time.[2] Newman's star has risen inexorably through the late twentieth and early twenty-first centuries. Maurice, by contrast, is unpublished and almost unread today. Despite some grudging mutual respect, neither devoted very much attention to the other, once Maurice had decisively rejected Tractarian theology in the late 1830s. It would be trivial merely to list points of comparison and contrast. Nor would it be valuable or perhaps convincing to set out to inflate Maurice's reputation at the expense of Newman's. But placing these two theologians – especially taking Newman in his Anglican phase – in putative dialogue on particular points of controversy is illuminating, not least because it helps to lay bare the presuppositions and shape of two quite different ecclesiological models in Anglicanism, both of which have continued to exert some influence on Anglican thinking on the Church right up to the present, and yet which have often been confused with one another. This is especially so when their ecclesiological theories are examined and compared in the light of the idea of Anglicanism as a *via media*, or middle way between extremes, a theory which proved tenacious in Anglican (and especially High Anglican) thinking in the 'ecumenical' era.

Exploration of both authors' defence of Anglicanism via a mediating relation to two fixed poles, Roman Catholicism and Protestantism, forms the centrepiece of this chapter. First, it is necessary to lay down some obvious differences and similarities in their use and treatment of history, which supply the context for their views of Anglicanism. After the central section, comparing aspects of

---

2   See, for example, B. C. Butler, *The Idea of the Church;* J. S. Coulson, *Newman and the Common Tradition;* and S. Prickett, *Romanticism and Religion:The Tradition of Coleridge and Wordsworth in the Victorian Church.*

their ecclesiological theories of Anglicanism, some further comments reasserting their strikingly different evaluations of the history of the Christian Church will be necessary before moving to a conclusion.

History and Ecclesiology

History was central to the ecclesiological theories of both men, a fact not necessarily evident from some critical views of them as anti- or unhistorical. Newman has been accused of excessive credulity about the lives of the saints.[3] Admittedly, this was offset by a sensitivity to the critical limitations of historical epistemology, which could lead, via the doctrine of probability, to the apparently opposite charge of rationalism.[4] Maurice's quasi-Platonic metaphysics led to a different accusation, namely that he subordinated historical events to a quite independent philosophical *schema*. Newman himself said as much, writing to Walter Hook in 1835 (*before* Maurice fell out with the Tractarians):

> He is a Coleridgian [sic] and a Platonist, I believe – and so though not far from a Catholic, when contrasted with Rationalists, yet some way off too. He is of the Cambridge School – and from the little I have seen of those men, they seem to me never satisfied to take things as they find them, but … to believe sacred doctrines, not because they have received them, but because they can prove them from philosophy.[5]

Maurice has been pursued by the charge ever since. Torben Christensen, for example, in one of the few systematic analyses of Maurice's theology, suggested that, for Maurice, 'the truth of an idea establishes the historical validity of its outward embodiment'.[6]

Both theologians in fact professed to take history seriously. They were certainly interested in it as a formal object of study.[7] But it also constituted a

---

3   Geoffrey Faber made great play of Newman's 'puerile love of supernatural and miraculous stories', quoting Mark Pattison: G. Faber, *Oxford Apostles*, p. 442.

4   The Congregationalist theologian Andrew Fairbairn asserted this, in *The Place of Christ in Modern Theology*, p. 204; Maurice made a similar point about the 'Catholic school', in *The Kingdom of Christ*, Vol. II, p. 407.

5   T. Gornall (ed.), *Letters and Diaries of John Henry Newman*, Vol. 5, p. 180.

6   T. Christensen, *The Divine Order: A Study of F. D. Maurice's Theology*, p. 187.

7   See, for example, J. H. Newman, *Arians of the Fourth Century*, and F. D. Maurice, *Lectures on the Ecclesiastical History of the First and Second Centuries*.

central feature of their respective theological methods. On Newman's side, briefly, one can mention his concern to trace the development of the doctrinal tradition of Catholic Christianity, his conviction of the authority of tradition, and his appeal to the experience of the Church in history: '[Christianity] has from the first had an objective existence, and has thrown itself upon the great concourse of men. Its home is in the world, and to know what it is, we must seek it in the world, and hear the world's witness of it.'[8] For Maurice, history itself could be providential, as the unfolding in time of the divine order of the universe, and so as a record of God's revelation of himself: 'The Acts of God are the true commentaries on his Word: For he is with us to interpret both.'[9] Historical arguments were at the very centre of both theologians' assessments of the Church of England.

There is perhaps nothing remarkable in two Victorian theologians sharing a common conviction of the theological significance of history.[10] Yet neither claimed to be a historian. Both read history teleologically, with the history of the Christian Church defined by its origins as normative. For Newman, with his attention to developing tradition, the history of the Church itself indicated cumulatively the authenticity of Christian origins. As he put it again memorably in the *Essay on Development*, 'from the nature of the human mind, time is necessary for the full comprehension and perfection of great ideas.'[11] On another view (consider the doctrine of infallibility), history illuminated the Church's indefectibility, taking 'Church', that is, as a visible and universal organisation.

For Maurice, the history of the Christian Church often seemed a process of continual decline and failure, a falling away from the primitive ideal. This was particularly clear in the first edition of the *Kingdom of Christ*, in a chapter on church history which he omitted from the revised (and much more widely read) second edition, published in 1842, and which demonstrated the presence of Catholicity in the Church despite the complexity and apparent contradictions of its history.[12] His providentialism was another aspect of his theology of revelation, connecting the revelation of a divine ordering of the world with the faith and experience of Christians throughout history. It presupposed an immediacy of experience which sidestepped the supposition of any cumula-

---

8   J. H. Newman, *An Essay on the Development of Christian Doctrine*, p. 69.

9   F. D. Maurice, *The Gospel of the Kingdom of Heaven*, p. ix.

10   Both Maurice and Newman feature in J. M. R. Bennett, 'Doctrine, progress and history: British religious debate 1845–1914', D.Phil. thesis, University of Oxford, 2015.

11   Newman, *Essay on Development*, p. 90.

12   Maurice, *Kingdom of Christ*, Vol. II (1838 edn.), pp. 261–352.

tive wisdom, or mediatorial tradition, embedded in the Church itself. Thus Maurice could present the Church in history almost as an obstacle to the realisation of its own object, the effecting of the communion of believers with God: 'She [the Church] can scarcely make her voice heard against schemes for reducing all things to a common stock, for establishing a fellowship upon a law of mutual selfishness, because she has not believed that the internal communion, the law of Love, the polity of members united in one Head ... is a real one.'[13] By the same token, Maurice professed great admiration for Luther, who had grasped the immediacy of faith.[14] It was not that Maurice simply assumed an individualistic understanding of faith. On the contrary, his perception of the Church as one of three constitutive categories of human experience and organisation (the others being the family and the nation) made its abiding presence in history as an idea – in the Coleridgean sense, a prototypical model embedded in the actual history of the institution – a permanent rebuke to the tendency of excessive individualism to reduce faith to a subjective egotism.[15] Yet, as his lectures on *The Conscience* (1868) suggested, the individual's experience remained of paramount concern for Maurice.[16] His habitual suspicion of historical institutions, ecclesiastical parties and Church leaders thus sat uneasily alongside an intrinsic valuation of certain institutional forms as divinely imprinted.

At this point, then, certain basic similarities and contrasts can be suggested. The history of the Christian Church was a central problematic for both Newman and Maurice, and so, by extension, for their understanding of Anglicanism. For both, history was theologically significant: it was the arena of human encounter with God, an encounter to be read in terms of the mutations of ecclesial organisation from its primitive form. But for Newman, the historical structures of the Catholic Church, including its dogmatic structures,

13   F. D. Maurice, *Sermons on the Prayer Book and the Lord's Prayer*, pp. 340–1.
14   Cf. J. N. Morris, 'Reconstructing the Reformation: F. D. Maurice, Luther, and Justification', pp. 487–500.
15   As Coleridge himself put it, 'By an *idea*, I mean ... that conception of a thing, which is not abstracted from any particular state, form, or mode, in which the thing may happen to exist at this or that time; but which is given by the knowledge of its ultimate aim': S. T. Coleridge, *On the Constitution of the Church and State*, p. 4; italics original. Maurice's debt to Coleridge was immense; it was explicitly mentioned in the 'Preface' to the second edition of *The Kingdom of Christ* (1842), and can be pursued in much of the secondary literature, including C. R. Sanders, *Coleridge and the Broad Church Movement: Studies in S. T. Coleridge, Dr. Arnold of Rugby, J. C. Hare, Thomas Carlyle and F. D. Maurice;* and T. E. Jones, *The Broad Church: A Biography of a Movement.*
16   See especially Lecture 1, 'On the Word 'I'': F. D. Maurice, *The Conscience*, pp. 1–23.

were themselves carriers of truth and life. As we shall see, there was a 'com-
pactness' about Newman's notion of Catholicity which confined it to one form
of ecclesial organisation. The Anglican Newman located this in the primitive
model, a view which the Catholic Newman came to see as unduly limited. For
Maurice, it seems, the historical structures, though also vehicles of the sacred,
in practice were often tenuously related to the revealed 'principles' they sought
to protect and to convey.[17]

Anglicanism and the Middle Way

These contrasting evaluations of the theological significance of Church history
gave rise to different assessments of Anglicanism, despite superficial similarities. Both theologians have been cast as apologists of the *via media*, Newman
self-consciously so, Maurice by later scholars.[18]

Newman's theory of the *via media* was laid out most famously in his *Lectures
on the Prophetical Office of the Church* (1836). As he wrote later, this was 'an
attempt at commencing a system of theology on the Anglican idea', which took
as its triple basis the 'fundamental points of dogma, the sacramental system,
and anti-Romanism'.[19] The book began by counterpointing the 'errors' of
Protestantism and Romanism, locating the Church of England's *via media* as a
'third system ... cutting between them'.[20] Newman acknowledged common
points of doctrine with both 'rival creeds'. Like Protestantism, the Church of
England recognised no other ultimate standard of appeal in doctrine than the
Bible, but it did not consider the Bible the *only* ground of appeal.[21] Protestantism
actually had no theory of the Catholic Church.[22] Like Romanism, the Anglican

---

17   This is most evident in *The Kingdom of Christ*, in which Maurice sought to explore the
      'principles' of the Catholic Church in the fragmented 'systems' of different churches and
      church parties which had appeared in history; cf. J. N. Morris, *F. D. Maurice and the Crisis
      of Christian Authority*, pp. 68–75.
18   Stephen Sykes went to so far as to call Maurice's 'theory of comprehensiveness' (itself a
      misleading designation) a 'reformulation of the theory [of the *via media*]': S. W. Sykes, *The
      Integrity of Anglicanism*, p. 16.
19   J. H. Newman, *Apologia Pro Vita Sua*, pp. 67 & 71.
20   J. H. Newman, *The Via Media of the Anglican Church*, Vol. 1, p. 16. The *Lectures on the Pro-
      phetical Office of the Church* were originally published in 1837, but they were reissued vir-
      tually unaltered, though with an entirely new Preface and title in 1877; this later edition is
      used here, referenced as *Via Media*.
21   Newman, *Via Media*, pp. 27–8.
22   Newman, *Via Media*, p. 7.

system conceded that appeal in matters of doctrinal dispute could also be made to tradition; but unlike Romanism, it located tradition in the witness of the early Church, and not in the corruptions which have been intruded into 'Antiquity' in subsequent centuries.[23]

Covertly, then, Newman had already made clear his starting-point, namely the perception that the *via media* of the Anglican system was in fact a replication (or, perhaps better, a continuation) of the Romanist system, but in a purer form. He admitted as much when he came to revise the work as a Roman Catholic: 'It [i.e. the Prophetical Office] only directly comes into collision with the theology of Rome ... while [the author] attacked it at considerable length, he adopted its main principles and many of its conclusions; and, as obliterating thereby or ignoring the very rudiments of Protestantism, he acted far more as an assailant of the religion of the Reformation than of what he called "Popery".'[24]

Newman's treatment of Protestantism throughout the volume was dismissive, identifying its appeal to the principle of *sola scriptura* as evidence that it smuggled in the principle of 'private judgment', since Scripture itself did not supply the principles by which it was to be interpreted authoritatively.[25] He was able to demonstrate skilfully the impossibility of a decisive appeal to Scripture alone; as he said in relation to some of the proof-texts Protestants were fond of citing, 'this does not show that the *private* reading of *Scripture* is the *one* essential requisite for gaining [wisdom].'[26] His case was superficially similar to Hooker's polemic against the Puritans in Books 1 to 4 of the *Laws of Ecclesiastical Polity*, but Newman's solution was a distinctive place for the rule of Antiquity, and not for Reason. If the conception of Protestantism presented here was startlingly (and almost unremittingly) negative, it is difficult to escape the conclusion that already Newman was drawing a notion of tradition from Romanism which would prove to be a powerful magnet for him. He distinguished the 'Prophetical Tradition' from the 'Apostolic' or 'Episcopal' tradition, as the means by which divine revelation was interpreted.[27] Now this was a *Church* office: it signified a comparable (and complementary) 'prophetic' function for the Church as a whole alongside the 'ruling' function of episcopal

23   Newman, *Via Media*, pp. 37–40.

24   Newman, *Via Media*, pp. xv-xvi.

25   '[A]cute men among them see that the very elementary notion ... of the Bible without note or comment being the sole authoritative judge in controversies of faith, is a self-destructive principle': Newman, *Via Media*, p. 27.

26   Newman, *Via Media*, p. 164; italics original.

27   Newman, *Via Media*, pp. 250–1.

tradition. It was therefore a possession of the Church as a whole, and at its clearest in the primitive Church. Underlying the work was an appeal to the Church of England to make its system 'live', that is, to recover and repristinate the doctrinal heritage which lay (as Newman saw it) dormant in its history.[28] The *Prophetical Office* was a clarion call to renewal, and despite its author's loss to Anglicanism in 1845, it continued to exert a profound influence on the mind of High Church Anglicanism over successive generations, as the statement of a 'middle' Anglican Catholicism that was historically validated and also had a forward-looking, revivalist agenda of its own.

Two other things are also noteworthy at this point. First, Newman's appeal to history in the *Prophetical Office* had a static form characteristic of Anglo-Catholic or High Church apologetic at this period. When Newman revisited the work as a Roman Catholic, he provided a lengthy preface which entirely recast his theory, giving an account of three offices of the Church – the prophetic, the priestly and the regulatory – which could be in tension with each other, and which therefore function as the motor of doctrinal development. But in the work as it was first written, the fact that the content of the prophetical tradition was supplied primarily by Antiquity suggested that the doctrinal tradition ceased to evolve at some specific point in history. Newman famously abandoned this position in the *Essay on Development*, the work which helped to propel him into the Roman Catholic Church. Second, Newman's conception of the *via media* could be amplified by its location within the emergent, radically new Tractarian concentration on the absolute importance of the apostolical succession, an emphasis that Newman had signalled himself in Tract I, 'On the Ministerial Commission', but which received its most systematic expression in Palmer's *Treatise on the Church of Christ*.

When we turn to Maurice's one great treatise on ecclesiology, *The Kingdom of Christ*, an altogether different picture emerges. Like Newman, Maurice perceived contemporary Anglicanism to be the inheritor of a period of lassitude and failure.[29] He placed the sacramental system of the Church, and the apostolic ministry, at the centre of his understanding of Catholicity.[30] Like Newman, too, he depicted Romanism as parasitic, through its corruption of the ordinances of the Catholic Church. But his evaluation of Protestantism was much more positive than Newman's. In formulating an ecclesiological theory for Anglicanism which ultimately took on the appearance of a notion of *via*

---

28   Newman, *Via Media*, p. 355.

29   Maurice, *Kingdom of Christ* (1842), Vol. II, pp. 380–97.

30   Maurice, *Kingdom of Christ* (1842), esp. Part Two, 'Of the Catholic Church and the Romish System'.

media, Maurice deployed a dialectical method of reading Church history. His aim in the work was to outline 'hints' of the 'principles, constitution and ordinances' of the Catholic Church – that is, to trace the Catholicity of the Church through its history, and to locate Anglicanism within that history.[31] So his method was reflexive: it *assumed* a Catholicity inhering within the separated churches of Christendom which it then set out to discern in the history of fragmentation and division within the Church. By this means, he could identify 'positive principles' in all of the main branches of Protestant Christianity, even though they had been encased in 'systems' which had obscured or subverted those very principles themselves.

However, this positive evaluation was partly dependent on Maurice's anatomy of the 'constitution' of the Church, something reflected in his constant use of the phrase 'spiritual constitution'. Three related levels of reality – family, nation and church – represented permanent features of the historical process and were grounded in God's creative and providential ordering of the universe.[32] These were harmonious and to an extent mutually balanced. Maurice's theory of nationality buttressed his claim that Protestantism was an essential complement to Catholicism, because Protestantism represented the principle of nationality acknowledged in the structure and organisation of the Church.[33] This framework linking the Church with the subordinate realities of family and nation enabled him to treat the various 'sects' of Protestantism seriously as separated communities of faith within which nevertheless lineaments of the Catholicity of the Church could be detected. By his historical dialectic, Maurice could separate the sects' 'positive principles' from the 'systems' in which historically they were embedded, and by affirming these principles, cast them as intrinsic aspects of the Catholicity of the Church. One example will have to suffice here: in chapter 2 of Part I, Maurice enumerated four leading principles of Protestantism – justification by faith, *sola scriptura*, election, and national distinctions – and then traced their distortion in the actual history of Protestantism.[34]

Maurice's 'hints' at the 'principles' and 'constitution' of the Church did not exhaust his ecclesiological method and his description of Anglicanism. The

---

31 The subtitle is simply *Hints to a Quaker respecting the Principles, Constitution, and Ordinances of the Catholic Church*. The significance of the word 'hints' is that no complete, systematic or definitive presentation of ecclesiology can be offered, presented as it is by Maurice as a complex reality intertwined with history.

32 Maurice, *Kingdom of Christ* (1842), Vol. I, pp. 260–9.

33 Cf. F. D. Maurice, *Three Letters to the Rev. William Palmer* (London, 1842), pp. 16–19.

34 Maurice, *Kingdom of Christ* (1842), Vol. I, pp. 62–130.

heart of the *Kingdom of Christ* consisted of a very long chapter in which the
'ordinances' of the Catholic Church were expounded as six 'signs', namely baptism, eucharist, creeds, Scripture, an ordered ministry, and a fixed liturgy
(characteristically this took national forms). The possession of all of these
signs indicated the Church of England's location within the universal Church.[35]

Again, it is worth noting several basic points. First, it is all too easy to suggest
– as did Stephen Sykes – that Maurice's method was synthetic.[36] But to assert
that is to miss the fundamental shape of Maurice's argument, which sought,
not to 'reconstruct' an ecclesiology for Anglicanism, but to identify what it is
about the Church of England which enabled it to be said of it: 'This is part of the
Catholic Church.' Maurice strenuously resisted the suggestion that his theory
could be systematised, or characterised as 'eclectic' or 'syncretist'.[37] It provided
'hints' deduced from the historical evidence; it amounted to a descriptive perspective on Anglicanism. But, second, we must distinguish between Maurice's
carefully-delineated idea of the 'spiritual constitution', with its associated
terminology, and his own tendency at times to fall back on the common designations of terms such as 'Protestant' and 'Catholic'. Strictly, according to his
view, most of the Protestant churches had retained Catholicity; and the terms
'Catholic' and 'Protestant' could not fairly be taken to represent different ecclesial communities between which the Church of England stood equidistant.
Third, in common with Newman in the 1830s and many of his contemporaries, Maurice was ill-informed about Roman Catholicism, and cannot be said
ever to have approached it with the same intended sympathy and insight with
which he approached the main traditions of Protestantism.

The contrasting characteristics of these different views of Anglicanism as
a *via media* can be stated briefly. Newman apparently took the notion much
along the lines adumbrated in, for example, George Herbert's famous poem
on 'The British Church', namely, 'The mean thy praise and glory is.'[38] But
he did not present a vision of Anglicanism as an actual mean equidistant
between two extremes. He defined the *via media* from the starting point of
a common identity with Roman Catholicism, seeing Protestantism as a more

35   The similarity of these 'signs', minus 'fixed liturgy', to the four points of the Lambeth
      Quadrilateral, is significant, as it has been argued that Maurice was an influence on Wil-
      liam Reed Huntington, who first theorized the quadrilateral in his book *The Church Idea*
      (1876): M. Woodhouse-Hawkins, 'Maurice, Huntington, and the Quadrilateral: an Explora-
      tion in Historical Theology'.
36   Sykes, *Integrity of Anglicanism*, p. 17: the phrase used is actually 'excessively synthetic
      theory'.
37   Maurice, *Kingdom of Christ* (1842), Vol. II, pp. 409–13.
38   George Herbert, *The Complete English Poems*, p. 101.

fundamental 'aberration' than Romanism. In doing so, he articulated a defence of the doctrinal tradition of Anglicanism which reflected the position of Tractarianism as a whole, and which continued to be important into the late twentieth century, but which nevertheless was vulnerable in its assumption of a fixed, authoritative point in history. This was a form of historicism: ultimately it made the content of the 'Prophetic Tradition' of the Church dependent on a notional reconstruction of Patristic norms (which was why, in the end, Newman had to modify his theory). For Maurice, there was no 'fixed point' of history from which the doctrinal character of Anglicanism could be evaluated. Guided by his theology of revelation, and by his conviction that God's ordering of the world was a continuous process, Maurice presented a providential defence of the Church of England. In his criticism of Newman's *Prophetical Office* – made in passing in his generally sympathetic examination of the *Essay on Development* – Maurice pointed out that Newman's argument seemed to deny to the present the possibility of an experience of faith as authentic as that of the past: it was a theory 'which must have left the impression deeply fixed on numbers of minds, that a living voice had spoken in the old time, and that since, only faint echoes of it are to be heard in tomes of divinity'.[39] Maurice did not use the language of *via media*, and even though he did use the term 'comprehensive' at times in relation to Anglicanism, nevertheless he described Anglicanism not as a definite position 'between' other doctrinal traditions, but as a polity containing within itself 'hints' of the greater reality of the universal Church.[40] Protestantism and Catholicism were complementary dimensions of this. The *history* of the Church of England was intrinsic to the analysis of its Catholic identity. By implication, there could be no 'general theory' of an Anglican *via media* which was not at the same time and by the same token a description of its actual existence. At the risk of extending this point a little further, a theory of 'comprehensiveness' derived from Maurice's ecclesiology cannot be projected as a normative ecclesiological theory, but can function only as a theorizing of practice.

---

39   F. D. Maurice, *The Epistle to the Hebrews*, p. xxxii.

40   For this very reason my use of the very term 'Anglicanism' here in relation to Maurice's views is anachronistic and misleading: Maurice would have been suspicious of the systematizing implications of the term, and would not have sought to expound an Anglican doctrinal system apart from its actual manifestation in the particular church, the Church of England.

The Visible Church and the Church of England

The contrasts between Newman and Maurice should not be exaggerated. I have already shown some significant points of comparison. There are others. Both theologians, for example, rejected the conventional Reformation distinction between the 'visible' churches and 'invisible' Church. Newman's stance was natural enough, given his general understanding of the force of tradition and of the abiding continuity of the Catholic Church, a view which developed more forcefully towards the end of his Anglican period and during his years as a Roman Catholic. Maurice's position is perhaps more surprising, but the evidence is unequivocal. In a letter to Sara Coleridge, written in 1843, Maurice asserted:

> The words Visible Church I confess I have never rightly understood. You seem to think that I have somewhere used them; I do not recollect ever to have done so – except in the preface to the first edition of my Kingdom of Christ wherein I protested against the whole method of considering the subject which is involved in the adoption of the words Visible and Invisible ... I left out the passage in the later edition because I had taken so much more pains to bring out my idea of the Church as a spiritual constitution that I thought the formal announcement of my objection to the other [mode] of speaking unnecessary and perhaps exasperating.[41]

How was this possible? It was entirely consistent with Maurice's conception of the absolute intersection of history and providence. The construction of a *systematic theory* of Catholicity was impossible, on Maurice's view for, as he would surely have pointed out, we have only *one* actual, historical Catholic Church about which we can theorize.

A second, relevant point of comparison is that both theologians had a profoundly sacramental view of the universe, which informed their understanding of the being and mission of the Church. Again and again, in Newman's *Parochial and Plain Sermons*, for example, one can find expressions strikingly similar to Maurice. These are not superficial similarities, either. Newman, for example, could speak of 'spiritual men', just as Maurice did.[42] He dwelt, like Maurice, on the abiding presence of the Spirit within the faithful.[43] He could write of the

---

41   Letter dated 23 November 1843, King's College London Archives (Relton Library, Box 5037-M4-R).

42   Newman, *Parochial and Plain Sermons*, Vol. I, p. 79.

43   Newman, *Parochial and Plain Sermons*, Vol. II, p. 19.

divine light originally implanted in us.[44] Such a string of examples could be extended considerably.

However, in turn the comparisons should not be overdone. There were serious differences of opinion between the two men on the status, role and theological character of the Church of England, as their respective views of its history demonstrated. By the late 1830s Newman had a profoundly unsympathetic view of the Reformation, which was influenced in part by his friend Hurrell Froude, whose antipathy to the Reformers was to become notorious on the posthumous publications of his literary *Remains* in 1838.[45] He saw the Catholicity of the Church as rooted in its apostolic order and faith, and transmitted through history through the apostolical succession of the ministry. Given the rule of Antiquity, what was Catholic about the Church of England essentially consisted of its conformity to the Primitive norm, which in itself contained the very institution – the apostolic ministry – through which the norm's continuing application in history could be validated. That implied, however, that the Church's authority was entirely separate from that of the State, derived as it was from a separate source. Newman upheld a high estimate of the spiritual autonomy of the Church, and was indifferent to, and suspicious of, Establishment. A revealing comment to Isaac Williams on the perils of Establishment illustrates this: he could never be sorry when a friend refused a bishopric in the Establishment, for 'How can a person enter upon the office of defender of the Church without almost a promise on entering it, that he will not defend it?'[46] The real nature of the Church of England was obscured by its contemporary malaise, remaining, in his own words, a 'paper religion', until it could be revived and made once more the centre of a living system of doctrine and practice.[47]

Maurice's understanding of the history of the Church of England was radically different. He too valued the early Church; but he did not elevate it into a norm.[48] Despite his sacramental theology, and his similarity to Tractarianism

---

44   Newman, *Parochial and Plain Sermons*, Vol. IV, p. 186.

45   Cf. P. B. Nockles, *The Oxford Movement in Context: Anglican High Churchmanship 1760–1857*, pp. 124–7.

46   Cited in I. Ker, *John Henry Newman: A Biography*, p. 178. Note, however, that S. A. Skinner cautions against taking Newman's view of Establishment as entirely negative: idem, *Tractarians and the 'Condition of England': The Social and Political Thought of the Oxford Movement*, pp. 123–6.

47   Newman, *Apologia*, p. 70.

48   Maurice's most sustained comments on the Fathers are in *Lectures on the Ecclesiastical History of the First and Second Centuries*, and in *Moral and Metaphysical Philosophy*, Vol. I, 'Contents of the First Six Centuries', pp. 263–419. In *The Kingdom of Christ* he rejected the

on ministerial order, Maurice was suspicious of what he saw as its clericalism, and of its efforts to emphasize the corporate, spiritual authority of the Church as a mediatorial authority. He conceived of Catholicity as a continuous presence in history, outworking itself even in the fragmentation of Christian churches and sects. Moreover, he effectively sacralised the Establishment, and the nation, through his understanding of national and ecclesial authorities as interlinked dimensions of the divine order. The Reformation was a providential act, reasserting the intrinsically national character of the English Church.[49] Maurice's historical idea of Catholicity, which may seem close to a notion of developing revelation, had definite and stable content, since he identified the elements of historical continuity (the 'ordinances' of the Church) through which its original 'principles' were defended in the real history of the Church of England. But it did mean that, on his view, the Church of England was already perfect *in potentia*, merely requiring its members to witness to authentic revelation, and to express their 'union with God' through the Church, to be once again fully itself.

Dissection of the contrasting ecclesiological bases of both thinkers in this way may seem to beg the question as to which version is the more convincing. But that would probably require a degree of oversimplification, and anyway is perhaps not necessary in a book which addresses the history of the High Church revival. Both approaches left their mark on subsequent discussion, as we shall see. Maurice's proved immensely productive for ecumenical relations in the twentieth century, but it had its difficulties too, not least in its estimate of the spiritual reality of the principle of nationality, and in its accordingly high valuation of an abstract and (some would say) idealised English national character.[50] Newman's approach had the merit – for some – of detaching Anglican ecclesiology altogether from the specificity of Establishment and national character. It is not surprising that, correspondingly, Anglo-Catholicism was often sceptical of the actions and stance of the Establishment. But, on the other hand, the rule of Antiquity did not prove to be as decisive as many hoped, partly *because* it was an appeal to history, and thereby its conclusions could never be as fixed and complete as its apologists hoped – the very nature of historical scholarship made this unlikely.

---

supposition that the Early Church could be resurrected directly as a model for the contemporary Church: ibid. (1842), Vol. II, pp. 302–26.

49 Cf. the second letter, 'The English Church', in *Three Letters to the Rev. William Palmer*, pp. 16–39.

50 Cf. the chapters on 'National Morality' and 'War' in F. D. Maurice, *Social Morality*.

Charles Gore and a Late-nineteenth Century Synthesis

That Newman and Maurice shared a number of presuppositions about the Church and about the nature of Christian faith is scarcely surprising. Their affinities in part arose from a shared intellectual and religious heritage and context. Both were profoundly influenced by Romanticism, with its revivification of a sacramental, mysterious conception of creation.[51] Both, though not to the same extent, admitted the influence of Coleridge. Both articulated criticisms of the rationalism embedded in much contemporary British theology and philosophy. Both, influenced by Patristic sources, expressed an understanding of the relation of human beings to God which drew on the language of 'participation' and 'communion'. Both, in summary, represented a reaction against a narrowly instrumental view of the Church. But there was as much difference in their intellectual backgrounds as similarity. Newman, emerging from an Evangelical upbringing, was influenced by the Aristotelianism and Anglican Orthodoxy of Oxford much more profoundly than Maurice. Maurice, in turn, was clearly marked by his upbringing as son of a Unitarian minister, and his education at Cambridge, and his exposure to Plato there, though it is true he was also shaped by his subsequent years of study at Oxford, if to a lesser extent than Newman, from 1830 to 1832.[52] In complex ways, the theological methods of both men which emerged from these converging and yet different streams of influence resulted in sharply contrasting methods of historical inquiry. It is possible to see a broad 'Platonic' method at work in Maurice's assumption of a Catholicity inhering in all the separated parts of Christianity, a Catholicity which could be accessed only by a careful consideration of their history, and correspondingly to see a characteristically Aristotelian method at work in Newman's assumption of a 'rule' (antiquity) according to which contemporary expressions of Christianity could be assessed, and in his assumption of Anglicanism as a 'mean' – though both characterisations should not be pushed very far.

What remains striking, however, is not so much that these different assessments of Church history, and of Anglicanism, should come into being at all, but rather that their influence should continue well into the twentieth century. The language of the *via media*, as it was often expressed in High Anglican thought after Newman and Maurice, was a fusion of the two theologian's arguments. Anglicanism was conceived as a 'mean' between two extremes, and yet at the

---

51   Cf. Prickett, *Romanticism and Religion*; also, J. R. Barth, *Romanticism and Transcendence: Wordsworth, Coleridge and the religious imagination.*

52   Morris, *F. D. Maurice*, pp. 49–54.

same time as a 'comprehensive' system, a fusion of different elements which were also found in the 'extreme' terms of the equation. It is certainly arguable that the very different bases of these two views of the Anglican position were fundamentally incompatible. Yet they did achieve a kind of compatibility in the arguments conventionally advanced by many High Churchmen by the end of the nineteenth century, and on into the twentieth century. The theologian and church leader who was probably more responsible than anyone else for this was Charles Gore (1853–1932), Bishop successively of Worcester, Birmingham and Oxford, and a figure self-confessedly standing in what he called a 'Liberal Catholic' tradition. Gore was two generations younger than the Oxford leaders, but always regarded himself as a follower – though not an uncritical one – of Tractarian principles.[53] He was a protégé of Henry Liddon, but also influenced by the idealist philosopher T. H. Green (1836–1882), whom he met at Balliol. Working in tandem with a group of other theologians who formed, with him, the 'Holy Party', Gore published *Lux Mundi: A Series of Studies in the Religion of the Incarnation* (1889), a volume which has been called 'a creative interaction between patristic theology, Anglo-Catholicism, and broad-church Liberalism'. Gore, it is argued, thus was primarily responsible for preserving the spirit of the Oxford Movement by adjusting its theological method to accommodate modern biblical and historical criticism.[54]

In two important respects, *Lux Mundi* seemed to represent an accommodation of High Church or Anglo-Catholic doctrine to Liberalism and the 'Broad Church'. In the first place, the pervasive yet somewhat unsystematic marriage of traditional Christian theology, and in particular the doctrine of the Incarnation, to a quasi-Hegelian metaphysic, derived ultimately from the work of Green, enabled the contributors to resist contemporary claims that it was impossible to reconcile High Church positions with modern thought. Gore's chapter, on 'The Holy Spirit and Inspiration' was the one which drew most attention, but arguably the more telling one was by John Illingworth (1848–1915) on 'The Incarnation and Development', for here the sense of forward movement in history – a sense thoroughly conversant with religious Liberalism – was specifically connected to the principle of God's intervention in history through the Incarnation of the Son of God. Taking his starting point in the theory of evolution, and its impact on theology, Illingworth contended that the 'perpetual development which we are learning to trace throughout the uni-

---

53   J. Carpenter, *Gore: A Study in Liberal Catholic Thought*, p. 59; see also P. D. L. Avis, *Gore: Construction and Conflict* for an excellent general account of Gore's thought.

54   A. Wilkinson, 'Charles Gore', ODNB.

verse' was 'the natural expression ... of that Logos Who is the Life'.[55] For Illingworth, as for Gore and others, traditional Christian doctrine simply *was* the most compelling and yet progressive framework through which the growth of modern knowledge could be interpreted. As Illingworth was to put it elsewhere, the doctrine of the Trinity 'preserves the divine transcendence which gives fixity to all relative existence without sacrificing the divine immanence which makes life and progress possible'.[56] This apparently abstract formula was preached to a congregation of undergraduates, and Illingworth's language at times did envelope conventional theological language in a philosophical haze. Nevertheless his position was shared in all essentials by the other contributors to *Lux Mundi*. Gore himself proceeded to elaborate their central emphasis on the Incarnation in particular at greater length in his Bampton lectures on the doctrine, published in 1891, and in a series of subsequent studies.[57]

But in the second place, this apparent marriage of the modern and the traditional also served as a useful hook for a much more concerted commitment by High Churchmen late in the century to a socially progressive approach to politics and welfare. Here Gore was also very much to the fore, as co-founder of the Community of the Resurrection (CR), a religious order which he conceived almost as a Christian Socialist community, and as a strong supporter of the Christian Social Union (CSU).[58] CR, created at Gore's initiative in 1892 after several years' rumination on the need for new models of Christian community, reflected his conviction that the time had come for the Church 'to put social morality, Christian living, in the forefront of its effort', so that, as a community bringing together celibate priests, it embodied the conviction that 'a religious community should be a paradigm for the right ordering of society.'[59] Formed in 1889, the same year as *Lux Mundi* appeared, the CSU brought together traditional High Churchmen and 'Liberal' followers of the Christian Socialism of Maurice, Charles Kingsley and others. Gore, Illingworth, Henry Scott Holland and other members of the 'Holy Party' often mentioned Maurice in particular as a sympathetic voice – his *Moral and Metaphysical Philosophy*, a massive and highly partial tour through the history of Western philosophy was especially

---

55   J. R. Illingworth, 'The Incarnation and Development', in C. Gore et al., *Lux Mundi: A Series of Studies in the Religion of the Incarnation*, p. 196.

56   J. R. Illingworth, *Sermons Preached in a College Chapel*, p. 172, quoted in A. L. Illingworth, *The Life and Work of John Richardson Illingworth*, p. 275.

57   C. Gore, *The Incarnation of the Son of God*; idem, *Dissertations on Subjects Connected with the Incarnation*.

58   A. Wilkinson, *Christian Socialism: Scott Holland to Tony Blair*, p. 53.

59   A. Wilkinson, *The Community of the Resurrection: A Centenary History*, p. 37.

commended by Illingworth – though they also approved of B. F. Westcott's theology of social engagement.[60] Exactly how close and powerful these influences were in practice is very hard to discern. Interest in social reform, and an accompanying concern for the appalling conditions in which people lived in the poorest parts of the great industrial cities, was a characteristic preoccupation of the mid- and late-Victorian clergy, and the term 'socialist' should not be taken in too narrow or prescriptive a sense, since it often denoted comprehensive social concern rather than a doctrinaire adherence to notions of collective ownership of the means of production. Nevertheless, as James Carpenter has observed, Gore and his circle 'decisively ranged themselves on the side of the Maurician strain of theology' and looked with favour on certain contemporary social movements.[61]

Yet Gore's own freedom of language about contemporary thought, and his confidence in the ability of Anglicanism to countenance a *rapprochement* with it, at certain times could give the impression of a greater latitude in his teaching than he really intended, and at other times could lead him to endorse positions which certainly would have been regarded with suspicion by an earlier generation of High Churchmen. For Gore, Catholicism, and indeed the Church of England itself, was 'Liberal' precisely in the sense that it was founded on Scripture and accepted an associated free inquiry as a check to mere dogmatism. It was the 'scriptural test', as he put it, that qualified the Catholicism of the Church of England as 'scriptural or liberal'.[62] As Carpenter recognised, Gore spoke freely of the Church of England's 'duty of private judgment', and was perfectly comfortable with a grateful acknowledgement of its Reformation heritage.[63] This was all language that would have been anathema to Newman, Keble and Froude. The defence of private judgement, of the Reformation heritage, and of critical limits to assertions of ecclesiastical tradition, were a significant step away from first-generation Tractarianism. Gore was sympathetic to ecumenical contacts not only with Roman Catholics, as a participant in the 'Malines conversations', the informal talks on corporate reunion held from 1921 to 1927 between a Roman Catholic group of theologians assembled by the Belgian Cardinal Mercier and a group of Anglicans, but also with the Free Churches, as a member of a group comprising Anglican and Free Church theologians who, during the First World War, supported the adoption of episcopacy as a basis for reunion in fact and 'not in any theory as to its character',

60   Illingworth, *Life and Work of John Richardson Illingworth*, p. 244.
61   Carpenter, *Gore*, p. 245.
62   C. Gore, *The Basis of Anglican Fellowship*, pp. 4–5, cited in Carpenter, *Gore*, p. 56.
63   Carpenter, *Gore*, p. 57.

and with the restoration of election by clergy and people.[64] He was also surprisingly open to the acknowledgement of truth in other faiths, since all
religions, he said, 'contain more or less considerable elements of truth'.[65] In
this, once again, there is more than an echo of Maurice, whose *Religions of the
World* (1847), exemplifying a 'hierarchy of truths' approach to the relationship
between Christianity and other faiths, had come to exert a powerful influence
on some missionary theologians towards the end of the nineteenth century.[66]

Though an astute and persuasive writer, Gore was perhaps not a creative or
original theologian of the very first rank: certainly he was not a Newman or a
Maurice. But he did manage to combine something of the spirit of both writers, not least in his popular writing on the Church of England. He definitely
wrote as a High Churchman, resting his view of the authority of the Church on
a 'classical' defence of the apostolic institution of the ministry. In his influential early work, *The Church and the Ministry* (1888), this was stated in a form
surely familiar enough to earlier generations of High Churchmen: 'the record
of history renders it practically indisputable that Jesus Christ founded a visible
society or Church, to be the organ of His Spirit in the world ... and in the unin-
terrupted history of the Church ... one such link [of connection across time]
has always existed in the apostolic successions of the ministry.'[67] Despite some
uncertainty about the exact mode by which the episcopal ministry arose in the
first and second centuries – here Gore showed himself in tune with moderately advanced strands of critical scholarship – the ministry 'advanced always
upon the principle of succession ... by regular devolution from the Apostles'.[68]
He did not flinch from the strong conclusion that non-episcopal ministries
were in some sense defective or invalid.[69] Nor, however, was he reluctant to
state strong reservations about the Roman position: 'No one can survey the
course of European thought ... without seeing that it [the Roman authority]
has been on many points, and not chiefly in virtue of the decrees for which
infallibility is claimed, the great misleader of Europe.'[70]

But whatever the formal strength of Gore's commitment to a traditional
High Church ecclesiology, positioning Anglicanism between Protestantism
and Roman Catholicism, at the same time he had imbibed elements of

---

64   C. Gore, *Dominant Ideas and Corrective Principles*, p. 49.

65   C. Gore, *The Mission of the Church*, p. 112.

66   See K. Cracknell, *Justice, Courtesy and Love: Theologians and Missionaries encountering
      World Religions, 1846–1914*.

67   C. Gore, *The Church and the Ministry*, p. 304.

68   Gore, *Church and Ministry*, p. 311.

69   Gore, *Church and Ministry*, p. 313.

70   C. Gore, *The Reconstruction of Belief*, p. 815.

Maurice's understanding of Anglicanism, as is clear from the many admiring references he made to Maurice's work. In a vein that would certainly not have commended itself to Newman, he acknowledged and valued the latitude implicit in the Anglican formularies: 'Indefinite formulae are not indeed satisfactory. They may appear to say much and in fact say little ... But none of greater definiteness drawn up at that moment could have failed to commit us to what, in the great issue, would have imperilled our position.'[71] On the sacraments, for example, the Church of England laid down 'certain broad limits' and within these there was 'a space which is left without further definition'.[72] He could even claim that this combination of definite dogma with a 'considerable degree of divergence of opinion' was perhaps 'the ideal of church government'.[73] And whilst affirming that there was no cause to be ashamed of 'this phrase *via media* which common consent has fixed upon Anglicanism', at the same time the terms in which Gore defended its use bore resemblance to Maurice's suspicion of system and appreciation of the core principles at stake in Protestantism and Catholicism:

> [The] principle of combination holds beyond the area of theology proper ... You may press the claims of the individual to freedom to the extent of annihilating all real unity, or you may press Church authority so as to annihilate the free development of the individual. The former extreme we call individualism, the latter imperialism or absolutism. Both are 'logical,' that is to say both are the logical application of a true principle, but they are the one-sided applications of it, and we should be inclined to call Protestantism on one side individualistic, and Romanism absolutist, on the other: while the *via media* undertakes the more difficult but not the less necessary task of preserving the balance by keeping hold of both terms.[74]

Conclusion

Whether or not this approach was ultimately a sustainable or consistent over-mapping of two very different methods is not for exploration here. But it is worth observing that the historical implications of Newman's and Maurice's

71   C. Gore, *The Mission of the Church*, p. 49.
72   Gore, *Mission of the Church*, p. 50.
73   Gore, *Mission of the Church*, p. 76.
74   C. Gore, *Roman Catholic Claims*, pp. 3–5.

arguments lead in different directions, and that a theory that tries to hold both together faces considerable difficulties. The assumption of a primitive norm, the 'rule of Antiquity', favoured by the Anglican Newman, remained a powerful weapon in the hands of Anglicans who were to oppose later developments such as the ordination of women. But it was a method which potentially imprisoned Anglicanism within a fixed framework of doctrine and practice itself synthesised from what we now know to have been a remarkably diverse history. As Pusey well knew – and as will be discussed in the following chapter – this made the distance between Anglicanism and Roman Catholicism potentially very great indeed, since significant elements of Roman Catholic doctrine and practice could not be grounded explicitly in the rule of Antiquity. It also had the incidental consequence of making Anglican ecclesiology vulnerable to the claims of other Christian churches that their polities were more authentically 'primitive' than Anglicanism.

Maurice's position was always much more difficult to evaluate, despite its immense influence on theologians such as Gore and his successors, partly because of the notorious complexities and obscurity of his work, and partly because, by its very nature, he could only provide 'hints' of a Catholicity projected as latent in all major Christian traditions. 'Comprehensiveness' – a term Maurice actually did not use very often – has never been a very adequate way of describing the implications of his ecclesiological theory. But his reflexive method, with its attention to the truth embedded in particular traditions, and to the patterns of their divergent histories, was to prove an immensely valuable tool in ecumenical discussion, and it thus positioned Anglicanism – for much of the twentieth century – to see itself as peculiarly well placed to develop relationships across the spectrum of both Catholic and Protestant churches. The Roman Catholic theologian Louis Bouyer, quoted by William Wolf, said as much himself: 'If there is anyone within Protestantism who saw with clarity and depth into the principle needed to resolve the crisis endemic within Protestantism, it is surely Maurice.'[75] The principle of attending to elements of positive truth within separated traditions was carried forward, after the Second Vatican Council, as Wolf acknowledged, in the work of ecumenical dialogue. In the statement of ARCIC II, *The Church as Communion* (1991), for example, we find a summary position remarkably close to the language and spirit of Maurice:

---

75   W. J. Wolf, 'Frederick Denison Maurice', p. 85, citing L. Bouyer, *The Spirit and Forms of Protestantism* (1956).

Whenever differences become embodied in separated ecclesial communities, so that Christians are no longer able to receive and pass on the truth within the one community of faith, communion is impoverished and the living memory of the Church is affected. As Christians grow apart, complementary aspects of the one truth are sometimes perceived as mutually incompatible.[76]

Maurice would surely have found *that* application of his theory encouraging.

It is a moot point whether Maurice is rightly described as 'High Church' or not. His eventual hostility to the Tractarians on some points may seem to set him apart, but he sustained good relationships with High Churchmen (including Henry Manning, Samuel Wilberforce, and William Palmer), and his defence of the objectivity of church order placed him close to the spirit of historic High Churchmanship – something recognised in the twentieth century by such theologians as Michael Ramsey and Gabriel Hebert.[77] Nonetheless, despite common convictions around the character and historical authenticity of traditional church order, theologically Anglican High Churchmanship was never a single body of doctrine or opinion, and it is striking that it was able to accommodate such contrasting views of Anglican identity as those of Newman and Maurice, and even to blend them into one seeming synthesis. This may have given it durability in the face of battles with Modernism, on the one hand, and with ultra-traditionalism or ultra-Evangelicalism on the other. But if it had a weakness, it lay in its very intellectual character. It depended on adherence to an understanding of church history, and in particular of the origins of doctrine and order, that itself required a fine-tuned appreciation of the past. Where clergy, theologians, church leaders and others might share a common culture and a common commitment to a defence of tradition, in time the erosion of widespread Christian belief in Britain in the second half of the twentieth century made it seem vulnerable, behind the times, slow or irrelevant. New storms over women's ministry, medical ethics, and sexual orientation and behaviour, were to press severely upon the delicate synthesis that Gore and others had striven to uphold. In that context, the competing claims of Anglicanism to be comprehensive or to be a 'middle way' came under attack as never before.

---

76   ARCIC II, *The Church as Communion*, p. 22.

77   A. M. Ramsey, *The Gospel and the Catholic Church*, p. 214; A. G. Hebert, *Liturgy and Society*, p. 108.

CHAPTER 8

Scripture and History: Mary and the Nature of Doctrine

In claiming to represent the authentic tradition of Anglicanism, High Churchmen nonetheless had to clarify and define their theological position on two fronts. Against those who argued that their revival (or, better, creative adaptation) of ritual and practice, that they claimed to be consistent with primitive tradition, was part of a 'Romanizing' agenda which would subvert the Protestant character of the Church of England, they had to demonstrate a clear difference from the Roman Catholic Church. But on another front – and as chapter six implied – they also had to differentiate their position from that of Evangelicals, who claimed to be the true guardians of the Reformation. If, as the last chapter showed, in fact High Churchmanship did not constitute one undifferentiated tradition, but was patient both of theological development and of considerable internal diversity, nevertheless on both fronts it was obliged to substantiate what amounted to a coherent, common perspective. In this chapter I shall explore the Romeward tension, looking at the theological 'border' between High Churchmen and Roman Catholicism.

In 1960 the Anglican philosopher Austin Farrer preached a sermon 'On being an Anglican', in the chapel of Pusey House, Oxford, which must have amazed his hearers. It began gently enough, with a teasing reference to a correspondent to the *Times* who had announced his disillusionment with the Church of England, but halfway through, the tone changed. Human perversity had rent the unity of the Church with schisms and heresies, Farrer said. How could he, 'truly and with a good conscience', stay in the Church of God? His reply was unequivocal: 'Only by remaining in the Church of England'.[1] He put down two markers for his Anglican identity. One was stated briefly and with restraint: 'I dare not dissociate myself from the apostolic ministry'. It was the other that must have startled his congregation:

> I dare not profess belief in the great Papal error. Christ did not found a Papacy ... Its infallibilist claim is a blasphemy, and never has been accepted by the oriental part of Christendom. Its authority has been employed to establish as dogmas of faith, propositions utterly lacking in

---

1   A. Farrer, 'On being an Anglican', in idem, *The End of Man*, p. 50.

© KONINKLIJKE BRILL NV, LEIDEN, 2016 | DOI 10.1163/9789004326804_009

historical foundation. Nor is this an old or faded scandal – the papal fact-factory has been going full blast in our own time, manufacturing sacred history after the event.[2]

Written close to the assembling of the Second Vatican Council, and from the standpoint of over half a century of improving Anglican-Catholic relations, Farrer's words seem to have a harsh and polemical ring. They are all the more surprising, considering his seemingly impeccable Anglo-Catholic credentials.[3] If we are to take seriously Farrer's participation in the discussions and report on Catholicity published in 1947 by a group convened by Gregory Dix, it cannot be the case that Farrer's objection to the 'great Papal error' involved objection to the concept of primacy *per se*.[4] Rather, there were two basic points of offence: the concept and declaration of infallibility itself, and of course the two Marian dogmas of the Immaculate Conception and the Assumption.

Farrer's wariness of these dogmas was symptomatic of the attitude of most leading Anglo-Catholic theologians until recently. Far from sharing enthusiastically in the swelling amplitude of Marian devotion, as Pickering seemed to imply, the theological heirs of the Tractarians (and certainly of the older or 'orthodox' High Church tradition) were ambivalent about it.[5] This chapter is an exploration of their ambivalence, largely through the lens of Farrer's attitude to the Marian dogmas. It will aim, first, to place Farrer's views in the context of the main streams of High Church theology after Pusey. In this way, it will demonstrate something of the way in which, theologically, High Churchmen actually sustained and promoted a distinction between their understanding of Anglicanism and the charge, made by their opponents, that they represented a 'Romanizing' tendency in the Church of England. Then it will return to Farrer, identifying points both of continuity and of development. Finally, it will contrast and examine the new perspective on Mary that began to emerge among

---

2   Farrer, 'On being an Anglican', pp. 50–1.

3   See, for example, his participation in three of the most significant Anglo-Catholic publications of the mid-twentieth century: 'Eucharist and Church in the New Testament', in A. G. Hebert, *The Parish Communion*, pp. 73–94; 'The Ministry in the New Testament', in K. E. Kirk (ed.), *The Apostolic Ministry: Essays on the History and Doctrine of Episcopacy*; and co-authorship with E. S. Abbott, Gregory Dix, Michael Ramsey *et alia*, *Catholicity: A Study in the Conflict of Christian Traditions in the West*.

4   'If such an institution as the 'universal Church' is to exist as more than a sentiment and an ideal ... then some such central institution [as the Papacy] would seem to be more than just a convenience': Abbott *et al.*, *Catholicity*, p. 36.

5   'Anglo-Catholics made a great deal of the feast of the Assumption': W. S. F. Pickering, *Anglo-Catholicism: A Study in Ambiguity*, p. 39.

Anglo-Catholic theologians in the 1950s and 1960s, and which arguably exercised a more decisive influence on the Anglican-Catholic theological rapprochement of the last half of the twentieth century.

The High Church Tradition and the Double Test

A survey of the broad history of High Church theologians' views of Mary naturally should begin, not with the Tractarians, but with the Reformers, and the impact of their views on the English Church after the Reformation. Martin Luther's position conventionally highlights the limits and ambiguities of Protestant reflection on Mary.[6] Rejecting as he did the late medieval *cultus*, for Luther Mary had no soteriological function apart from her historical one. What could be said about her had to be evident from Scripture. The principle of *Sola scriptura* left some latitude of interpretation in practice, but operated as a mechanism of doctrinal control, distinguishing between what may be held of Mary as a matter of private devotion, and which therefore was, in 'classic' Reformation terminology, *adiaphora*, and what must be affirmed of her as a matter of holding to the Catholic faith. Nonetheless, nurtured as he was in a religious world saturated with Marian piety, Luther valued Mary as the highest example of Christian obedience and discipleship. Calvin strengthened and made more rigorous the biblical control, and this emphasis was carried across into the Anglican settlement through the views of those English Reformers who were increasingly influenced by the Reformed strand of Continental Protestantism.[7] This did not preclude, however, a growing readiness in some Anglican writers to praise and honour Mary as Christian exemplar and – when influenced by Patristic and Eastern sources – even as 'mother of God', whilst at the same time stopping short of saying anything beyond what Scripture itself could plainly validate. As a recent survey of Anglican views on Mary in the sixteenth and seventeenth centuries concluded, the theological issues involved in ideas of immaculate conception and assumption 'were hardly discussed: they seemed too far afield from Scripture, and too religiously controversial'.[8]

This remained the basic position even for most Anglo-Catholic theologians, let alone the more cautious, 'orthodox' High Church, in the nineteenth

---

6   Cf. G. Maron, 'Mary in Protestant theology', in H. Küng and J. Moltmann (eds), *Mary in the Churches*, pp. 40–2.

7   Cf. M. Nazir-Ali & N. Sagovsky, 'The Virgin Mary in the Anglican tradition of the sixteenth and seventeenth centuries'.

8   Nazir-Ali & Sagovsky, 'The Virgin Mary in the Anglican tradition', p. 144.

century. In effect, the Reformers had laid down a primary scriptural control or 'test' of doctrine, and this remained paramount for Anglican theologians of all shades of opinion, though High Churchmen generally added a second test, namely primitive tradition. Thus Keble, cited by Donald Allchin as one whose appreciation of Mary marked a significant enhancement of Anglican reflection, himself would not go further than Scripture indicated.[9] His poem 'Mother out of sight' displayed what appeared to be a novel and exalted appreciation of Mary's place in the economy of salvation:

> ... Mother of God! O, not in vain
> We learn'd of old thy lowly strain.
> Fain in thy shadow would we rest,
> And kneel with thee, and call thee blest;
> With thee would 'magnify the Lord, '
> And if thou art not here adored,
> Yet seek we, day by day, the love and fear
> Which bring thee, with all saints, near and more near.
>
> What glory thou above hast won,
> By special grace of thy dear Son,
> We see not yet, nor dare espy
> Thy crowned form with open eye.
> Rather beside the manger meek
> Thee bending with veiled brow we seek,
> Or where the angel in the thrice-great Name
> Hail'd thee, and Jesus to thy bosom came ...
>
> Fair greeting, with our matin vows
> Paid duly to the enthroned Spouse,
> His Church and Bride, here and on high,
> Figured in her deep purity,
> Who, born of Eve, high mercy won,
> To bear and nurse the Eternal Son.
> O, awful station, to no seraph given,
> On this side touching sin, on the other heaven![10]

---

9   A. M. Allchin, *The Joy of all Creation: An Anglican Meditation on the Place of Mary*, Part II, 'The Witness Continued', chapter 7, 'John Keble and B. F. Westcott'.

10   J. T. Coleridge, *A Memoir of the Rev. John Keble*, pp. 305–9.

Written originally for the *Lyra Innocentium* (1846) – poems which took their starting point as children's thoughts and experiences – the poem was never published. Keble sent it, along with other poems for the volume, to various friends and advisers, who seemingly took objection. It contained allusions and explicit references which would have fanned the flames of the critics of Tractarian 'Romanizing' – including, from the verses quoted above, 'crowned form', suggesting of course the title of 'Queen of Heaven', and 'Mother of God' recalling the ancient *theotokos*. Keble was taken aback at the reaction, and writing to his friend and biographer, John Coleridge (who later published the poem in full, after Keble's death), disavowed any essential novelty in the poem: 'You see when I recommend the Ave, I mean merely the Scripture part.'[11] But Keble was also known for advocating the necessity of studying the Fathers for guiding the interpretation of Scripture, and on this he was entirely at one both with the older High Church tradition, and with his Tractarian colleagues. In his sermon *Primitive Tradition recognised in Holy Scripture* (1836) he pointed out the probability of the existence of an unwritten tradition of the early Church, on which Scripture itself rested: it was accordingly 'matter of investigation in each case, whether any given rule, interpretation, or custom, be traditionary in the required sense'.[12]

If Keble's defence of primitive tradition put down a clear marker for what Tractarian teaching would become best known as advocating, namely the expansion of doctrine, rites and devotional practice within the Church of England along lines that they professed to find validated in the Fathers, it is perhaps not so widely recognised that it also reflected the assertion of a significant boundary between what was required and what was – at best – permissible. This was precisely the role of the double test of Scripture and tradition, and it was most strenuously asserted not by Keble, but by Pusey. Pusey was resolutely attached to the double test. In his first *Eirenicon* (1865), published in the wake of Newman's *Apologia* but stung in particular by Henry Manning's suggestion (in *The Workings of the Holy Spirit in the Church of England*, 1864) that the Holy Spirit was not much in evidence in the Church of England, he surveyed the teaching and popular devotion of Roman Catholicism concerning Mary. The recent declaration of the dogma of the Immaculate Conception, he claimed, had smuggled in a principle 'which made all evidence as to fact superfluous', namely that 'the Church, being incapable of erring, any thing taught through-

---

11   A letter to J. T. Coleridge, dated 18 June 1845, cited in Coleridge, *Memoir of John Keble*, p. 281.

12   J. Keble, *Primitive Tradition recognised in the Holy Scriptures: A Sermon, preached in the Cathedral Church of Winchester*, p. 34.

out the Church ... was necessarily true'.[13] To those who believed in the Pope's personal infallibility, 'the fact that he pronounced any thing to be true was to be a proof that it had been always taught'.[14] For Pusey (as for Luther, we might say) the only justification for Marian titles (such as the thoroughly orthodox *theotokos*) was that they 'pointed to the central truth of Christian faith, the doctrine of the incarnation.[15]

   The operation of this double test of Scripture and tradition, as articulated by Tractarians such as Keble and Pusey, was entirely consistent with the 'older' or orthodox High Church position. Only a couple of examples will suffice here. Hook of Leeds, preaching to the clergy of Manchester in 1839 against the 'novelties of Romanism', placed his first emphasis on the appeal to Scripture, and then on a requisite second 'test', namely 'the testimony of the Church from the beginning'.[16] Hook was writing before the declaration of the dogma of the Immaculate Conception, but still noted how Romanism 'added' to the biblical doctrine professed by the Church of England: the Romanist held with Anglicans the doctrine that Christ was a mediator, but then 'he *adds* the mediation of the Virgin, saints, and angels'.[17] The real question, Hook averred, was not whether or not Papists held doctrines in common with the Church of England, but rather 'whether we adhere to their additions to the Gospel truth'.[18] Christopher Wordsworth, perhaps a more 'muscular' High Churchman even than Hook, certainly agreed with him on exactly the same grounds when it came to evaluating distinctly Romanist doctrine. In his response to the dogma of the Immaculate Conception, preached in Westminster Abbey in December 1854, he asserted as much in terms not all that different from Farrer over a hundred years later. The new dogma was not a declaration of a primitive doctrine, but the assumption of a power 'to *make a new doctrine*, and to add it to Christ's Gospel'.[19] Such an act struck 'at the root of the Authority and Inspiration of Holy Scripture'.[20] Wordsworth perhaps went even further than Hook in his deduction from this newly-claimed power: 'If the Church of Rome can make a

---

13   E. B. Pusey, *The Church of England a Portion of Christ's One Holy Catholic Church, and a Means of Restoring Visible Unity: An Eirenicon*, p. 148.

14   Pusey, *Eirenicon*, p. 149.

15   E. B. Pusey, *First Letter to the Very Rev. J. H. Newman* [Eirenicon II], p. 29.

16   W. F. Hook, *The Novelties of Romanism: Or, Popery refuted by Tradition; A Sermon preached in St Andrew's Church, Manchester*, p. 8.

17   Hook, *Novelties of Romanism*, p. 18; emphasis original.

18   Hook, *Novelties of Romanism*, p. 19.

19   C. Wordsworth, *On 'The Immaculate Conception': A sermon preached at Westminster Abbey, 17 December 1854*, p. 12.

20   Wordsworth, *On 'The Immaculate Conception'*, p. 16.

new Article of Faith ... if the dogmatic coin just issued from the Papal mint, is to become the spiritual currency of Christendom ... then, my brethren, Almighty God is dethroned, and the Pontiff of Rome is King of the Universe.'[21] What is noteworthy in both of these authors, from a modern perspective, is not so much the application of the double test *per se* to distinguish between true doctrine and innovation, but rather that it was *High Churchmen* saying all this.

The same position was shared by the younger generation of Tractarian or Anglo-Catholic theologians, nonetheless. Henry Liddon, for example, wrote in 1864 that 'I never pass the Festival of the Assumption ... without being thankful that I am not a Roman Catholic. For here you have an instance of a presumed fact, resting on no historical basis whatsoever, yet itself made the basis of a devotional system.'[22] The immaculate conception, he argued in his Bampton lectures, 'appears to presuppose a Church ... which is empowered to make actual additions to the number of revealed certainties'.[23] Yet Liddon's position did not rule out a high estimate of Mary; according to George Russell, he revered 'the unique prerogative and Perpetual Virginity of Mary, Mother of God'.[24]

Liddon's position was also almost identical with that of Charles Gore, whose 'Liberal Catholicism' is usually contrasted by historians with Liddon's conservatism. Far apart though they may have been on the question of Biblical inspiration, their conception of the *content* of the apostolic faith was virtually the same. The Church's dogmas, argued Gore, were justified on the basis of the dual appeal to primitive history and Scripture.[25] Where doctrines such as the 'actual sinlessness of the blessed Virgin' could not call in support the authority of Scripture nor the universal consent of the Church, even when it had been commonly held by Christians, it would 'rank rather as a pious opinion than as an article of faith'.[26] Further, where doctrines lacked *any* Scriptural warrant, but came to prevail only in a later age of the Church – and Gore included specifically the doctrine of the Immaculate Conception – then 'even without condemning them as positively heretical, we shall have no hesitation in declining them with emphatic decision'.[27] For the testimony of history, after Scripture, was absolutely decisive, and he resolutely defended the historicity of

21   Wordsworth, *On 'The Immaculate Conception'*, p. 22.
22   J. O. Johnston, *Life and Letters of Henry Parry Liddon*, p. 93.
23   H. P. Liddon, *The Divinity of Our Lord and Saviour Jesus Christ*, p. 433.
24   G. W. E. Russell, *Dr. Liddon*, p. 135.
25   C. Gore, *The Creed of the Christian*, p. 17.
26   Gore, *Roman Catholic Claims*, p. 70.
27   Gore, *Roman Catholic Claims*, pp. 70–1.

Scripture and of faith; his acceptance of critical history went hand in hand
with his acceptance of the faith of the ancient creeds: 'I do not ... want you to
be like Romanists, who ask for the same faith in the Immaculate Conception of
the Blessed Virgin – which can claim no historical evidence whatever – as for
the Resurrection of our Lord or His Virginal Birth.'[28]

Nor is it easy to find other High Church or Anglo-Catholic theologians in the
late nineteenth and early twentieth centuries who disagreed substantially with
the position laid down by Pusey and others. Almost at the furthest reaches of
what could be professed in the Church of England – though admittedly from
what was a minority view even within Anglo-Catholicism – lay Darwell Stone,
the conservative Principal of Pusey House, Oxford, in the early twentieth
century, and, according to his biographer, 'leader of the Romeward-leaning
Anglo-Catholic group'.[29] A contemporary and occasional critic of Gore, Stone
went much further in his recognition of the growing tide of Marian devotion in
the Church of England, and in terms of what he regarded as permissible: 'In
teaching, in private and public prayer, in hymns, veneration of Our Lady and
invocation of her and the other saints have become very prominent.'[30] But
even he, in his *Outlines of Christian Dogma* (1903), resisted the view that either
the Immaculate Conception or the Assumption could ever be viewed as anything other than permissible opinions.[31] He reiterated this view a quarter of a
century later, confirming that the issue was one of plain evidence. Stone did
not assert explicitly the question of scriptural grounds, but it is implicit in his
discussion, and included in his understanding of 'evidence', as was the second
test, the question of primitive tradition. On the Assumption, for example, he
could say that the opinion, 'though widely held' in East and West, 'has never
been made to be of faith in any part of the Church'.[32]

Citing a string of authors – Pusey, Keble, Hook, Wordsworth, Liddon, Gore,
Stone – in this way can give the impression that there was a vigorous and lively
debate amongst High Churchmen about Mary. But that was far from the case,
if one excludes polemical writing against Roman Catholics. There is little evidence of any strong interest in Marian doctrine amongst High Church writers,
including those self-identifying as Anglo-Catholics, even in the first half of the
twentieth century. Surveying the work of Kenneth Kirk, Oliver Quick, Leonard
Hodgson, Lionel Thornton, Gregory Dix, to name but a few, one struggles to

28   C. Gore, *Can We Then Believe?*, p. 95.
29   F. L. Cross, 'Darwell Stone (1859–1941), ODNB.
30   D. Stone, *The Faith of an English Catholic*, p. 86.
31   D. Stone, *Outline of Christian Dogma*, pp. 57–9.
32   Stone, *The Faith of an English Catholic*, p. 88.

find more than a few passing references, and even the broad continuity with Pusey is evident. Quick, for example, completely ignored Marian doctrine in his best-selling *Doctrines of the Creed* (1939).[33] Nor did it feature in the influential essay collections *Essays Catholic and Critical*, *Essays Catholic and Missionary*, and *Northern Catholicism*.[34]

Yet this absence of theologians' interest before the middle of the twentieth century is certainly not reflected in the popular devotional culture and history of Anglo-Catholicism. The *Book of Common Prayer* had cut out from English devotion almost every sign of the medieval cult of the Blessed Virgin Mary. But Anglo-Catholics were increasingly susceptible to the influence of Roman Catholic practice, following a trajectory we have seen already hinted at in Keble and Liddon, and indeed Stone. The formation of a number of Marian societies, such as the Confraternity of Our Lady in 1880, and later the Union of the Holy Rosary and the League of Our Lady, reflected growing interest in Marian devotion.[35] The revival of Walsingham in the early twentieth century, encouraged by influential Anglo-Catholic laity such as Lord Halifax, though controversial, was to create a significant centre of Anglican Marian devotion.[36] Marian hymns began to appear, such as those by Stuckey Coles, whose 'Ye who own the faith of Jesus', with its rousing chorus 'Hail Mary, full of grace', had already become something of an anthem for High Churchmen and Anglo-Catholics by the time of the first Anglo-Catholic Congress in 1923.[37] In time, as Pickering pointed out, Anglo-Catholics and 'Anglo-Papalists', as he called them, were to adopt Marian devotions such as the recitation of the rosary, the angelus, and the litany and vespers of the Blessed Virgin.[38]

By the middle of the twentieth century, a gap had opened up in Anglo-Catholicism. Laity and clergy were adopting a richness in Marian devotion which was perhaps bound, in time, to drag doctrinal reflection in its wake. Anglo-Catholic theologians, on the other hand, like their close colleagues of a more moderate High Church persuasion, even conceding some space for the development of Marian devotion, neither considered the question of Marian

---

33   O. C. Quick, *Doctrines of the Creed*, p. 160.

34   E. G. Selwyn (ed.), *Essays Catholic and Critical*; E. R. Morgan (ed.), *Essays Catholic and Missionary*; N. P. Williams and C. Harris, *Northern Catholicism*.

35   J. S. Reed, *Glorious Battle: The Cultural Politics of Victorian Anglo-Catholicism*, p. 89; P. G. Cobb, 'The development of modern day pilgrimage', p. 157.

36   Guild of Our Lady of Ransom, *Walsingham 1061–1997*, pp. 85–8. Cf. also M. Yelton, *Alfred Hope Patten and the Restoration of the Shrine of Our Lady of Walsingham*; also G. Waller, *Walsingham and the English Imagination*.

37   Pickering, *Anglo-Catholicism*, pp. 50–2.

38   Pickering, *Anglo-Catholicism*, p. 38.

doctrine to be of much significance, nor were prepared to countenance development beyond the scriptural and patristic norms.

Farrer, Mary and Doctrine

Given this background, the provenance of Austin Farrer's views on Mary is clear. Yet the sermon 'On being an Anglican' is not by any means the only thing he wrote on this. Instead, it is necessary to turn to two articles published some years later, after the Second Vatican Council had begun its work. These are 'Mary, Scripture and Tradition', and 'Infallibility and historical revelation'.[39] In the latter, Farrer repeated his earlier charge: the two Marian decrees, he claimed, had the 'alarming appearance of an infallible fact-factory going full blast'.[40]

In both, Farrer's broad continuity with Pusey and the High Church tradition that I have described is evident from his appeal to historical and scriptural fact:

> It is my special concern, as a reformed Christian, to emphasize the necessity of a constant overhaul of dogmatic development by the standard of Christian origins; and 'Christian origins' can only mean in practice the *evidences we have* for Christian origins; and they come down pretty nearly to the New Testament writings, and the primitive sacramental usage.[41]

For Farrer, then, revelation was 'the concordant testimony of Gospel fact and inspired Church'.[42] Scripture, reflected in the primitive *regulum fidei*, imposed a limit on authentic doctrinal decision-making: the Church could not definitely infer as presumed fact doctrines for which there was no historical testimony.[43] The Marian dogmas were a 'surely vicious' application of the principle that the Church could deduce what was historically fitting, since not only was there no evidence that God had acted this way, but there was 'no possibility ever that there should be'.[44]

---

39   A. M. Farrer, 'Mary, Scripture and Tradition'; A. M. Farrer, 'Infallibility and historical revelation'; the latter was reprinted after Farrer's death, in A. M. Farrer, *Interpretation and Belief*, and that is the edition used here.

40   Farrer, 'Infallibility and historical revelation', p. 164.

41   Farrer, 'Infallibility and historical revelation', p. 158; italics original.

42   Farrer, 'Mary, Scripture and Tradition', in Mascall and Box, *Blessed Virgin Mary*, p. 118.

43   Farrer, 'Mary, Scripture and Tradition', p. 122.

44   Farrer, 'Mary, Scripture and Tradition', pp. 121–2.

Farrer appeared to be pushing his argument further than Pusey. 'Mary, Scripture and Tradition' contained an extended examination of the grounds of the virginal conception. Farrer noted that the scriptural evidence for the doctrine was both late (Matthew, Luke, and John, but not Paul or Mark) and not *prima facie* harmonious.[45] This was – in Farrer's terms – historical evidence, but not strong evidence. Consequently, the main prop of the doctrine was the Church's decision that it was 'absolutely fitting', from which it 'presumed the soundness' of the scriptural testimony.[46] In essence, Farrer said, the Church 'judged Christ to have been virginally conceived because they thought he must have been, not because they had evidence that he was'.[47] This was certainly language that would have sounded incautious to nineteenth-century High Churchmen, even if formally Farrer's position on the concordant testimony of Scripture and tradition was the same as theirs.

Like his High Church forebears, Farrer was troubled too by the relationship of Scripture, history, and faith. Studying for a time under Emil Brunner at Zürich in the early 1930s, and noted as much for his forays into New Testament exegesis as for his philosophical theology, he was well equipped to probe the epistemological and hermeneutic conditions of Christian doctrine.[48] His defence of the virginal conception, and his criticism of the Marian dogmas, was not one more instance of the lamentable history of liberal Protestantism's attempt to trim Christian faith. Rather, it aimed to understand the inner rationale of the Church's proclamation of truth. Farrer's approach did not give priority to the independently-verified conclusions of historical scholarship over the traditional facts of revelation. Instead it insisted on the presumed historicity of revealed fact itself. He did see as established without question in the nineteenth century the view that scholarship is revisable, and that scholarship affects what we can conclude to be the teaching of Scripture – 'to admit primitivity as a judge or as a control is to submit to scholarship or historianship.'[49] But the appearance of deviation from Pusey's position was just that – appearance, not substance. The basic ground of Farrer's acknowledgement of the virginal conception and his rejection of the Marian dogmas was the same as that of Pusey – history and inspired text.

---

45   Farrer, 'Mary, Scripture and Tradition', p. 116.
46   Farrer, 'Mary, Scripture and Tradition', p. 117.
47   Farrer, 'Mary, Scripture and Tradition', p. 112.
48   On Farrer's studies in Germany and Switzerland, see P. Curtis, *A Hawk among Sparrows: A Biography of Austin Farrer*, pp. 75–80, 96–103.
49   Farrer, 'Infallibility and historical revelation', p. 158.

Farrer contended, then, not that the Marian dogmas were demonstrably untrue, but that there was nothing demonstrable about them. The Church, Farrer insisted, is inspired 'to proclaim facts, and to interpret facts; but not to create facts'.[50] For Farrer, infallibility was 'an expression of the faith that God will effectively guide his Church in the way of truth and salvation'.[51] But it had the status of a regulative idea; it could not be 'spotted, pinned down, identified with an ecclesiastical organ, or demanded on a given occasion'.[52] Like Pusey, Farrer implicitly conceded two dimensions in Christian belief about Mary. In one, authoritative teaching rested on the facts of Scripture and primitive faith, and constituted the essence of the Christian faith. In the other, particular teaching about Mary rested on no such basis, could not be required of Christians, and could not be regarded as essential.[53]

Yet even Farrer was not averse to Marian devotion. If generally restrained in his language on Mary, still there is sufficient indication of a high regard for her: 'Her glory is that she is the virgin mother of God: what more can be added to it?'[54] Though Mary could not be regarded as the 'archetype, or universal matrix of the Church', still she was glorified 'by being taken up' into the Church's function of being mother to the children of God, and that in a 'unique way', through her motherhood of Christ.[55] In his preaching, Farrer rarely succumbed to an idealised portrait of Mary. He could even claim that the point of John's telling of the miracle at Cana was to show the foolishness of human beings – in this case Mary herself.[56] Yet he could also explore imaginatively the life and maternal feeling of Mary with immense sensitivity, as in his posthumously-published sermon, 'The friendship of Jesus', in which he described Mary's faith growing through her separation from Jesus: 'Once he had been hers, now she was proud to be called his, and found her happiness in the bond with a son whose works

---

50   Farrer, 'Mary, Scripture and Tradition', p. 113.

51   Farrer, 'Infallibility and historical revelation', p. 162.

52   Farrer, 'Mary, Scripture and Tradition', p. 163.

53   The compatibility of this position with the Protestant tradition of 'fundamentals of faith' is evident: see, for example, S. W. Sykes, 'The fundamentals of Christianity', in idem, *Unashamed Anglicanism*, pp. 64–80. Though Sykes assumed here a general Tractarian hostility to the use of the term, the use of the concept itself was, as I have indicated, more widespread in High Church thought than he acknowledged.

54   Farrer, 'Mary, Scripture and Tradition', p. 123.

55   Farrer, 'Mary, Scripture and Tradition', p. 124.

56   Farrer, *The End of Man*, p. 155. This was in a sermon preached in Keble College Chapel in 1966.

and words were full of godhead.'[57] Five years before delivering the sermon with which this chapter began, Farrer had already signalled a change of heart on the rosary by publishing his own commentary on it and prayers for it.[58]

Farrer himself, then, was a sign of a developing Marian sensibility within High Churchmanship. What is striking now about his criticism of the evidential basis of the Marian dogmas is that it was expressed just at the time when other theologians were beginning to reflect a fundamental shift in Anglo-Catholic perceptions of them. Farrer's article on 'Mary, Scripture and Tradition' was already somewhat at odds with other contributions to the collection in which it appeared. H. S. Box, for example, affirmed the immaculate conception of Mary on grounds opposed to Farrer, assuming it as fact: 'The Immaculate Conception was a privilege bestowed upon Mary ... to the honour of the Second Person of the Blessed Trinity.'[59] In 1968, the year of Farrer's death, Eric Mascall tentatively affirmed the persuasiveness of the doctrine, attributing it to greater sophistication in our understanding of original sin.[60] By the late 1970s, John Macquarrie, in a bold side-stepping of Farrer's position, could insist that Christian truth was 'mutually implicate or coinherent', and that this removed the need for truths lower in the hierarchy of truth to be grounded explicitly on Scripture and tradition.[61] For him, the immaculate conception was 'a clear implicate of basic Christian doctrines which we all accept'.[62] To Box, Mascall, and Macquarrie, we could add, amongst others, Donald Allchin, and other contributors to the Ecumenical Society of the Blessed Virgin Mary.[63]

Conclusion

Why – briefly – did the theological climate change towards the end of Farrer's life? Three possible reasons stand out. First, as the whole history of Anglo-Catholicism arguably indicates, theological development often follows as much as it precedes popular devotion. The flowering of Marian devotion in

---

57 A. M. Farrer, *Words for Life*, p. 13. Though undated, the sermon was probably preached in Trinity College Chapel, Oxford, before Farrer left to go to Keble College as Warden in 1960: see Leslie Houlden's introduction, pp. i-xiii.

58 In A. M. Farrer, *Lord I believe*, pp. 80–95.

59 H. S. Box, 'The Immaculate Conception', p. 88.

60 E. L. Mascall, 'The Mother of God', p. 95.

61 J. Macquarrie, 'Immaculate Conception', in Stacpoole, *Mary's Place*, p. 100.

62 Macquarrie, 'Immaculate Conception', p. 106.

63 Allchin, *Joy of all Creation*; Stacpoole, *Mary's Place*; Mcloughlin Pinnock, *Mary is for Everyone*.

Anglo-Catholicism perhaps subtly eroded the determination of its theologians to maintain a sharp distinction between the required truth of faith and permissible expressions of it. We may say, then, that the gradual acceptance of the Marian dogmas by many High Churchmen was a classic example of the principle of *lex orandi, lex credendi*. Even so, it should be noted that this development marked a new and distinct phase in the theological history of Anglo-Catholicism in particular. Much of the ritual development of the late nineteenth and early twentieth centuries, as we have seen, was predicated on a common reinterpretation or renewal of eucharistic theology, placing it in what we can now see as a Europe-wide change in the ethos and shape of Christian worship and belief. The same could not be said for Marian devotion: here was a dimension of Christian faith and practice which involved different and more contested grounds of appeal.

Second, the effects of Vatican II and the changes it initiated in the Roman Catholic Church on many Anglicans was paradoxical. The seeming readiness of Roman Catholics to acknowledge the weight of Protestant criticism, far from reinforcing wholeheartedly Anglican determination to maintain articulated grounds of objection to 'Romanist innovation', instead blunted it. It became harder to argue forcefully against infallibility, for example, and easier to countenance the possibility of agreement on matters such as the Petrine primacy. Correspondingly, more latitude opened up for Anglicans to acknowledge the Marian dogmas, albeit in largely unofficial ways. In this context, the restoration of the feast day of the Blessed Virgin Mary on 15 August (the feast day of the Assumption of Mary) to the Anglican calendar in the 1990s was surely significant.

Third, hand in hand with this greater openness to receiving Roman Catholic views sympathetically went the growing participation of Roman Catholics in the ecumenical movement. This opened up increasingly the possibility of the joint study of Marian doctrine, and a greater freedom and sympathy of approach from many Protestant theologians. A brief initial statement by the first Anglican-Roman Catholic International Commission emphasised considerable areas of agreement on Mary's role and significance, before noting continuing differences on the status of the dogmas of the Immaculate Conception and Assumption.[64] The full statement produced by the second commission in 2004, *Mary: Grace and Hope in Christ*, went further than any 'official' report to which Anglicans were party had gone before in seeking to explore how the dogmas could be interpreted so as to be compatible with Anglican belief. In concert with its previous report, *The Gift of Authority* (1999),

---

64   ARCIC I, *The Final Report*, pp. 93–4.

ARCIC II deployed the concept of 're-reception' to explicate how the Church could receive afresh elements of the apostolic tradition which had been forgotten or abused.[65] A detailed discussion of New Testament texts which either mentioned Mary or had clear implications for her status – including an exegesis of the wedding at Cana which runs counter to that of Farrer[66] – and of the witness of Church tradition concluded that the proper context for viewing the Marian dogmas was eschatological and ecclesiological: 'Mary thus embodies the 'elect Israel' of whom Paul speaks – glorified, justified, called, predestined.'[67] The double test of Scripture and tradition was not explicitly abandoned – indeed the statement confirms the requirement of conformity to Scripture[68] – but, somewhat along the lines indicated by Macquarrie, the eschatological reading was used to urge both communions to re-receive Marian doctrine together, so that 'the Marian teaching and devotion within our respective communities, including differences of emphasis, would be seen to be authentic expressions of Christian belief'.[69] The statement seemed to be opening up the prospect of what, in ecumenical circles, is called 'reconciled diversity', namely that in a reunited Church exactly the same interpretation of the Marian dogmas would not be required, provided that consonance with Scripture was secured.

The work of ARCIC II in particular thus seemed to consummate the theological trend towards the amplification of Marian devotion which I noted as beginning even within Farrer's own lifetime. That trend perhaps implied that his position in 'On being an Anglican', for all its force of language and argument, was already outmoded in tone, almost before the ink was dry. Yet the lukewarm response with which *Mary: Grace and Hope in Christ* was received by the General Synod of the Church of England, along with substantial criticism by others, opened up another possibility. Even as theological intelligibility was increasingly conceded to the Marian dogmas by Anglo-Catholic theologians and others, tensions on this front became more acute for the larger proportion of the Anglican faithful (including especially Evangelicals) who had never felt drawn in that direction. Pusey's instincts were proved correct. Anglicans – and particularly Anglo-Catholics – continued to be troubled by the question of Anglican identity throughout the second half of the twentieth century. The longer tradition of High Church reflection on Mary marked out a

---

65   ARCIC II, *Mary: Grace and Hope in Christ*, p. 5.
66   ARCIC II, *Mary*, pp. 22–4.
67   ARCIC II, *Mary*, p. 51.
68   ARCIC II, *Mary*, pp. 59–60.
69   ARCIC II, *Mary*, p. 63.

position that at least was distinct from that of Roman Catholics, for all its apparent openness to Marian devotion. Despite his strong defence of the plea of historical and revelatory fact, as we have seen Farrer himself was not immune to the attraction of Marian devotion. Yet his published work suggests that, had he lived, he would not have been impressed by the changing theological climate associated with his friend Eric Mascall and others, but would have maintained the critical responsibility of the Christian philosopher and theologian to point to the requirement that Church teaching should be authenticated by the united testimony of Scripture and primitive tradition. In Farrer's words, 'the Catholic historian, however Catholic, is as much an historian as any other. He has Catholic expectations, he cannot force facts.'[70]

---

70   Farrer, 'Infallibility and historical revelation', p. 162.

Conclusion

∴

CHAPTER 9

Modern Destinies: The Revival into the Twentieth Century

The central preoccupation of this book has been the nature and course of the High Church revival in the Church of England, which I have sought to place in a broader social and religious context than is usual. For many good and some bad reasons both supporters and critics of the revival – to say nothing of historians – have been tempted to see it as an eccentric development in English religion. Certainly it had its distinct characteristics. It had its flamboyant characters, and it had its absurd episodes, as surely any strong movement of opinion or renewal must. It positioned itself as a critical current in Anglican opinion, both in the sense that it called for a renewal of the faith and devotion that it presumed had stagnated in earlier generations, and in the sense that it set itself apart from other 'party' traditions in the Church of England and in English religious life. It was critical of Evangelicals' apparent indifference to Primitive tradition and Church order, their suspicion of the authority of the Church as the interpreter of Scripture, and their seeming 'worldliness' in their apparent individualism and their lack of concern for the ordinances of the Church, including its sacramental system. It was also critical of 'Broad' churchmen, or Liberals, on the grounds of their seeming indifference to doctrine and tradition, and their apparent capitulation to rationalism. It had very little sympathy indeed for Protestant Nonconformity, which – to most High Churchmen – had all the weaknesses of Anglican Evangelicalism with none of the assurances secured by fidelity to the historic structures of the Church, and which they assumed to be schismatic, if not downright heretical. Many of these criticisms were quite unfair. Moreover, they rested on a profound misreading of the history of the Church of England itself, assuming that the High Church vision of Catholicity had always been central to the identity of Anglicanism.

Nonetheless, the High Church revival was part of a broader movement of renewal in nineteenth-century religion, and its distinctiveness has to be picked out by the historian with a great deal of care, so that its quintessential character is not obscured by a temptation to cast it as a species of exotica. That requirement for care is strengthened by the wider European perspective. Much more could have been said on that than I have been able to say here. In chapters four and five I offered just two complementary angles – church tourism, and French Catholic commentary – on the relationship between Anglican High

© KONINKLIJKE BRILL NV, LEIDEN, 2016 | DOI 10.1163/9789004326804_010

Churchmanship and European movements of religious opinion. Historians recently have reasserted the strength of Christian renewal across Europe in the nineteenth century. Once we grasp how far that process ran, and how similar in many respects these movements between confessional contexts and countries were, the apparent 'oddity' of Anglican High Churchmanship looks much less so.

That in turn requires a reckoning with the tangled history of what social historians have learnt to call the 'secularisation' thesis. I touched in passing on this in the first chapter.[1] For our purposes, the salient points are these. For a long time historians – following in the footsteps of sociologists of religion – believed that, from the late eighteenth century on, organised religion (i.e. the religion of the churches) was in retreat in western Europe, marginalised and undermined by rapid processes of social and economic change, and by the political challenges which emerged out of the ferment of ideas that produced the French Revolution. Some saw this as an intellectual change first and foremost.[2] For others, drawing on the sociological theories of Max Weber, it was implied in, and required by, the social changes that underpinned industrialisation and modernisation.[3] Both views could call in evidence the baleful commentary of generations of Christians for whom the urban context seemed more and more resistant to their efforts.[4] There are different theories about how and why this perception of decline became so firmly entrenched in the minds of social historians in the mid-twentieth century.[5] But by the 1980s a new wave of historical scholarship had begun to challenge the theory of decline, citing the strong evidence of congregational expansion in the nineteenth century.[6] There is as yet no new consensus as to when, and how, decline did finally set in, for that is clearly what happened in the course of the twentieth century, but the balance

---

1   A good introduction to the historiographical issues is D. H. McLeod, *Secularisation in Western Europe, 1848–1914*; for the most provocative contribution to the debate, cf. C. G. Brown, *The Death of Christian Britain: Understanding Secularisation 1800–2000*.

2   Cf. W. O. Chadwick, *The Secularization of the European Mind in the Nineteenth Century*.

3   Here one of the most noteworthy accounts was B. R. Wilson, *Religion in Secular Society*.

4   Cf. E. R. Wickham, *Church and People in an Industrial City*, and K. S. Inglis, *The Churches and the Working Classes in Victorian England*.

5   For a recent assertion that secularisation theory was a response, not to sociology, but to radical theology, cf. S. Brewitt-Taylor, "Christian Radicalism' in the Church of England, 1957–70', unpub. DPhil. thesis, University of Oxford, 2012.

6   D. H. McLeod, 'New perspectives on Victorian working-class religion: the oral evidence'; also C. G. Brown, 'Did urbanization secularize Britain?'; the pioneering work of Sarah Williams, *Religious Belief and Popular Culture in Southwark,c. 1880–1939*, built on these and other insights.

of probability looks increasingly to lie with those, such as Simon Green and Jeffrey Cox, who have argued that it had certainly begun by the 1930s, though it steepened dramatically in the 1960s.[7]

Even granting the force of criticisms of the theory of nineteenth-century decline, it is unquestionably true that church people of all persuasions faced formidable obstacles to their evangelistic, pastoral and philanthropic strategies in the nineteenth century, not least in those places where the population was increasing rapidly, drawing in migrants from a countryside that was confronting the churches with the corresponding challenges of poverty and depopulation. Yet, as we have seen, High Church Anglicans displayed as much vigour and ingenuity in rising to these challenges as did other Christians in Britain. In the past, much weight has been placed on the justification put forward for ritual and liturgical innovation, namely that its colour and ceremonial were more likely to appeal to the labouring population than the restrained, cerebral culture of the 'older' High Church tradition.[8] Evidence in favour of this contention, as we saw in chapter 2, was mixed. Hugh McLeod argued that Ritualist churches in London were no better than other churches in attracting larger congregations: 'The sort of community the Anglo-Catholic was trying to recreate did not exist in the English countryside, let alone in the metropolis.'[9] Ritual innovation did attract significant opposition, or indifference. Active hostility was fading in most places by the end of the century, however, and 'advanced' Ritualist churches, along with other churches run on High Church lines, were no less successful in embedding their particular beliefs and practices in the local context than other traditions – the 'flip side' of the observation made by McLeod.

Put that alongside a re-reading of the nineteenth century as predominantly an era of religious revival and consolidation (though one not without its own difficulties too), and the notion that the High Church revival was an 'eccentric' or counter-cultural development in English religion looks tenuous. The advance of High Church principles and practice in the Church of England in the localities was the result of a complex interaction of factors – personal, institutional, legal, political, social, to name but a few. Where these worked in favour of local High Church initiatives, they demonstrated the revival's ability to adapt and to achieve success even in situations of conflict. After all, it

---

7 J. Cox, *The English Churches in a Secular Society: Lambeth, 1870–1930*; S. J. D. Green, *The Passing of Protestant England: Secularisation and social change c. 1920–1960*.

8 J. S. Reed, *Glorious Battle: The Cultural Politics of Victorian Anglo-Catholicism*, pp. 60–3 & 72–4.

9 D. H. McLeod, *Class and Religion in the Late Victorian City*, p. 80.

included much thoroughly characteristic of the religious ideals of the nineteenth century, including its energy, commitment, earnestness and austerity, and its conviction that Christian faith could not be compartmentalised into a discrete realm of activity marked off from the rest of life. Both detractors and admirers of the revival have allowed their descriptions of it to be shaped largely by its ritual and liturgical innovations. But that is at best a limitation: High Church Anglicanism was as much a moral, social and devotional philosophy of life as it was an approach to worship. This last point perhaps needs more substantiation – more research – than I have been able to give it here. But, as chapter 3 showed, in terms of parish life High Churchmen increasingly sought to recast their local communities as in essence eucharistic communities. Underpinning that was undoubtedly a particular theological anthropology, not only – following Augustine's famous dictum at the beginning of the *Confessions* (in Pusey's influential translation) 'Thou awakest us to delight in Thy praise; for Thou madest us for Thyself, and our heart is restless, until it repose in Thee' – seeing man as a creature made first and foremost for worship of God, but as one who was easily misled from the way of devotion to God, needing both the support of the sacraments of the Church and an attention to private devotional practice, including confession, to keep heart and soul concentrated on the pursuit of God.[10] This was a very different religious philosophy from Evangelicalism, no matter how much it also shared with it.

Moreover that religious philosophy had broad political dimensions, even if High Churchmen themselves inevitably displayed a typical variety of actual political opinion. Its readiness to express new forms of ecclesial belonging and organisation, as well as liturgy and ceremonial, in the clothing (the architecture, art, and language) of the Middle Ages was more than Romantic nostalgia for a lost world: it was born of a deep inner conviction that the political, economic and social upheavals of the modern world had broken the threads of continuity which bound traditional ways of being community into the life of the Church. High Churchmen – whether politically conservative, liberal or Christian Socialist – all aspired to rebuild an idea of community in which the Church was central to social relationships, and not marginalised as it seemed to have been by the political crisis of 1828–32, by the upsurge of Protestant Nonconformity and Roman Catholicism, and by the emergence of an industrial economy and its concomitant consumerism. Once again, there were echoes of parallel movements on the continent of Europe, though it was an English High Churchman, Neville Figgis (1866–1919), who was to give perhaps the most powerful theoretical expression to this 'political' High Churchmanship

---

10   Augustine, *Confessions*, p. 1.

in the early twentieth century with his theory of corporate, mediating institutions as a necessary barrier between the individual citizen and the otherwise unrestrained power of the modern State.[11]

If High Churchmanship was a movement of wide scope and ambition, then, which merits historians' attention as a substantial and in its own way popular movement, if a minority one, what was its contribution to Anglicanism? High Churchmen claimed to have defended, rediscovered or re-emphasised the true character of the Church of England, as a body which had retained the Catholic order of the western, Latin Church whilst undergoing reform in the sixteenth century. There was more than a touch of invention in their medievalism: just as neo-Gothic architects 'restored' neglected church buildings to a more 'authentic' representation of their past, in the process ignoring the untidiness of the real history of the buildings, so the 'revivers' of historic ceremonial, liturgy and vestments were creating new traditions even as they claimed to follow Patristic and medieval English precedent. But this creative 'reinvention' went beyond liturgical and ceremonial practice to include High Church views of Anglican history itself. Nowhere was this more evident than in the conviction that the Prayer Book validated High Church claims about the character of the Church of England. It did not. Evangelicals such as Nathaniel Dimock and William Goode were keen to point that out. The Tractarian controversies triggered a flurry of hostile commentary from Evangelicals, and a major venture in republishing long-forgotten English Reformation texts, through the Parker Society. Some aspects of the Prayer Book – including its doctrine of baptismal regeneration – were uncomfortable for modern Evangelicals. That was a measure, however, not of the overall 'Catholic' character of the Prayer Book, but of the changing history of Evangelicalism or 'low' church Anglicanism. It was the gradual realisation that the Prayer Book did *not* defend High Church claims that underlay emergent calls for its revision towards the end of the nineteenth century. High Churchmen were on very thin ice indeed attempting to argue that their position was in continuity with the Anglican settlement of the sixteenth and seventeenth centuries – something that is underscored by the work of modern Reformation historians.[12] Even men such as Richard Hooker and George Herbert who, at first glance, fitted into a High Church, 'via media' interpretation of Anglicanism, on closer inspection turn out to have been much

---

11   Cf. D. Nicholls, *The Pluralist State: The Political Ideas of J. N. Figgis and his Contemporaries*;
      D. Runciman, *Pluralism and the Personality of the State*.

12   Cf. D. MacCulloch, *Thomas Cranmer: A Life*, pp. 614–32; also A. Ryrie, *Being Protestant in Reformation Britain*, pp. 317–29.

more complicated.[13] As Brown Patterson has recently argued, the 'Puritan' William Perkins was more representative of pre-Restoration Anglicanism than was Richard Hooker, though even the latter arguably ought to be interpreted as a 'Reformed' theologian rather than as the proto-Tractarian that Keble assumed him to be.[14] Inasmuch as High Churchmen in the nineteenth century could cite continuity with earlier Anglican theologians, they relied on a handful of Caroline divines, heavily selected, and on the shift in the centre of gravity which occurred in the Church of England *after* the Restoration settlement and the effective excision of the 'Puritan' wing in 1662.[15]

Was High Churchmanship as it came to be by the end of the nineteenth century and the beginning of the twentieth, then, an alien intrusion into Anglicanism, an imported, hybrid system drawing on elements of Roman Catholic theology grafted onto surviving institutional features such as episcopacy and the accident of the preservation of the tactile succession of ministry via ordination? That was evidently the view of opponents.[16] But it is important to try to get away from the idea that there is a real, 'authentic' Anglicanism utterly true to the spirit, practice and principles of the Anglican Reformers still to be dug out of the historical record and applied without adaptation to the present. There is no such thing at hand, nor could there be, given the utter 'strangeness' of the world of the sixteenth century from that of Britain today. The mistake of High Churchmen may have been, from one angle, a kind of blind historicism – an assumption that they could claim for themselves the historic heart of the Church of England – but the same mistake could be posited of their rivals too. Anglican theology has always been subject to change and development, even as it has sought to remain faithful to some degree to its historic heritage and to the biblical witness.[17] High Churchmen were not simply inventing a new religion to suit themselves. They were attempting to give real expression to what they interpreted as the long-term historical experience and form of the Christian Church, in the particular context of the Church of England. High Church theology had a real theological 'centre', both in its conviction of the normative character of the threefold order of ministry and in its fidelity to the main outlines of Christian doctrine as it had been settled largely

---

13   Cf., for example, N. Atkinson, 'Hooker's Theological Method and Modern Anglicanism'.

14   Cf. W. B. Patterson, *William Perkins and the Making of a Protestant England*.

15   Cf. P. B. Nockles, 'The Reformation Revised? The Contested Reception of the English Reformation in Nineteenth-Century Protestantism'.

16   Cf. the survey in M. Wellings, *Evangelicals Embattled: Responses of Evangelicals in the Church of England to Ritualism, Darwinism and Theological Liberalism*, pp. 40–60.

17   Cf. the excellent account by Mark Chapman, *Anglican Theology*.

by the fifth century. Its border with Roman Catholicism was – despite many conversions – maintained with some determination and consistency, as we saw in chapter 8. Yet it also self-consciously marked out its position over and against other elements of Anglicanism. Its case could perhaps be summed up in the following way. It typified a 'reformed Catholicism' also to be found in other portions of the western Church, holding (and here there are echoes of Austin Farrer) both to the threefold order of ministry and to a refusal to accept the Papal primacy as currently constituted. In spirit, as ecumenical agreements were to confirm in the twentieth century, it brought Anglicanism close to Scandinavian Lutheranism, and to the non-aligned 'Old' Catholic churches that were to be included, in 1889, into a union under the Declaration of Utrecht, as well as to some of the Orthodox churches. Through the Chicago-Lambeth Quadrilateral of 1886–88, it helped to mark out an ecclesial position that could be hospitable to different doctrinal views within Anglicanism, and also be patient of some development in different ecumenical directions.

Yet, however persuasive this theological position may have been to High Churchmen and their followers themselves, their ambition to transform the life and practice of the Church of England was partially successful at best. The Church of England did eventually adjust to the new liturgical and ceremonial changes that Ritualists and others introduced. Opposition largely faded by the early twentieth century. Many 'low' or 'middle' Anglican parishes adopted some of the controversial innovations of the mid-nineteenth century, such as surpliced choirs, 'Anglican' chanting and lit candles on the altar. Liturgical reform was eventually engineered by High Church leaders and theologians, though not without significant setbacks such as Parliament's defeat of Prayer Book revision in 1927–28. As Arthur Burns has shown, High Churchmen were instrumental in the adoption and implementation of organisational changes which helped the Church of England to thrive in the mid and late nineteenth century.[18] Moreover, by the mid-twentieth century, Anglo-Catholicism had even acquired a fashionable, cultivated literary following, in writers such as T. S. Eliot, Dorothy L. Sayers, Barbara Pym, and W. H. Auden, among others. All these things were so, and yet the High Church revival faced definite limits. It never succeeded in changing decisively the piety of the majority of English parishes. Its role in the institutional revival of the Church of England came to a head, it seems, in the early twentieth century, just at the point at which churchgoing in Britain began to falter. It was confronted by powerful currents of popular anti-Catholic opinion, which began to fade in the late nineteenth century, but which lingered on as a predominantly 'Protestant' idea of national

---

18   R. A. Burns, *The Diocesan Revival in the Church of England c. 1800–1870.*

identity well into the twentieth century.[19] And it also struggled to change an associated, long-run 'default' in popular English religion which was wary of sacramentalism.

High Churchmanship, then, was fraught with signs of promise and portents of failure. Nowhere is this clearer, perhaps, than in its involvement in the emergence of the modern Church of England's representative system. That is a suitable point from which to assess its limits.

High Churchmen and the Representative System: An Organisational Defeat

The creation of a representative system of governance was one of the most significant ways in which the Church of England reacted to change in the nineteenth century.[20] The revival of the (entirely clerical) Convocations of Canterbury and York owed something to Tractarian pressure for spiritual independence for the Church of England, particularly in the wake of the Gorham judgement, but more moderate High Churchmen were arguably more important in the expansion of the system to encompass local as well as national layers of the system.[21] High Church support for *lay* representation was more mixed, however. Some Anglo-Catholics were openly hostile, fearing that it could undermine the doctrinal authority of the clergy. Luke Rivington, for example, claimed that the inclusion of the laity in Church government, where matters of doctrine would be concerned, would be 'unscriptural and uncatholic'.[22] Some, such as R. F. Littledale, were more supportive, though still wary of lay involvement in doctrinal matters.[23] Others, such as Charles Gore,

---

19   Cf. J. Maiden, *National Religion and the Prayer-Book Controversy, 1927–8*, pp. 133–62.

20   The main accounts are in: K. A. Thompson, *Bureaucracy and Church Reform: The Organizational Response of the Church of England to Social Change, 1800–1965*; M. J. D. Roberts, 'The Role of the Laity in the Church of England c. 1850–1885, D.Phil. thesis, Oxford University, 1974; B. Heeney, *The Women's Movement in the Church of England 1850–1930*; and Burns, *Diocesan Revival*.

21   Burns, *Diocesan Revival*, pp. 10 & 218–21.

22   Speech to the English Church Union, reported in the *Church Times* for 18 January 1868, and quoted in G. Byrne, 'Consulting the Faithful: The Role of the Laity in the Government of the Church of England 1861–1904', M.Phil. thesis, Cambridge University, 1998, p. 31. I am much in debt in this and the following paragraph to Georgina Byrne's study.

23   Littledale's views on lay representation were propagated in a number of publications, including his *Church Reform: A Lecture Delivered in the Corn Exchange, Lincoln*.

were more enthusiastic.[24] But despite disagreement on the *principle* of lay representation, by the end of the nineteenth century most High Churchmen accepted confirmation and regular communion as the franchise for lay representation.

By the 1880s, the basic structure of the modern Anglican representative system was established. A report on lay representation prepared by Canterbury Convocation in 1872 presupposed four fundamental principles: separate but parallel representation for clergy and laity; a hierarchy of authorities, rising from parish councils to national convocations or assemblies; the connection of representative bodies with traditional ecclesiastical units of jurisdiction (parish, deanery, diocese, and province); and an indirect, rather than mass or 'democratic', election of representatives to the higher authorities.[25] The system was voluntary, and lacked legislative foundation. Lay representation did not exist at the national level until the formation of the Representative Church Council (RCC), combining both Convocations and lay assemblies, in 1903; even then, its powers were largely consultative.

In some parishes, parish councils may have evolved out of the communicants' guilds. St Luke's, Chesterton, was perhaps a case in point. A new parish on the northern outskirts of Victorian Cambridge, St Luke's was at first moderate High Church, but under its vicar from 1892 it moved towards a more 'advanced' Ritualism.[26] It had a Guild, but one never formally integrated into the management of the parish, so far as the evidence of vestry minutes suggests.[27] There were meetings of male communicants, however (the gender exclusivity here was not unusual), particularly for important decisions. So, for example, in September 1883 a meeting of male communicants recommended the collection of a voluntary church rate to maintain the church's fabric.[28] In 1904, it was a meeting of male communicants again which decided to institute a church council, with the electorate as confirmed men in the parish.[29] The council oversaw a wide range of practical, administrative matters; the only

---

24   As Byrne points out, the contrasting views of Littledale and Gore may be attributable in part to the fact that Gore was writing later, signifying a theological development in the Anglo-Catholic understanding of authority in the Church: idem, 'Consulting the Faithful', p. 47.

25   Little attention has been paid to this report by historians: Chadwick, for example, says nothing of it in *The Victorian Church*, Vol. 2, nor does K. A. Thompson. Cf. Byrne, 'Consulting the Faithful', pp. 36–9.

26   RCED, *Report*, Vol. 2, para. 5941.

27   Vestry minutes, St Luke's, Chesterton: CambRO, P40A/8/1.

28   Vestry minutes, 17 September 1883, St Luke's, Chesterton: CambRO, P40A/8/1.

29   St Luke's Church Council Minutes, 30 October 1904: CambRO, P40A/8/3.

excluded items were doctrine and ritual.[30] But this merely reflected wider trends. By the early twentieth century the communicant franchise, though not absolutely universal, was very widespread, going well beyond the circle of 'advanced' Anglo-Catholic parishes.[31]

Full legislative implementation of a representative system for the Church of England had to wait until after the First World War, with the Enabling Act in 1919. Probably the most significant single piece of legislation passed by Parliament for the Church of England in the twentieth century, it led to the full integration of lay representatives with the two houses of clergy and bishops into a new Church Assembly. It provided some legislative autonomy for the Church, thus drawing the sting of anti-establishmentarian criticism, and instituted at local level the Parochial Church Councils which constitute the bedrock of the Church of England's representative system today. Euphoria at the creation of the Church Assembly was short-lived, however, dented as it was by the Prayer Book controversy of 1927–28, when it became evident just how limited the Church's new-found independence really was. Even so, on a long perspective the 1919 measure was the axis of the Church of England's development of a synodical system of government, producing for the first time a uniform system of lay and clerical representation from parish to national level.

The strong support of High Churchmen for the creation of a representative system has been largely forgotten in the mythology of the Enabling Act. It is widely assumed that much of the credit for the measure has to go to the Life and Liberty movement, formed in 1917 by a formidable group of clergy and laity led by William Temple.[32] Life and Liberty aimed to 'win for the Church full power to control its own life, even at the cost, if necessary, of disestablishment'.[33] The energy and idealism of Temple chimed in with the mood of a younger generation's impatience with the cumbersome nature of the Church of England's governance, exposed by its failure to raise enthusiasm for religious revival during the war.[34]

---

30   Ibid.

31   One probable exception was the new diocese of Southwell, where the first bishop, George Ridding, insisted on a 'wide' franchise, a description that almost certainly indicates baptism rather than confirmation: J. N. Morris, 'George Ridding and the diocese of Southwell: A Study in the National Church Ideal', p. 140.

32   Lloyd called Life and Liberty 'one of the most remarkable fellowships which have ever changed a Church's history': R. Lloyd, *The Church of England in the Twentieth Century*, p. 248.

33   Letter in *The Times* of 20 June 1917 announcing the formation of Life and Liberty, quoted in Thompson, *Bureaucracy and Church Reform*, p. 156.

34   Cf. A. Wilkinson in *The Church of England and the First World War*, p. 71.

Some credit should go to Life and Liberty for intensifying pressure on Archbishop Randall Davidson. But in fact Davidson himself was the guiding force behind the legislation. Far from being a product of the war, the final scheme was pre-war in origin. Its immediate context was Welsh Church Disestablishment. Concerned to head off a similar challenge to the Church of England, Sir Alfred Cripps had moved (in the RCC in 1913) the appointment of a committee of enquiry to secure the 'fuller expression of the spiritual independence of the Church and the national recognition of religion'.[35] The committee reported in 1916, advocating the universal establishment of PCCs, the full integration of lay representation in the assembly, and the devolution of powers of self-government to the new assembly, though Davidson resisted implementation until after the war.[36] Thus, by the time Life and Liberty was formed, the main outlines of the scheme eventually adopted had already been formulated and received episcopal approval.

Historians' opinions vary over what influence Life and Liberty wielded, and over whether or not Davidson would have pushed the 1916 proposals through to implementation without external pressure.[37] But in one crucial respect the pressure group's influence was decisive. That was the nature of the franchise for the new PCCs. The 1916 scheme envisaged a confirmation franchise, a proposal in line (as we have seen) with existing practice. But by late 1917 the mood was changing: a number of speakers in the RCC urged the adoption of the baptismal franchise, despite strong opposition from Gore and others.[38] The Council of Life and Liberty eventually followed Temple on the matter, supporting the baptismal franchise.[39] In the February 1919 debates in the RCC, opinion swung heavily in favour of Life and Liberty's line, and the baptismal franchise secured substantial majorities in all three houses.[40]

Why did opinion change during the war? There are at least three possible explanations, by no means mutually exclusive: women, social class, and Establishment. First, in debate in the RCC in July 1914 some speakers pointed

35 G. K. A. Bell, *Randall Davidson, Archbishop of Canterbury*, p. 957.

36 Bell, *Randall Davidson*, p. 959.

37 E. W. Kemp, *Counsel and Consent: Aspects of the Government of the Church*, pp. 195–7, and Thompson, *Bureaucracy and Church Reform*, pp. 156–73, thought Temple decisive; but against this cf. J. H. S. Kent, *William Temple: Church, State and Society in Britain, 1880–1950*, pp. 74–5 & 91–3, D. M. Thompson, 'The Politics of the Enabling Act (1919)', and of course George Bell himself, in his *Randall Davidson*, p. 980.

38 *Proceedings of the RCC* for 27 November 1917.

39 F. A. Iremonger, *William Temple, Archbishop of Canterbury*, p. 260.

40 *Proceedings of the RCC* for 28 February 1919.

out that many more women than men were confirmed.[41] There was still sufficient controversy over the inclusion of women as electors in 1919 to require
specific debate on the issue. Did some representatives fear that the confirmation franchise would unduly favour women? Second, early opinion in favour of
special representation for working men (it is nearly always 'men' in the record
of debate) was transmuted into a widening of the church electorate overall.
The *Modern Churchman* claimed that the confirmation franchise was socially
divisive, favouring the middle-class churchgoers who were the staple of most
communicating congregations.[42] Third (and this was reflected in debate), the
failure of the Church of England's National Mission during the war convinced
'Broad' churchmen that participation in church matters had to be widened to
include as much of the nation as possible.[43] As John Kent has argued, Temple
'was bound to favour an inclusive against an exclusive voting qualification,
because he desired a truly national establishment'.[44]

Temple himself was somewhat disingenuous on the matter of Life and
Liberty's position, claiming in the RCC that none of his colleagues in the movement was 'a protagonist for any one franchise against the others', but laying out
a clear case himself for baptism.[45] There was evidently a serious division in the
movement. Gore resigned his bishopric in 1919, citing defeat of the confirmation franchise as one of his reasons: 'I am convinced that ... we have sacrificed
principle to the desire for larger numbers on our rolls, and that largely for the
sake of maintaining the 'national' position of the Church.'[46] Francis Underhill
wrote privately to Temple to protest that the movement's position 'would do
much to stop progress in a Catholic direction by giving too much power to
an ultra-conservative laity'.[47] Opposition to the new franchise in discussion
in the RCC was almost entirely from Anglo-Catholic members, as noted by the
strongly pro-Anglo-Catholic *Church Times*.[48]

In summary, the outcome of the short-lived but heated dispute over the
electoral qualification was a decisive vote in favour of the proposal adopted by
'Broad' Church or Liberal Anglicans, and supported by Evangelical laity and

---

41   *Proceedings of the RCC* for 9 & 10 July 1914.
42   Quoted in Thompson, *Bureaucracy and Church Reform*, p. 172.
43   Edward Talbot, Bishop of Winchester, friend and associate of Gore (but on this his oppo-
     nent) argued to this effect: *Proceedings of the RCC* for 28 February 1919.
44   Kent, *William Temple*, p. 74.
45   Iremonger, *William Temple*, p. 260; see also *Proceedings of the RCC* for 27 February 1919.
46   Bell, *Randall Davidson*, p. 970; Davidson persuaded Gore to change the word 'established'
     to 'national' in the passage cited, when the letter was released for publication.
47   Cited in Thompson, *Bureaucracy and Church Reform*, p. 173.
48   *Church Times*, 7 March 1919.

clergy. A bitter disappointment for many Anglo-Catholics, it marked a definite shift in the organisation of the Church's representative system away from the assumption that the real test of 'membership' of the Church of England was regular communion. According to his biographer, Gore accused the Church of 'treating the spiritual obligations of Church membership with something like contempt'.[49] The sensitivities were plain in the reporting of the *Church Times*. In its issue of 7 March 1919, during the RCC debates, it emasculated Temple's speech, turning him into an apparent supporter of the confirmation franchise, alongside Gore, Lord Cecil, the Earl of Selborne, and others.[50] A week later, after the franchise defeat, it carried a rather paranoid article by Francis Underhill under the title 'What are Catholics to do?' Almost all the bishops, Underhill asserted, 'are against us; they use us and abuse us, and slight our work, they treat us generally as if we were naughty school-boys, they seldom let slip an opportunity of attacking us'.[51]

It may seem to be claiming too much to suggest that this defeat marked the outer limit of the High Church revival in Anglicanism, especially since Temple's hope that the baptismal franchise would draw millions of working-class electors into active participation in church affairs proved illusory. But consider its ecclesiological implications. By making baptism co-extensive with the condition for participation in the Church's local administration, the franchise strengthened the argument that the Church of England's polity reflected a 'baptismal ecclesiology'. It placed at the very heart of the Church's governance a challenge to the Anglo-Catholic assumption that the constitution and authority of the Church resided decisively in the hierarchical order of the ministry. This was recognised at the time. For the Evangelical *Churchman,* Gore's resignation showed that he and his friends 'see that their influence is passing away, and that there is reason to believe that real power will ultimately – perhaps soon, perhaps late – be vested in a body which, with the laity largely represented, is not specially impressed by sacerdotal pretensions'.[52] The decision to adopt a baptismal franchise could be read as a reaffirmation of a historic Anglican position on the catholicity of the Church, reaching back well before Tractarianism to embrace the view that baptism was what was supremely important in determining the identity of the Church. This 'baptismal ecclesiology' remained implicit for much of the twentieth century, masked, if anything,

---

49   Though intriguingly he does not indicate the exact source of this statement: G. L. Prestige, *The Life of Charles Gore, a Great Englishman,* p. 422.

50   *Church Times,* 7 March 1919.

51   *Church Times,* 14 March 1919.

52   *The Churchman,* 33 (May 1919), p. 231.

by the apparent strength of the Anglo-Catholic movement in the 1920s and 1930s. It came to be articulated most fully in the late twentieth century, in the work of Stephen Sykes, Paul Avis and others.[53] But at the 1920 Lambeth Conference the baptismal constitution of the Church was vigorously affirmed. The appeal 'To all Christian People' acknowledged 'all those who believe in Our Lord Jesus Christ and have been baptized into the name of the Holy Trinity, as sharing with us membership in the universal Church of Christ which is his Body'.[54] That in turn was to prove vital for the Church's later exploration of ecumenical relationships with non-episcopal churches.

Symbolically, then, the decision to reject the cumulative precedent of years of development at local level, and to adopt the baptismal franchise instead of the confirmation franchise, may well have marked the beginning of the end of Anglo-Catholic influence in the Church of England – and in that sense its 'failure'. Certainly, the mood of Anglo-Catholics generally remained buoyant through the following forty years or so, and their influence was immense. But it is difficult not to see this as a turning point, the beginning of a trajectory of increasing defensiveness on the part of Anglo-Catholics, in which they fought bitterly and then lost over a series of issues which included the revised Prayer Book and the formation of the Church of South India. At the very least, it cut short abruptly the trend towards the adoption of regular communion as the basic test of church membership pioneered by Anglo-Catholic parishes in the late nineteenth century, and so landed the Church of England with an organisational 'definition' of church membership which did not reflect the convictions of most High Churchmen.

But in any event the model of eucharistic community which underlay support for the communicant franchise in 1919 was liturgically and devotionally premature: its theological basis was a theory of church membership defined by eucharistic participation which was not matched by the actual practice of many Anglican congregations. The persistence of Mattins as a main Sunday service in many parishes well into the mid-twentieth century is evidence of that. Moreover, there is the awkward fact of the very high level of non-receiving attendance even at many of the most 'advanced' Ritualist churches to contend with. As liturgical historians have long recognised, not until the emergence of the 'Parish Communion' in the middle years of the twentieth century could Anglican eucharistic practice really be said to reflect adequately the

---

53   Cf. S. W. Sykes, 'Foundations of an Anglican Ecclesiology', in *Unashamed Anglicanism*, pp. 122–39; also P. D. L. Avis, *The Identity of Anglicanism: Essentials of an Anglican Ecclesiology*, pp. 109–17.

54   H. Bettenson (ed.), *Documents of the Christian Church*, p. 441.

sacramental doctrine of the High Church revival – and even then, at first in but a small proportion of parishes.[55]

The Limitations of Success

Although the 1920s and 1930s have been hailed as the high-water mark of Anglo-Catholicism in the Church of England, High Churchmen had already conceded a reorganisation of the church's institutional governance which marginalised their distinctive perspective on church membership. Their ability to organize large rallies such as the London congress of 1923, with over 16,000 attenders, belied the fact that theirs was a minority view in the Church of England as a whole. Defeat of Prayer Book revision in Parliament in 1927–8 merely confirmed this, exposing not only the limited nature of the legislative autonomy granted to the Church just eight years before, but the abiding force of popular Protantism and anti-Catholicism. It was a coalition of Evangelical and Liberal Anglican MPs with Nonconformist MPs that voted the 'Deposited Book' down, but the politicians were certainly reflecting wider currents of popular opinion.[56] The revised book passed into wide use, in fact, since bishops could licence its use on a voluntary basis. But the damage had been done. Parliament's blocking of the Church's own proposals for liturgical revision left High Church parishes in a liturgical no man's land, unable to express their characteristic devotional principles satisfactorily in what remained the only officially-sanctioned book of services for the Church of England. They had no choice but to carry on quietly editing, adapting, ignoring or dismantling the Prayer Book, if they were to remain faithful to the main currents of High Church development in doctrine and practice since the mid-nineteenth century.

As if this institutional constraint were not enough, it is also worth bearing in mind that High Church devotional ideals were intense and demanding, and unlikely ever to have commanded the full assent of more than a proportion even of the highest or most 'advanced' Anglo-Catholic parishes. The small numbers of those receiving communion in the early twentieth century was a sign of that. All the effort poured into increasing celebrations of communion

---

55   The principal authorities are A. G. Herbert, *Liturgy and Society*; idem, *The Parish Communion*; D. Gray, *Earth and Altar: The Evolution of the Parish Communion in the Church of England to 1945;* and J. Fenwick and B. Spinks, *Worship in Transition: The Twentieth Century Liturgical Movement.*

56   Maiden, *National Religion*, pp. 63–5.

and enhancing the beauty and splendour of High Mass in these churches ran up against the austere ideal of fasting communion. Though he was a defender of fasting communion, Gabriel Hebert aptly summarised the quandary in which Anglo-Catholic parishes found themselves in the early twentieth century: the clergy maintained in principle that the eucharist was 'the sacrament of the fellowship of the Body ... [but in fact] Holy Communion is commonly regarded as a service of private devotion for the few'.[57] Almost certainly this is an indication also of the limitations that High Churchmen – and especially Anglo-Catholics – faced in their commendation of auricular confession. Again great efforts were made to encourage congregants to make their confession privately and regularly, in the face of much controversy. No figures for 'take up' exist – nor, by the very nature of private confession, could they – but it seems likely that practice never matched precept, and never caught up with the frequency of confession in Roman Catholic parishes, even granting the common complaint of Catholic clergy that their parishioners were not attentive enough to confession. But again Anglo-Catholics had to reckon here with a powerful countervailing culture in the Church of England which, insisting on public confession as in itself necessary and sufficient for reception of communion, made it difficult to make much headway with recommending private confession.[58]

None of this is to deny the very great impact that High Churchmen had made on the modern Church of England by the middle of the twentieth century. If the revival had reached its limit by then, it had already embedded High Church theology and devotional practice solidly in parishes the length and breadth of the Church of England. It was unquestionably a lively, dynamic element of modern Anglicanism, and its achievement in England was matched by its influence in the worldwide Anglican Communion. Why, then, was it to falter in the next half-century, so that by the end of the twentieth century many critics could even proclaim its death? To answer that question would require another book altogether. I can offer only a few comments here. Commonly attention has been drawn to the theological fragility of High Church theology in the face of arguments over women's ministry, liturgical reform, and human sexuality. The divisions that flared up in western Anglicanism in the 1970s and 1980s over women's ministry and homosexuality exacerbated underlying strategic differences in Anglican High Churchmanship over how

---

57   Hebert, *Liturgy and Society*, p. 165.

58   Even Vernon Staley quoted approvingly Pusey's *Letter to the Bishop of London*: 'I have never taught that confession to man was necessary to forgiveness': idem, *The Catholic Religion: A Manual of Instruction for members of the Anglican Church*, p. 352.

to respond constructively to a rapidly-changing world. These differences have been characterised by an acerbic critic of Anglicanism, the Dominican Aidan Nichols, as lying between an 'Orthodox' Anglican Catholicism and an Anglican 'Modernism'.[59] Unquestionably Nichols is right to draw attention to internal divisions. Anglican High Churchmanship may have cohered around common theological convictions about church order and fundamental doctrine, but it always contained a range of different views, and the very lack of an Anglican *magisterium* to compare with that of the Roman Catholic Church meant that fidelity to core doctrine and practice was never really policed in the Church of England.

The problem with theological division as an explanation for High Church decline, however, is that it ignores the possibility of longer-run, underlying changes that helped to weaken the popular base of the High Church tradition in Anglicanism *before* these divisions really emerged into the open. Here, it is surely the case that the very distinctiveness of High Churchmanship as an approach to piety and practice proved to be a weakness when confronted with the revolution in popular culture after the Second World War. It was, after all, a religiously demanding way of life requiring the kind of regular, institutional commitment which people increasingly fought shy of. Unlike popular Evangelicalism, what had made Anglo-Catholic worship so distinctive was not readily adaptable to elements of the new popular culture. Its characteristic mode was a kind of self-conscious formality, supported by a 'high' culture of choral music, distinctive dress, and a hierarchical reading of ministerial authority, which could not adapt easily to the casual, informal and somewhat subversive mood promoted by the new media.

Was the High Church revival ultimately a failure, then? I am tempted to follow Chairman Mao who, asked about the impact of the French Revolution, is supposed to have replied, 'It is too soon to say.' It is certainly too soon to say whether or not the relative weakening of High Church or Anglo-Catholic influence in the contemporary Church of England is likely to continue or to stabilize. Any estimate about the future of High Churchmanship would require a much more detailed assessment of its position at the beginning of the twenty-first century. So the judgement to make about the revival's success or failure must necessarily be a provisional one, based on a summing up of its historic achievements. These are many. They include a substantial contribution to the Church of England's ecumenical relationships, a broadening of its awareness of currents of theological opinion elsewhere in Europe, a notable role in the

---

59   At least, this is implicit in his comments on the mixed legacy of the Oxford Movement: A. Nichols, *The Panther and the Hind: A Theological History of Anglicanism*, p. 128.

foundation of theological colleges and the development of theological education, a decisive influence in many of the organisational developments of the nineteenth and early twentieth centuries and in liturgical revision, enrichment of the musical heritage of Anglicanism, a long list of outstanding pastors, theologians, apologists and missionaries, and the revival of Anglican religious orders. If, under the influence of Tractarianism, High Churchmen have accentuated or even exaggerated the importance of the doctrine of apostolic succession and, as a result, sometimes projected a distorted image of the historic identity of the Church of England, the fading of popular anti-Catholic prejudice in English culture has enabled us to see that they have nonetheless also helped Anglicanism to 'reconnect' itself with much of the spirit and history of Catholic Christianity. The anti-Evangelical and anti-Liberal polemics of the nineteenth century surely caused much damage within Anglicanism, though 'party spirit' was hardly something confined to High Churchmen. High Church aspirations to change the religious life of the Church of England achieved much, but ultimately hit the 'invisible' wall of a popular religious culture which proved largely resistant to their brand of sacramentalism. But they did, all the same, create space for a reformed Catholicism within its generous bounds, and that is a significant and lasting achievement. The very fact that some modern scholars have to work hard to argue how much the Oxford Movement misled the mind of modern Anglicanism is testimony to that.

Bibliography

[NB: This bibliography does not include individual entries in the ODNB, which are credited in the chapter footnotes.]

Unpublished Primary Sources

Bodleian Library, Oxford
  George Ridding papers
Cambridge University Library
  Ely diocesan visitation records
Cambridgeshire Record Office, Cambridge
  Barrington parish records
  St Clements, Cambridge, parish records
  All Saints, Cambridge, parish records
  St Luke's, Cambridge, parish records
King's College, London
  Relton Library, F. D. Maurice papers
Lambeth Palace Library
  Records of the CBS
  J. M. Neale papers
Medway Archives & Record Centre, Rochester
  Papers of St Mary, Chatham
Pusey House, Oxford
  H. P. Liddon papers
Somerset Record Office, Taunton
  Axbridge parish records
  St Mary, Bathwick, parish records
Satffordshire Record Office, Stafford [check]
  St Modwen's, Burton-on-Trent, parish records

Published Primary Sources (pre-1914)

Abbeloos, J. -B., *La crise du Protestantisme en Angleterre* (Louvain: chez Peeters, 1870).
[Alford] *Life and Letters of Henry Alford, DD, Late Dean of Canterbury, edited by his widow* (London: Rivingtons, 1873).
Alford, H., *Letters from Abroad* (2nd edn, London: Strahan, 1865).

Allies, T. W., *Journal in France in 1845 and 1848, with Letters from Italy in 1847, of Things and Persons concerning the Church and Education* (London: Longman, Brown, Green & Longman, 1849).

———, *A Life's Decision* (London: Kegan Paul, 1880).

Anonymous, 'An Enquirer', *A re-print of a letter addressed to a Revd Member of the Cambridge Camden Society ... with a few remarks and queries* (London: Edwards, 1845).

———, *St Andrew's Church for the Poor* (Croydon: privately published, 1858).

———, *Remarks on the Primary Charge of the Bishop of Brechin* (Edinburgh, 1858).

———, *Manual of the Confraternity of the Blessed Sacrament* (London: CBS, 1862).

———, (ed.), *Memorials and Correspondence respecting the recent appointment of an Incumbent for St Saviour's Church, Croydon* (London: privately published, 1869).

———, 'John Hodgson', in *Croydon Crayons* (Croydon: Croydon Advertiser, 1873).

———, *Ritual Notes on the Order of Divine Service* (London: Mowbray, 1890).

Arnold, M., 'Emerson', in M. Arnold, *Discourses in America*, in *Works*, Vol. 4 (London: Macmillan, 1903).

Arnold, T., *Travelling Journals*, ed. A. P. Stanley (London: Fellowes, 1852).

Augustine, *Confessions* (new edn, transl. E. B. Pusey, London: Dent, 1907).

Ayres, J. (ed.), *Paupers and Pig Killers: The diary of William Holland, a Somerset Parson 1799–1818* (Gloucester: Alan Sutton, 1984).

[Baunard], *Épiscopat Français depuis le Concordat jusqu'à la Séparation* ("ouvrage publié sous la Direction de la Société Bibliographique ... et une introduction par Mgr. Baunard" (Paris: Librairie de Saint-Pères, 1907).

Bennett, F., *The Story of W. J. E. Bennett* (London: Longmans, 1909).

Bennett, W. J. E., *Distinctive Errors of Romanism: a series of lecture-sermons* (London: Cleaver, 1842).

———, *The Church, the Crown, and the State: Their Junction or their Separation* (London: Cleaver, 1850).

Benson, A. C., *Edward White Benson* (new edn, London: Macmillan, 1901).

Birks, T. R., *Memoir of the Rev. Edward Bickersteth, late Rector of Watton, Herts* (3rd edn, London: Seeleys, 1852).

Blunt, J. H., *Directorium Pastorale: Principles and Practice of Pastoral Work in the Church of England* (London: Rivingtons, 1864).

———, *The Sacraments and Sacramental Ordinances of the Church: Being a plain exposition of their history, meaning, and effects* (London: Rivingtons, 1867).

———, *A Key to the Knowledge and Use of the Book of Common Prayer* (London: Rivingtons, 1868).

Bowden, J. E., *The Life and Letters of Frederick William Faber DD* (London: Burns & Oates, 1869).

Brajeul, M., *Lettres d'un Catholique à un Protestant de l'église Anglicane* (Dinan: J.-B. Huart, 1839).

[British Weekly], *The Religious Census of London: Reprinted from the British Weekly* (London: British Weekly, 1887).

Bumpus, T. F., *London Churches Ancient and Modern* (London: T. Werner Laurie, 1908).

Burgon, J. W., *Lives of Twelve Good Men* (4th edn, London: Murray, 1889).

[Burnouf], *Choix de lettres d'Eugène Burnouf 1825–1852* (Paris: H. Champion, 1891).

Census of Great Britain, 1851: Religious Worship (England and Wales), Report and Tables (London: Routledge, 1853).

Chéry, 'Le R. P. M.', *Appel à l'Église Russe et à l'Église Anglicane* (Paris: Victor Palmé, 1866).

Church, M. C., *Life and Letters of Dean Church* (London: Macmillan, 1895).

Church, R. W., *The Oxford Movement: Twelve Years: 1833–1845* (new edn, London: University of Chicago Press, 1970).

Coleridge, J. T., *A Memoir of the Rev. John Keble* (Oxford & London: Parker, 1869).

Coleridge, S. T., *On the Constitution of the Church and State* (new edn, London: Dent, 1972).

Compton, B., *Edward Meyrick Goulburn, D.D., D.C.L., Dean of Norwich: A Memoir* (London: Murray, 1899).

Conybeare, W., 'Church Parties', ed. R. A. Burns, in S. Taylor (ed.), *From Cranmer to Davidson: A Church of England Miscellany* (Woodbridge: Boydell, 1999), pp. 245–385.

Copleston, W. J., *Memoir of Edward Copleston, DD, Bishop of Llandaff* (London: Parker, 1851).

Cornish, F. Warre, *A History of the English Church in the Nineteenth Century* (2 vols., London: Macmillan, 1910).

Cox, G. W., *The Life of John William Colenso, Bishop of Natal* (2 vols., London: Ridgway, 1888).

Crouch, W., *Bryan King and the Riots at St. George's-in-the-East* (London: Methuen, 1904).

d'Aubigné, J. H. Merle, ed. E. Bickersteth, *A Voice from the Alps: Or, a Brief Account of the Evangelical Societies of Paris and Geneva* (London: Seeley & Burnside, 1838).

Davidson, R. T., & Benham, W., *Life of Archibald Campbell Tait: Archbishop of Canterbury* (London: Macmillan, 1891).

Draper, W. H., *Recollections of Dean Fremantle, chiefly by himself* (London: Cassell, 1921).

Faber, F., *Sights and Thoughts in foreign churches and among foreign peoples* (London: Rivingtons, 1842).

Fairbairn, A., *The Place of Christ in Modern Theology* (London: Hodder & Stoughton, 1893).

Falloux, F. A. P. [Comte de], *Mémoires d'un Royaliste* (Paris: Perrin , 1888).

Fowler, J. T., *Life and Letters of John Bacchus Dykes* (London: Murray, 1897).

Gerbet, P., *Considerations on the Eucharist, viewed as the Generative Dogma of Catholic Piety* (London: Dolman, 1840).

Gondon, J., *Du Mouvement Religieux en Angleterre, ou Les Progrès du Catholicisme et le Retour de l'Église Anglicane à l'Unité; par un Catholique* (Paris: Sangier & Bray, 1844).

———, *Conversion de soixante ministres Anglicans* (Paris: Sangier, 1846).

———, *Motifs de conversion de dix ministres Anglicans, exposés par eux-mêmes, et rétraction du Révérend J. H. Newman* (Paris: Sangier & Bray, 1847).

———, *Notice biographique sur le R. P. Newman* (Paris: Sangier & Bray, 1853).

Gore C., et al., *Lux Mundi: A series of studies in the religion of the Incarnation* (London: Murray, 1889).

Gore, C., *The Incarnation of the Son of God* (London: Murray, 1891).

———, *The Mission of the Church* (London: Murray, 1892).

———, *Dissertations on Subjects Connected with the Incarnation* (London: Murray, 1895).

———, *The Creed of the Christian* (London: Wells Gardner Darton, 1895).

———, *Roman Catholic Claims* (London: Longmans, 1900).

———, *The New Theology and the Old Religion* (London: Murray, 1908).

Gray, J. H., *Letter to the Rt Hon and Rev. the Lord Bishops of London, on the State of the Anglican Congregations in Germany* (London: Rivingtons, 1843).

Gresley, W., *Ecclesiastes Anglicanus: Being a Treatise on the Art of Preaching, as adapted to a Church of England Congregation* (London: Rivingtons, 1835).

———, *The Necessity of Zeal and Moderation: The Present Circumstances of the Church, enforced and illustrated in five sermons preached before the University of Oxford* (London: Rivingtons, 1839).

———, *Practical Sermons* (London: Joseph Masters, 1848).

———, *The Present State of the Controversy with Rome: Three Sermons preached in S. Paul's Church, Brighton* (London: Joseph Masters, 1855).

Grovestins, Le Baron Sirtema de, *Considérations sur l'église Anglicane et l'église Catholique, à l'occasion de la création de l'évêché Anglican de Jérusalem et du rétablissement de la hiérarchie catholique en Angleterre* (Paris: chez Dentu, 1851).

Headlam, S., *The Meaning of the Mass: Five lectures* (London: Brown Langham, 1905).

Heitland, L., *Ritualism in Town and Country: A Volume of Evidence* (London: Murray, 1902).

Herbert, George, *The Complete English Poems* (Harmondsworth: Penguin, 1991).

[Holland, H. S.], *Impressions of the Ammergau Passion Play, by an Oxonian* (London: Swift, 1870).

Hook, W. F., *The Novelties of Romanism: or, Popery refuted by Tradition. A Sermon preached in St Andrew's Church, Manchester* (London: Rivingtons, 1839).

———, *The Eucharist a Sacrament and a Sacrifice* (London: Rivingtons, 1846).

Hutchings, W. H., *Life and Letters of Thomas Thellusson Carter* (London: Longmans, 1903).

Illingworth, A. L., *The Life and Work of John Richardson Illingworth* (London: Murray, 1917).

Illingworth, J. R., 'The Incarnation and Development', in C. Gore et al., *Lux Mundi: A Series of Studies in the Religion of the Incarnation* (2nd edn., London: Murray, 1890).

Johnston, J. O., *Life and Letters of Henry Parry Liddon* (London: Longmans, 1904).

Joseph, F. P., *Du Protestantisme suivi d'une dissertation sur le casuel et d'une abrégé de la religion Anglicane* (Campiègne: Dubois, & Paris: Debécourt, 1842).

Jouffroy, Count Achille de, *Adieux à l'Angleterre* (Paris: Méguignon, 1832).

Jowett, B., *et al.*, *Essays and Reviews* (London: Parker, 1860).

Keble, J., *National Apostasy Considered* (Oxford: Parker, 1833).

———, *Primitive Tradition recognised in the Holy Scriptures: A Sermon, preached in the Cathedral Church of Winchester* (London: Rivingtons, 1836).

———, *On Eucharistical Adoration* (2nd ed., Oxford: Parker, 1859).

———, *Sermons, Occasional and Parochial* (Oxford: Parker, 1868).

———, *Letters of Spiritual Guidance and Counsel* (London: Parker, 1870).

———, *Sermons for the Christian Year* (Oxford: Parker, 1876).

———, *Sermons for the Christian Year. Sermons for Lent to Passiontide* (Oxford: Parker, 1877).

Kilvert, F., *Diary* (ed. W. Plomer, 3 vols., London: Cape, 1939).

King, B., *Sacrilege and its Encouragement, being an Account of the St George's Riots and of their Successes, in a Letter of Remonstrance to the Lord Bishop of London* (London: Joseph Masters, 1860).

———, *Disestablishment the Present Hope of the Church: An Appeal to his Brother Churchmen* (London: Palmer, 1882).

[Lacordaire], *Correspondence du R. P. Lacordaire et de Madame Swetchine, publiée par le Cte de Falloux* (Paris: Auguste Vaton, 1864).

Lecanuet, É., *Montalembert: Sa jeunesse (1810–1836)* (2nd edn., Paris: Poussielgue, 1898).

Liddon, H. P., *The Divinity of Our Lord and Saviour Jesus Christ* (London: Rivingtons, 1869).

———, *Walter Kerr Hamilton, Bishop of Salisbury: A Sketch, reprinted, with additions and corrections, from 'The Guardian'* (London: Rivingtons, 1869).

———, *A. Rosmini, Of the Five Wounds of the Holy Church* (London: Rivingtons, 1883).

———, *Life of Edward Bouverie Pusey* (4 vols, London: Longmans, 1893).

———, *Clerical Life and Work: A Collection of Sermons* (2nd edn, London: Longmans, 1895).

Littledale, R. F., *Church Reform: A Lecture Delivered in the Corn Exchange, Lincoln* (London: Palmer, 1870).

Lupton, J. H., *Archbishop Wake and the Project of Union (1717–1720) between the Gallican and Anglican Churches* (London: Bell, 1896).

MacColl, M., *The Ammergau Passion Play* (London: Rivingtons, 1870).

Mann, H. (ed.), *Census of Religious Worship in England and Wales* (London: Routledge, 1854).

Mansel, H. L., *The Limits of Religious Thought Examined* (London: Murray, 1858).

Maskell, W., *Monumenta Ritualia Ecclesiae Anglicanae* (3 vols, London: Pickering, 1846–47).

———, *A Second Letter on the Present Position of the High Church Party in the Church of England* (London, Pickering, 1850).

Maurice, F., *Life of F. D. Maurice* (2 vols, London: Macmillan, 1884).

Maurice, F. D., *Subscription no Bondage, or the Practical Advantages Afforded by the Thirty-Nine Articles as Guides in all the Branches of Academical Education* (Oxford: Parker, 1835).

———, *The Kingdom of Christ, or, Hints on the principles, ordinances, and constitution of the Catholic Church in letters to a member of the Society of Friends* (1st edn, London: Darton & Clark, 1838).

———, *The Kingdom of Christ, or Hints to a Quaker respecting the Principles, Constitution and Ordinances of the Catholic Church* (1842; 4th edn, London: Macmillan, 1891).

———, *Three Letters to the Revd William Palmer* (London: Rivingtons, 1842).

———, *The Epistle to the Hebrews* (London: Parker, 1846).

———, *The Prayer-Book Considered Especially in Reference to the Romish System* (3rd edn, London: Parker, 1849).

———, *Lectures on the Ecclesiastical History of the First and Second Centuries* (Cambridge: Macmillan, 1854).

———, *Moral and Metaphysical Philosophy* (2 vols, London: Macmillan, 1862).

———, *The Conscience* (London: Macmillan, 1868).

———, *Social Morality* (London: Macmillan, 1869).

———, *Sermons on the Prayer Book and the Lord's Prayer* (3rd edn, London: Macmillan, 1880).

———, *The Gospel of the Kingdom of Heaven* (London: Macmillan, 1893).

Monro, E., *Parochial Work* (2nd edn., Oxford: Parker, 1850).

Montalembert, Charles [le Comte] de, *A Letter addressed to a Rev. Member of the Camden Society, on the Subject of Catholic Literary Societies, on the Architectural, Artistical, and Archaeological Movements of the Puseyites* (Liverpool: Booker, 1844).

———, *The Political Future of England* (London: Murray, 1856).

———, *Journal intime inédit* (9 vols, various eds., Paris: Honoré Champion, 1990–2009).

Moore, T., *Travels of an Irish Gentleman in Search of a Religion* (London: Longman, 1833).

Moule, H. C. G., *Memories of a Vicarage* (London: Religious Tract Society, 1913).

Mozley, T., *Reminiscences chiefly of Oriel College and the Oxford Movement* (London: Longmans, 1882).

Neale, J. M., *Notes, Ecclesiological and Picturesque on Dalmatia, Croatia, Istria, Styria: with a visit to Montenegro* (London: Hayes, 1861).

————, *Sermons for the Church Year* (London: Hayes, 1876).

————, *Letters, edited by his daughter* (London: Longmans, 1910).

Newman, J. H., *Arians of the Fourth Century* (London: Rivingtons, 1833)

————, *Lectures on Justification* (2nd edn, Oxford: Rivingtons & Parker, 1840).

————, *Fifteen Sermons preached before the University of Oxford* (Oxford: Rivingtons, 1843).

————, *An Essay on the Development of Christian Doctrine* (1845; new edn., Harmondsworth: Penguin, 1974).

————, *Parochial and Plain Sermons* (8 vols, new edn, London: Rivingtons, 1868).

————, *Apologia Pro Vita Sua* (1864; new edn, London: Oxford University Press, 1964).

————, *The Via Media of the Anglican Church* (2 vols, London: Pickering, 1877).

————, *Discussions and Arguments on Various Subjects* (new edn, London: Longmans, 1891).

————, *Letters and Diaries* (32 vols, various editors (Oxford: Oxford University Press, 1961- 2015).

Northcote, J. S., *Pilgrimage to La Salette, or, a Critical Examination of all the facts* (London: Burns & Lambert, 1852).

Oakeley, F., *Personal Reminiscences of the 'Oxford Movement'* (London: Teulon, 1855).

————, *Historical Notes on the Tractarian Movement* (London: Longmans, 1865).

Oldknow, J., *A Month in Portugal* (London: Longmans, 1855).

Osborne, C. E., *The Life of Father Dolling* (London: Arnold, 1903).

Paget, F. E., *Sermons on Duties of Daily Life* (Rugeley: John Thomas Walters, 1849).

————, *The Parish and the Priest: Colloquies on the Pastoral Care, and Parochial Institutions of a Country Village* (London: Joseph Masters, 1858).

Palmer, W. [of Worcester College], *Treatise on the Church of Christ* (London: Rivingtons, 1838).

————, *Origines Liturgicae or Antiquities of the English Ritual* (4th edn, Oxford: Rivingtons, 1845).

————, *Narrative of events connected with the publication of the Tracts for the Times* (1843; new edn, expanded; London: Rivingtons, 1883).

Palmer, W. [of Magdalen College], *Notes of a Visit to the Russian Church in the Years 1840, 1841, selected and arranged by Cardinal Newman* (London: Kegan Paul Trench, 1882).

Perceval, A. P., *Results of an ecclesiastical tour in Holland and Northern Germany* (London: Leslie, 1846).

Perry, T. W., *Lawful Church Ornaments: Being an historical examination of the Judgement of the Right Hon. Stephen Lushington* (London: Joseph Masters, 1857).

Pollen, A., *John Hungerford Pollen 1820–1902* (London: Murray, 1912).

Prevost, G. (ed.), *The Autobiography of Isaac Williams* (London: Longmans, 1892).

Prothero, R. E., *The Life and Correspondence of Arthur Penrhyn Stanley* (London: Murray, 1893).

Purcell, E. S., *Life and Letters of Ambrose Phillipps de Lisle* (2 vols, edited & finished by Edwin de Lisle; London: Macmillan, 1890).

———, *Life of Cardinal Manning, Archbishop of Westminster* (2 vols, London: Macmillan, 1896).

Purchas, J., *Directorium Anglicanum: Being a Manual of Directions for the right Celebration of the Holy Communion, for the Saying of Matins and Evensong, and for the Performance of the other Rites and Ceremonies of the Church* (London: Joseph Masters, 1858).

Pusey, E. B., *An Historical Enquiry into the Probable Causes of the Rationalist character lately predominant in the Theology of Germany* (new edn, London: Rivingtons, 1830).

———, *The Church the Converter of the Heathen: Two Sermons preached in conformity with the Queen's Letter on behalf of the Society for the Propagation of the Gospel* (Oxford: Parker & Rivingtons, 1838).

———, (ed.), *Sermons on Selected Lessons of the New Testament, by S. Augustine* (Oxford: Parker, 1844).

———, *A Course of Sermons on Solemn Subjects chiefly bearing on Repentance and Amendment of Life, preached at St Saviour's, Leeds, during the week of its Consecration* (Oxford: Parker, 1845).

———, *Sermons during the Season from Advent to Whitsuntide* (Oxford: Parker, 1848).

———, *The Church of England a Portion of Christ's One Holy Catholic Church, and a Means of Restoring Visible Unity: An Eirenicon* (Oxford: Parker, 1865).

———, *First Letter to the Very Rev. J. H. Newman [Eirenicon II]* (Oxford: Parker, 1869).

———, *This is my Body: A Sermon preached before the University at St Mary's* (Oxford, 1871).

———, *Lenten Sermons* (Oxford: Parker, 1874).

———, 'Advertisement', to J. Keble, *Sermons for the Christian Year. Sermons for Lent to Passiontide* (Oxford: Parker, 1877).

———, *Lenten Sermons, preached chiefly to young men at the Universities* (London: Walter Smith, 1883).

———, *Spiritual Letters* (London: Longman, Green & Co., 1901).

Robert, Jean-François, *Souvenirs d'Angleterre et considérations sur l'église Anglicane* (new edn, Lille & Paris: Librairie de J. Lefort, 1878).

Rogers, C. F., *Principles of Parish Work: An Essay in Pastoral Theology* (London: Longmans, 1905).

Rose, H. J., *The State of the Protestant Religion in Germany; in a series of discourses preached before the University of Cambridge* (Cambridge: Deighton & Son, 1825).

Rose, H. J. [son of above], *Untrodden Spain, and her Black Country* (London: Tinsley, 1875).

———, *Among the Spanish People* (London: Bentley, 1877).

[Royal Commission on Ecclesiastical Discipline], *Report of the Royal Commission on Ecclesiastical Discipline* (London: HMSO, 1906).

Russell, G. W. E., *Dr. Liddon* (London: Mowbray, 1905).

Scott, J., *Visit to Paris in 1814: Being a review of the moral, political, intellectual and social condition of the French capital* (London: Longman, Hurst, Rees, Orme & Brown, 1815).

Simeon, C. S., *Horae Homilecticae or, Discourses (principally in the form of skeletons) now first digested into one continued series and forming a commentary upon every book of the Old and New Testament* (11 vols., London: Watts, 1819–28).

Smith, R. Mudie, *The Religious Life of London* (London: Hodder & Stoughton, 1904).

Spencer, G. S., *The Testimony of Primitive Antiquity against the peculiarities of the Latin Church: being a supplement to the Difficulties of Romanism: in reply to an Answer to the difficulties of Romanism, by J. F. M. Trévern, Bishop of Strasbourg* (London: Rivingtons, 1828).

Staley, V., *Ceremonial of the English Church* (London: Mowbray, 1899).

———, *Christian Duty. A Plain Guide to the Knowledge and Practice of Religion* (Oxford: Mowbray, 1901).

———, *The Practical Religion* (3rd edn, Oxford: Mowbray, 1901).

———, *The Catholic Religion: A Manual of Instruction for members of the Anglican Church* (12th edn., Oxford: Mowbray, 1903).

———, *The Holy Communion: Addresses and Instruction Doctrinal, Practical, and Ceremonial concerning the Sacrament of the Body and Blood of Christ* (Oxford: Mowbray, 1905).

Stanley, A. P., *Sinai and Palestine in connection with their history* (London: Murray, 1856).

———, *Lectures on the History of the Eastern Church* (London: Murray, 1861).

Stephens, W. R. W., *The Life and Letters of Walter Farquhar Hook* (6th edn, London: Bentley, 1881).

Stone, D., *Outlines of Christian Dogma* (London: Longmans, 1903).

Sumner, J. B., *Apostolical Preaching considered in an Examination of St Paul's Epistles* (London: Hatchard, 1815).

Talbot, J., *Letter to Ambrose Lisle Phillipps, Esq.: descriptive of the Estatica of Caldaro and the Addolorata of Capriano* (London: Dolman, 1842).

Trévern, J. F. M., *Discussion amicale sur l'église Anglicane, et en générale sur la Réformation, dediée au clergé de toutes les communions Protestants,* (1817; 2nd edn, 2 vols, Paris: chez Potey, 1824).

Veuillot, E., *Louis Veuillot* (4 vols, Paris: Victor Retaux, 1899–1913).

Veuillot, L., *Mélanges religieux, historiques, politiques et littéraires (1842–1856)* (12 vols, Paris: L. Vivès, 1856–61).

Walsh, W., *The Secret History of the Oxford Movement* (London: Swan Sonnenschein, 1898).

———, *History of the Romeward Movement in the Church of England: 1833–1864* (London: Swan Sonnenschein, 1900).

Webb, B., *Sketches of Continental Ecclesiology, or Church Notes in Belgium, Germany, and Italy* (London: Joseph Masters, 1848).

Wesley, J., *Standard Sermons: Consisting of Forty-Four Discourses* (new edn, London: Epworth, 1964).

Weston, F., *The One Christ: An inquiry into the manner of the Incarnation* (London: Longmans, 1914).

Whewell, W., *Architectural notes on German churches: with notes written during an architectural tour in Picardy and Normandy* (Cambridge: Deighton, 1842).

White, J. H., *A Short History of the Foundation and Progress of the Church of St Augustine, South Croydon* (Croydon: privately published, 1909).

Williams, I. (ed.), *Plain Sermons by Contributors to the 'Tracts for the Times'* (London: Rivingtons, 1839).

————, *Tract 80, On Reserve in Communicating Religious Knowledge*, in *Tracts for the Times*, Vol. IV (London: Rivingtons, 1840).

————, *A Series of Sermons on the Epistle and Gospel for each Sunday in the Year* (London: Rivingtons, 1853).

————, (ed.), *Sermons, Plain and Practical, by the late Rev. R. A. Suckling* (London: Joseph Masters, 1853).

————, *Plain Sermons on the Catechism* (new edn, London: Rivingtons, 1882).

Wilson, D., *Revival of Spiritual Religion the Only Effectual Remedy for the Dangers which now Threaten the Church of England* (London: Hatchard, 1851).

Wordsworth, C, *Diary in France, mainly on topics concerning Education and the Church* (London: Rivingtons, 1845).

————, *Letters to M. Gondon, author of 'mouvement religieux en Angleterre'* (London: Rivingtons, 1847).

————, *Notes at Paris, particularly on the State and Prospects of Religion* (London: Rivingtons, 1854).

————, *On 'The Immaculate Conception': A sermon preached at Westminster Abbey, 17 December 1854* (London: Rivingtons, 1857).

Worley, G., *The Catholic Revival of the Nineteenth Century: A brief popular account of its origin, history, literature, and general results* (London: Elliot Stock, 1894).

Primary Sources – Journals & Newspapers

Cheshire Observer
Churchman
Church Times
Crockford's Clerical Directories
Croydon Advertiser

Croydon Chronicle
L'Ami de la Religion
L'Univers

Secondary Sources

Abbott, E. S., Dix, G., *et alia, Catholicity. A Study in the Conflict of Christian Traditions in the West* (Westminster: Dacre,1947)

Agulhon, M., *Pénitents et francs-maçons de l'ancienne Provence* (Paris: Fayard, 1968)

Allchin, A. M.,*The Silent Rebellion: Anglican religious communities, 1845–1900* (London: SCM, 1958)

———, *Participation in God: a Forgotten Strand in Anglican Tradition* (London: DLT, 1988)

———, *The Joy of all Creation. An Anglican Meditation on the Place of Mary* (new edn., London: DLT, 1993)

Allen, L., 'Letters of Phillipps de Lisle to Montalembert', *Dublin Review*, 228 (1954), pp. 53–64

——— (ed.), *John Henry Newman and the Abbé Jager. A Controversy on Scripture and Tradition (1834–1836)* (London: OUP, 1975)

Altholz, J. L., *The Liberal Catholic movement in England: the 'Rambler' and its contributors, 1848–1864* (London: Burns & Oates, 1962)

Anonymous, *St Peter's, Croydon: The First Hundred Years* (Croydon: privately published, 1951)

Anson, P. F., *The Call of the Cloister: religious communities and kindred bodies in Anglicanism* (London: SPCK, 1955)

Archer, A., *The Two Catholics Churches. A Study in Oppression* (London: SCM, 1986)

ARCIC I, *The Final Report* (London: CTS/CHP, 1982)

ARCIC II, *Church as Communion* (London: CTS/CHP, 1991)

ARCIC II, *Mary: Grace and Hope in Christ* (London: CTS/CHP, 2004)

Atherstone, A., 'The Martyrs' Memorial at Oxford', *JEH*, 54 (2003), pp. 278–301

Atkin, N., &. Tallett, F., *Priests, Prelates and People. A History of European Catholicism since 1750* (Oxford: OUP, 2005)

Atkinson, N., 'Hooker's Theological Method and Modern Anglicanism', *The Churchman*, 114 (2000), pp. 40–70

Aubert, R. (ed.), *Correspondance entre Charles de Montalembert et Adolphe Dechamps 1838–1870* (Louvain: Bibliothèque de la Revue d'Histoire Ecclésiastique , 1993)

Avis, P. D. L., *Gore: Construction and Conflict* (Worthing: Churchman, 1988)

———, *Anglicanism and the Christian Church* (new edn., Edinburgh: T & T Clark, 2002)

————, *The Anglican Understanding of the Church: Theological Resources in Historical Perspective* (new edn., London: SPCK, 2013)

————, *The Identity of Anglicanism. Essentials of an Anglican Ecclesiology* (London: T & T Clark, 2007)

Bailey, S., *A Tactful God: Gregory Dix Priest, Monk and Scholar* (Leominster: Gracewing, 1995)

Balteau, J., et al., *Dictionnaire de Biographie Française*, vol. 14 (Paris: Librairie Letouzey et Ané, 1979)

Barrett, P., *Barchester: English Cathedral Life in the Nineteenth Century* (London: SPCK, 1993)

Barth, J. R., *Romanticism and Transcendence: Wordsworth, Coleridge and the religious imagination* (Columbia: University of Missouri Press, 2003)

Barth, K., *Protestant Theology in the Nineteenth Century* (new edn., London: SCM, 2001)

Bateman, H. W., *A Short History of the Church of St John the Evangelist, Upper Norwood 1871–1937* (Croydon: privately published, 1937)

Battiscombe, G., *John Keble. A Study in Limitations* (London: Constable, 1963)

Bebbington, D. W., *Evangelicalism in Modern Britain. A History from the 1730s to the 1980s* (London: Unwin Hyman, 1989)

————, *The Dominance of Evangelicalism* (Leicester: IVP, 2005)

————, *Holiness in Nineteenth-Century England* (Carlisle: Paternoster, 2000)

Beeson, T., *The Bishops* (London: SCM, 2002)

Bell, G. K. A., *Randall Davidson. Archbishop of Canterbury* (3rd ed., Oxford: OUP, 1952)

Bellenger, A., *The French Exiled Clergy in the British Isles after 1789. A Historical Introduction and Working List* (Bath: Downside Abbey, 1986)

Bentley, J., *Ritualism and Politics in Victorian Britain: the Attempt to Legislate for Belief* (Oxford: OUP, 1978)

Berghoff, H., Korte, B., Schneider, R., &. Harvie, C. (eds.), *The Making of Modern Tourism. The Cultural History of the British Experience, 1600–2000* (Basingstoke: Palgrave, 2002)

Best, G. F. A., *Temporal Pillars: Queen Anne's Bounty, the ecclesiastical commissioners and the Church of England* (Cambridge: CUP, 1964)

Bettany, F. G., *Stewart Headlam* (London: Murray, 1926)

Bettenson, H. (ed.), *Documents of the Christian Church* (Oxford: OUP, 1943)

Blackbourn, D., *The Marpingen Visions. Nationalism, Religion and the Rise of Modern Germany* (new edn., London: Fontana, 1995)

Bossy, J., 'The Mass as a Social Institution', *Past & Present*, 100 (1983), pp. 29–61

Boudon, J. -O., *L'Episcopat Français à l'Époque Concordataire (1802–1905)* (Paris: Cerf, 1996)

Box, H. S., 'The Immaculate Conception', in Mascall, E. L., and Box, H. S. (eds.), *The Blessed Virgin Mary* (London: DLT, 1963), pp. 77–88

Bradshaw, P. F., *The Anglican Ordinal* (London: Acluin Club/SPCK, 1971)

Brendon, P., *Hurrell Froude and the Oxford Movement* (London: Elek, 1974)

————, *Thomas Cook. 150 Years of Popular Tourism* (London: Secker & Warburg, 1991)

Brent, R., *Liberal Anglican Politics: Whiggery, Religion and Reform, 1830–1841* (Oxford: Clarendon, 1987)

Brilioth, Y., *The Anglican Revival. Studies in the Oxford Movement* (London: Longmans, 1925)

————, *Eucharistic Faith and Practice* (London: Longmans, 1930)

Broad, J., 'Parish Economies of Welfare, 1650–1834', *HJ*, 42 (1999), pp. 985–1006

Brose, O., *Church and Parliament, the reshaping of the Church of England, 1828–1860* (Stanford, CA: Stanford University Press, 1959)

Brown, C. G., 'Did urbanization secularize Britain?', *Urban History Yearbook* (Leicester: Leicester University Press, 1988), pp. 1–11

————, *The Death of Christian Britain. Understanding Secularisation 1800–2000* (2001; new edn., London: Routledge, 2009)

Brown, Ford K., *Fathers of the Victorians: the age of Wilberforce* (Cambridge: CUP, 1961)

Bryant, C., *Possible Dreams: A Personal History of British Christian Socialists* (London: Hodder & Stoughton, 1996)

Budge, G., *Charlotte M. Yonge: Religion, Feminism and Realism in the Victorian Novel* (Oxford & New York: Peter Lang, 2007)

Burns, R. A., *The Diocesan Revival in the Church of England c. 1800–1870* (Oxford: Clarendon, 1999)

————, 'Beyond the "Red Vicar": Community and Christian Socialism in Thaxted, Essex, 1910–84', *History Workshop Journal*, 77 (2013), pp. 101–24

Bushaway, R. W., *By Rite. Custom, Ceremony and Community 1700–1880* (London: Junction Books, 1982)

Bussche, J. V., *Ignatius (George) Spencer, Passionist (1799–1864), Crusader of Prayer for England and pioneer of ecumenical prayer* (Leuven: University Press, Peeters, 1991)

Butler, B. C., *The Idea of the Church* (London: DLT, 1962)

Carpenter, J., *Gore: A Study in Liberal Catholic Thought* (London: Faith Press, 1960)

Castle, V., & Castle, S., *Richard Trew 1793–1874, Mayor of Axbridge. A History of Axbridge in the Nineteenth Century* (Wedmore: S. Castle, 1993).

Cattanéo, B., *Montalembert: un catholique en politique* (Chambray: CLD, 1990)

Chadwick, W. O., *The Victorian Church* (2 vols., London: A & C Black, 1966–70)

————, *The Secularization of the European Mind in the Nineteenth Century* (Cambridge: CUP, 1975)

————, *Michael Ramsey: A Life* (Oxford: OUP, 1990)

————, *The Spirit of the Oxford Movement. Tractarian Essays* (Cambridge: CUP, 1990)

Chandler, M., *The Life and Work of John Mason Neale, 1818–1866* (Leominster: Gracewing, 1995)

————, *The Life and Work of Henry Parry Liddon* (Leominster: Gracewing, 2000)

Chapman, M. D., 'The Fantasy of Reunion: The Rise and Fall of the Association for the Promotion of the Unity of Christendom', *JEH*, 58 (2007), pp. 49–74

——, *Anglican Theology* (London: T & T Clark, 2012)

——, *The Fantasy of Reunion: Anglicans, Catholics, and Ecumenism, 1833–1882* (Oxford: OUP, 2014)

Chapman, R., *Faith and revolt: studies in the literary influence of the Oxford Movement* (London: Weidenfeld & Nicolson, 1970)

Chard, C., *Pleasures and Guilt on the Grand Tour: Travel Writing and Imaginative Geography, 1600–1830* (Manchester: Manchester University Press, 1999)

Cherry, B., & Pevsner, N., *The Buildings of England: London 2: the South* (Harmondsworth: Penguin, 1983)

Christensen, T., *The Origins and History of Christian Socialism 1848–1854* (Aarhus: Universitetsforlaget, 1962)

——, *The Divine Order: A Study of F. D. Maurice's Theology* (Leiden: Brill, 1973)

Clark, C., & Kaiser, W. (eds.), *Culture Wars: Secular-Catholic Conflict in Nineteenth-Century Europe* (Cambridge: CUP, 2003)

Claydon, T., and McBride, I. (eds.), *Protestantism and national identity. Britain and Ireland, c. 1650–c. 1850* (Cambridge: CUP, 1998)

Cobb, P. G., 'The development of modern day pilgrimage', in Anon., *Walsingham: Pilgrimage and History* (Walsingham: R. C. National Shrine, 1999), pp. 155–64

Cobban, A., *A History of Modern France. II: 1799–1871* (2nd edn., Harmondsworth: Penguin, 1965)

Cocksworth, C. J., *Evangelical Eucharistic Thought in the Church of England* (Cambridge: CUP, 1993)

Cohen, M. N. (ed.), *The Russian Journal – II: A record kept by Henry Parry Liddon of a tour taken with C. L. Dodgson in the summer of 1867* (New York: Lewis Carroll Society of America, 1979)

Coleman, B. I., *The Church of England in the Mid-Nineteenth century. A Social Geography* (London: Historical Association, 1980)

Corsi, P., *Science and Religion. Baden Powell and the Anglican debate 1800–1860* (Cambridge: CUP, 1988)

Coulson, J. S., *Newman and the Common Tradition* (Oxford: OUP, 1970)

Cox, J., *The English churches in a secular society: Lambeth, 1870–1930* (Oxford: OUP, 1982)

Cracknell, K. *Justice, Courtesy and Love. Theologians and Missionaries encountering World Religions, 1846–1914* (London: Epworth, 1995)

Crumb, L. N., *The Oxford Movement and its leaders: a bibliography of secondary and lesser primary sources* (3 vols., Metuchen, NJ: American Theological Library Association & Scarecrow, 1988–1993, and 2009)

Currie, R., *Methodism Divided: A Study in the Sociology of Ecumenicalism* (London: Faber, 1968)

Curtis, P., *A Hawk among Sparrows. A Biography of Austin Farrer* (London: SPCK, 1985)

Dark, S. (ed.), *Conrad Noel: An Autobiography* (London: Dent, 1945)

Davidoff, L., & Hall, C., *Family Fortunes. Men and Women of the English middle class 1780–1850* (London: Hutchinson, 1987)

Davie, P., *Raising up a Faithful People* (Leominster: Gracewing, 1997)

De Lubac, H., *The Splendour of the Church* (new edn., London: Sheed & Ward, 1979)

Dewey, C., *The Passing of Barchester* (London: Hambledon, 1991)

Dix, [Dom] G., *A Detection of Aumbries* (Westminster: Dacre, 1942)

Donajgrodski, A. P., (ed.), *Social Control in Nineteenth-Century Britain* (London: Croom Helm, 1977)

Douglas, B., *A Companion to Anglican Eucharistic Theology, I: The Reformation to the Nineteenth Century* (Leiden: Brill, 2011)

———, *The Eucharistic Theology of Edward Bouverie Pusey. Sources, Context and Doctrine within the Oxford Movement and Beyond* (Leiden: Brill, 2015)

Douglas, M., *Natural Symbols. Explorations in Cosmology* (Harmondsworth: Penguin, 1973)

Duffy, E., *The Stripping of the Altars: Traditional Religion in England 1400–1580* (New Haven: Yale University Press, 1992)

———, 'The reception of Turner's Newman: a reply to Simon Skinner', *JEH*, 63 (2012), pp. 534–48

Ellis, I., *Seven against Christ: a Study of Essays and Reviews* (Leiden: Brill, 1980)

Ellsworth, L., *Charles Lowder and the Ritualist Movement* (London: DLT, 1982)

Erdozain, D., 'The secularisation of sin in the nineteenth century', *JEH*, 62 (2011), pp. 59–88

Everitt, A. M., *The Pattern of Rural Dissent: the Nineteenth Century* (Leicester: Leicester University Press, 1972)

Faber, G., *Oxford Apostles* (London: Faber, 1933)

Farrer, A. M., 'Eucharist and Church in the New Testament', in A. G. Hebert, (ed.), *The Parish Communion* (London: SPCK, 1937), pp. 73–94

———, 'The ministry in the New Testament', in K. E. Kirk (ed.), *The Apostolic Ministry. Essays on the History and Doctrine of Episcopacy* (London: Hodder & Stoughton, 1946), pp. 113–82

———, *Lord I believe* (London: SPCK, 1955)

———, 'Mary, Scripture and Tradition', in E. L. Mascall and H. S. Box (eds.), *The Blessed Virgin Mary* (London: DLT, 1963), pp. 27–52

———, et al., *Infallibility in the Church: an Anglican-Catholic Dialogue* (London: DLT, 1968)

———, *The End of Man* (London: SPCK, 1973)

———, *Interpretation and Belief* (London: SPCK, 1976)

———, *Words for Life* (London: SPCK, 1993)

Fenwick, J., and Spinks, B., *Worship in Transition. The Twentieth Century Liturgical Movement* (Edinburgh: T & T Clark, 1995)

Fox-Genovese, E., & Genovese, E. D., *The Mind of the Master Class: History and Faith in the Southern Slaveholders' Worldview* (Cambridge & New York: CUP, 2005)

Franklin, R. W., *Nineteenth-century churches : the history of a new Catholicism in Württemberg, England, and France* (New York & London: Garland, 1997)

Frere, W., *Recollections of Malines. A Contribution to the Cause of Christian Reunion* (London: Centenary, 1935)

Galloway, P., *A Passionate Humility: Frederick Oakeley and the Oxford Movement* (Leominster: Gracewing, 1999)

Gammon, V., 'Babylonian Performances: the Rise and Suppression of Popular Church Music, 1660–1870', in E. & C. S. Yeo (eds.), *Popular Culture and Class Conflict 1590–1914: Explorations in the History of Labour and Leisure* (Brighton: Harvester, 1981), pp. 62–88

Gay, J. D., *The Geography of Religion in England* (London: Duckworth, 1971)

Gilbert, A. D., *Religion and Society in Industrial England: Church, Chapel and Social Change 1740–1914* (London: Longman, 1976)

Gilley, S., *Newman and his Age* (new edn., London: DLT, 2003)

———, 'Edward Irving: Prophet of the Millennium', in J. Garnett & H. C. G. Matthew (eds.), *Revival and Religion since 1700: Essays for John Walsh* (London: Hambledon, 1993), pp. 95–110

Gore, C., *Dominant Ideas and Corrective Principles* (London: Mowbray, 1918)

———, *Can We Then Believe?* (London: Murray, 1926)

Gorer, G., 'English Character in the Twentieth Century', *Annals of the American Academy of Political and Social Science*, 370 (1967), pp. 174–81

Gougaud, L., and Joynt, M, 'The Isle of Saints', *Studies: An Irish Quarterly Review*, 13 (1924), pp. 363–80

Gough, A., *Paris and Rome: The Gallican Church and the Ultramontane Campaign 1848–1853* (Oxford: Clarendon, 1986)

Gouldstone, T., *The Rise and Decline of Anglican Idealism in the Nineteenth Century* (London: Palgrave, 2005)

Gray, D., *Earth and Altar. The Evolution of the Parish Communion in the Church of England to 1945* (Norwich: Alcuin Club/Canterbury, 1986),

———, *Percy Dearmer: a parson's pilgrimage* (Norwich: Canterbury, 2000)

———, *The 1927–28 Prayer Book crisis*. 2 vols. I. *Ritual, royal commissions, and reply to royal letters of business*. II. *The cul-de-sac of the deposited book...until further order be taken* (London: SCM/Canterbury, 2005–6)

Greaves, R. W., 'The Jerusalem Bishopric, 1841', *EHR*, 64 (1949), pp. 328–52

Green, S. J. D., 'Religion and the Rise of the Common Man: Mutual Improvement Societies, Religious Associations and Popular Education in Three Industrial Towns in the West Riding of Yorkshire c. 1850–1900', in D. Fraser (ed.), *Cities, Class and Communication: Essays in Honour of Asa Briggs* (London: Harvester Wheatsheaf, 1990), pp. 25–43

———, *Religion in the Age of Decline. Organisation and Experience in Industrial Yorkshire 1870–1920* (Cambridge: CUP, 1996)

———, *The passing of Protestant England. Secularisation and social change c. 1920–1960* (Cambridge: CUP, 2011)

Griffin, J. R., *The Oxford Movement: a revision* (Edinburgh: Pentland, 1984)

———, *John Keble: Saint of Anglicanism* (Macon, Georgia: Mercer University Press, 1987)

Guild of Our Lady of Ransom, *Walsingham 1061–1997* (London: Guild of Our Lady of Ransom, 1998)

Gury, J. (ed.), *Le voyage Outre-Manche. Anthologie de voyageurs français de Voltaire à Mac Orlan du XVIIIe au XXe siècle* (Paris: Robert Laffront, 1999)

Härdelin, A., *The Tractarian Understanding of the Eucharist* (Uppsala: Uppsala Universitet, Acta Universitatis Upsaliensis, 1965)

Harris, R., *Lourdes. Body and Spirit in the Secular Age* (London: Allen Lane, 1999)

Hastings, A., *A History of English Christianity 1920–1985* (London: Fount, 1986)

Heazell, F. N., *The History of St Michael's Church, Croydon: a Chapter in the Oxford Movement* (London: Mowbray, 1934)

Hebert, A. G., *Liturgy and Society* (London: Faber, 1935)

——— (ed.), *The Parish Communion* (London: SPCK, 1937)

Heeney, B., *The Women's Movement in the Church of England 1850–1930* (Oxford: OUP, 1988)

Heimann, M., *Catholic Devotion in Victorian England* (Oxford: OUP, 1995)

Hempton, D., *Evangelical Disenchantment. Nine Portraits of Faith and Doubt* (New Haven & London: Yale University Press, 2008)

Hilliard, D., 'Unenglish and unmanly: Anglo-Catholicism and Homosexuality', *VS*, 25 (1982), pp. 181–210

Hilton, B., *The age of atonement: the influence of evangelicalism on social and economic thought, 1795–1865* (Oxford: Clarendon, 1988)

Hinchliff, P. B., *God and history: aspects of British theology, 1875–1914* (Oxford: Clarendon, 1992)

How, J., *Epistolary Spaces: English letter-writing from the foundation of the Post Office to Richardson's Clarissa* (Aldershot: Ashgate, 2003)

Inglis, K. S., 'Patterns of religious worship in 1851', *JEH*, 11 (1960), pp. 74–86

———, *Churches and the Working Classes in Victorian England* (London, 1963)

Iremonger, F. A. ,*William Temple. Archbishop of Canterbury* (Routledge Kegan Paul London: OUP, 1948)

Jacob, W. M., 'The Diffusion of Tractarianism: Wells Theological College 1840–49', *Southern History*, 5 (1983), pp. 189–209

Janes, D., *Victorian Reformation. The Fight over Idolatry in the Church of England, 1840–1860* (Oxford: OUP, 2009)

Jay, E., 'Charlotte Mary Yonge and Tractarian Aesthetics', *Victorian Poetry*, 44 (2006), pp. 43–59

Jenkins, T. D., *Religion in English Everyday Life. An Ethnographic Approach* (Oxford: Berghahn, 1999)

Jones, H. S., *Victorian Political Thought* (Basingstoke: Macmillan, 2000)

Jones, T. E., *The Broad Church: a Biography of a Movement* (Lanham, MD: Lexington Books, 2003)

Jones, P. D'A., *The Christian Socialist Revival 1877–1914: Religion, Class and Social Conscience in Late Victorian England* (Princeton: Princeton University Press, 1968)

Jungmann, J. A., *The Mass of the Roman Rite. Its Origins and Development* (London: Burns & Oates, 1959)

Kemp, E. W., *Counsel and Consent. Aspects of the Government of the Church* (London: SPCK, 1961)

Kent, D., 'High Church Rituals and Rituals of Protest: the "Riots" at St George-in-the-East, 1859–1860', *London Journal*, 24 (2007), pp. 145–66

Kent, J. H. S., *Holding the Fort: Studies in Victorian Revivalism* (London: SCM, 1978)

———, *William Temple. Church, State and Society in Britain, 1880–1950* (Cambridge: CUP, 1992),

Ker, I., *John Henry Newman. A Biography* (Oxford: OUP, 1988)

Koenker, E. B., *The Liturgical Renaissance in the Roman Catholic Church* (St Louis: Concordia, 1954)

King, B., *Newman and the Alexandrian Fathers. Shaping doctrine in Nineteenth-Century England* (Oxford: OUP, 2009)

Knight, F., 'The influence of the Oxford Movement in the Parishes: a Reassessment', in P. Vaiss, *From Oxford to the People. Reconsidering Newman and the Oxford Movement* (Leominster: Gracewing, 1996), pp. 127–40

Knox, E. A., *The Tractarian movement, 1833–1845: a study of the Oxford movement as a phase of the religious revival in Western Europe in the second quarter of the nineteenth century* (London: Putnam, 1933)

Langlois, C., 'Les effectifs des congrégations féminin au XIXe siècle: de l'enquête statistique à l'histoire quantitative', *Revue d'histoire de l'église de France*, 60 (1974), pp. 44–53

Larsen, T., *Crisis of doubt: honest faith in nineteenth-century England* (Oxford: OUP, 2006)

———, *A People of One Book: the Bible and the Victorians* (Oxford: OUP, 2011)

La Trobe-Bateman, W. F., *Memories Grave and Gay* (London: Longmans, 1927)

Lee, R., *Rural Society and the Anglican Clergy, 1815–1914. Encountering and Managing the Poor* (Woodbridge: Boydell, 2006)

Leslie, S., *The Oxford Movement, 1833–1933* (London: Burns & Oates, 1933)

Lindon, J., 'Alessandro Manzoni and the Oxford Movement: His Politics and Conversion in a New English Source', *JEH* , 45 (1994), pp. 297–318

Litvack, L., *John Mason Neale and the quest for sobornost* (Oxford: OUP, 1994)

Lloyd, R., *The Church of England in the Twentieth Century* (London: Longmans, 1946)

Lockhart, J. G., *Charles Lindley Viscount Halifax,* (London: Bles, 1935)

MacCulloch, D., *Thomas Cranmer. A Life* (New Haven & London: Yale University Press, 1996)

————, 'Protestantism in Mainland Europe: New Directions', *Renaissance Quarterly*, 59 (2006), pp. 698–706

McLeod, D. H., *Class and Religion in the Late Victorian City* (London: Croom Helm, 1974)

————, *Religion and the People of Western Europe 1789–1970* (Oxford: OUP, 1981)

————, 'New perspectives on Victorian working-class religion: the oral evidence', *Oral History*, 14 (1986), pp. 31–49

————, *Religion and Society in England, 1850–1914* (Basingstoke: Macmillan, 1996)

————, *Secularisation in Western Europe, 1848–1914* (Basingstoke: Macmillan, 2000)

Macquarrie, J., 'Immaculate Conception', in A. Stacpoole (ed.), *Mary's Place in Ecumenical Dialogue* (St Paul, Slough, 1982), pp. 98–107

Machin, G. I. T., 'The Last Victorian Anti-Ritualist Campaign, 1895–1906', *VS*, 25 (1982), pp. 277–302

Maiden, J., *National Religion and the Prayer-Book Controversy, 1927–8* (Woodbridge: Boydell, 2009)

Maron, G., 'Mary in Protestant theology', in H. Küng and J. Moltmann (eds.), *Mary in the Churches* (T & T Clark, Edinburgh, 1983), pp. 40–7

Marsh, P. T., *The Victorian Church in Decline. Archbishop Tait and the Church of England* (London: RKP, 1969)

Marshall, P., '(Re)defining the English Reformation', *JBS*, 48 (2009)

Mascall, E. L., 'The Mother of God', in A. Stacpoole (ed.), *Mary's Place in Ecumenical Dialogue* (St Paul, Slough, 1982), pp. 91–7

————, *Saraband* (Leominster: Gracewing, 1992)

Matthew, H. C. G., *Gladstone 1809–1874* (Oxford: OUP, 1986)

May, A. R., 'The Falloux Law, the Catholic Press, and the Bishops: Crisis of Authority in the French Church', in FHS, 8 (1973), pp. 77–94

May, J. L., *The Oxford Movement: its history and future* (London: Bodley Head, 1933)

Mills, H. M., 'Negotiating the Divide: Women, Philanthropy and the "Public Sphere" in Nineteenth-Century France', in F. Tallett & N. Atkin, *Religion, Society and Politics in France since 1789* (London: Hambledon, 1991), pp. 29–54

Moody, J. N., 'The French Catholic Press in the Education Conflict of the 1840s', *FHS*, 7 (1972), pp. 394–415

Morgan, E. R. (ed.), *Essays Catholic and Missionary* (London: SPCK, 1928)

Morris, J. N., 'Church and People Thirty-Three Years On: A Historical Critique', *Theology*,
94 (1991), pp. 92–101

———, *Religion and Urban Change: Croydon 1840–1914* (Woodbridge: Boydell, 1992)

———, 'The Regional Growth of Tractarianism', in P. Vaiss, *From Oxford to the People.
Reconsidering Newman and the Oxford Movement* (Leominster: Gracewing, 1996), pp.
141–59

———, 'Reconstructing the Reformation: F. D. Maurice, Luther, and Justification', in
R. N. Swanson (ed.), *The Church Retrospective. Studies in Church History*, 33
(Woodbridge: Boydell, 1997), pp. 487–500

———, *F. D. Maurice and the Crisis of Christian Authority* (Oxford: OUP, 2005)

———, *Renewed by the Word: The Bible and Christian Revival since the Reformation*
(Ropley: John Hunt, 2005)

———, 'The Spirit of Comprehension: Examining the Broad Church Synthesis', *Anglican
and Episcopal History*, 75 (2006), pp. 423–43

———, 'George Ridding and the Diocese of Southwell: a Study in the National Church
Ideal', *JEH*, 61 (2010), pp. 125–43

———, 'Secularization and Religious Experience: Arguments in the Historiography of
Modern British Religion', *HJ* (2012), pp. 195–219

———, '"Separated Brethren": French Catholics and the Oxford Movement', in S. J.
Brown & P. Nockles (ed.), *The Oxford Movement: Europe and the Wider World 1830–1930*
(Cambridge: CUP, 2012), pp. 203–20

Mumm, S., *Stolen daughters, virgin mothers: Anglican sisterhoods in Victorian Britain*
(Leicester: Leicester University Press, 1999)

Nazir-Ali, M., & Sagovsky, N., 'The Virgin Mary in the Anglican tradition of the sixteenth
and seventeenth centuries', in A. Denaux & N. Sagovsky (eds.), *Studying Mary. The
Virgin Mary in Anglican and Roman Catholic Theology and Devotion* (London: T & T
Clark, 2007), pp. 131–46

Neill, S. C., *Anglicanism* (Harmondsworth: Penguin, 1958)

———, *The Interpretation of the New Testament 1861–1961* (Oxford: OUP, 1964)

Newsome, D., *The Parting of Friends: A Study of the Wilberforces and Henry Manning*
(London: Murray, 1966)

———, *Two Classes of Men: Platonism and English Romantic Thought* (London: Murray,
1974)

———, *Convert Cardinals: Newman and Manning* (London: Murray, 1993)

Nichols, A., *The Panther and the Hind. A Theological History of Anglicanism* (Edinburgh:
T & T Clark, 1993)

Nicholls, D., *The Pluralist State: the Political Ideas of J. N. Figgis and his Contemporaries*
(2nd edn., Basingstoke: Macmillan, 1994)

Nockles, P. B., *The Oxford Movement in Context: Anglican High Churchmanship 1760–1857*
(Cambridge: CUP, 1994)

————, '"Our brethren of the north": The Scottish Episcopal Church and the Oxford Movement', *JEH*, 47 (1996), pp. 655–82

————, '"Lost Causes and…Impossible Loyalties": The Oxford Movement and the University', in M. G. Brock & M. C. Curthoys, *The History of the University of Oxford, Vol. VI. Nineteenth-Century Oxford, Part I* (Oxford: Clarendon, 1997), pp. 195–266

————, 'Church or Protestant Sect? The Church of Ireland, High Churchmanship, and the Oxford Movement, 1822–1869', *HJ*, 41 (1998), pp. 457–93

————, 'The Reformation Revised? The Contested Reception of the English Reformation in Nineteenth-Century Protestantism', in P. Nockles & V. Westbrook (eds.), *Reinventing the Reformation in the Nineteenth Century: A Cultural History*, Bulletin of the John Rylands Library, 90 (2014), pp. 231–56

————, & Westbrook, V. (eds.), *Reinventing the Reformation in the Nineteenth Century: A Cultural History*, Bulletin of the John Rylands Library, 90 (2014)

————, 'Newman's Tractarian Reception', in F. D. Aquino & B. King (eds.), *Receptions of Newman* (Oxford: OUP, 2015), pp. 137–55

Noll, M., *The Rise of Evangelicalism* (Leicester: IVP, 2004)

Norman, E. R., *Anti-Catholicism in Victorian England* (London: Allen & Unwin, 1968)

————, *Church and Society in England, 1770–1970* (Oxford: Clarendon, 1975)

————, *Roman Catholicism in England* (Oxford: OUP, 1985)

————, *The Victorian Christian Socialists* (Cambridge: CUP, 1987)

Obelkevich, J., *Religion and Society: South Lindsey 1825–1875* (Oxford: OUP, 1976)

Orens, J., *Stewart Headlam's Radical Anglicanism: the Mass, the masses, and the music hall* (Urbana: University of Illinois Press, 2003)

Orford, B. A., *H. P. Liddon and the Priestly Ideal* (London: Anglo-Catholic History Society, 2009)

Palmer, B., *Reverend rebels: five Victorian clerics and their fight against authority* (London: DLT, 1993)

Patterson, W. B., *William Perkins and the making of a Protestant England* (Oxford: OUP, 2014)

Pattison, R., *The Great Dissent: John Henry Newman and the Liberal Heresy* (Oxford: OUP, 1991)

Pawley, M., *Faith and Family: the Life and Circle of Ambrose Phillips de Lisle* (Norwich: Canterbury, 1993)

Paz, D. G. *Popular Anti-Catholicism in Mid-Victorian England* (Stanford, CA: Stanford University Press, 1992)

Peart-Binns, J. S., *Wand of London* (London: Mowbray, 1987)

Pereiro, J., *Cardinal Manning: An Intellectual Biography* (Oxford: OUP, 1998)

————, 'Ethos' and the Oxford Movement. At the heart of Tractarianism (Oxford: OUP, 2008)

Pickering, W. S. F., 'The 1851 religious census: a useless experiment?', *British Journal of Sociology*, 18 (1967), pp. 382–407

———, *Anglo-Catholicism: A Study in Ambiguity* (London: SPCK, 1991)

Pinnock, M., *Mary is for Everyone* (Leominster: Gracewing, 1997)

Ploeger, M., *High Church Varieties. Three Essays on Continuity and Discontinuity in Nineteenth-Century Anglican Catholic Thought* (Amersfoort: Stichting Oud-Katholiek Seminaire, 2001)

Prestige, G. L., *The Life of Charles Gore, a Great Englishman* (London: Heinemann, 1935)

———, *St Paul's in its Glory. A Candid History of the Cathedral 1831–1911* (London: SPCK, 1955)

Prickett, S., *Romanticism and Religion. The Tradition of Coleridge and Wordsworth in the Victorian Church* (Cambridge: CUP, 1976).

Quick, O. C., *The Christian Sacraments* (London: Nisbet, 1927)

———, *Doctrines of the Creed* (London: Nisbet, 1939)

Rahner, K., *The Church and the Sacraments* (London: Burns & Oates, 1974)

Railton, N., *No North Sea: the Anglo-German Evangelical Network in the Middle of the Nineteenth Century* (Leiden: Brill, 2000)

———, *Transnational Evangelicalism: the Case of Friedrich Bialloblotzky, 1799–1869* (Göttingen: Vandenhoeck & Ruprecht, 2002)

Ramsey, A. M., *The Gospel and the Catholic Church* (London: Longmans & Green, 1936)

———, *From Gore to Temple: The Development of Anglican Theology between Lux Mundi and the Second World War 1889–1939* (London: Longmans, 1960)

Rapp, F. (ed.), *Le Diocèse de Strasbourg* (Paris: Beauchesne, 1982)

Raven, C. E., *Christian Socialism 1848–54* (new edn., London: Frank Cass, 1968)

Ravitch, N., *The Catholic Church and the French Nation 1589–1989* (London: Routledge, 1990)

Reardon, B. M. G., *Liberalism and tradition: aspects of Catholic thought in nineteenth-century France* (Cambridge: CUP, 1976)

———, *Religious thought in the Victorian age: a survey from Coleridge to Gore* (London: Longmans, 1980)

Reckitt, M. B., *Maurice to Temple: A Century of the Social Movement in the Church of England* (London: Faber, 1947)

Reed, J. S, *Glorious Battle: The Cultural Politics of Victorian Anglo-Catholicism* (new edn., London: Tufton, 1998)

Reynolds, M., *Martyr of ritualism: Father Mackonochie of St Alban's, Holborn* (London: Faber, 1965)

Ricoeur, P., *Freud and Philosophy: An Essay on Interpretation* (New Haven: Yale University Press, 1970)

Roberts, M. J. D., 'Private Patronage and the Church of England, 1800–1900', *JEH*, 32 (1981), pp. 199–223

Roe, W. G., *Lamennais and England: the Reception of Lamennais's Religious Ideas in England in the Nineteenth Century* (Oxford: OUP, 1996)

Rousseau, O., *The Progress of the Liturgy. An Historical Sketch from the Beginning of the Nineteenth Century to the Pontificate of Pius X* (Westminster, MD: Newman, 1951)

Rowell, G., *The Vision Glorious. Themes and Personalities of the Catholic Revival in Anglicanism* (Oxford: OUP, 1983)

———— (ed.), *The English religious tradition and the Genius of Anglicanism* (Wantage: IKON, 1992)

Royle, E., *Radicals, Secularists and republicans : popular freethought in Britain, 1866–1915* (Manchester: Manchester University Press, 1980)

Rubin, M., *Corpus Christi. The Eucharist in Late Medieval Culture* (Cambridge: CUP, 1991)

Runciman, D., *Pluralism and the Personality of the State* (Cambridge: CUP, 1997)

Russell, G. W. E., *Arthur Stanton: a memoir* (London: Longmans, 1917)

Ryrie, A., *Being Protestant in Reformation Britain* (Oxford: OUP, 2013)

Sagovsky, N., *On God's Side: A Life of George Tyrrell* (Oxford: OUP, 1990)

Sanders, C. R., *Coleridge and the Broad Church movement: studies in S. T. Coleridge, Dr. Arnold of Rugby, J. C. Hare, Thomas Carlyle and F. D. Maurice* (Durham, N. C.: Duke University Press, 1942)

Sauvigny, G. de B. de, 'The young Montalembert: Liberal, Catholic, and Romantic', *Catholic Historical Review*, 77 (1991), pp. 485–8

Sell, A. P. F., *Philosophical Idealism and Christian Belief* (Cardiff: University of Wales Press, 1995)

Selwyn, E. G. (ed.), *Essays Catholic and Critical, by members of the Anglican Communion* (London: SPCK, 1926)

Skinner, S. A., *Tractarians and the 'Condition of England': The Social and Political Thought of the Oxford Movement* (Oxford: Clarendon, 2004)

————, 'History *versus* Hagiography: The Reception of Turner's *Newman*', in *JEH*, 61 (2010), pp. 764–81

————, 'A response to Eamon Duffy', *JEH*, 63 (2012), pp. 549–67

Smith, P. T., 'The London Police and the Holy War: Ritualism and St.George's-in-the-East, London, 1859–1860', *Journal of Church and State*, 28 (1986), pp. 107–19

Snell, K. D., & Ell, P. S., *Rival Jerusalems. The Geography of Victorian Religion* (Cambridge: CUP, 2000)

Spencer, P., *Politics of Belief in Nineteenth-Century France: Lacordaire, Michon, Veuilliot* (London: Faber, 1954)

Stone, D., *The Faith of an English Catholic* (London: Longmans, 1926)

Strong, R., *Alexander Forbes of Brechin: The First Tractarian Bishop* (Oxford: OUP, 1995)

————, *Episcopalianism in Nineteenth-Century Scotland. Religious Responses to a Modernising Society* (Oxford: OUP, 2002)

————, & Engelhardt, C. (eds.), *Edward Bouverie Pusey and the Oxford Movement* (London: Anthem, 2012)

Stunt, T. C. F., *From awakening to secession: radical evangelicals in Switzerland and Britain, 1815–35* (Edinburgh: T & T Clark, 2000)

Sykes, N., *Edmund Gibson, bishop of London, 1669–1748; a study in politics & religion in the eighteenth century* (London: OUP, 1926)

————, *The church of England and non-episcopal churches in the sixteenth and seventeenth centuries: an essay towards an historical interpretation of the Anglican tradition from Whitgift to Wake* (London: SPCK, 1948)

————, *Old priest and new presbyter; episcopacy and Presbyterianism since the Reformation* (Cambridge: CUP, 1956)

Sykes, S. W., *The Integrity of Anglicanism* (London: Mowbray, 1978)

————, *Unashamed Anglicanism* (London: DLT, 1995)

Taylor, J. G., *Our Lady of Batersey* (Chelsea: George White, 1925)

Taylor, S. (ed), *From Cranmer to Davidson. A Church of England Miscellany* (Woodbridge: Boydell, 1999)

Thompson, D. M., 'The 1851 religious census: problems and possibilities', *Victorian Studies*, 11 (1967), pp. 87–97

————, 'The Politics of the Enabling Act (1919)', in D. Baker (ed.), *Church, Society and Politics* (Studies in Church History, 12, Oxford: Blackwell, 1975), pp. 383–92

————, *Baptism, Church and Society in Modern Britain* (Milton Keynes: Paternoster, 2005)

————, *Cambridge theology in the nineteenth century: enquiry, controversy and truth* (Aldershot: Ashgate, 2008)

Thompson, K. A., *Bureaucracy and Church Reform: The Organizational the Church of England to Social Change, 1800–1965* (Oxford: Clarendon, 1970)

Thompson, P., 'All Saints' Church, Margaret Street, Reconsidered', *Architectural History*, 8 (1965), pp. 73–94

Toon, P., *Evangelical Theology, 1833–1856: A Response to Tractarianism* (London: Marshall, Morgan & Scott, 1979)

Tovey, P., *Anglican Confirmation 1662–1820* (Farnham: Routledge, 2014)

Turner, F. M., *John Henry Newman: The Challenge to Evangelical Religion* (New Haven & London: Yale University Press, 2002)

Tyler, C. (ed.), *Unpublished Manuscripts in British Idealism: Political Philosophy, Theology, and Social Thought* (Exeter: Imprint Academic, 2008).

Vidler, A. R., *Prophecy and papacy; a study of Lamennais, the Church, and the Revolution* (London: SCM, 1954)

————, *The Church in an Age of Revolution* (Harmondsworth: Penguin, 1961)

Vincent, A., & Plant, R., *Philosophy, Politics and Citizenship: the Life and Thought of British Idealists* (Oxford: Blackwell, 1984)

Voll, D., *Catholic evangelicalism: the acceptance of Evangelical traditions by the Oxford Movement during the second half of the nineteenth century* (London: Faith Press, 1963)

Waller, G., *Walsingham and the English Imagination* (Farnham: Ashgate, 2011)

Wand, J. W. C., *A History of the Modern Church from 1500 to the Present Day* (London: Methuen, 1930)

———, *Anglicanism in History and Today* (London: Weidenfeld & Nicolson, 1961)

Ward, W. R., *The Protestant Evangelical awakening* (Cambridge: CUP, 1992)

Webster, A. B., *Joshua Watson: the story of a layman* (London: SPCK, 1954)

Webster, C., & Elliott, J. (eds.), *"A church as it should be": the Cambridge Camden Society and its influence* (Stamford: Shaun Tyas, 2000)

Welch, P. J., 'Blomfield and Peel: a study in co-operation between Church and State, 1841–46', *JEH*, 12 (1961), pp. 71–84

Wellings, M., *Evangelicals Embattled: Responses of Evangelicals in the Church of England to Ritualism, Darwinism and Theological Liberalism* (Carlisle: Paternoster, 2003)

White, J. F., *The Cambridge Movement: the ecclesiologists and the gothic revival* (Cambridge: CUP, 1962)

Wickham, E. R., *Church and People in an Industrial City* (London: Lutterworth, 1957)

Wilkinson, A., *The Community of the Resurrection. A Centenary History* (London: SCM, 1992

———, *The Church of England and the First World War* (new ed., London: SCM, 1996)

———, *Christian Socialism: From Scott Holland to Tony Blair* (London: SCM, 1998)

Williams, N. P., and Harris, C. (eds.), *Northern Catholicism* (London: SPCK, 1933)

Williams, S. C., *Religious Belief and Popular Culture in Southwark, c. 1880–1939* (Oxford: OUP, 1999)

Wilson, B. R., *Religion in Secular Society: A Sociological Comment* (London: Watts, 1966)

Witheridge, J., *Excellent Dr Stanley. The Life of Dean Stanley of Westminster* (Norwich: Michael Russell, 2013)

Wolf, W. J., 'Frederick Denison Maurice', in ibid., J. E. Booty and O. C. Thomas, *The Spirit of Anglicanism: Hooker, Maurice and Temple* (Edinburgh: T & T Clark, 1982), pp. 49–98

Wolffe, J., *The Protestant Crusade in Great Britain, 1829–1860* (Oxford: OUP, 1991)

———, *The expansion of Evangelicalism: the age of Wilberforce, More, Chalmers and Finney* (Nottingham: IVP, 2006)

Woodhouse-Hawkins, M., 'Maurice' Huntington, and the Quadrilateral: an Exploration in Historical Theology', in J. Robert Wright (ed.), *Quadrilateral at One Hundred* (Oxford: Mowbray, 1988), pp. 61–78

Yates, W. N., 'The Parochial Impact of the Oxford Movement in South West Wales', in T. Barnes & W. N. Yates (eds.), *Carmarthenshire Studies* (Carmarthen: Carmarthenshire County Council 1974), pp. 221–47

———, *Leeds and the Oxford Movement* (Leeds: Thoresby Society, 1975)

————, *The Oxford Movement and Parish Life: St Saviour's, Leeds, 1839–1929* (York: University of York, Borthwick Papers, 1975)

————, *Ritual Conflict at Farlington and Wymering* (Portsmouth: Portsmouth City Council, 1978)

————, *The Anglican Revival in Portsmouth* (Portsmouth: Portsmouth City Council, 1983)

————, 'The Religious Life of Victorian Leeds', in D. Fraser (ed.), *A History of Modern Leeds* (Manchester: Manchester University Press, 1980), pp. 250–69

————, 'Bells and Smells: London, Brighton and South Coast Religion Reconsidered', *Southern History*, 5 (1983)

————, *Kent and the Oxford Movement* (Gloucester: Alan Sutton, 1983)

————, *The Oxford Movement and Anglican Ritualism* (London: Historical Association, 1983)

————, *Anglican Ritualism in Victorian Britain, 1830–1910* (Oxford: OUP, 1999)

————, Hume, R. & Hastings, P., *Religion and Society in Kent, 1640–1914* (Woodbridge: Boydell, 1994)

Yelton, M., *Alfred Hope Patten and the Restoration of the Shrine of Our Lady of Walsingham* (Norwich: Canterbury, 2006)

Theses

Bennett, J. M. R., 'Doctrine, progress and history: British religious debate 1845–1914', D.Phil. thesis, University of Oxford, 2015

Brewitt-Taylor, S., '"Christian Radicalism" in the Church of England, 1957–70', D.Phil. thesis, University of Oxford, 2012

Byrne, G., 'Consulting the Faithful: the Role of the Laity in the Government of the Church of England 1861–1904', M.Phil. thesis, University of Cambridge, 1998

Cowl, R., '"London, Brighton and South Coast Religion"? Tractarianism and ritualism in Brighton, Hove and Worthing', PhD thesis, University of Keele, 1996

Herring, G. W., 'From Tractarianism to Ritualism: A Study of Some Aspects of Tractarianism outside Oxford, from the time of Newman's conversion in 1845 until the First Ritual Commission in 1867', D.Phil. thesis, University of Oxford, 1984

Hughes, A., 'The gospel of divine action: Oliver Chase Quick and the search for a Christocentric metaphysic', PhD thesis, University of Cambridge, 2011

Piggot, A., '"An educated sense of fitness": Liberal Anglo-Catholicism 1900–1940', D.Phil. thesis, University of Oxford, 2004

Roberts, M. J. D., 'The Role of the Laity in the Church of England c. 1850–1885', D.Phil. thesis, University of Oxford, 1974

Wilson, R. A., 'G. A. Selwyn, the colonial episcopate and the formation of the Anglican Communion', PhD thesis , University of Cambridge, 2010

Index

Printed in the United States
By Bookmasters